Cybernetical Intelligence

Cybernetical Intelligence

Engineering Cybernetics with Machine Intelligence

Kelvin K. L. Wong

Published by John Wiley & Sons, Inc., Hoboken, New Jersey.
Published simultaneously in Canada.

For general information on our other products and services or for technical support, please contact our Customer Care Department within the United States at (800) 762-2974, outside the United States at (317) 572-3993 or fax (317) 572-4002.

Wiley also publishes its books in a variety of electronic formats. Some content that appears in print may not be available in electronic formats. For more information about Wiley products, visit our web site at www.wiley.com.

Library of Congress Cataloging-in-Publication Data applied for:

Hardback: 9781394217489

Cover Design: Wiley
Cover Image: Courtesy of author

Set in 9.5/12.5pt STIXTwoText by Straive, Pondicherry, India

Contents

Preface

Life evolves into existence from the edge of chaos and builds up a new mechanism based on a set of rules that governs the law of survival, reproduction, and evolution. This complex set of rules that allows a living thing to interact with its environment comes into being from the beginning of life itself, which is something one can understand as intelligence. All the wonders of art, design, sciences, etc., in the world make us ponder upon the question of the ages, on the origin of creation and the existence of life itself and the evolution of intelligence that comes into being.

"The important thing is not to stop questioning," is a famous quotation by Albert Einstein from 1955. A robot gains intelligence by questioning and seeking answers, which form examples for the labels for the unseen examples. However, will the robot have a creative mind similar to that of Einstein? This leads us to the question of whether creativity can be programmed. Can an analogy be bridged between the robot's experience in developing multiple search way paths for the optimal solution and an intelligent being's intuition to design creative solutions?

Artificial intelligence (AI) is built on the pillars of a few major branches of science and engineering, namely, systematology, information theory, and cybernetics, which is typically based on control theory that was derived from the studies of Norbert Wiener, the world-renowned father of cybernetics. In 1954, Hsue-sen Tsien founded engineering cybernetics by publishing the famous engineering cybernetics in America. On the basis of cybernetics, a predictive system may be regarded as a multiple feedback system. The framework of a multilayer perceptron as well as that of a backpropagation neural network can be based on the theoretic of system control in modern cybernetics. With this type of thinking, perceptron theory offers a cohesive approach to the statistical mechanics and principles of cybernetics as a basis for the successful neural network modeling.

A feedback controller's operation is to change the behavior of a system fundamentally. Feedback control systems sample a system's outputs, compare them to a set of desired outputs, and then utilize the resulting error signals to compute the system's control inputs in such a way that the errors are minimized. Artificially built feedback control systems, which are utilized to govern industrial, automotive, and aeronautical systems, are responsible for today's aerospace achievements. Biological systems are full of naturally occurring feedback controls. The cell, one of the most basic of all life forms, regulates the potential difference across the cell membrane to preserve homeostasis. Although neural network controllers are adaptive learning systems, they do not need the conventional assumptions of adaptive control theory, such as parameter linearity and the presence a regression matrix. It is demonstrated in detail the process to create neural network based controllers for cybernetical systems, a general category of nonlinear systems, complicated industrial systems with vibrations and flexibility effects, force control, motor dynamics control, and other applications. These are given for both continuous-time and discrete-time weight tuning.

Integration of AI and cybernetics can produce applications in predictive control, pattern recognition, and classification, which essentially are based on the same fundamentals. This book proposes for the first time the novel perspective of machine intelligence, which is termed as *Cybernetical Intelligence*. Such a new field will have extensive and practical applications in not just the combinatorial optimization problems but also in pattern recognition, data mining, and other related machine intelligence based cybernetics problems.

The key concept of *Cybernetical Intelligence* grew from a desire to understand and build systems that can achieve goals, whether complex human goals or just goals. It is even deeper underlying conceptual term. Cybernetics holds the world sufficiently to gain feedback in order to correct the actions to achieve goals. It is mutual combination of automated communication and control system between artificially intelligent machines and the environment with subsequent strong support from machine learning; the concepts of systems thinking and systems theory became integral parts of the established scientific language of *Cybernetical Intelligence* and can lead to numerous new methodologies and applications.

The basic ideas of *Cybernetical Intelligence* can be treated without reference to electronics, but they are fundamentally challenging; so although advanced techniques may be necessary for advanced applications, a great deal can be done, especially in biological sciences, by the use of mathematical derivations, provided they are used with a clear and deep understanding of the principals involved.

This book is intended to provide a concise conceptualization of *Cybernetical Intelligence*. It starts from common place and well-understood concepts and proceeds, step by step, to show how these concepts can be made exact and how they can be developed until they lead into subjects such as feedback, stability, regulation, ultrastability, information, coding, noise, and other cybernetic topics. Closed-loop applications and features of neural network are examined and developed in great detail in this book, employing mathematical stability proof approaches that illustrate how to construct neuro-controllers while also ensuring their stability and performance. Control engineering based concepts, a family of multi-loop neuro-controllers for various applications have been created methodically.

There are strategies for both continuous-time and discrete-time weight tuning given. The book is intended for students taking a second semester in control theory, as well as engineers in academia and industry who construct feedback controllers for complex systems found in commercial, industrial, and military applications. The many types of neuro-controllers are organized in tables for simple reference when it comes to design procedures.

This material is a comprehensive exploration of the advanced terminologies in AI and cybernetics. In Chapter 1, the concept of AI and its relation to cybernetics are introduced. Chapter 2 delves into the theory of cybernetical intelligence and control. Chapter 3 covers the basics of perceptron, including its activation function. The structure of the multilayer perceptron neural network is discussed in Chapter 4, while Chapter 5 covers the backpropagation algorithm and its derivatives, as well as the resampling rate. Chapter 6 focuses on neural network applications in learning and recognition. Chapter 7 explores self-organizing and its applications in AI, and Chapter 8 covers support vector machines and their applications. Chapters 9 and 10 delve into bio- and life-inspired *Cybernetical Intelligence*. Chapters 11 and 12 revisit cybernetics and its relation to *Cybernetical Intelligence* and Turing machines. Entropy concepts and sampling methods in *Cybernetical Intelligence* are covered in Chapters 13 and 14. Chapters 15 and 16 describe linear systems and deep learning, including their methods and applications. Finally, Chapter 17 focuses on neural architecture search, including its methods and applications. Every chapter presents its own characteristic concept, and the concatenation of these concepts generates a mind map and general framework for the formulation of machine learning from the cybernetics perspective and encompassing the *Cybernetical Intelligence* philosophy. The philosophical insights and mathematical theories in this book will give us the adequate knowledge necessary for building AI.

It is the author's belief that the subject founded is well understood and is then built up carefully, step by step, with advanced mathematical, computing, and engineering knowledge. Having spent years consolidating and developing the conceptual roadmap of machine learning from the cybernetics perspective, the author is proud to present the novel work on *Cybernetical Intelligence* to the academic community with the ultimate aim of training the next generation of AI cybernetists.

About the Author

 Prof. Dr. Kelvin K. L. Wong is a distinguished expert in medical image processing and computational science, who earned his Ph.D. from The University of Adelaide. With a strong academic background from Nanyang Technological University and The University of Sydney, he has been at the forefront of merging the fields of cybernetics and artificial intelligence (AI). He is widely recognized for introducing the term "Cybernetical Intelligence" and is the inventor and founder of the Deep Red AI system. Dr. Wong's impactful research in AI has yielded significant achievements with the potential to positively impact humanity. He is the author of influential books such as *Methods in Research and Development of Biomedical Devices* and *Computational Hemodynamics–Theory, Modelling, and Applications*. With extensive experience as an associate editor and guest editor for esteemed biomedical engineering and computational intelligence journals, he has contributed extensively to the field. As an internationally recognized biomedical engineering scientist and AI cybernetist, Dr. Wong was named among Stanford University's top 1.3% biomedical engineering researchers in 2020. He has actively participated in researching the management and control of COVID-19 and is a dedicated supporter and donor to UNICEF, advocating for kindness and human rights. Throughout his professorship, he has mentored numerous students, providing invaluable guidance and shaping their careers. Leading a team of experts in AI, healthcare, disease management, and diagnosis, Dr. Wong's expertise has been instrumental in supporting government projects and initiatives in developing countries.

About the Companion Website

This book is accompanied by a companion website:

www.wiley.com/go/cyberintel

This website includes:

- Assignments and Solutions

1

Artificial Intelligence and Cybernetical Learning

Artificial intelligence (AI) is a field of engineering cybernetics that focuses on the development of intelligent machines that can simulate human-like behaviors such as learning, problem-solving, reasoning, and decision-making. AI technology involves the use of algorithms and computational models to analyze vast amounts of data, recognize patterns and make predictions, and interact with humans through natural language processing (NLP) and other forms of communication.

This chapter will comprehensively explore various aspects of AI, including its relation to cybernetics and the fundamental principles governing it. Additionally, it will delve into the nuances of parametric and nonparametric algorithms and core concepts of cybernetical intelligence (CI). Through a systematic and rigorous exposition, readers will acquire a robust understanding of the key principles and algorithms that underlie AI. Consequently, they will be well equipped with the requisite knowledge to develop their own AI applications, leveraging the insights gained from this chapter.

1.1 Artificial Intelligence Initiative

Intelligence includes the capacity for abstraction, logic, learning, reasoning, communication, and inference. It can learn from the environment both actively and passively and use the knowledge to obtain adaptive ability. AI can be defined as a human-made machine with human-like intelligence. The use of AI in education has produced effective pedagogical effects in addition to technical advancements and theoretical developments. Automated target identification, automatic medical diagnosis, and audio recording are a few interesting uses. AI may be utilized to provide customized assistance and increase knowledge-gap awareness, allowing educators to deliver individualized and adaptable education with efficiency and effectiveness. Enabling computers to simulate intelligent behavior using prestored world models is the main goal of AI. The AI simulates human cognitive processes such as reasoning, learning, pattern recognition, knowledge reasoning, and machine learning (ML). ML refers to the creation of automated systems capable of processing massive volumes of data for data mining and is one of the more traditional fields of computing intelligence.

ML is a part of AI that allows machines to obtain intelligence from data without being explicitly programmed. Therefore, it often associates ML with data mining. ML enables a cyber system to possess intelligence by using massive data. Based on that data, ML models or algorithms can mine the knowledge, rules, and laws behind the data. ML identifies underlying functional links in systems between sets of variables and individual variables. The goal of combining the fields of ML and cybernetics is to identify different ways that systems interact with one another through various methods for learning from data. Equation (1.1) illustrates how ML may be summed up as learning a function (f) that maps input variables (x) to output variables (y).

$$y = f(x). \tag{1.1}$$

The configuration of the function is unknown, but the ML algorithms learn to map the target function from the training data. It is necessary to assess many algorithms to determine which one is best at modeling the underlying function because they all reach different conclusions or exhibit biases on the function's structure. In theory, there are two types of ML algorithms: parametric algorithms and nonparametric algorithms. Additionally, three well-known techniques are used to train ML algorithms. Supervised learning, unsupervised learning, and reinforcement learning are the three categories of ML.

The most significant methodology in ML is supervised learning, which is especially crucial in the processing of multimedia data. This kind of learning is comparable to how humans learn from their past experiences to obtain new information and improve their capacity to carry out activities in the actual world. Models for supervised learning are designed to predict the appropriate label for newly presented data. Unsupervised learning is typically used to identify patterns in the input data that propose candidate features prior to the application of supervised learning, and feature engineering changes these candidate features to make them more appropriate for supervised learning. It is quite time-consuming to identify the correct category or response for every observation in the training set in addition to the characteristics. With the help of semi-supervised learning, one may train models with very little labeled data, which will reduce the labeling work.

Unsupervised learning can be motivated from information-theoretic and Bayesian principles. It empowers the model to work independently to identify previously unnoticed patterns and information. Take into account a device (or living thing) that gets a series of inputs, such as $x_1, x_2, ..., x_t$, where x_t is the sensory input at time t. This input, which is known as sensory data, can be a representation of a retinal image, a camera's pixels, or a sound waveform. The most famous technique is clustering in which each observation belongs to at least one of the k clusters, while i and j belong to centroid of each cluster. Furthermore, variation within each cluster is achieved by minimizing the sum of the squared Euclidean distance between each observation within a cluster, as shown in Equation (1.2).

$$\underset{\{C_k\}, \forall k \in 1, ...K}{\text{argmin}} \sum_{k=1}^{k} \sum_{i \in C_k} \|X_i - \mu_k\|^2, \tag{1.2}$$

where μ_k represents the centroid of the kth cluster, X_i is the ith data point in the kth cluster, and C_k represents the set of indices of data points assigned to the kth cluster. Reinforcement learning, on the other hand, is heavily influenced by the theory of Markov decision processes and deals with the ability to learn the associations between stimuli, actions, and the occurrence of positive events. The agents are taught a reward and punishment scheme in reinforcement learning. For wise actions, the agent is rewarded, and for poor ones, they are penalized. While doing this, the agent tries to minimize the undesirable motions while maximizing the desirable ones. It is hardly unexpected that reinforcement learning has been noticed in the really distant past given its clear adaptive benefit. A few cybernetics experiments have made use of reinforcement learning. Robots can learn skills that a human instructor is unable to teach, adapt a learned ability to a new task, and accomplish optimization even in the absence of an analytical formulation with the help of this sort of ML. The predicted total of the immediate reward and the long-term reward under the best feasible policy (Max Policies), as given in Equation (1.3), is utility u (over a limited agent lifespan):

$$u(s_t, a) = \mathbb{E} \, R(s_t, a) + \text{MaxPolicies} \sum_{j=1}^{N-1} R(t+j), \tag{1.3}$$

where s_t is the state at time step t, $R(s_t, a)$ is the immediate reward of executing an action in state s_t, N is the number of steps in the lifetime of the agent, and R is the reward time step t. The operator $\mathbb{E}$ stands for taking an expectation over all sources of randomness in the system. Here, s_t denotes the state at time step t, $R(s_t, a)$ is the instantaneous benefit of carrying out an action in state s_t, and N denotes the total number of steps the agent will take throughout its lifespan. Taking an expectation across all system randomness sources is what the operator.

The configuration of the function is unknown, but the ML algorithms learn to map the target function from the training data. It is necessary to compare multiple algorithms to determine which one is the best successful at modeling the underlying function since different algorithms reach different conclusions or have different biases on the structure of the function. As a result, ML algorithms may be divided into parametric and nonparametric varieties, which will be covered in the following subsections.

1.2 Intelligent Automation Initiative

Intelligent automation initiative (IAI) is an emerging technology-driven approach to optimize business processes and decision-making through a combination of AI, robotic process automation (RPA), and other advanced technologies. It aims to streamline repetitive and mundane tasks, improve productivity, reduce errors, and enable employees to focus on higher-value-added activities. The IAI strategy involves the integration of different technologies to automate various aspects of the business, including customer service, supply chain management, finance, human resources, and more. The main components of IAI include:

- Artificial intelligence (AI): A subset of computer science that focuses on developing algorithms that can mimic human intelligence, such as speech recognition, NLP, ML, and computer vision. AI helps organizations to make sense of vast amounts of data, predict trends, and make informed decisions.
- Robotic process automation (RPA): A software tool that uses bots to automate repetitive and rule-based tasks, such as data entry, invoice processing, and report generation. RPA can reduce operational costs, improve accuracy, and increase efficiency.
- Advanced analytics: It involves the use of statistical models, data mining, and predictive analytics to analyze data and extract insights. This can help organizations to make informed decisions and improve business outcomes.
- Chatbots: AI-powered virtual assistants that can interact with customers, answer queries, and resolve issues in real time. Chatbots can improve customer satisfaction, reduce response times, and free up resources for other tasks.
- Machine learning: A subset of AI that focuses on developing algorithms that can learn from data without being explicitly programmed. ML can be used to make predictions, identify patterns, and automate decision-making.
- Cognitive automation: Involves the use of AI and other advanced technologies to automate complex tasks that require human-like reasoning and decision-making. This can include tasks such as fraud detection, risk analysis, and supply chain optimization.

1.2.1 Benefits of IAI

IAI is a strategic approach to integrating advanced technologies, such as AI, RPA, and ML, to automate business processes and workflows. Here are some of the benefits of implementing IAI:

- Increased productivity: Automation can perform repetitive and time-consuming tasks faster and with fewer errors than humans, leading to increased productivity and efficiency. By freeing up employees from these mundane tasks, they can focus on higher-value tasks that require creativity and critical thinking.
- Cost savings: Automation can help reduce labor costs, as companies no longer need to hire additional staff to perform repetitive tasks. Additionally, automation can help reduce operational costs by streamlining processes and reducing the potential for errors and delays.
- Improved accuracy and quality: Automation can perform tasks with a high degree of accuracy, consistency, and quality, reducing the potential for errors and improving the quality of work produced.
- Faster processing times: Automation can help speed up processing times for tasks such as data entry, data analysis, and report generation. This can lead to faster decision-making and improved business agility.
- Enhanced customer experience: Automation can help improve the customer experience by enabling faster response times to inquiries, reducing errors, and providing more accurate and personalized services.
- Increased scalability: Automation can help businesses scale their operations more easily by enabling them to handle higher volumes of work without the need for additional staff.
- Better data insights: Automation can help businesses gather and analyze data more quickly and accurately, enabling them to make better-informed decisions.

Overall, the benefits of IAI can help businesses streamline their operations, reduce costs, and improve their ability to compete in an increasingly fast-paced and competitive market.

1.3 Artificial Intelligence Versus Intelligent Automation

AI and intelligent automation (IA) are two related technologies that are transforming the way businesses operate. AI is the simulation of human intelligence processes by machines, while IA refers to the automation of processes using AI and other advanced technologies. IA combines RPA, ML, and other AI technologies to automate repetitive and time-consuming tasks. It allows businesses to automate processes that were previously done manually, which saves time, reduces costs, and improves accuracy.

AI, on the other hand, is a broader field that encompasses a range of technologies, including ML, NLP, and computer vision. These technologies enable machines to perform tasks that would typically require human intelligence, such as understanding language, recognizing images, and making decisions based on data. When AI and IA are combined, businesses can achieve even greater benefits. For example, IA can be used to automate processes such as data entry and document processing, while AI can be used to analyze that data and provide insights for decision-making. This can help businesses make more informed decisions faster, which can lead to improved efficiency, productivity, and profitability. Moreover, AI can help automate decision-making processes by analyzing vast amounts of data and providing recommendations based on that data. IA can then be used to execute those decisions automatically, further streamlining business processes. The complete workflow of how IA works is shown in Figure 1.1.

1.3.1 Process Discovery

Process discovery involves using mathematical equations and algorithms to analyze business processes and identify areas where automation can be applied. One example of a mathematical equation used in process discovery is the process cycle efficiency (*PCE*), as shown in Equation (1.4).

$$PCE = \frac{VT}{CT} \times 100\%, \tag{1.4}$$

where value-added time (*VT*) is the time spent on activities that directly add value to the customer, and cycle time (*CT*) is the total time taken to complete the process, including both value-added and non-value-added activities. The *PCE* formula helps businesses identify areas where there is wastage or inefficiency in the process. A high *PCE* indicates that a process is highly efficient and that there is minimal wastage, while a low *PCE* suggests that there is a lot of wastage that can be eliminated through automation.

The first step in process discovery is to collect data on the current business processes. This can be done by conducting interviews with key stakeholders, analyzing documentation such as process maps, or observing the processes

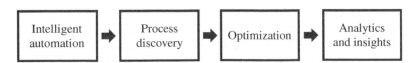

Figure 1.1 Workflow of intelligent automation.

in action. Once the data has been collected, the next step is to map out the processes using visual diagrams such as flowcharts or swim lane diagrams. This helps to identify the different steps involved in the process, as well as the inputs and outputs at each stage. After the process has been mapped out, the next step is to analyze it in detail. This involves looking for inefficiencies or bottlenecks in the process that could be improved through automation or optimization. Based on the analysis, the process can be optimized by identifying areas where automation can be applied to reduce manual effort, speed up processing times, or reduce errors. This may involve using RPA to automate repetitive tasks or using ML or AI to analyze data and make predictions about future outcomes.

Once the process has been optimized, it is important to test it thoroughly to ensure that it works as intended. This may involve conducting user acceptance testing (UAT) or running pilot programs to ensure that the process is reliable and effective. Once the testing is complete, the optimized process can be implemented into production. Overall, process discovery is an essential part of IA, as it helps organizations identify and optimize their existing business processes, reducing costs, increasing efficiency, and improving the overall customer experience. By leveraging technologies, such as RPA, ML, and AI, organizations can automate repetitive tasks, make better decisions based on data, and streamline their operations to stay competitive in a rapidly evolving business landscape.

1.3.2 Optimization

Optimization is an important aspect of IA. It refers to the process of improving the efficiency and effectiveness of automated processes over time by continuously analyzing and refining them. Optimization involves using advanced technologies such as ML and AI to analyze data generated by automated processes. By analyzing this data, businesses can identify areas where the process can be improved and make adjustments to improve efficiency and effectiveness.

One example of how optimization can be achieved is with predictive analytics. Predictive analytics uses statistical algorithms and ML techniques to analyze historical data and make predictions about future outcomes. By using predictive analytics, businesses can identify potential problems in their automated processes before they occur, allowing them to take corrective action to prevent issues from arising. Optimization is an ongoing process in IA, and it requires businesses to continuously monitor and analyze their automated processes to identify areas for improvement. By doing so, businesses can improve efficiency, reduce costs, and improve the quality of products or services produced, leading to improved customer satisfaction and profitability. Here are the key steps involved in optimizing processes using IA:

- Identify the processes to be optimized: The first step is to identify the processes that are causing bottlenecks, delays, or inefficiencies. This can be done by analyzing data, conducting surveys, or observing the workflow. Once the processes have been identified, it is important to prioritize them based on their impact on the business.
- Define the objectives: The next step is to define the objectives of the optimization process. This could be reducing costs, improving quality, increasing productivity, or enhancing customer satisfaction. The objectives should be specific, measurable, and achievable.
- Collect data: Data is essential for IA to work effectively. It is important to collect relevant data related to the processes being optimized, such as CT, throughput, error rates, and customer feedback. The data can be collected from various sources, such as sensors, databases, or manual inputs.
- Analyze the data: The data collected needs to be analyzed using advanced analytics techniques, such as ML or statistical analysis. This will help identify patterns, trends, and correlations that can provide insights into the root causes of the problems. Based on these insights, it is possible to develop strategies to optimize the processes.
- Implement intelligent automation: The next step is to implement IA to automate the processes. This can be done using a combination of technologies, such as RPA, NLP, and ML. The automation can be used to eliminate manual tasks, reduce errors, and speed up the process.
- Monitor and refine: Once the optimization process has been implemented, it is important to monitor the performance of the processes and refine the strategies if needed. This can be done using key performance indicators (KPIs) such as CT, cost per unit, and customer satisfaction scores. The data collected can be used to fine-tune the automation algorithms and make continuous improvements.

Overall, the combination of optimization and IA can provide significant benefits to organizations, such as cost savings, increased productivity, and improved customer satisfaction. By following these steps, businesses can create a data-driven approach to process optimization that leverages the power of advanced technologies.

1.3.3 Analytics and Insight

Analytics and insights are critical components of IA. They refer to the process of collecting and analyzing data generated by automated processes to gain insights into how the processes are performing and identify areas for improvement.

Analytics involves the use of advanced technologies such as ML and AI to analyze large volumes of data and identify patterns and trends. For example, businesses can use analytics to identify bottlenecks in their processes, areas where there is wastage or areas where automation can be applied to improve efficiency. Insights involve using the data generated by analytics to inform business decisions. For example, businesses can use insights gained from analytics to identify opportunities for process improvement, inform strategic decision-making, or identify areas where additional automation can be applied. Analytics and insights are essential in IA because they help businesses identify areas for improvement, optimize processes, and make data-driven decisions. By continuously analyzing data generated by automated processes and using insights to inform decision-making, businesses can improve efficiency, reduce costs, and improve the quality of products or services produced. IA is the use of AI and ML technologies to automate processes, tasks, and workflows. When applied to analytics, IA can significantly enhance the speed, accuracy, and efficiency of data processing and analysis.

By leveraging IA, businesses can quickly and easily extract insights from large amounts of data, identify trends and patterns that might be difficult to spot manually, and make data-driven decisions based on accurate and reliable information. This can help companies improve their performance, optimize their processes, reduce costs, and stay ahead of the competition.

In conclusion, AI and IA are two powerful technologies that are transforming the way businesses operate. By combining these technologies, businesses can automate processes, analyze data, and make more informed decisions faster, which can lead to improved efficiency and profitability.

1.4 The Fourth Industrial Revolution and Artificial Intelligence

AI has played a crucial role in every industrial revolution from the first to the fourth. In the First Industrial Revolution, machines were primarily powered by steam, water, and coal. However, the Second Industrial Revolution brought about the rise of electricity and the development of the telegraph and telephone. The use of computers and automation in manufacturing was first introduced during the Third Industrial Revolution, which led to the development of AI. Then, AI technology was further improved in the Fourth Industrial Revolution (4IR), which brought about the Internet of Things (IoT), Big Data, and cloud computing. The use of AI in these revolutions has brought about increased efficiency, productivity, and automation of various industries. In the 4th Industrial Revolution, AI is being used to optimize manufacturing processes, improve supply chain management, and revolutionize healthcare by developing more accurate diagnoses and personalized treatments. AI has become a crucial tool in various industries, and it is expected to continue playing an essential role in future revolutions.

The 4IR is a term used to describe the current era of rapid technological advancement that is transforming the way of living, working, and communicating. It builds upon the previous industrial revolutions, which were characterized by the mechanization of production (1IR), the introduction of mass production and assembly lines (2IR), and the automation of production through the use of computers and robotics (3IR). The 4IR is characterized by the integration of physical, digital, and biological systems and the use of technologies such as AI, the IoT, and robotics to drive innovation and productivity.

AI is one of the key technologies driving the 4IR. It refers to the ability of machines to perform tasks that typically require human intelligence, such as learning, reasoning, problem-solving, and perception. AI systems are designed to simulate human cognitive abilities and can be used to automate a wide range of tasks across different industries. One of the most significant impacts of AI is its ability to analyze vast amounts of data quickly and accurately. This makes it particularly useful for applications, such as predictive analytics, where it can be used to identify patterns and make predictions based on historical data. AI is also increasingly being used for NLP, which enables computers to understand and process human language. Another key application of AI in the 4IR is in the development of autonomous systems, such as self-driving cars and drones. These systems use a combination of sensors, algorithms, and ML to navigate their environment and make decisions in real time.

AI is also being used to improve healthcare, with applications such as personalized medicine, medical imaging, and drug discovery. In the financial sector, AI is being used for fraud detection and risk assessment, while in manufacturing, it is being used to optimize production processes and improve product quality. However, the increasing use of AI also raises concerns about issues such as job displacement, bias in decision-making, and data privacy. As such, there is a growing need for ethical frameworks and regulations to ensure that AI is used in a responsible and transparent manner. The Fourth Industrial Revolution will be characterized by the widespread use of AI and Big Data. AI can be categorized into three stages: narrow artificial intelligence (ANI), artificial general intelligence (AGI), and super artificial intelligence (ASI). The ultimate goal is to achieve intelligence or even wisdom.

1.4.1 Artificial Narrow Intelligence

Artificial Narrow Intelligence (ANI) is a type of AI that is designed to perform specific tasks within a limited range of functions. ANI systems are built using ML algorithms and statistical models, and they are trained on large amounts of data to perform specific tasks. ANI systems use mathematical equations and algorithms to process data and make decisions based on that data. These mathematical models are often complex and can involve several different types of algorithms and techniques. One example of an ANI system is a computer vision system that is designed to recognize objects in images. This type of system uses deep learning algorithms, such as convolutional neural networks (CNNs), to analyze images and identify patterns that are associated with specific objects.

The mathematical equations used in ANI systems vary depending on the specific application, but they generally involve techniques such as linear algebra, probability theory, and optimization. Here are some examples of mathematical equations that are commonly used in ANI:

Linear regression is a statistical technique that is used to model the relationship between two variables. In ANI, linear regression can be used to predict the value of an output variable based on the values of one or more input variables. The equation for linear regression is:

$$y = b_0 + b_1 x_1 + b_2 x_2 + \ldots + b_n x_n, \tag{1.5}$$

where y is the output variable, $x_1, x_2, \ldots, x_n$ are the input variables, and $b_0, b_1, b_2, \ldots, b_n$ are the coefficients of the regression equation. Bayes' Theorem is a mathematical equation that is used to calculate the probability of an event based on prior knowledge of related events. In ANI, Bayes' Theorem can be used to make predictions based on data that has been collected previously. The equation for Bayes' Theorem is:

$$P(A \mid B) = \frac{P(B \mid A)P(A)}{P(B)}, \tag{1.6}$$

where $P(A \mid B)$ is the probability of event A given that event B has occurred, $P(B \mid A)$ is the probability of event B given that event A has occurred, $P(A)$ is the prior probability of event A, and $P(B)$ is the prior probability of event B.

Gradient descent is an optimization algorithm that is used to find the minimum of a function. In ANI, gradient descent can be used to adjust the parameters of an ML model to minimize the error between predicted and actual values. The equation for the gradient descent algorithm is:

$$b = a - \gamma \nabla f(a), \tag{1.7}$$

where b is the next position of the migrating point, while a represents its current position. The minus sign refers to the minimization part of the gradient descent algorithm. The γ is a waiting factor and the gradient term $\nabla f(a)$ is simply the direction of the steepest descent.

In summary, ANI is a type of AI that uses mathematical equations and algorithms to process data and perform specific tasks. The specific mathematical models and equations used in ANI systems depend on the specific application, but they generally involve techniques such as linear algebra, probability theory, and optimization.

1.4.2 Artificial General Intelligence

Artificial General Intelligence (AGI) is a theoretical type of AI that can perform tasks that typically require human-level intelligence.

The idea behind AGI is that an AI system would be able to learn and adapt to new situations, just as a human would. This would require the AI to be able to reason, make decisions, and solve problems in a variety of contexts. One of the key challenges in creating AGI is developing algorithms that can handle the complexity of human-like thinking.

One approach to developing AGI is through deep learning, which uses neural networks to simulate the function of the human brain. Neural networks consist of interconnected nodes that perform computations based on input data. These computations are typically represented as mathematical equations. The connections between nodes are weighted based on the strength of the correlation between the input and output data. The weights are adjusted during the learning process, allowing the neural network to improve its predictions over time.

Another approach to developing AGI is reinforcement learning, which involves training an AI system to make decisions based on feedback from its environment. Reinforcement learning uses a reward-based system to encourage the AI to take actions that lead to positive outcomes. The goal is to develop an AI system that can learn from its mistakes and make better decisions over time. There are many mathematical equations used in the development of AGI, including:

- Gradient descent: This equation is used in deep learning to adjust the weights of the connections between nodes in a neural network. It involves calculating the gradient of the error function with respect to the weights and then adjusting the weights in the direction of the gradient.
- Bellman equation: This equation is used in reinforcement learning to calculate the expected value of a decision based on the potential future rewards. It takes into account the immediate reward as well as the expected future reward based on the decision.
- Bayes' Theorem: This equation is used in probabilistic reasoning to update the probability of a hypothesis based on new evidence. It is often used in ML algorithms that involve uncertainty.

Overall, AGI is a complex and challenging field of study that involves many different mathematical approaches. While still there has not been a fully functioning AGI system, ongoing research is pushing the boundaries of what is possible with AI and bringing us closer to creating machines that can reason, learn, and adapt like humans.

1.4.3 Artificial Super Intelligence

Artificial Super Intelligence (ASI) refers to the hypothetical future state of AI where machines will surpass human intelligence and become capable of performing tasks that are currently considered impossible for machines. While there is no universally accepted definition of super AI, one way to conceptualize it is through the concept of an AGI. An AGI is an AI system that is capable of understanding or learning any intellectual task that a human being can, including those that are currently beyond the capabilities of any machine. ASI could be seen as an even more advanced version of AGI, capable of not just performing any intellectual task but surpassing human intelligence in all areas. The development of ASI would likely involve significant advances in fields such as ML, artificial neural networks (ANNs), and reinforcement learning, as well as the development of entirely new approaches to AI. Some possible mathematical equations and concepts that could be involved in the development of super AI include:

- Neural networks: ANNs are a mathematical model that is inspired by the structure and function of biological neural networks in the brain. ANNs consist of layers of interconnected nodes (also known as neurons), which are capable of processing information and making predictions. ANNs can be trained using algorithms such as backpropagation to adjust the weights and biases of the nodes to improve their performance. Super AI could potentially involve the development of more advanced and complex neural networks, with a greater number of layers and nodes.
- Reinforcement learning: A type of ML that involves an agent learning through trial and error in an environment where it receives feedback in the form of rewards or punishments. The agent's goal is to learn a policy (i.e. a set of actions) that maximizes its long-term reward. Super AI could potentially involve the development of more advanced reinforcement learning algorithms, such as deep reinforcement learning, which uses deep neural networks to represent the agent's policy.
- Bayesian networks: A probabilistic graphical model that represents a set of random variables and their conditional dependencies using a directed acyclic graph. Bayesian networks can be used for reasoning, prediction, and decision-making

under uncertainty. Super AI could potentially involve the development of more advanced Bayesian networks, capable of handling larger and more complex data sets.

- Information theory: Information theory is a mathematical framework for quantifying and analyzing the amount of information in a message or data set. Information theory can be used for tasks such as data compression, error correction, and signal processing. ASI could potentially involve the development of more advanced information-theoretic approaches to AI, such as the use of entropy-based measures to optimize learning algorithms.
- Optimization theory: A branch of mathematics that deals with finding the best solution to a problem within a set of constraints. Optimization theory can be used to solve a wide range of problems in AI, such as parameter tuning, feature selection, and hyperparameter optimization. ASI could potentially involve the development of more advanced optimization algorithms, such as stochastic gradient descent with adaptive learning rates.

Overall, the development of super AI would likely involve significant advances in a wide range of mathematical fields, as well as interdisciplinary collaborations between computer scientists, mathematicians, and other experts. While it is difficult to predict the exact form that super AI will take, these mathematical concepts and approaches are likely to play a central role in its development.

1.5 Pattern Analysis and Cognitive Learning

Pattern analysis and cognitive learning are two important concepts in the field of AI and ML. These approaches have been used in various applications, such as image recognition, NLP, and speech recognition, to name a few.

Pattern analysis is the process of identifying patterns or regularities in data. It involves analyzing large amounts of data and looking for commonalities or trends that can be used to make predictions or draw conclusions. In ML, pattern analysis is often used in unsupervised learning, where the algorithm must identify patterns on its own without any explicit training or guidance.

Cognitive learning, on the other hand, is a subfield of AI that is focused on mimicking the way humans learn and process information. This approach is based on the idea that human learning involves more than just identifying patterns in data. It involves reasoning, problem-solving, and decision-making. Cognitive learning algorithms attempt to replicate these processes by using techniques such as neural networks and decision trees.

One of the key advantages of pattern analysis and cognitive learning is their ability to handle large amounts of data. This makes them particularly useful in applications where there is a lot of data to analyze, such as in social media monitoring or financial forecasting. Another advantage is their ability to learn and adapt over time. ML algorithms can be trained on new data as it becomes available, allowing them to improve their predictions or recommendations over time. There are several applications of pattern analysis and cognitive learning in various industries. For example, in healthcare, pattern analysis can be used to identify early warning signs of diseases, while cognitive learning can be used to help doctors diagnose and treat patients.

1.5.1 Machine Learning

ML is a field in AI that deals with developing algorithms and models that can learn patterns and relationships in data without being explicitly programmed. The key idea behind ML is to use data to train a model to make predictions or decisions based on new data. ML can be broadly classified into three categories: supervised learning, unsupervised learning, and reinforcement learning.

Supervised learning involves training a model on a labeled dataset, where the desired output is known. In supervised learning, the model is trained to learn the relationship between input variables and their corresponding output variables. The model is then used to predict the output variable for new input variables. Examples of supervised learning algorithms include linear regression, logistic regression, decision trees, random forests, and neural networks.

Unsupervised learning involves training a model on an unlabeled dataset, where the desired output is not known. In unsupervised learning, the model is trained to learn the structure of the data and identify patterns and relationships between the input variables. Examples of unsupervised learning algorithms include clustering algorithms, such as K-means clustering and hierarchical clustering, and dimensionality reduction algorithms, such as principal component analysis (PCA) and t-distributed stochastic neighbor embedding (t-SNE).

Reinforcement learning involves training a model to interact with an environment and learn from its experiences. In reinforcement learning, the model is rewarded or punished based on its actions, and it learns to take actions that maximize its reward. Examples of reinforcement learning algorithms include Q-learning, SARSA, and deep reinforcement learning. The process of ML typically involves the following steps:

- Data collection: Collecting and preprocessing the data is the first step in ML. The data is collected from various sources and is cleaned and preprocessed to remove any noise, outliers, or missing values.
- Feature engineering: Involves selecting and transforming the input variables to improve the performance of the model. The features are selected based on their

relevance to the output variable and are transformed to ensure that they are in the appropriate format for the model.

- Model training: Involves selecting an appropriate algorithm and training the model on the dataset. The model is trained using a portion of the data, and the remaining portion is used for validation and testing.
- Model evaluation: Involves measuring the performance of the model on the validation and testing datasets. The performance metrics used to evaluate the model depend on the problem being solved and the type of algorithm used.
- Model deployment: Involves integrating the trained model into the production environment and using it to make predictions or decisions on new data.

1.5.1.1 Parametric Algorithms

The foundation of parametric algorithms is a mathematical representation of the input–output connection. They have fewer applications than nonparametric algorithms as a result, but they are quicker and simpler to learn. The most suitable problems for parametric algorithms have well-defined and predictable input data. A parametric model is a learning model that uses a collection of fixed-size parameters to summarize data (regardless of the number of training samples). The methods consist of two steps: choosing a function's form in the first step and learning the function's coefficients from training data in the second. Equation (1.8) illustrates a functional form for the mapping function f.

$$(x_1, x_2) = b_0 + b_1 x_1 + b_2 x_2. \tag{1.8}$$

where x_1 and x_2 are two input variables, and b_0, b_1, and b_2 are the line's coefficients that determine the intercept and slope.

By assuming a line's functional form, the learning process may be greatly streamlined. All that is needed to turn this into a predictive model for the circumstance is to guess the coefficients of the line equation. Since the assumed functional form is generally a linear combination of the input variables, parametric ML algorithms are sometimes referred to as "linear machine learning algorithms." The coefficients must be estimated with respect to Equation (1.4). As a consequence, a predictive model is produced for the specified job. Any value may be predicted using the intercept and coefficients. Parametric models are often referred to as linear ML models. This is because the function's expected form is linear. Figure 1.2 also displays a few examples of parametric algorithms.

In the context of cybernetics, parametric algorithms can be used to model complex systems and predict their behavior. The process of estimating these parameters often involves optimization techniques, such as gradient descent, that seek to minimize the difference between the predicted output and the actual output. For instance, in the development of control systems for autonomous vehicles.

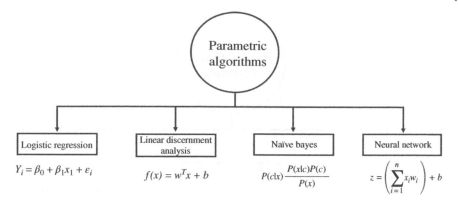

Figure 1.2 Examples of parametric algorithms along with their characteristic mathematical equations.

By modeling the relationships between inputs such as speed and steering angle and outputs such as vehicle trajectory and speed, parametric algorithms can be used to predict the behavior of the vehicle and adjust its controls to optimize its performance. These algorithms can also be used to learn from feedback and improve their predictions over time, leading to more efficient and reliable control systems.

Overall, parametric algorithms are a powerful tool in the field of cybernetics, as they allow researchers to model complex systems and make predictions about their behavior. By optimizing these models through the estimation of parameters, researchers can create systems that are more efficient, adaptable, and robust.

1.5.1.2 Nonparametric Algorithms

Algorithms for nonparametric ML do not place a lot of reliance on the characteristics of the mapping function. Since they are not making any assumptions, they are free to learn any functional form of the training data. Nonparametric techniques are the best option when there is a lot of data, no previous knowledge, and no need to worry about choosing the right features.

Nonparametric methods make an effort to produce the mapping function that fits the training data the best while keeping some generalizability to unknown data. They may thus accommodate a variety of functional shapes. The k-Nearest Neighbor method is a simple nonparametric model that makes predictions based on the k most similar training patterns for fresh data instances. The method's only mapping function shape assumption is that patterns with similar characteristics are likely to have similar output variables. For nonparametric ones, the quantity of training data affects how many parameters are used. The number of parameters

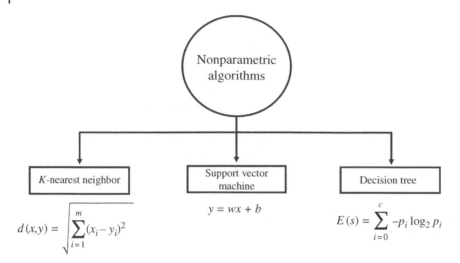

Figure 1.3 Examples of nonparametric algorithms along with their characteristics mathematical equations.

increases with the amount of training data. This has the effect of making nonparametric algorithms' training times significantly longer. Figure 1.3 also displays a few examples of nonparametric methods.

After a detailed understanding of AI, ML algorithms, and their different categories, it is important to understand how AI and cybernetics are related to each other. AI and cybernetics are sometimes confused with each other, as to which deals with the creation of intelligent cyborgs and robots. In reality, cybernetics and AI are two different perspectives on intelligent systems or systems that may act to achieve a purpose. Furthermore, both AI and cybernetics are built on the notion of human–machine interaction and are based on binary logic. Moreover, the feature-wise difference between parametric and nonparametric algorithms is shown in Table 1.1.

They are two distinct but linked fields. Cybernetics is based on a constructivist understanding of the universe, whereas AI is based on a realist notion that machines can operate and behave like humans. Cybernetics constitutes a closed-loop feedback control system, while neural networks serve as multiple control mechanisms for interconnected neurons in a system. This shows that creating these meta-systems calls for new technology. It is crucial to take your time and pay attention to it in order to do this. Participant observation and self-observation are two techniques mentioned by Martelaro that may provide a feedback loop on the designer's own creative process. It is a reality that in the future, more designers need to get familiar with cybernetics. More critically,

Table 1.1 Feature-wise difference between parametric and nonparametric algorithm.

Feature	Parametric Algorithm	Nonparametric Algorithm
Definition	Makes assumptions about the underlying data distribution	Makes no assumptions about the underlying data distribution
Model complexity	Often simpler, with fewer parameters to estimate	More complex, with more parameters or even infinite parameters
Data size requirements	Typically requires a larger sample size to estimate parameters accurately	Can often work with smaller sample sizes
Flexibility	Less flexible, as the assumptions made about the data can limit the types of data that can be analyzed	More flexible, as they can be applied to a wider range of data types and distributions
Robustness	More sensitive to outliers and violations of assumptions	More robust to outliers and violations of assumptions
Common examples	Linear regression, ANOVA, t-tests	k-nearest neighbors, decision trees, support vector machines

engineers should consider including feedback systems into design tools that may help designers with both the current design project and the design process. Once it is understood that how AI and cybernetics are relating to each other further, there is need to understand the mathematics of cybernetics. According to Wiener who proposed the study of control and communication in the animal and the machine, it is suggested that learning, cognition, adaptability, emergence, communication, and efficiency are all ideas in cybernetics that are fundamental to the comprehension of complex systems.

The nonparametric algorithms are particularly useful when the underlying relationship between inputs and outputs is unknown or difficult to model. For instance, in the development of control systems for unmanned aerial vehicles. These systems must be able to adapt to changing conditions, such as wind speed and direction, while maintaining stability and control of the vehicle. Nonparametric algorithms such as support vector machines and decision trees have been used to model the relationship between inputs such as airspeed and altitude, and outputs such as pitch and roll angles, allowing for more accurate and adaptable control systems. Overall, nonparametric algorithms offer a flexible and adaptable approach to modeling complex systems in cybernetics, particularly when the underlying relationships between inputs and outputs are unknown or difficult to model using traditional parametric approaches.

Neural networks are a class of cybernetic systems that are modeled on the structure and function of the human brain. They is a type of ML algorithm that is capable of learning complex patterns in data and making predictions based on that learning. Neural networks are composed of layers of interconnected nodes, or neurons, that process and transmit information. They are used for tasks such as classification, regression, and pattern recognition. The basic unit of a neural network is the artificial neuron, which computes a weighted sum of its inputs and applies an activation function. The output of a neuron is given by $y = f(w \cdot x + b)$, where y is the output, x is the input, w is the weight vector, b is the bias, and f is the activation function.

Neurons are typically organized into layers within a neural network. The input layer receives data from the outside world, while the output layer produces the final output of the network. In between the input and output layers, there may be one or more hidden layers that perform computations on the data as it passes through the network. During the training process, a neural network is presented with a set of input–output pairs, known as training data. The network adjusts the weights of the connections between its neurons in order to minimize the difference between its predicted outputs and the true outputs of the training data. This process is known as backpropagation, and it allows the neural network to learn complex patterns in the data and make accurate predictions on new, unseen data.

Neural networks are highly versatile and can be used in a wide range of applications, including image and speech recognition, NLP, and predictive analytics. They are particularly effective at tasks that involve large amounts of data and complex patterns, such as detecting fraud in financial transactions or predicting stock prices.

One of the key advantages of neural networks is their ability to learn from experience and improve their performance over time. As they are presented with more data and experience, they can refine their internal representations of the data and make more accurate predictions. This ability to learn and adapt makes neural networks a powerful tool for solving complex problems in a wide range of domains.

1.5.2 Deep Learning

Deep learning is a subfield of ML that uses neural networks with multiple layers to learn and recognize complex patterns in data. It is a form of AI that allows machines to learn from data, rather than being explicitly programmed. At a high level, ML is the process of teaching a computer to make predictions or decisions based on data, without being explicitly programmed. This can be done using a variety of algorithms, including linear regression, decision trees, support vector machines, and neural networks. In contrast to traditional programming, where rules and instructions are explicitly defined by the programmer, ML algorithms "learn" from data, iteratively improving their performance as they are exposed to more examples.

Deep learning is a specific type of ML that uses neural networks with many layers to learn hierarchical representations of data. In a neural network, information is processed through a series of interconnected nodes, or neurons, which are organized into layers. The input layer receives data, which is then transformed by a series of hidden layers before being output as a prediction or decision. Each layer in a neural network can be thought of as learning increasingly complex features of the data, allowing the network to make more accurate predictions.

Deep learning has gained popularity in recent years due to its ability to achieve state-of-the-art performance on a wide range of tasks, including image recognition, speech recognition, NLP, and game playing. It has been particularly effective in domains where there is a large amount of data available, as deep learning models can leverage this data to learn complex patterns that may be difficult or impossible for humans to detect. In summary, deep learning is a subfield of ML that uses neural networks with multiple layers to learn hierarchical representations of data. It is a form of AI that allows machines to learn from data, rather than being explicitly programmed. While ML encompasses a wide range of algorithms and techniques, deep learning specifically focuses on neural networks with many layers.

1.5.2.1 Convolutional Neural Networks in Advancing Artificial Intelligence

Neural networks are a type of ML algorithm that is designed to mimic the structure and function of the human brain. They are composed of multiple interconnected processing units called neurons, which are arranged in layers. Each neuron takes in input, processes it, and produces an output, which is then passed on to the next layer of neurons. Neural networks have been used extensively in advancing AI in a number of ways, including:

- Image recognition: One of the most widely used applications of neural networks is in image recognition. Neural networks can be trained to recognize and classify images based on patterns and features present in the image data. This has many practical applications, such as in self-driving cars, where the car needs to be able to recognize and respond to objects in its environment.
- Natural language processing: Neural networks can also be used for NLP, which involves teaching machines to understand and generate human language. This has many applications, such as in chatbots, language translation, and speech recognition.
- Predictive analytics: Neural networks are also used in predictive analytics, where they are trained on historical data to make predictions about future events. This has many practical applications, such as in financial forecasting, fraud detection, and weather prediction.

- Robotics: Neural networks are also used in robotics, where they can be used to control the movement of robots and make decisions based on sensor data. This has many practical applications, such as in manufacturing and logistics.
- Gaming: Neural networks are also used in gaming, where they can be used to create intelligent opponents that can learn and adapt to the player's behavior.

1.5.2.2 Future Advancement in Deep Learning

Deep neural networks have seen significant advancements in recent years, and they are expected to continue evolving in the future. Here are some potential advancements that one can expect in the field of neural networks:

- Deep reinforcement learning: Reinforcement learning involves the use of a reward system to train an AI model. Deep reinforcement learning involves using neural networks to learn from the data generated by a reward-based system. This technique has already been used to teach machines to play complex games like Go and Chess. In the future, deep reinforcement learning will become more sophisticated and could be used to solve more complex problems in industries like robotics and autonomous vehicles.
- Explainable AI: The ability to interpret and explain the decisions made by AI models is becoming increasingly important. Explainable AI (XAI) aims to make AI more transparent by providing insights into the decision-making process of AI models. In the future, XAI techniques will become more sophisticated and will be able to provide more detailed and accurate explanations of AI model decisions.
- Generative adversarial networks (GANs): A type of neural network that can generate synthetic data that closely resembles real-world data. GANs are already being used to create realistic images and videos. In the future, GANs will become more advanced and can be used to create highly realistic virtual environments for gaming and training purposes.
- Transfer learning: Involves taking a pretrained neural network and fine-tuning it for a specific task. This technique allows for faster and more efficient training of neural networks. In the future, transfer learning will become more prevalent, and pretrained neural networks will become more widely available.
- Edge computing: Involves processing data at the edge of a network, rather than sending it to a centralized server for processing. This approach is becoming more important as the amount of data generated by IoT devices continues to grow. In the future, edge computing will become more sophisticated, and AI models will be designed to work effectively in edge computing environments.
- Quantum neural networks: Quantum computing is a rapidly growing field, and quantum neural networks (QNNs) are an area of active research. QNNs could

potentially outperform classical neural networks in certain applications. In the future, QNNs will become more sophisticated and can be seen the development of hybrid classical–QNNs that combine the strengths of both approaches.

- Neuromorphic computing: Involves designing hardware that mimics the structure and function of the human brain. This approach could lead to highly efficient and powerful AI models. In the future, neuromorphic computing will become more prevalent.

The future of neural networks looks bright, and one can expect to see continued advancements in this field in the years to come. These advancements will make AI models more powerful, efficient, and transparent, and will enable them to solve increasingly complex problems.

1.5.3 Cybernetical Learning

Cybernetics is a transdisciplinary field of study that explores the behavior of complex systems and how they can be controlled or regulated through feedback mechanisms. At its core, cybernetics seeks to understand the interactions between systems, and how they can be optimized for a desired outcome. Cybernetics has been influential in the development of AI, as many of the concepts and techniques used in AI are based on cybernetic principles. For example, feedback mechanisms are critical to the functioning of many AI systems, as they allow the system to adapt and learn from its environment. Additionally, cybernetics has contributed to the development of control systems, which are used to regulate the behavior of autonomous agents in AI applications such as robotics and autonomous vehicles. By drawing on the principles of cybernetical learning, researchers in AI are able to create systems that are more efficient, adaptable, and resilient and thereby giving rise to CI. At its core, cybernetic learning is about creating a feedback loop between a learner and their environment or task. This feedback loop allows the learner to adjust their behavior and improve their performance over time. The learner receives information about their progress and uses that information to make adjustments and improve their approach. There are several key components to cybernetic learning:

- Feedback loops: A crucial aspect of cybernetic learning. Learners need to receive feedback on their progress and performance so they can adjust their behavior and improve. Feedback can come in many forms, such as grades, test scores, or verbal feedback from a teacher.
- Control systems: The mechanisms that govern how the feedback loop operates. They set the parameters for what is considered successful performance and adjust those parameters based on feedback from the learner.

- Adaptation: Cybernetic learning is about adapting and adjusting behavior over time. As the learner receives feedback and makes changes, the control system also adjusts to ensure that the feedback loop remains effective.
- Communication: Effective communication is critical for cybernetic learning. The learner needs to be able to understand the feedback they receive and communicate their progress and challenges effectively.

One example of cybernetic learning is adaptive learning software, which uses feedback loops and control systems to adjust the difficulty of tasks based on the learner's performance. The software can adapt to the learner's needs and provide targeted feedback and support, helping them to improve their performance over time. The study of how systems control themselves and act in support of goals depending on input from the environment is included in cybernetics more broadly. Cybernetics is related to creating intelligent cyborgs and robots. In actuality, cybernetics and AI are different ways of thinking about intelligent systems or systems that can act toward reaching a goal. CI presents cogent and non-vital explanations for continuously ordered natural and biological phenomena that have previously been examined by scientific thinkers relying on vital functions. Cybernetics is a relatively new science concerned with the study of mechanical, biological, physical, and cognitive regulating systems. It is a broad concept that encompasses information processing, feedback regulation, and decision-making.

1.6 Cybernetical Artificial Intelligence

Cybernetics is the interdisciplinary study of the structure, function, and control of complex systems, including mechanical, biological, and social systems. It is often described as the science of communication and control of the animal and the machine. Cybernetics uses mathematical equations to model and analyze systems.

1.6.1 Artificial Intelligence Control Theory

Control theory is a branch of cybernetics that deals with the analysis and design of systems that can be controlled or regulated. It is concerned with the study of how systems behave, how they can be controlled, and how to optimize their performance. Control theory deals with the design of controllers that can manipulate a system to achieve a desired response. The most commonly used controller is the Proportional–Integral–Derivative (PID) controller, which is defined by the Equation (1.9).

$$u(t) = k_p e(t) + K_i \int_0^t e(t)dt + K_d \frac{de(t)}{dt}, \tag{1.9}$$

where $u(t)$ is the control input, $e(t)$ is the error signal, k_p, K_i, and K_d are the proportional, integral, and derivative gains, respectively. The main objective of control theory is to design control systems that can regulate the behavior of a system in order to achieve a desired outcome. This is typically done by introducing feedback mechanisms that allow the system to adjust its behavior in response to changes in the environment or its own internal state.

There are several types of control systems that can be used to regulate the behavior of a system, including open-loop control, closed-loop control, and adaptive control. Open-loop control involves setting the input to the system based on a predetermined set of rules or instructions. Closed-loop control, on the other hand, involves using feedback mechanisms to adjust the behavior of the system in response to changes in the environment or its own internal state. Adaptive control involves using ML algorithms to adjust the behavior of the control system based on real-time data.

Control theory is used in a wide variety of applications, including robotics, manufacturing, aerospace, and automotive industries. It is an important field of study in engineering, computer science, and mathematics and has contributed significantly to the development of modern control systems and automation technologies.

Artificial Intelligence Control Theory (AICT) is an emerging field that combines principles of control theory with AI techniques to design intelligent systems that can control complex dynamic systems. AICT is used to create adaptive, predictive, and autonomous control systems that can learn from data and optimize their performance over time.

Control theory is a well-established field of engineering that deals with the analysis and design of systems that can be controlled to achieve specific goals. It involves the study of dynamic systems, feedback control, stability analysis, and optimal control. Control theory is widely used in many applications such as aerospace, chemical process control, and robotics.

AI, on the other hand, deals with the development of algorithms and techniques that enable machines to learn from data and make decisions based on that knowledge. AI techniques such as ML, deep learning, and reinforcement learning have been widely used in various applications such as image recognition, speech recognition, and NLP.

AICT combines these two fields to create intelligent control systems that can learn from data and adapt to changing environments. AICT algorithms use ML and other AI techniques to learn the dynamic behavior of the system and predict its future behavior. These predictions are used to adjust the control inputs to achieve the desired performance.

AICT algorithms can be classified into three categories: model-based control, data-driven control, and hybrid control. Model-based control uses mathematical models of the system to design control algorithms. Data-driven control, on the other hand, uses data-driven models such as neural networks to design control algorithms. Hybrid control combines both approaches and uses both mathematical models and data-driven models to design control algorithms. One of the main advantages of AICT is its ability to handle complex and uncertain systems. AICT algorithms can learn from data and adapt to changing environments, making them more robust and reliable than traditional control systems. AICT algorithms can also optimize their performance over time, leading to better control and higher efficiency. Applications of AICT include autonomous vehicles, robotics, industrial automation, and smart grids. AICT is also being used in healthcare to develop intelligent systems that can monitor patients and provide personalized care.

In conclusion, machine intelligence-based control is an emerging field that combines principles of control theory with AI techniques to design intelligent systems that can control complex dynamic systems. AICT algorithms use ML and other AI techniques to learn from data, adapt to changing environments, and optimize their performance over time. AICT has the potential to revolutionize many applications and industries, leading to more efficient and reliable systems.

1.6.2 Information Theory

Information theory is a branch of mathematics that deals with the quantification and transmission of information. It was initially developed by Claude Shannon in the 1940s as a way to study the transmission of information over communication channels. Since then, it has become an essential tool in various fields such as telecommunications, computer science, engineering, and cybernetics. One of the key concepts in information theory is entropy, which measures the amount of uncertainty or randomness in a system. The entropy of a discrete random variable X is given by:

$$H(X) = -\sum_x p(x) \log_2 p(x), \tag{1.10}$$

where $p(x)$ is the probability distribution of X. In cybernetics, information theory plays a crucial role in understanding and analyzing complex systems. Cybernetics is the study of systems that are self-regulating and can adjust to changes in their environment. These systems can be biological, mechanical, or social, and they all have the common feature of being able to communicate with their environment.

In information theory, information is measured in terms of bits. A bit is the basic unit of information, and it represents the choice between two alternatives, usually expressed as 0 or 1. Information theory considers communication channels as a way of transmitting information, and it measures the efficiency of communication channels by determining how much information can be transmitted over the channel.

One of the key concepts in information theory is entropy. Entropy is a measure of the uncertainty or randomness of a message or signal. The higher the entropy, the greater the uncertainty or randomness. Shannon's entropy is the most common measure of entropy used in information theory. It measures the average number of bits needed to represent a message or signal, and it is based on the probability distribution of the symbols in the message or signal. Another important concept in information theory is channel capacity. Channel capacity is the maximum rate at which information can be transmitted over a communication channel without error. It depends on the properties of the channel, such as its bandwidth and noise level, and it can be calculated using Shannon's channel capacity formula. Information theory has also been used to study feedback and control systems, which are common in cybernetics. Feedback is a process by which a system can adjust its behavior based on information about its current state. Information theory has provided insights into how feedback can be used to control complex systems and how the quality of feedback can affect system performance. In conclusion, information theory is an essential tool in cybernetics for understanding and analyzing complex systems. It provides a mathematical framework for measuring and quantifying information, and it has led to significant advances in communication, control, and computing.

1.6.3 Cybernetic Systems

Cybernetic systems are systems that incorporate feedback loops to maintain a desired state. The behavior of these systems can be modeled using differential equations. One common model is the predator–prey model. Consider two populations whose sizes at a reference time t are denoted by $x(t)$ and $y(t)$, respectively. The functions x and y might denote population numbers or concentrations or some other scaled measure of the population sizes, but are taken to be continuous functions. Changes in population size with time are described by the time derivatives $\dot{x} \equiv \frac{dx}{dt}$ and $\dot{y} \equiv \frac{dy}{dt}$, respectively, and a general model of interacting populations is written in terms of two autonomous differential equations

$$\dot{x} = x \cdot f(x, y)$$
$$\dot{y} = y \cdot g(x, y),$$

(1.11)

where the time t does not appear explicitly in the functions $x \cdot f(x, y)$ and $y \cdot g(x, y)$. The functions f and g denote the respective per capita growth rates of the two species. At the heart of a cybernetic system is a feedback loop that allows the system to monitor its own performance and adjust its behavior accordingly. The feedback loop typically consists of three components:

- Sensor: The sensor detects changes in the system's environment or behavior and converts them into a signal that can be processed by the system.
- Controller: The controller processes the sensor signal and makes decisions about how to adjust the system's behavior in response.
- Actuator: The actuator receives the controller's instructions and carries out the necessary changes to the system's behavior.

This feedback loop allows the system to adjust its behavior in response to changes in its environment, ensuring that it operates effectively and efficiently. For example, a thermostat uses a simple feedback loop to regulate the temperature in a room. The sensor detects the current temperature, the controller compares it to the desired temperature, and the actuator turns the heating or cooling system on or off as necessary to maintain the desired temperature. Cybernetic systems can range in complexity from simple feedback loops to highly complex, multilayered systems that incorporate ML and AI algorithms. Examples of complex cybernetic systems include self-driving cars, which use a combination of sensors, controllers, and actuators to navigate roads and respond to changing traffic conditions, and industrial control systems that regulate the operation of large-scale manufacturing processes.

One key advantage of cybernetic systems is their ability to adapt to changing environments and operating conditions. By monitoring their own performance and making adjustments in real time, these systems can optimize their behavior to achieve the best possible outcomes. This adaptability makes cybernetic systems ideal for use in a wide range of applications, from consumer electronics to industrial automation to aerospace and defense.

1.7 Cybernetical Intelligence Definition

The area of cybernetics and intelligent machines arose from an intellectual revolution based on the belief that at least part of our mental descriptions can be translated into machines that can be rendered into the specifications for the design of machines, systems, and programs. The application of cybernetics is vast in various aspects of life such as control theory, information theory, and many more, as shown in Figure 1.4. Until recently, the concept that humans are able to build something far more complicated and intelligent than themselves can only be considered a dream. This began to change when scientists and mathematicians began to consider new approaches to making machines smarter and hyperintelligent.

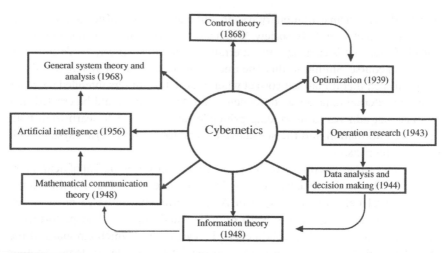

Figure 1.4 Historical overview and development of cybernetics.

Cybernetics has successfully blended human intelligence with machines. The best instances of this human–machine fusion are AI and cybernetics. Both AI and cybernetics are founded on the binary logic premise. Both phrases are frequently used interchangeably, resulting in confusion of their terminology. Cybernetics is an interdisciplinary discipline that examines how a system processes information, responds to it, and changes or is altered in order to improve its performance. It is a broad concept that encompasses information processing, feedback regulation, and decision-making.

AI is founded on the realist belief that machines can operate and behave like humans, whereas cybernetics is based on a constructivist worldview. According to research, the differences between AI and cybernetics are conceptual rather than semantic. The science of human–machine interaction based on the principles of feedback, control, and communication is known as cybernetics. Cybernetics is a relatively new science concerned with the study of mechanical, biological, physical, and cognitive regulating systems. It investigates control and communication principles in live creatures, machines, and groups, as well as self-organization. Cybernetics is an interdisciplinary discipline that examines how a system processes information, responds to it, and changes or is altered in order to improve its performance. It is a broad theory of information processing, control, and decision-making.

Similar to an individual with a specific job in life who learns from a variety of external inputs via a feedback mechanism, AI systems should be built with a purpose that allows them to learn from external interaction or data while being true to their aim. The system's operational principles may guide the goal. Survival of the fittest is the aim of an evolutionary system, but maximization of economic production is the aim of a capitalist society. When a system's guiding principle notices an outside factor that is causing it to act erratically, it adjusts the system's course to keep it on course. Similar to this, the underlying idea of an AI system should be designed such that it may self-correct when it deviates from its intended behavior owing to external data. As a consequence, an AI system should be created in a manner that adheres to its guiding principles and allows it to learn from both objective information and the subjective experience of the external system with which it interacts.

One of the earliest examples of this connection is the development of neural networks, which were inspired by the biological neural networks found in the human brain. Neural networks are a type of AI algorithm that is based on feedback mechanisms, allowing them to learn from data and improve their performance over time. This approach was influenced by cybernetics, which emphasized the importance of feedback in controlling and regulating complex systems. Another example of the link between cybernetics and AI is in the development of reinforcement learning algorithms. Reinforcement learning is a type of ML that involves training an agent to make decisions in an environment in order to maximize a reward signal. This approach was influenced by cybernetics, which emphasized the importance of feedback in controlling and regulating complex systems.

The connection between cybernetics and AI is also evident in the development of control systems for autonomous vehicles. These systems use a combination of feedback mechanisms and ML algorithms to predict the behavior of the vehicle and adjust its controls to optimize its performance. This approach draws on both the principles of cybernetics, which emphasize the importance of feedback in controlling and regulating complex systems, and the techniques of AI, which provide powerful tools for modeling and predicting system behavior. Overall, the connection between cybernetics and AI reflects a shared interest in understanding and controlling complex systems through the use of feedback mechanisms and learning algorithms. This has led to the development of a wide range of AI algorithms that are inspired by the principles of cybernetics and that have the potential to revolutionize our ability to control and regulate complex systems in a wide range of domains.

1.8 The Future of Cybernetical Intelligence

CI has the potential to transform our society in many ways, from improving healthcare and education to revolutionizing transportation and manufacturing. However, as CI becomes more integrated into our lives, there are growing concerns about its safety and ethical implications. This section is going to discuss how CI could change our society and how one can ensure that CI is developed and used safely and responsibly.

- Healthcare: CI has already started to transform healthcare by improving disease diagnosis and treatment. In the future, CI could help doctors identify early warning signs of diseases, develop personalized treatment plans for patients, and even perform complex surgeries. However, it is important to ensure that CI is developed and used in a way that prioritizes patient safety and privacy.
- Education: CI has the potential to personalize education and help students learn more efficiently. CI could be used to develop personalized learning plans for students, provide instant feedback on their work, and even help teachers identify struggling students. However, it is important to ensure that CI is not used to replace teachers but rather to enhance their abilities and improve the overall quality of education.
- Transportation: Self-driving cars and drones are already starting to revolutionize transportation, and CI could make transportation even safer and more efficient. CI could be used to optimize traffic flow, reduce congestion, and improve public transportation. However, it is important to ensure that CI is developed and used in a way that prioritizes safety and reduces the risk of accidents.
- Manufacturing: CI could transform manufacturing by automating production processes, reducing costs, and improving product quality. CI could be used to optimize production lines, predict maintenance needs, and even develop new products. However, it is important to ensure that CI is developed and used in a way that prioritizes worker safety and job security.
- Ethical implications: CI raises many ethical concerns, including issues of bias, transparency, and accountability. It is important to ensure that CI is developed and used in an ethical and responsible manner, with the well-being of humans and society as a top priority. This includes ensuring that CI systems are transparent and accountable and that they do not discriminate against individuals or groups based on their race, gender, or other factors.
- Safety concerns: CI also raises concerns about safety, particularly when it comes to autonomous systems such as self-driving cars and drones. It is important to ensure that these systems are designed and tested in a way that prioritizes safety and reduces the risk of accidents. This includes developing robust safety protocols and ensuring that autonomous systems are able to respond appropriately to unexpected situations.

In light of abovementioned applications and implications, the future of CI is full of possibilities and potential, but it is important to ensure that CI is developed and used in a way that prioritizes safety, ethics, and responsibility. By working together to address these concerns by ensuring that, the CI is a force for good that benefits everyone in our society.

Summary

This chapter discussed various aspects of AI and its related technologies, including IA, cybernetics, the 4IR, and AICT. Started by exploring the origins of AI, which can be traced back to cybernetics—the study of communication and control in living organisms and machines. This discipline provided a theoretical framework for understanding how machines and living organisms can interact and learn from each other. Then this book delved into IA, which is the use of AI technologies to automate business processes and improve productivity. IA combines various technologies, including AI, RPA, and other tools, to create intelligent systems that can learn and adapt to changing business needs.

Moreover, the chapter discussed the 4IR, which refers to the current technological revolution that is transforming the manufacturing and industrial sectors by integrating advanced technologies such as AI, the IoT, and blockchain. This transformation is expected to have a profound impact on the global economy. The chapter also explored AICT, a branch of control theory that deals with the design of controllers for AI systems. AICT is concerned with developing algorithms that can control AI systems to achieve desired outcomes and ensure safety and reliability, which gives rise to a form of CI.

The future of AI with the exploding utilization of CI looks promising. With advancements in technology, AI is expected to become more advanced and ubiquitous in our daily lives, leading to greater automation and efficiency in various industries. However, this could also raise concerns about job displacement and ethical considerations surrounding AI. Cybernetics will likely continue to develop and merge with AI, leading to the creation of more advanced and intelligent systems that can be controlled and optimized in real time. Overall, it presents exciting possibilities for innovation and progress, but also poses important ethical and societal questions that will need to be addressed as the technology continues to evolve.

Exercise Questions

Q.1.1 Define artificial intelligence.

Q.1.2 Discuss how AI and cybernetics are related to each other.

Q.1.3 Describe machine learning and differentiate between parametric and non-parametric machine learning algorithms.

Q.1.4 Explain cybernetics with mathematical expressions.

Q.1.5 What is third-order cybernetics?

Q.1.6 Are cybernetic models more predictive in AI?

Q.1.7 What is the Bayes' rule in probability theory, and how is it used in Bayesian inference to update prior probabilities based on new evidence?

Q.1.8 What is the formula for calculating the sigmoid function in a neural network, and how is it used in the activation function?

Q.1.9 Can you explain the difference between L1 and L2 regularization in machine learning, and how they are mathematically expressed in the loss function?

Further Reading

Martelaro N, Ju W. Cybernetics and the design of the user experience of AI systems. *Interactions*. 2018 Oct 25;25(6):38 41.

Wiener N. *God & Golem, Inc.: a comment on certain points where cybernetics impinges on religion*. MIT press; 1966 Mar 15.

2

Cybernetical Intelligent Control

Control theory is a field of engineering and mathematics that deals with the analysis and design of systems that are able to control the behavior of other systems. It involves the use of mathematical models to describe the dynamics of a system and the design of control algorithms to manipulate the inputs of the system in order to achieve desired outcomes.

In a control system, there is a process or system that is being controlled and a controller that receives information about the process and generates an output signal to adjust the process, as shown in Figure 2.1. The controller's output is typically a function of the input signal (which represents the desired outcome or set point) and the feedback signal (which represents the actual state of the process).

There are two main types of control systems: open loop and closed loop. In an open-loop system, the controller sends an output signal to the process without any feedback on the process state, which can result in errors or instability. In a closed-loop system, the feedback signal is used to adjust the output signal and achieve better control of the process. Control theory also involves the study of stability and controllability of systems. Stability refers to the ability of a system to return to a steady state after a disturbance or change, while controllability refers to the ability to manipulate the system's output through the input signal. The analysis of stability and controllability is important in designing robust control systems that can adapt to changes in the environment and operate reliably.

2.1 Control Theory and Feedback Control Systems

Control theory is a branch of engineering and mathematics that deals with the analysis and design of feedback control systems. A feedback control system is a type of system where the output of the system is fed back to the input, in order

Cybernetical Intelligence: Engineering Cybernetics with Machine Intelligence, First Edition.
Kelvin K. L. Wong.
© 2024 The Institute of Electrical and Electronics Engineers, Inc.
Published 2024 by John Wiley & Sons, Inc.
Companion website: www.wiley.com/go/cyberintel

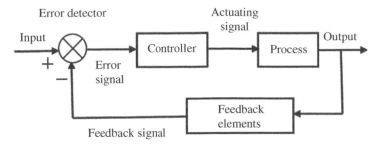

Figure 2.1 Understanding the concept of control system.

to regulate the output and maintain it at a desired level. The purpose of control theory is to design controllers that can regulate the output of a system in the presence of disturbances and uncertainties, in order to achieve the desired performance and stability.

The main components of a feedback control system are the plant, the controller, the sensors, and the actuator. The plant is the physical system that is being controlled, the sensors measure the output of the plant, the actuator adjusts the input to the plant, and the controller processes the sensor information and generates the control signal for the actuator. The performance of a feedback control system can be analyzed using mathematical models that describe the dynamics of the plant and the controller. These models can be represented in the form of differential equations, transfer functions, or state–space models. One of the most important concepts in control theory is feedback, which is the process of feeding the output of the system back to the input. Feedback control systems can be divided into two main categories: open-loop and closed-loop control systems.

In an open-loop control system, the control signal is generated based on a set point or reference signal, without any feedback from the output of the system. The performance of an open-loop control system is often limited by the uncertainties and disturbances in the plant. In a closed-loop control system, the output of the system is fed back to the input, in order to regulate the output and maintain it at a desired level. The performance of a closed-loop control system can be improved by designing a feedback controller that can compensate for the disturbances and uncertainties in the plant.

The design of a feedback controller involves selecting the appropriate control structure and tuning the controller parameters to achieve the desired performance and stability. There are several methods for controller design, such as classical control, modern control, and robust control.

Classical control methods, such as proportional–integral–derivative (PID) control, are based on linear time-invariant models and can be easily implemented in hardware. Modern control methods, such as state–space control and optimal control, are based on more advanced mathematical models and require computations that are more complex. Robust control methods, such as H-infinity control and sliding mode control, are designed to be more tolerant to uncertainties and disturbances in the plant and can provide better performance and stability in harsh environments. The performance and stability of a feedback control system can be analyzed using various techniques, such as root locus, Bode plot, Nyquist plot, and frequency response analysis. These techniques can provide insights into the stability margins and frequency characteristics of the system. In summary, control theory and feedback control systems play a crucial role in the design and analysis of intelligent control systems. They provide a mathematical framework for understanding the behavior of complex systems and designing controllers that can regulate the output of these systems in the presence of disturbances and uncertainties. Moreover, summarizing the key aspects of control theory and feedback control systems is shown in Table 2.1.

2.2 Maxwell's Analysis of Governors

Governors are devices used to regulate the speed of steam engines. They work by controlling the flow of steam into the engine in response to changes in the engine's speed. Maxwell was interested in understanding how governors work and how they could be optimized to achieve better performance. Maxwell's analysis of governors began with a study of the basic principles of control theory. He recognized that the behavior of a governor could be modeled as a system with an input (the speed of the engine), an output (the position of the governor's valve), and a feedback loop (the position of the valve affecting the speed of the engine). By analyzing the dynamics of this system, Maxwell was able to derive a set of equations that described how the governor would respond to changes in the engine's speed. One of the key insights that Maxwell had was that the design of a governor could be optimized by adjusting the position of the balls or weights that are used to regulate the valve. He showed that by changing the shape and position of these balls, it was possible to achieve a faster response time and greater stability in the governor's control of the engine's speed.

Maxwell's analysis of governors provided an early example of how control theory could be applied to engineering problems. His work laid the foundation for the development of modern control theory, which has since been applied to a wide range of applications, from aerospace and robotics to industrial automation and process control. The spindle is connected to a steam engine, and the balls are connected to a valve that controls the flow of steam into the engine. As the engine's

Table 2.1 Key aspects of control theory and feedback control systems.

Aspect	Description
Definition	Control theory is an interdisciplinary branch of engineering and mathematics that deals with the analysis and design of systems that behave in a desired manner. Feedback control systems are a type of control system that uses feedback mechanisms to adjust the behavior of the system.
Purpose	Control theory aims to design systems that behave in a desired manner. Feedback control systems aim to maintain a system's output at a desired level by adjusting the input based on feedback from the system.
Mathematical models	Control theory uses mathematical models of physical systems to analyze their behavior and design control algorithms. Feedback control systems use mathematical models of the system being controlled to determine how to adjust the input based on feedback.
Feedback mechanisms	Control theory often uses feedback mechanisms to adjust the system's behavior. Feedback control systems always use feedback mechanisms to adjust the system's behavior.
Control algorithms	Control theory designs algorithms for adjusting a system's behavior. Feedback control systems use feedback to adjust the input to the system, which can be done using a wide range of control algorithms, including proportional–integral–derivative (PID) control, adaptive control, and model predictive control.
Applications	Control theory and feedback control systems are used in a wide range of applications, including manufacturing, robotics, aerospace, chemical processes, and automotive systems.
Key features	Both control theory and feedback control systems require a deep understanding of the system being controlled, use mathematical models to analyze behavior, and aim to maintain desired levels of output. Feedback control systems use feedback mechanisms to adjust the system's behavior in real time.
Challenges	Designing effective control algorithms, addressing issues of stability and control, and ensuring the system remains responsive to changes in the environment. Feedback control systems also require accurate sensors to provide feedback, which can be a challenge in some applications.

speed changes, the spindle and balls move up and down, causing the valve to open or close and regulating the speed of the engine. Maxwell modeled this system as a feedback control system with an input signal (the engine speed), an output signal (the valve position), and a feedback signal (the spindle position). The feedback signal is used to adjust the output signal to maintain the desired engine speed. Mathematically, Maxwell represented the system as follows:

The input signal is the engine speed, denoted by ω. The output signal is the valve position, denoted by y. The feedback signal is the spindle position, denoted by x. The system dynamics are described by the equation:

$$m\left(\frac{d^2x}{dt^2}\right) = mg - F(x,y) - k\left(\frac{dx}{dt}\right), \tag{2.1}$$

where m is the mass of the spindle and balls, g is the acceleration due to gravity, $F(x, y)$ is the force exerted by the valve on the spindle, and k is the damping coefficient. The force $F(x, y)$ is given by:

$$F(x,y) = \frac{1}{2}\left(m\omega^2 r^2 - m(g + y)h\right)\sin 2\theta, \tag{2.2}$$

where r is the length of the spindle, h is the distance from the center of the spindle to the valve, and θ is the angle between the spindle and the vertical axis. The feedback control law that Maxwell proposed is given by:

$$y = k(x - x_0) + y_0, \tag{2.3}$$

where k is the gain of the feedback loop, x_0 and y_0 are the desired values of the spindle position and valve position, respectively.

Maxwell's analysis showed that the stability and performance of the governor system can be improved by adjusting the position of the balls and the gain of the feedback loop. This work laid the foundation for modern control theory, which has since been applied to a wide range of systems in engineering and science.

2.3   Harold Black

Harold Black's contributions to control theory are centered around the concept of negative feedback amplification. He showed that by introducing a negative feedback loop into an amplifier, the performance of the amplifier could be improved, making it more stable and reducing distortion. The principle of negative feedback is used in many control systems today, where the output of the system is fed back and used to modify the input in order to achieve a desired response. Mathematically, the principle of negative feedback can be represented as follows:

$$y = G(s)(u - y \cdot H(s)), \tag{2.4}$$

where y is the output of the system, u is the input, $G(s)$ is the forward transfer function of the system, and $H(s)$ is the feedback transfer function. The negative feedback loop subtracts a portion of the output from the input so that the input to the system is modified to reduce the error between the desired output and the actual output. The transfer function of a negative feedback system can be derived by substituting the equation for y into the equation. The input u the transfer function of a negative feedback system can be analyzed to determine its stability and performance characteristics:

$$\frac{y}{u} = \frac{G(s)}{1 + H(s)G(s)}.$$ (2.5)

The poles and zeros of the transfer function can be used to determine the frequency response and transient response of the system. Black's work on negative feedback amplification laid the foundation for modern control theory, and the principle of negative feedback is used in many different types of control systems, including mechanical systems, electrical systems, and biological systems.

2.4 Nyquist and Bode

Harry Nyquist's contributions to control theory include his work on sampling theory, which is a fundamental aspect of digital signal processing and control. Nyquist's sampling theorem states that in order to accurately reconstruct a continuous-time signal from its samples, the sampling rate must be at least twice the maximum frequency component of the signal. This principle is essential for the design and analysis of digital control systems.

Consider $x(t)$ to be a continuous-time signal, and $x(nT)$ to be its samples, where T the sampling interval, and n is is an integer. The sampled signal can be expressed as:

$$x_s(t) = \sum_{n=-\infty}^{\infty} x(nT)p(t-nT),$$ (2.6)

where $p(t)$ is the impulse response of the sampling process, also known as the sampling kernel. The impulse response is a function that describes how the continuous-time signal is sampled, and it plays a critical role in determining the accuracy and fidelity of the sampled signal. The Fourier transform of the sampled signal can be derived by taking the Fourier transform of both sides of the equation:

$$x_s(\omega) = \frac{x(\omega)p(\omega T)}{T},$$ (2.7)

where $x(\omega)$ is the Fourier transform of the continuous-time signal, and $x_s(\omega)$ is the Fourier transform of the sampled signal. The $p(\omega T)$ is the Fourier transform of the sampling kernel, which determines the frequency response of the sampling process. Nyquist's sampling theorem states that in order to accurately reconstruct the continuous-time signal from its samples, the sampling rate must be at least twice the maximum frequency component of the signal. This is known as the Nyquist–Shannon sampling theorem, and it is a fundamental principle of digital signal processing and control. Nyquist's work on sampling theory has had a profound impact on the development of digital control systems. By accurately sampling and processing signals, digital control systems can achieve high precision and accuracy, and they can be implemented using efficient and cost-effective hardware. Today, digital control systems are used in a wide variety of applications, including aerospace, automotive, and industrial control.

Hendrik Wade Bode was an American engineer and control theorist who made significant contributions to the field of intelligent control. Bode is best known for his work on frequency domain analysis and the development of Bode plots, which are graphical representations of the frequency response of a control system. Bode's work laid the foundation for the design and analysis of modern feedback control systems. Bode's contributions to intelligent control can be summarized as follows:

- Frequency domain analysis: Bode's work focused on the frequency response of control systems, which describes how the system responds to inputs of different frequencies. Bode introduced the concepts of gain margin and phase margin, which are measures of the stability and performance of a control system. The gain margin and phase margin can be used to analyze the robustness of a control system to disturbances and uncertainties.
- Bode plots: Bode developed the concept of Bode plots, which are graphical representations of the frequency response of a control system. Bode plots show the magnitude and phase of the system's transfer function as a function of frequency. Bode plots provide a powerful tool for analyzing the stability and performance of control systems, and they are widely used in the design and analysis of feedback control systems.
- Loop shaping: Bode introduced the concept of loop shaping, which is a design technique for achieving desired performance specifications in a control system. Loop shaping involves adjusting the magnitude and phase of the system's transfer function at different frequencies to achieve a desired response. Loop shaping is a powerful tool for designing robust and efficient control systems.
- Intelligent control: Bode's work on frequency domain analysis and loop shaping laid the foundation for the development of intelligent control systems, which use advanced algorithms and techniques to achieve high performance and robustness. Intelligent control systems are used in a wide variety of applications, including robotics, aerospace, and industrial automation.

Bode's contributions to intelligent control have had a profound impact on the development of modern control systems. By providing powerful tools for the design and analysis of feedback control systems, Bode's work has enabled engineers to develop control systems with high performance, efficiency, and robustness. Today, intelligent control systems are used in a wide variety of applications, from aerospace and automotive to biomedical and environmental control.

2.5 Stafford Beer

Stafford Beer was a British management theorist and cybernetician who made important contributions to the field of intelligent control. Beer's work was focused on developing a cybernetic approach to management, which involved using feedback control systems to improve organizational performance. Here are some of Beer's key contributions to cybernetical intelligent control, along with relevant math equations:

2.5.1 Cybernetic Control

Beer's approach to management was based on the principles of cybernetics, which is the study of systems that regulate themselves through feedback. Cybernetic control involves using feedback mechanisms to regulate the behavior of a system, in order to achieve a desired goal. Beer's work focused on applying cybernetic principles to the management of organizations.

The mathematical basis of cybernetic control is the feedback loop, which consists of a sensor, a controller, and an actuator. The sensor measures the current state of the system, and the controller calculates the corrective action needed to achieve the desired goal. The actuator then applies the corrective action to the system. The feedback loop provides a mechanism for regulating the behavior of the system and ensuring that it remains within acceptable limits.

2.5.2 Viable Systems Model

Beer developed the viable systems model (VSM), which is a cybernetic model of organizational structure and function. The VSM is designed to ensure that an organization is capable of adapting to changing circumstances and maintaining its viability over time. The VSM consists of five levels, each of which corresponds to a different function within the organization. The five levels are:

- Level 1: Operations—the activities that produce the organization's outputs.
- Level 2: Coordination—the activities that coordinate the work of the operations.
- Level 3: Control—the activities that monitor and control the performance of the operations and coordination.
- Level 4: Intelligence—the activities that collect and analyze information about the environment and the organization's performance.
- Level 5: Policy—the activities that determine the organization's goals and strategies.

The VSM provides a framework for designing organizations that are capable of adapting to changing circumstances and maintaining their viability over time.

2.5.3 Cybernetics Models of Management

Beer developed a number of cybernetics models of management, which are designed to help managers understand and improve the performance of their organizations. One such model is the management cybernetics model, which consists of three feedback loops:

- The performance feedback loop—which measures the current performance of the organization and provides feedback to the management.
- The learning feedback loop—which allows the organization to learn from its experiences and improve its performance over time.
- The strategic feedback loop—which ensures that the organization's strategies are aligned with its goals and its environment.

The management cybernetics model provides a framework for designing feedback control systems that can help organizations improve their performance and adapt to changing circumstances.

Overall, Stafford Beer's work on cybernetical intelligent control provided important insights into the use of feedback control systems to improve organizational performance. His work on cybernetics, the VSM, and cybernetic models of management helped to lay the foundation for the development of modern approaches to organizational design and management.

2.6 James Lovelock

James Lovelock is a British scientist who is best known for his work on the Gaia hypothesis, which suggests that the Earth is a self-regulating system. Lovelock's work on cybernetics intelligent control is based on the idea that the principles of cybernetics can be applied to the study of ecological systems.

2.6.1 Cybernetic Approach to Ecosystems

Lovelock's work on cybernetics intelligent control is based on the principles of cybernetics, which involves the study of systems that regulate themselves through feedback. Lovelock's approach involves applying these principles to the study of ecological systems, in order to understand how they regulate themselves and maintain their stability.

The mathematical basis of Lovelock's approach to cybernetic ecosystems is the feedback loop, which consists of a sensor, a controller, and an actuator. The sensor measures the current state of the system, and the controller calculates the corrective action needed to achieve the desired goal. The actuator then applies the corrective action to the system. The feedback loop provides a mechanism for regulating the behavior of the ecosystem and ensuring that it remains within acceptable limits.

2.6.2 Gaia Hypothesis

Lovelock's most famous contribution to the field of cybernetics intelligent control is the Gaia hypothesis, which suggests that the Earth is a self-regulating system that maintains its own stability through feedback loops. According to the Gaia hypothesis, the Earth's biosphere, atmosphere, oceans, and geology are all interconnected and work together to maintain a stable environment for life. The mathematical basis of the Gaia hypothesis is the feedback loop, which is responsible for maintaining the Earth's stability. The feedback loop involves the exchange of information between the Earth's systems, which allows them to adjust their behavior in response to changes in the environment. The feedback loop helps to maintain a stable environment for life on Earth and ensure that the Earth's systems are able to adapt to changing circumstances over time.

The mathematical basis of the Daisyworld model is the feedback loop, which involves the exchange of information between the daisies and the atmosphere. The daisies absorb and reflect sunlight, which affects the temperature of the atmosphere. The temperature of the atmosphere affects the growth and reproduction of the daisies. This feedback loop helps to regulate the behavior of the ecosystem and ensures that it remains within acceptable limits.

Overall, James Lovelock's work on cybernetics intelligent control provided important insights into the use of feedback control systems to understand ecological systems. His work on the Gaia hypothesis, cybernetic models of ecosystems, and the Daisy world model helped to lay the foundation for the development of modern approaches to the study of ecology and environmental science.

2.7 Macy Conference

The Macy Conferences were a series of interdisciplinary meetings that were held in New York City between 1946 and 1953. The Josiah Macy Jr. Foundation, a philanthropic organization that aims to support research in medicine, the social sciences, and the humanities, organized the conferences. The meetings brought together leading researchers and thinkers from a wide range of disciplines, including mathematics, engineering, psychology, biology, and philosophy. One of the main objectives of the Macy conferences was to explore the emerging field of cybernetics, which was concerned with the study of communication, control, and feedback in both natural and artificial systems. The mathematician Norbert Wiener, who was one of the key figures at the conferences, coined the term "cybernetics." Wiener defined cybernetics as "the study of control and communication in the animal and the machine."

At the Macy Conferences, researchers discussed topics such as information theory, neural networks, artificial intelligence, and the relationship between man and machine. They explored the idea of feedback and control systems in both biological and technological systems, leading to new insights into the operation of complex systems and the possibility of creating artificial systems that could learn and adapt. One of the key contributions of the Macy Conferences was the development of the concept of feedback. Feedback, in this context, refers to the process by which a system receives information about its own behavior and uses that information to adjust its behavior in response. The idea of feedback was applied to both biological and technological systems, leading to new insights into the operation of complex systems and the possibility of creating artificial systems that could learn and adapt.

The Macy Conferences also had an impact on the development of the field of artificial intelligence. Many of the early pioneers of AI, such as John McCarthy and Marvin Minsky, were influenced by the discussions at the conferences and drew on ideas from cybernetics and related fields to develop their own theories of intelligent systems. Overall, the Macy Conferences were an important forum for the exchange of ideas and the development of new concepts related to communication, control, and feedback in both natural and artificial systems. The interdisciplinary nature of the conferences helped to foster a new way of thinking about complex systems, and their influence can still be seen today in fields such as cybernetics, artificial intelligence, and systems theory.

2.8 McCulloch–Pitts

The McCulloch–Pitts model, proposed by Warren McCulloch and Walter Pitts in 1943, is a simple mathematical model of a neuron that is often used in the study of cybernetics and intelligent control. The model consists of a binary threshold function that takes in input signals and produces an output signal based on whether the inputs exceed a certain threshold. The mathematical basis of the McCulloch–Pitts model is a set of binary threshold functions, which can be represented as follows:

Consider $x_1, x_2, ..., x_n$ to be the input signals to the neuron, and $w_1, w_2, ..., w_n$ to be the weights associated with each input signal. Then, the neuron's output y is given by:

$$y = f(w_1 x_1 + w_2 x_2 + ... + w_n x_n), \tag{2.8}$$

where f is the threshold function, which takes the form, $f(x) = 1$, if $x \geq 0$ $f(x) = 0$, if $x < 0$. In other words, the output of the neuron is determined by whether the weighted sum of the inputs exceeds a certain threshold.

The McCulloch–Pitts model is often used to represent simple decision-making processes in intelligent control systems. For example, a control system might use a set of neurons to determine whether a certain action should be taken based on a set of input signals. Each neuron might represent a different criterion for taking action, and the output of the neurons would be combined to make a decision.

Figure 2.2 is the McCulloch–Pitts neuron model, which can also be written in the form on the right, and the output y can be expressed by Equation (2.9).

$$y = \varphi \left(\sum_{i=1}^{n} w_i x_i + b \right). \tag{2.9}$$

The McCulloch–Pitts model can be seen as the foundation of artificial neural networks and machine-learning algorithms. Its key concept of using binary threshold functions to simulate the behavior of neurons has been built upon and expanded to create more complex and powerful models. For example, modern neural networks can contain multiple layers of interconnected neurons, with each layer performing a different level of processing on the input data. The output of one layer is passed as input to the next layer, allowing the network to learn and

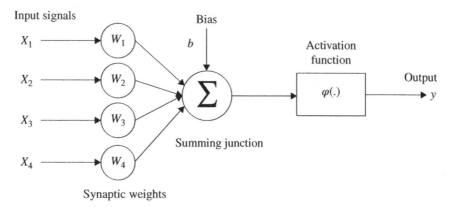

Figure 2.2 McCulloch and Pitts neuron model.

recognize complex patterns in the data. Furthermore, the weights assigned to the input signals can be adjusted through a process called training, where the network is presented with a large set of input–output examples and its weights are adjusted to minimize the difference between the predicted and actual outputs. This allows the network to learn from experience and improve its accuracy over time.

The McCulloch–Pitts model has also been used in other areas of intelligent control, such as in the development of fuzzy logic systems. Fuzzy logic systems use membership functions and fuzzy sets to represent uncertain or imprecise information and make decisions based on a set of rules. In summary, the McCulloch–Pitts model has been a foundational concept in the development of artificial intelligence and intelligent control systems. Its simplicity and elegance have inspired countless research efforts and practical applications, making it an important contribution to the field of cybernetics.

2.9 John von Neumann

John von Neumann was one of the key participants in the Macy Conferences on cybernetics, which were held in the 1940s and 1950s and brought together scientists from a wide range of fields to discuss the emerging field of cybernetics and its applications in areas such as intelligent control and artificial intelligence. At the Macy Conferences, von Neumann contributed to discussions on a variety of topics related to intelligent control and artificial intelligence. Some of his key contributions included:

2.9.1 Discussions on Self-Replicating Machines

One of John von Neumann's key contributions to the Macy Conferences on cybernetics was his work on self-replication. He was interested in the idea of designing machines that could reproduce themselves, and he believed that such machines would be a key feature of intelligent control systems. Von Neumann argued that self-replication was a fundamental characteristic of life and that machines capable of self-replication would have the potential to explore new frontiers in space and other domains. He also believed that self-replication was essential for the sustainability of any intelligent control system.

At the Macy Conferences, von Neumann contributed to discussions on the design and construction of self-replicating machines. He proposed a model for a self-replicating machine that consisted of a set of instructions or "blueprint" for building a copy of itself, as well as a set of tools or "universal constructor" for carrying out the instructions. Von Neumann's model for self-replicating machines was based on the idea of cellular automata, which are simple computational systems that consist of a grid of cells that can be in different states. In von Neumann's model, each cell represented a unit of information or "bit," and the machine's "blueprint" was encoded in the state of the cells. Von Neumann's work on self-replication was groundbreaking, and it laid the foundation for the development of self-replicating machines and other forms of artificial life. His ideas have had a profound impact on the field of artificial intelligence, and they continue to inspire research in the field today.

2.9.2 Discussions on Machine Learning

Von Neumann was interested in the idea of machine learning and contributed to discussions on the design of learning algorithms and the use of machine learning in intelligent control systems. In particular, he focused on the use of statistical methods for machine learning.

Von Neumann recognized that machine learning could be used to improve the performance of intelligent control systems by allowing them to adapt to changing environments and learn from experience. He also recognized that statistical methods were essential for machine learning, as they provided a way to make inferences and predictions based on data. One of von Neumann's contributions to the development of machine learning was his work on the theory of games. He recognized that games provided a natural framework for studying decision-making processes, and he developed mathematical models to describe these processes. This work laid the foundation for modern game theory, which is used to study decision-making processes in a wide range of fields.

Von Neumann also contributed to the development of artificial neural networks, which are machine-learning algorithms that are loosely modeled on the structure and function of the human brain. He recognized that artificial neural networks could be used to solve a wide range of problems in intelligent control and artificial intelligence, and he developed mathematical models to describe their behavior. Overall, von Neumann's contributions to the development of machine learning and artificial intelligence have had a profound impact on modern technology and continue to be studied and refined today.

Summary

Cybernetical intelligent control is a field of study that involves the use of control theory and feedback control systems to design intelligent machines that can learn and improve their performance over time. It has its roots in the work of scientists such as James Clerk Maxwell, who developed mathematical models for governors that were used to regulate the speed of machines. The concept was further developed during the Macy Conferences in the mid-20th century, where scientists discussed the potential of cybernetics to create intelligent machines. One of the key contributions to cybernetics was the McCulloch and Pitts model, which provided a theoretical framework for understanding how neurons in the brain work. John von Neumann, who attended the Macy Conferences, contributed to the development of self-replicating machines, machine-learning algorithms, and the use of game theory in intelligent control systems. The future of cybernetical intelligent control and artificial intelligence is promising. With the rapid advancements in technology, it is likely that intelligent control systems will become even more sophisticated and capable of performing complex tasks with greater efficiency and accuracy. Another important area is the integration of intelligent control systems with other technologies such as robotics and the Internet of Things (IoT), enabling these systems to operate in real-world environments and interact with the physical world.

Additionally, the ethical and social implications of intelligent control systems and artificial intelligence will need to be considered and addressed, including issues such as privacy, transparency, and accountability. Overall, the future of cybernetical intelligent control and artificial intelligence holds great potential for transforming various industries and improving human lives.

Exercise Questions

Q.2.1 Explain the current limitations of cybernetical intelligent control and artificial intelligence systems?

Q.2.2 How can cybernetical intelligent control and artificial intelligence systems be made more transparent and explainable?

Q.2.3 What are the ethical considerations involved in the development and use of intelligent control and artificial intelligence systems?

Q.2.4 In which directions the intelligent control and artificial intelligence systems be made more resilient to attacks and disruptions?

Q.2.5 How can intelligent control and artificial intelligence systems be used to enhance human decision-making and problem-solving?

Q.2.6 How can one ensure that intelligent control and artificial intelligence systems are aligned with human values and goals?

Q.2.7 What are some of the emerging applications of intelligent control and artificial intelligence systems in various industries and domains?

Q.2.8 Describe how intelligent control and artificial intelligence systems be used to address some of the world's most pressing challenges, such as climate change and inequality?

Q.2.9 Explain how one can ensure that intelligent control and artificial intelligence systems are developed and used in a responsible and sustainable manner?

Q.2.10 What are some of the emerging technologies and research areas that are likely to shape the future of intelligent control and artificial intelligence?

Further Reading

Åström KJ. *Computer aided tools for control system design*. Department of Automatic Control, Lund Institute of Technology (LTH); 2016.

Bateson MC. Angels fear revisited: Gregory Bateson's cybernetic theory of mind applied to religion-science debates. In: *A legacy for living systems: Gregory Bateson as precursor to biosemiotics*. Taylor & Francis; 2008: pp. 15–25.

Kirchner JW. The Gaia hypotheses: are they testable? Are they useful. *Scientists on Gaia*. 1991:38–46.

Mead M. *Cybernetics of cybernetics*. éditeur non identifié; 1968.

Warwick K. Cybernetic enhancements. *Reshaping the Human Condition Exploring Human Enhancement*. 2008:123.

3

The Basics of Perceptron

3.1 The Analogy of Biological and Artificial Neurons

To understand and build a neural network, one may compare the structure and function of neurons in the brain to the artificial neurons in a mathematically constructed neural topology. Both biological and artificial neurons receive input, process it, and produce an output. In the case of biological neurons, the information comes in the form of electrical signals from other neurons, and the output is also an electrical signal sent to other neurons. Neural network concept is derived from the human brain, and learning is achieved by simulating the work of the brain. The human brain is made up of neurons and the neural network is made up of artificial neurons (Figure 3.1).

In artificial neurons, the input is typically numerical values, and the output is also numerical. The processing in both types of neurons is similar, as it involves using mathematical functions to transform the input into the output. This analogy aims to mimic the functioning of biological neurons in artificial neural networks to improve their performance and make them more similar to the human brain. Another critical aspect of the brain's information processing is lateral and feedback connections. Lateral connections allow neurons to communicate with each other within the same layer of neurons, while feedback connections allow neurons to communicate with neurons in higher layers. This can be mimicked in artificial neural networks by using recurrent connections, where the output of one neuron is used as input to another neuron.

Additionally, sparsity can be used to extend the analogy further. In the brain, only a small percentage of neurons are active at any given time, while the majority of neurons are not active. This concept of sparsity can be mimicked in artificial neural networks by using sparse representations, where only a small percentage

Cybernetical Intelligence: Engineering Cybernetics with Machine Intelligence, First Edition.
Kelvin K. L. Wong.
© 2024 The Institute of Electrical and Electronics Engineers, Inc.
Published 2024 by John Wiley & Sons, Inc.
Companion website: www.wiley.com/go/cyberintel

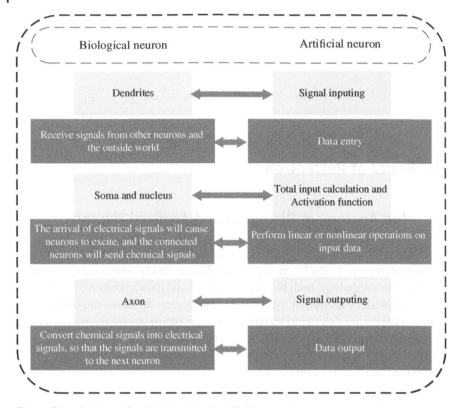

Figure 3.1 Analogy of real neurons and artificial neurons.

of neurons are active at any given time. This can help reduce the network's complexity and improve its performance. Another essential aspect of biological neurons is the biological noise and stochasticity, which can be mimicked in artificial neurons by adding some noise or randomness in the processing. This can help to improve the robustness and generalization of the network. It is also worth noting that the analogy between biological and artificial neurons is limited to the structure of neurons and the way they process information, as well as the way they are organized and connected in networks. The brain has a hierarchical organization where information is processed in different areas, and it is also parallel, where many neurons process the same information simultaneously.

3.1.1 Biological Neurons and Neurodynamics

According to the Hodgkin–Huxley model, the behavior of biological neurons is a set of four differential equations describing neurons' electrical activity.

The equations model the flow of ions through the neuron's membrane and how this flow changes over time. The equations are as follows:

$$C_m \frac{dv}{dt} = I_{ion} - g_{Na}\, m^3 h(V - V_{Na}) - g_K\, n^4(V - V_K) - g_L(V - V_L) \tag{3.1}$$

$$\frac{dm}{dt} = \frac{m_\infty - m}{\tau_m} \tag{3.2}$$

$$\frac{dn}{dt} = \frac{n_\infty - n}{\tau_n} \tag{3.3}$$

$$\frac{dh}{dt} = \frac{h_\infty - h}{\tau_h}, \tag{3.4}$$

where C_m is the membrane capacitance, I_{ion} is the total ionic current, g_{Na}, g_K, and g_L are conductance of sodium, potassium, and leak channels, respectively. While m, n, and h are the gates of the sodium, potassium, and leak channels, respectively. The V_{Na}, V_K, and V_L are reversal potentials of the sodium, potassium, and leak channels, respectively, and m_∞, n_∞, and h_∞ are steady-state values of the gates τ_m, τ_n, and τ_h are the time constants of the gates.

According to the FitzHugh–Nagumo model, it is a set of two nonlinear differential equations that describe the electrical activity of neurons are defined in Equations (3.5) and (3.6).

$$\frac{dx}{dt} = c\left(y - \frac{x^3}{3} + x\right) \tag{3.5}$$

$$\frac{dy}{dt} = -\left(\frac{x - a + by}{C}\right), \tag{3.6}$$

where x is the neuron's membrane potential, y is a recovery variable, and a, b, $c =$ parameters of the model. Cybernetic intelligence studies machine systems that can learn and adapt to new information. Artificial neural networks are machine-learning algorithms that mimic the structure and function of biological neurons. The analogy of biological and artificial neurons refers to comparing the structure and function of biological neurons to the artificial neurons in artificial neural networks. Artificial neurons receive inputs, process them through an activation function, and produce an output. Summarizing the key differences between artificial and biological neurons is shown in Table 3.1.

3.1.2 The Structure of Neural Network

A neural network has at least two physical components: the processing elements and the connections between them. The processing elements are called neurons,

Table 3.1 Summarizing the key differences between artificial and biological neurons.

Aspect	Artificial Neuron	Biological Neuron
Definition	A mathematical model designed to simulate the behavior of a biological neuron in an artificial neural network.	A specialized cell is the basic building block of the nervous system in animals and humans.
Components	Typically consists of an input, an activation function, and an output.	Consists of a cell body (soma), dendrites, an axon, and axon terminals (synaptic terminals).
Input	Receives input signals from other neurons or from sensors.	Receives input signals from other neurons or from sensory receptors.
Activation function	A mathematical function that transforms the input signals into an output signal.	The neuron integrates the input signals and, if the combined input is above a certain threshold, generates an action potential.
Output	Produces an output signal that is transmitted to other neurons or to an output device.	Transmits output signals to other neurons via axons, or to muscle cells or glands via neuromuscular junctions or neuroglandular junctions.
Learning	Typically uses supervised or unsupervised learning algorithms to adjust the weights of the inputs to the neuron.	Biological neurons can modify the strength of their connections (synaptic plasticity) based on the activity of the synapse.
Speed	Artificial neurons can process input signals much faster than biological neurons.	Biological neurons operate much more slowly than artificial neurons.
Power consumption	Artificial neurons consume much less power than biological neurons.	Biological neurons consume a significant amount of energy, primarily to maintain ion gradients across the cell membrane.
Reproduction and repair	Artificial neurons can be easily duplicated or replaced if damaged.	Biological neurons cannot be easily duplicated or replaced if damaged.
Applications	Artificial neurons are used in artificial neural networks for tasks, such as image and speech recognition, and in robotics and control systems.	Biological neurons are involved in a wide range of physiological processes, including sensation, perception, movement, and cognition.

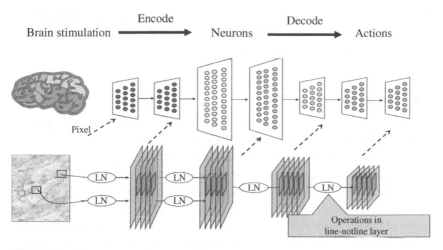

Figure 3.2 The structure of the neural network.

and the connections between the neurons are known as links. Every link has a weight parameter associated with it. Figure 3.2 describes the working process of the neural network.

The overall structure of a neural network is hierarchical, with multiple layers of neurons organized in a feedforward or recurrent configuration. The input layer receives data from the outside world, the hidden layers process the data, and the output layer produces the final result. The data processing in the network is guided by the learning rule, which adjusts the network weights to minimize the error between the network's prediction and the desired outcome.

The error or loss function evaluates the network's performance and guides the learning process. Standard error functions include the mean squared error (MSE) and cross-entropy loss, as shown in Equations (3.7) and (3.8), respectively.

$$\text{MSE} = \frac{1}{2N} \sum_{i=1}^{N} (y_i - y_i')^2 \tag{3.7}$$

$$\text{loss} = -\frac{1}{N} \sum_{i=1}^{N} y_i \log(y_i') + (1 - y_i) \log(1 - y_i'). \tag{3.8}$$

The gradient descent algorithm uses the gradient of the error concerning the weights to update the consequences in the direction of the minimum error, as shown in Equation (3.9):

$$w_{new} = w_{old} - \eta \frac{\partial L}{\partial w}, \tag{3.9}$$

where w_{old} and w_{new} are the old and updated new weights, respectively, L represents the loss, η represents the learning rate, and $\frac{\partial L}{\partial w}$ represents the gradient of the loss with respect to the weight.

3.1.3 Encoding and Decoding

Encoders are a type of neural network architecture that is commonly used for dimensionality reduction and feature extraction. They consist of two main components: an encoding part that maps the input data to a lower-dimensional representation, and a decoding part that maps the lower-dimensional representation back to the original input space. The encoding part is typically implemented as a feedforward neural network, such as a multilayer perceptron (MLP), with a smaller number of hidden units compared to the input size. This reduces the dimensionality of the input data by compressing it into a lower-dimensional representation, which is then fed into the decoding part. There are various types of encoders, including auto encoders, variation auto encoders, and de-noising auto encoders, each with slightly different architecture and training objectives. These encoders are widely used in various applications, including computer vision, natural language processing, and anomaly detection.

- The x is the input data, with dimensions (n, d), where n is the number of samples and d is the number of features.
- The encoding function h maps the input data to a lower-dimensional representation z, with dimensions (n, m), where m is the number of hidden units in the encoding layer. The encoding function is typically implemented as a feedforward neural network, with parameters θ, $h(x, \theta) = z = \sigma(Wx + b)$. Where W is the weight matrix, b is the bias vector, and σ is the activation function (e.g. sigmoid, ReLU).
- The decoding function g maps the lower-dimensional representation z back to the original input space $\hat{x}$, with dimensions (n, d). The decoding function is also implemented as a feedforward neural network, with parameters φ, $g(z, \varphi) = \hat{x} = \sigma(W'z + b')$. Where W' is the weight matrix, b' is the bias vector, and σ is the activation function.
- The loss function is defined as the reconstruction error between the original input x and the reconstructed input $\hat{x}$, $J(\theta, \varphi) = ||x - \hat{x}||^2$.

The decoding part is also typically implemented as a feedforward neural network, with a structure that is symmetrical to the encoding part. The goal of the decoding part is to reconstruct the original input data from the lower-dimensional representation.

- The hidden representation of the data is represented by z, with dimensions (n, m), where n is the number of samples and m is the number of hidden units in the encoding layer.
- The decoding function g maps the hidden representation z back to the original input space $\hat{x}$, with dimensions (n, d), where d is the number of features. The decoding function is typically implemented as a feedforward neural network, with parameters $\varphi, g(z, \varphi) = \hat{x} = \sigma(W'z + b')$.

3.2 Perception and Multilayer Perceptron

Perception is the simplest type of artificial neural network, made up of a single layer of input nodes connected to output nodes, used for binary classification tasks. The input nodes pass their values to the output nodes via weighted connections, which are then transformed by an activation function to produce the final prediction. The weights of the connections can be adjusted through learning algorithms to improve the model's accuracy over time. Given an input vector x, the output y can be calculated as $y = f(Wx + b)$, where W is a matrix of weights, b is a bias vector, and f is an activation function.

The activation function f introduces nonlinearity into the model and can be chosen based on the solved problem. Common activation functions include the step function, sigmoid, tanh, and ReLU. The weights W, and biases b, are adjustable parameters that determine the model's output. They are typically updated during training using an optimization algorithm, such as gradient descent, to minimize a cost or loss function, which measures the difference between the predicted output and the true output. Training a perception aims to find the optimal values for W and b that produce the most accurate predictions for a given input data.

MLP fully connects the most straightforward and classic neural network. One will take MLP as an example to illustrate the specific structure of the neural network. The network consists of an input, hidden, and output layer. The number of neurons in the input layer is determined by the number of feature vectors of the input data, the number of neurons in the output layer depends on the problem type, and the hidden layer determines the complexity of the network. In the classification problem, only one output neuron is required for the two-classification problem, and the multi-classification problem has as many output neurons representing different types. Given an input vector x, the output y can be calculated as $y = f_i(...f_2(W_{2h_1} + b_2)...)$, where f_i is the activation function of the ith layer, w_i is the weight matrix of the ith layer, b_i is the bias vector of the ith layer, and h_i is the output of the ith layer, given by $h_i = f_{i-1}(w_{i-1}h_{i-2} + b_{i-1})$.

The activation function f_i, is used to introduce nonlinearity into the model and can be chosen based on the problem being solved. Common activation functions include the sigmoid, tangent, and ReLU. The weights w_i, and biases b_i, are adjustable parameters that determine the output of the model. They are typically updated during training using an optimization algorithm, such as gradient descent, to minimize a cost or loss function, which measures the difference between the predicted output and the true output. Training an MLP aims to find the optimal values for all the weights and biases that produce the most accurate predictions for a given input data. Table 3.2 summarizing the differences between perception and MLP.

Table 3.2 Summarizing the differences between perception and multilayer perceptron.

Aspect	Perceptron	Multilayer Perceptron (MLP)
Definition	A type of artificial neuron that can make a binary decision.	A type of neural network composed of multiple layers of artificial neurons that can make complex decisions.
Architecture	Consists of a single layer of artificial neurons with no hidden layers.	Consists of multiple layers of artificial neurons, including one or more hidden layers between the input and output layers.
Learning algorithm	Uses the Perceptron learning rule, a type of supervised learning algorithm, to adjust the weights of the inputs to the neuron.	Uses backpropagation, a type of supervised learning algorithm, to adjust the weights of the inputs to the neurons in the hidden and output layers.
Activation function	Typically uses a step function as the activation function.	Can use a variety of activation functions, such as sigmoid, ReLU, or tanh.
Output function	Produces a binary output signal, i.e. either 0 or 1.	Can produce a continuous or binary output signal, depending on the problem being solved.
Capability	Can only solve linearly separable problems.	Can solve more complex problems that are not linearly separable.
Performance	Performs well on simple problems with a small number of input variables.	Performs well on complex problems with a large number of input variables.
Overfitting	Prone to overfitting when the number of input variables is large.	Can be prone to overfitting when the number of hidden layers or neurons is large.
Applications	Used in simple classification problems, such as image recognition.	Used in a wide range of applications, including image and speech recognition, natural language processing, and predictive modeling.

3.2.1 Back Propagation Neural Network

Back Propagation (BP) neural network is a classic algorithm for obtaining started in machine learning. BP neural network is a "universal model + error correction function" each time the error analysis is performed according to the training and expected results. Then the weights and thresholds are modified to obtain a model that can output consistent with the desired results. It is currently the most widely used and successful model in deep learning tasks.

Given training dataset $D = \{(x_1, y_1), (x_2, y_2), ..., (x_n, y_n)\}$, where $x_i \in R^d$, $y_i \in R^l$, and x_i is a $d \times 1$ matrix that represents the input features, y_i is a 1×1 matrix that represents the components for the output.

Figure 3.3 shows a neural network whose input layer has d neurons, the hidden layer has q neurons, and output layer has l neurons. The neuron for the input layer has a threshold θ_j, the neuron of the hidden layer has a threshold γ_h. The weight between the input layer's neuron and the hidden layer's neuron is v_{ih}, the weight between the hidden layer's neuron and the output layer's neuron is w_{hj}. The input of the hidden layer's neuron is $\alpha_h = \sum_{i-1}^{d} v_{ih} x_i$, the input of the output layer's neuron is $\beta_j = \sum_{h=1}^{q} w_{hj} b_h$.

3.2.2 Derivative Equations for Backpropagation

For training example (x_k, y_k), one may assume the output of the output layer is $\hat{y}_k = (\hat{y}_1^k, \hat{y}_2^k, ..., \hat{y}_l^k) = f(\beta_j - \theta_j)$, then the mean square error $E_k = \frac{1}{2} \sum_{j=1}^{l} (\hat{y}_j^k - y_j^k)^2$, in this neural network, their parameter space has $(d + l + 1)q + l$ components. The weight between the input layer neuron and the hidden layer's neuron has $d \times q$ features, and the weight between the hidden layer's neuron and the output layer's neuron has $q \times l$ components. The threshold of the hidden layer and output layer has $q + l$ components.

The backpropagation algorithm is an iterative gradient descent strategy. With a given learning rate η, the parameter increment is described in Equation (3.10) (Algorithm 3.1).

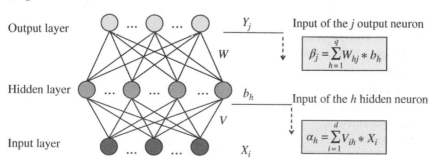

Figure 3.3 Schematic diagram of neural network.

$$\Delta w_{hj} = -\eta \frac{\partial E_k}{\partial w_{hj}}. \tag{3.10}$$

One can use the chain rule in calculus to obtain Equation (3.11):

$$\frac{\partial E_k}{\partial w_{hj}} = \frac{\partial E_k}{\partial \hat{y}_j^k} \cdot \frac{\partial \hat{y}_j^k}{\partial \beta_j} \cdot \frac{\partial \beta_j}{\partial w_{hj}}. \tag{3.11}$$

According to the definition of β_j, one has

$$\frac{\partial \beta_j}{\partial w_{hj}} = b_h. \tag{3.12}$$

If the active function is sigmoid, then the derivative can be easily obtained as:

$$f'(x) = f(x)(1 - f(x)). \tag{3.13}$$

Then it is to update w as follows:

$$\Delta w_{hj} = \eta g_j b_h. \tag{3.14}$$

Similarly, one can obtain

$$
\begin{aligned}
e_h &= -\frac{\partial E_k}{\partial b_h} \cdot \frac{\partial b_h}{\partial \alpha_h} \\
&= -\sum_{j=1}^{l} \frac{\partial E_k}{\partial \beta_j} \cdot \frac{\partial \beta_j}{\partial b_h} f'(\alpha_h - \gamma_h) \\
&= \sum_{j=1}^{l} w_{hj} g_j f'(\alpha_h - \gamma_h) \\
&= b_h (1 - b_h) \sum_{j=1}^{l} w_{hj} g_j.
\end{aligned}
\tag{3.15}
$$

Algorithm 3.1 The Definition of the Backpropagation Algorithm Using Pseudo-Code

---

Input: training data x_i
Process: backpropagation
1: for iteration in 1 to N
2: for each training data x_i
3: obtain output y_i
4: calculate $\Delta w_{hj}, \Delta \theta_j, \Delta v_{ih}, \Delta \gamma_h$
5: update parameters
Output: none

3.3   Activation Function

Activation functions are mathematical functions that are applied to the output of a neuron in a neural network to introduce nonlinearity in the network's decision-making process. They help to transform the inputs of the neuron into outputs that can be interpreted by the next layer of the neural network.

The importance of activation functions in neural networks cannot be overstated. Without activation functions, the network would simply be a linear model, and would not be able to learn complex patterns in the data. Activation functions are essential in enabling neural networks to model nonlinear relationships between the inputs and the outputs.

Some of the key roles that activation functions play in neural networks include:

- Introducing nonlinearity: Activation functions help to introduce nonlinearity into the neural network, which is critical for enabling the network to learn complex patterns and relationships in the data.
- Modeling complex functions: Activation functions can be used to model complex functions that are difficult to represent using simple linear models.
- Determining the output range: Activation functions can be used to constrain the output of a neuron to a particular range, such as between 0 and 1 or between -1 and 1, which is useful in certain types of problems, such as classification.
- Regularization: Some activation functions, such as the Dropout regularization technique, can be used to prevent overfitting in the neural network.

Overall, activation functions are a fundamental component of neural networks and play a crucial role in enabling them to learn and model complex patterns and relationships in the data.

3.3.1   Sigmoid Activation Function

The Sigmoid Activation Function is a widely used activation function that outputs values between 0 and 1. The sigmoid function has a characteristic S-shaped curve, as shown in Figure 3.4, which allows it to introduce nonlinearity into the neural network.

The function approaches 0 as x approaches negative infinity and approaches 1 as x approaches positive infinity. At $x = 0$, the sigmoid function has a value of 0.5. One limitation of the sigmoid function is that it can suffer from the "vanishing gradient" problem, which can make it difficult to train deep neural networks. As the input to the sigmoid function becomes very large or very small, the gradient of the function approaches zero, which can slow down the learning process. As a result, other activation functions, such as the ReLU and its variants, have become more popular in recent years.

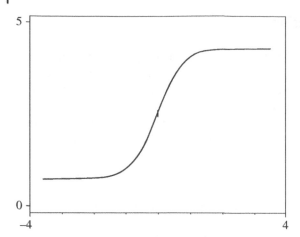

Figure 3.4 Sigmoid activation function.

3.3.2 Hyperbolic Tangent Activation Function

The Hyperbolic Tangent activation function is a commonly used activation function in neural networks. It maps the input to a value between −1 and 1. The mathematical equation for the hyperbolic tangent function is:

$$f(x) = \tanh(x) = \frac{e^x - e^{-x}}{e^x + e^{-x}}, \tag{3.16}$$

where x is the input to the neuron, e is the mathematical constant approximately equal to 2.718, and $f(x)$ is the output of the neuron. The hyperbolic tangent function is a scaled version of the sigmoid function and has a similar shape. However, the hyperbolic tangent function maps the input to a range between −1 and 1, which can be useful in certain types of classification problems.

Like the sigmoid function, the hyperbolic tangent function is also differentiable, which makes it suitable for use in backpropagation algorithms for training neural networks (Figure 3.5).

In summary, the hyperbolic tangent activation function is a commonly used activation function that maps the input to a range between −1 and 1 and is useful in certain types of classification problems. It is also differentiable, which makes it suitable for use in backpropagation algorithms for training neural networks.

3.3.3 Rectified Linear Unit Activation Function

The Rectified Linear Unit (ReLU) Activation Function is a popular activation function that is widely used in neural networks. It is defined mathematically as:

$$f(x) = \max(0, x), \tag{3.17}$$

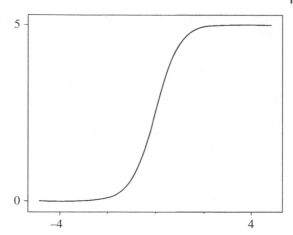

Figure 3.5 Tangent activation function.

where x is the input to the neuron. The ReLU function outputs 0 if x is negative, and x if x is positive. The function has a simple implementation and is computationally efficient.

The ReLU function introduces nonlinearity into the neural network, which allows it to model complex relationships between inputs and outputs. The ReLU function is also less prone to the vanishing gradient problem than some other activation functions, such as the sigmoid and tanh functions (Figure 3.6).

The leaky ReLU function is a variant of the ReLU function that introduces a small slope for negative values of x. It is defined mathematically as:

$$f(x) = \max(ax, x), \tag{3.18}$$

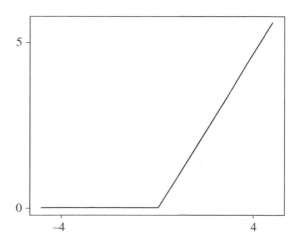

Figure 3.6 Rectified linear unit.

where x is the input to the neuron, and a is a small positive constant that is usually set to 0.01.

The parametric ReLU function is a variant of the Leaky ReLU function that allows the slope for negative values of x to be learned during training.

One drawback of the ReLU function is that it can suffer from the "dying ReLU" problem. This occurs when the input to the ReLU function is negative, and the output is 0. In this case, the gradient of the function is also 0, which means that the weights of the neuron are not updated during backpropagation. This can lead to neurons becoming "dead," or inactive, and can result in reduced performance of the neural network.

To address the "dying ReLU" problem, several variants of the ReLU function have been proposed, including the Leaky ReLU, the Parametric ReLU, and the Exponential ReLU. These variants introduce a small slope for negative values of x, which helps to prevent the gradient from becoming 0.

3.3.4 Linear Activation Function

The linear activation function is a simple activation function that returns the input value without any transformation. The mathematical equation for the linear activation function is shown in Equation (3.18) and graphically shown in Figure 3.7.

$$f(x) = x, \tag{3.19}$$

where x is the input to the neuron. In a neural network, the input to a neuron is typically multiplied by a weight before being passed through the activation function. The weighted linear function is expressed mathematically as:

$$f(x) = wx, \tag{3.20}$$

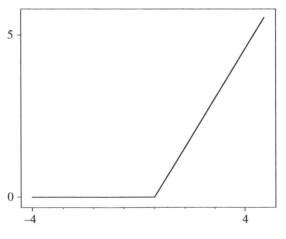

Figure 3.7 Linear activation function.

where x is the input to the neuron, w is the weight associated with the input, and $f(x)$ is the output of the neuron. In some cases, the input to a neuron may be transformed before being passed through the activation function. This can be expressed mathematically as:

$$f(x) = wx + b, \tag{3.21}$$

where x is the input to the neuron, w is the weight associated with the input, b is a bias term, and $f(x)$ is the output of the neuron. The linear activation function is rarely used in deep learning models because it does not introduce nonlinearity into the network. As a result, it can be difficult for the network to learn complex relationships between inputs and outputs.

Instead, nonlinear activation functions like the sigmoid, ReLU, and tanh functions are more commonly used because they introduce nonlinearity into the network, allowing it to learn more complex patterns in the data. The linear activation function is useful in cases where the output needs to be proportional to the input, such as in linear regression problems. However, it is not commonly used in deep learning models because it does not introduce nonlinearity into the network, which can limit the network's ability to learn complex relationships between inputs and outputs.

A comparative table of commonly used activation functions in neural networks, including their mathematical formulations, range, monotonicity, differentiability, advantages, and disadvantages, is presented in Table 3.3.

Summary

This chapter discusses the analogy of biological and artificial neurons and their similarities in structure and function. The chapter described how the structure of neurons in the brain can be mimicked in artificial neural networks and how this has led to the development of powerful machine-learning algorithms and also explored the structure of neural networks, including the derivative equations used in backpropagation, which train the network to learn from data. The chapter also discussed how these equations allow the network to adjust its weights and biases to improve its performance. Finally, by looking at the generalization of neural networks, which refers to their ability to make predictions about new data based on what they have learned from previous data, one have seen how this generalization ability can be improved using regularization and dropout techniques.

In summary, this chapter has provided an overview of the analogy between biological and artificial neurons and how this analogy has led to the development of powerful machine-learning algorithms. One has also discussed the key concepts and techniques used in the structure and training of neural networks and how these techniques can be used to improve their performance.

Table 3.3 Comparative of various activation functions in neural network.

Activation Function	Mathematical Formulation	Range	Monotonicity	Differentiability	Advantages	Disadvantages
Linear	$f(x) = x$	$(-\infty, \infty)$	Yes	Yes	Simple and fast computation	Limited representation power for nonlinear data
Sigmoid	$f(x) = \dfrac{1}{1 + e^{-x}}$	$(0, 1)$	No	Yes	Smooth and interpretable output	Vanishing gradient problem
Hyperbolic tangent (Tanh)	$f(x) = \tan h(x) = \dfrac{e^x - e^{-x}}{e^x + e^{-x}}$	$(-1, 1)$	Yes	Yes	Nonlinear and zero-centered output	Vanishing gradient problem
Rectified linear unit (ReLU)	$f(x) = \max(0, x)$	$(0, \infty)$	No	No (except at 0)	Simple and effective for deep networks	Dying ReLU problem
Leaky ReLU	$f(x) = \max(\alpha x, x)$ where α is a small constant (e.g. 0.01)	$(-\infty, \infty)$	Yes	Yes	Solves dying ReLU problem	Can lead to non-smooth derivatives
Softmax	$f(x_i) = \dfrac{e^{x_i}}{\sum_{j=1}^{C} e_j^x}$ where C is the number of classes	$(0, 1)$	No	Yes	Outputs probability distribution over classes	Requires multiple outputs for multi-class classification

Exercise Questions

Q.3.1 Explain the analogy of biological and artificial neurons and how it is applied in artificial neural networks.

Q.3.2 Describe a neural network's structure and the different layers' roles.

Q.3.3 Explain the backpropagation algorithm and how it is used to train a neural network.

Q.3.4 What is the role of bias terms in artificial neural networks, how do they relate to the resting potential of biological neurons, and what is the mathematical expression for the bias term?

Q.3.5 What is the role of regularization and dropout in improving the generalization of a neural network?

Q.3.6 How does the structure of a biological neuron compare to that of an artificial neuron in a neural network?

Q.3.7 Describe the dynamics of the gates of the channels in a biological neuron and how it is related to the activation function of an artificial neuron.

Q.3.8 Describe the importance of the membrane potential and the ion channels in a biological neuron and how they relate to the weights and biases of an artificial neuron.

Q.3.9 Discuss the similarity of the synaptic connections in a biological neuron and the weights of an artificial neuron.

Q.3.10 Explain the role of the learning rate in the backpropagation algorithm and how it affects the training of a neural network.

Further Reading

Rogers SK, Kabrisky M. *An introduction to biological and artificial neural networks for pattern recognition.* SPIE press; 1991.

Rosenblatt F. *Principles of neurodynamics. perceptrons and the theory of brain mechanisms.* Cornell Aeronautical Lab Inc, Buffalo NY; 1961 Mar 15.

4

The Structure of Neural Network

A neural network is a machine learning model that is inspired by the structure and function of the brain. It is a network of interconnected nodes, which are called artificial neurons that process information and make predictions.

4.1 Layers in Neural Network

4.1.1 Input Layer

A neural network is composed of multiple layers of artificial neurons, each layer performing a different computation. The layers in a neural network can be grouped into two main categories: input layers and hidden layers. The input layer in a neural network receives the raw input data and passes it on to the next layer. The mathematical representation of the input layer is straightforward and can be represented as a vector $x = [x_1, x_2, ..., x_n]$, where x_i is the ith input feature and n is the number of features.

This input vector x is used as the input to the first hidden layer, which performs computations on the input data to extract features that can be used to make predictions. However, in some cases, it may be necessary to normalize or preprocess the input data before passing it on to the next layer. One common method for normalizing the input data is min–max normalization, which scales the input features to a specific range (e.g. [0, 1]). The mathematical equation for min–max normalization can be given by:

$$x_i = \frac{x_i - x_{\min}}{x_{\max}} - x_{\min},\tag{4.1}$$

Cybernetical Intelligence: Engineering Cybernetics with Machine Intelligence, First Edition.
Kelvin K. L. Wong.
© 2024 The Institute of Electrical and Electronics Engineers, Inc.
Published 2024 by John Wiley & Sons, Inc.
Companion website: www.wiley.com/go/cyberintel

where x_i is i^{th} input feature, x_{min} and x_{max} are the minimum and maximum values of the features.

4.1.2 Hidden Layer

The hidden layer is where the bulk of the computation in a neural network takes place. The hidden layer performs nonlinear transformations on the input data and extracts features that can be used to make predictions. The mathematical representation of a single artificial neuron in the hidden layer can be given by the following equation:

$$z = \sum_{i=1}^{n} w_i x_i + b$$

$$y = f(z),$$

(4.2)

where z is the weighted sum of inputs, w_i is the weight for the ith input, x_i is the ith input, b is the bias, and $f(z)$ is the activation function. Common activation functions include the sigmoid function and rectified linear unit (ReLU). Table 4.1 summarizes the different layers that can be present in a neural network.

4.1.3 Neurons

Each neuron has one or more inputs, which are combined using weights, and an activation function is applied to the weighted sum to produce the output of the neuron. The mathematical equation for the output of a single neuron can be given by:

$$z = \sum_{i=1}^{n} w_i x_i + b$$

$$y = \varphi(z),$$

(4.3)

where z is the weighted sum of inputs, x_i is the ith input, w_i is the weight associated with the ith input, b is the bias term, and $\varphi(z)$ is the activation function. The activation function $\varphi(z)$ is applied to the weighted sum to produce the output of the neuron. The mathematical equation for the output of the neuron is $y = \varphi(z)$. The learning process adjusts these parameters to minimize the difference between the predicted output of the network and the true output, as determined by a loss function. If the activation function is the sigmoid function, the mathematical equation for the activation function is shown in Equation (4.4), the equation transforms

Table 4.1 Summarizing the different layers that can be present in a neural network.

Layer Type	Description
Input layer	The layer that receives the input data. The number of neurons in this layer corresponds to the number of input variables.
Hidden layer(s)	One or more layers of artificial neurons that receive input from the previous layer and apply a nonlinear transformation to produce an output. The number of neurons and layers can vary depending on the complexity of the problem being solved.
Output layer	The final layer of the neural network that produces the output prediction. The number of neurons in this layer corresponds to the number of output variables.
Convolutional layer	A type of layer used in convolutional neural networks (CNNs) that performs feature extraction from image or video data. These layers typically include a set of learnable filters that are convolved with the input data to produce a feature map.
Pooling layer	Another type of layer used in CNNs that reduces the spatial size of the feature maps produced by the convolutional layer. This helps to make the network more computationally efficient and reduces the risk of overfitting.
Recurrent layer	A layer used in recurrent neural networks (RNNs) that allows the network to process sequential data by maintaining an internal memory state. These layers are useful for natural language processing and time series prediction.
Normalization layer	A layer that normalizes the output of the previous layer to make the network more stable and reduce the impact of vanishing or exploding gradients during training.
Dropout layer	A layer that randomly drops out a percentage of the neurons in the previous layer during training to reduce overfitting.
Batch normalization layer	A layer that normalizes the output of a previous layer for each mini-batch during training. This can improve the training speed and stability of the network.

the weighted sum of inputs into a value between 0 and 1, which can be interpreted as the probability of a certain class or output.

$$\varphi(z) = \frac{1}{1 + e^{-z}}. \tag{4.4}$$

4.1.4 Weights and Biases

In a neural network, the weights and biases are the parameters that are learned during the training process. They determine the strength and direction of the connections between neurons and affect the output of the network.

The mathematical equation for the weighted sum of inputs for a single neuron is given by:

$$z = \sum_{i=1}^{n} w_i x_i + b, \qquad (4.5)$$

where z is the weighted sum of inputs, x_i is the ith input, w_i is the weight associated with the ith input, and b is the bias term. The weights w_i represent the strength of the connection between the ith input and the neuron, and the bias term b represents an offset or a baseline for the weighted sum of inputs. The learning process adjusts the weights and biases to minimize the difference between the predicted output of the network and the true output, as determined by a loss function. The adjustment of the weights and biases is typically done through gradient descent, where the gradient of the loss function with respect to the weights and biases is computed and used to update the parameters in the direction that reduces the loss.

4.1.5 Forward Propagation

In a neural network, forward propagation refers to the process of computing the output of the network given an input, by successively applying the activation function to the weighted sum of inputs for each neuron. Given an input x and a set of weights w and biases b, the weighted sum of inputs z for a single neuron can be computed as:

$$z = \sum_{i=1}^{n} w_i x_i + b. \qquad (4.6)$$

The activation function g is then applied to the weighted sum of inputs to produce the output y of the neuron, $= g(z)$.

Where g can be any activation function, such as a sigmoid, ReLU, or others. For a multilayer neural network, the process of forward propagation is repeated for each layer, where the output of one layer serves as the input to the next.

4.1.6 Backpropagation

Backpropagation is the process of computing the gradient of the loss function with respect to the parameters (weights and biases) of the neural network so that the parameters can be updated during the training process.

Given a loss function J, the gradient of the loss with respect to the parameters (weights and biases) of the neural network can be computed using the chain rule of differentiation.

For a single neuron in the output layer, the gradient of the loss with respect to the weights w and biases b can be written as:

$$\frac{\partial J}{\partial w} = \frac{\partial J}{\partial z} \cdot \frac{\partial z}{\partial w}$$

$$\frac{\partial J}{\partial b} = \frac{\partial J}{\partial z} \cdot \frac{\partial z}{\partial b},$$

(4.7)

where z is the weighted sum of inputs to the neuron, and ∂ represents the partial derivative. The gradients are used in the backpropagation algorithm to update the weights and biases during the training process of a neural network. The backpropagation algorithm computes the gradients of the loss with respect to the parameters by repeatedly applying the above equations, starting from the output layer and working backward through the hidden layers to the input layer. The computed gradients are then used to update the parameters using an optimization algorithm, such as gradient descent, to minimize the loss and train the neural network. These are the main concepts and mathematical equations involved in the structure of a neural network. Neural networks are powerful machine learning models that can learn complex relationships between inputs and outputs, and they have been used to solve a wide range of problems, such as image classification, speech recognition, and natural language processing.

4.2 Perceptron and Multilayer Perceptron

The Perceptron is a simple linear binary classifier algorithm introduced in the 1950s as one of the earliest models of artificial neural networks. The Perceptron model consists of a single layer of neurons and uses a linear decision boundary to classify the input data into two classes.

Given an input vector x, the Perceptron predicts the output y using a weighted sum of the inputs and a bias term, which is then passed through an activation function, $y = f(w^T x + b)$. The w is the weight vector that determines the importance of each input feature, b is the bias term that shifts the activation function f is the activation function, typically a step function or a sigmoid function, which maps the weighted sum of inputs to binary output.

The Perceptron algorithm updates the weights and biases iteratively based on the errors made on the training data until convergence or a maximum number of iterations is reached. Despite its simplicity, the Perceptron has several limitations, such as being unable to model nonlinearly separable data, and it has been largely replaced by more complex models such as Multilayer Perceptron and

Convolutional Neural Network (CNN). For a single training sample (x_i, y_i), the Perceptron algorithm updates the weights and bias using the following update rule:

$$w_{new} = w_{old} + \eta(y_i - y^i)x_i$$
$$b_{new} = b_{old} + \eta(y_i - y^i). \tag{4.8}$$

The η is the learning rate, a hyperparameter that determines the step size of the updates, y^i is the predicted output for the sample x_i, y_i is the true label for the sample x_i.

The prediction y^i is obtained by passing the weighted sum of inputs through the activation function, which for a step function, the perceptron algorithm repeats this update rule for each sample in the training set until convergence, i.e. until the model's predictions match the true labels for all the training samples, or until a maximum number of iterations is reached.

Once the Perceptron has been trained, it can be used to make predictions for new unseen data by applying the same weighted sum and activation function to the inputs. An MLP typically consists of an input layer, one or more hidden layers, and an output layer. The input layer receives the raw features of the data and passes them through the weighted connections to the hidden layers, where the inputs are transformed through nonlinear activation functions. The transformed inputs are then passed to the output layer, which generates the final prediction.

A common activation function used in the hidden layers of an MLP is the sigmoid function, which was previously defined in Equation (3.17). The prediction y of an MLP for a given input x is obtained by passing x through the multiple layers of the network and computing the weighted sum of inputs for each neuron in the output layer, with the sigmoid function applied to the weighted sums.

The error between the predicted output and the actual output is typically calculated using a loss function, such as mean squared error (MSE) or cross-entropy loss. For instance, L be the loss function, y be the actual output, and $\hat{y}$ be the predicted output, the error can be defined as:

$$L(y, \hat{y}) = \frac{1}{n}\sum_{i}^{n}(y_i - \hat{y}_i)^2, \tag{4.9}$$

where n is the number of instances in the training data. The gradient of the loss with respect to the weights and biases can be computed using the gradient of the loss with respect to the output of the layer. These gradients are then used to update the weights and biases using gradient descent or a variant thereof. The weights and biases are updated in the opposite direction of the gradient, to minimize the loss and reduce the error between the predicted output and the actual output.

4.3 Recurrent Neural Network

A recurrent neural network (RNN) is a type of neural network designed to handle sequential data. It has a loop that allows information to persist across many time steps by updating hidden state information with new input data. The hidden state is used to make predictions at each time step, and the process is repeated until the final prediction is made. RNNs can be used for various applications such as language modeling, speech recognition, and time-series forecasting. In RNNs, mathematical equations are used to model the relationships between input sequences and their corresponding outputs. RNNs use a dynamic computational graph, which allows them to process sequences of inputs by looping over the same set of weights at each time step.

In the Figure 4.1, the architecture of RNN is shown where, one can see that the new hidden state h is generated using both its corresponding input x, as well as the previous hidden state h_1, which captures any dependencies that might have come from earlier samples. The output y_2 is then a function of the hidden state h_2 and finally, w is the weight vector over the layer. Mathematically, the way we combine the current input with the previous hidden state. The hidden state in a RNN is an internal representation of the current time step of a sequence. At each time step, the hidden state is updated based on the previous hidden state and the current input. The hidden state contains information about the entire sequence processed so far, and it is used to make predictions at each time step. The equations for updating the hidden state in a simple RNN can be represented as:

$$h(t) = f(w_{hh}h(t-1) + w_{xh}x(t) + b_h), \tag{4.10}$$

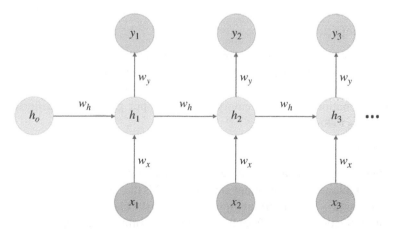

Figure 4.1 Architecture of recurrent neural network.

where f is the activation function, w_{hh} and w_{xh} are the weights matrices for the hidden-to-hidden and input-to-hidden connections, b_h is the bias term, $h(t)$ is the hidden state at time t, $h(t-1)$ is the hidden state at the previous time step, and $x(t)$ is the input at time t.

The output state in a RNN is the result produced by the final activation function in the network for a given input sequence. It is based on the hidden state computed at each time step of the sequence and represents a summary of the input sequence processed by the network. The output state can be represented mathematically by a vector $y(t)$, where t represents the current time step. It is usually computed using an activation function $g(h(t))$ and the hidden state $h(t)$ as input, such as $y(t) = g(w_h y (h(t))) + b_y$, where w_h and b_y are the weight matrix and bias vector for the output state, respectively.

4.3.1 Long Short-Term Memory

Long Short-Term Memory (LSTM) is a type of RNN designed to handle the problem of vanishing gradients in traditional RNNs by introducing a memory cell, input gate, forget gate, and output gate. The memory cell maintains its state across time steps, while the input and forget gates control the flow of information into and out of the cell, and the output gate produces the final output. This structure allows LSTM networks to better preserve long-term dependencies, leading to improved performance on tasks such as language modeling and sequential prediction. The LSTM network uses a set of gates, including the input gate, forget gate, and output gate, to control the flow of information into and out of the cell state. The equation for the cell state is given by:

$$\tilde{c}_t = \tanh(w_c[h_{t-1}, x_t] + b_c)$$
$$c_t = f_t c_t - 1 + i_t \tilde{c}_t \tag{4.11}$$
$$h_t = o_t \tanh(c^t),$$

where c_t is the cell state at timestamp t, $\tilde{c}_t$ represents candidate for cell state at timestamp t, h_{t-1} is the output of previous LSTM block, x_t is the input at current timestamp, o_t is the output gate. The input gate in a LSTM network is used to control the flow of information into the memory cell. The input gate can be defined mathematically as follows:

$$i_t = \sigma(w_i[h_{t-1}, x_t] + b_i), \tag{4.12}$$

where i_t is the input gate activation at time step t, σ is the sigmoid activation function, w_i is the weight matrix for the input gate, (h_{t-1}, x_t) is the concatenation of the previous hidden state h_{t-1} and current input x_t. The b_i is the bias for the input gate. The input gate activation i_t ranges from 0 to 1, and it determines the proportion of new information that will be added to the memory cell at time step t.

The forget gate in an LSTM network is a sigmoid function that helps control the flow of information from the cell state to the output state. The math equation for the forget gate f can be represented as:

$$f = \sigma\left(w_f[h_{t-1}, x_t] + b_f\right), \tag{4.13}$$

where w_f is the weight matrix, h_{t-1} is the previous hidden state, x_t is the current input, b_f is the forget gate bias, and σ is the sigmoid activation function. The output of the forget gate is then used to determine how much of the previous cell state will be forgotten and how much will be kept. The output gate in LSTM is determined by the following mathematical equation:

$$O_t = \sigma(w_o[h_{t-1}, x_t] + b_0), \tag{4.14}$$

where σ is the sigmoid activation function. w_o is the weight matrix for the output gate. h_{t-1} is the hidden state from the previous time step. x_t is the input at time step t. b_0 is the bias for the output gate. The output gate calculates how much of the hidden state should be output at time step t.

4.4 Markov Neural Networks

Markov Neural Network (MNN) is a type of neural network that combines neural networks with Markov models. It consists of an underlying graph structure where each node represents a hidden state and each edge represents a transition between hidden states. The transition probabilities are determined by neural network parameters, and the outputs are generated based on these probabilities and the observed inputs. MNNs can be used for various applications such as image segmentation, speech recognition, and natural language processing. The key feature of MNN is its ability to model temporal dependencies and relationships between different inputs and outputs. The mathematical equations behind MNNs can be complex, involving a combination of Markov models, RNNs, and deep neural networks.

4.4.1 State Transition Function

Given the current state of the system, the state transition function maps the state to the next state. The state transition function can be represented mathematically as $s_t = f(s_{t-1}, A_{t-1})$. Where s_t is the current state, s_{t-1} is the previous state, and A_{t-1} is the previous action.

4.4.2 Observation Function

Given the current state of the system, the observation function maps the state to the observation. The observation function can be represented mathematically as $O_t = g(S_t)$. Where O_t is the current observation.

4.4.3 Policy Function

The policy function maps the current state and observation to the action. The policy function can be represented mathematically as $A_t = \pi(S_t, O_t)$. Where A_t is the current action. In MNN, the policy function is implemented as a neural network, which takes the state and observation as inputs and outputs the action.

4.4.4 Loss Function

The loss function measures the difference between the predicted action and the actual action. The loss function can be represented mathematically as

$$L(\theta) = \sum_{t=1}^{T} A_t - \pi(s_t, O_t, \theta)^2, \tag{4.15}$$

where T is the number of time steps, θ is the set of parameters of the policy function. The goal of MNN is to minimize the loss function by updating the parameters of the policy function using gradient-based optimization methods such as stochastic gradient descent.

4.5 Generative Adversarial Network

A Generative Adversarial Network (GAN) is composed of two parts: a generator and a discriminator. The generator creates fake data that is meant to resemble real data, while the discriminator determines whether each sample is real or fake. The generator and discriminator are trained together in an adversarial process, where the generator tries to create data that will fool the discriminator, and the discriminator tries to correctly identify whether each sample is real or fake.

The mathematical structure of a GAN can be described as follows:

- Input data: Let x be a sample of real data, drawn from a real data distribution $P_{data}(x)$.
- Generator: The generator, $G(z)$, maps a random noise vector z to a sample x'.
- Discriminator: The discriminator, $D(x)$, outputs a scalar probability that x is a real sample, drawn from $P_{data}(x)$.

- Loss functions: The generator and discriminator have opposite loss functions. The generator's loss is given by the negative log-likelihood of the discriminator's prediction that x' is real:

$$L_G = - \log D(G(Z)), \qquad (4.16)$$

the discriminator's loss is given by the negative log-likelihood of the real samples being real, and the fake samples being fake:

$$L_D = - \log(D(x) + \log(1 - D(G(Z)))). \qquad (4.17)$$

The generator and discriminator are trained alternately, updating their weights and biases to minimize their respective loss functions. The generator tries to create samples that will fool the discriminator, while the discriminator tries to correctly identify real and fake samples. The training process continues until the discriminator can no longer distinguish between real and fake samples.

In summary, a GAN consists of a generator that creates fake data and a discriminator that determines whether each sample is real or fake. The generator and discriminator are trained in an adversarial process to produce realistic fake data.

Summary

Neural networks are machine learning models inspired by the structure and function of the human brain. They consist of interconnected nodes called neurons, which process information and make predictions based on input data. There are several types of neural networks, including the Perceptron and Multilayer Perceptron. In a neural network, data is processed through various layers including the input layer, hidden layer, and output layer. The neurons in each layer use mathematical equations to calculate weights and biases, which are then used in the forward and backward propagation steps to make predictions and adjust the model based on the accuracy of those predictions. Performance measures such as the confusion matrix, receiver operating characteristic (ROC) curve, and area under the ROC curve are used to evaluate the accuracy of a neural network model. These measures use mathematical equations to compare the predicted output of the model with actual output.

In summary, neural networks are complex mathematical models that use a combination of equations and algorithms to process and analyze data. The choice of which type of neural network to use, and the specific mathematical equations used, depends on the type and size of the data being analyzed, as well as the desired outcome.

Exercise Questions

Q.4.1 How does the number of layers in a neural network affect its performance and why?

Q.4.2 In a perceptron, the activation function used is a step function defined as:

$$f(x) = 1, \text{if } x >= 0 \quad f(x) = 0, \text{if } x < 0$$

Consider a perceptron with the following weights and inputs:
Weight $w_1 = 0.5$; Weight $w_2 = -0.3$; Input $x_1 = 0.7$; Input $x_2 = -0.2$; Calculate the weighted sum and the output of the perceptron.

Q.4.3 How does the sequential nature of Recurrent Neural Network (RNN) make it better suited for processing sequences of data?

Q.4.4 What is the role of gating mechanism in Long Short-Term Memory (LSTM) networks and how does it prevent vanishing gradients?

Q.4.5 How does the Markov property influence the design and training of Markov Neural Network (MNN)?

Q.4.6 What is the mathematical expression for the backpropagation algorithm in neural networks, and how is it used to compute the gradients of the loss function with respect to the weights?

Q.4.7 What are some popular activation functions used in neural networks and why are they important?

Q.4.8 How do weight initialization techniques affect the performance and convergence of a neural network?

Q.4.9 What is the vanishing gradient problem in deep neural networks and how can it be addressed?

Q.4.10 How does the choice of optimization algorithm impact the training of a neural network?

Q.4.11 How can regularization techniques such as dropout and weight decay be used to prevent overfitting in neural networks?

Q.4.12 How is the structure of a recurrent neural network (RNN) designed to handle sequential data, and what is the mathematical expression for the hidden state update in a basic RNN?

Q.4.13 In a multilayer perceptron, the activation function used in the hidden layer is the sigmoid function defined as:

$$f(x) = \frac{1}{1 + e^{-x}}$$

Consider a multilayer perceptron with a single hidden layer having the following weights and inputs:

Weight $w_1 = 0.6$; Weight $w_2 = -0.4$; Input $x_1 = 0.8$; Input $x_2 = -0.5$; Calculate the weighted sum and the output of the hidden layer neuron.

Further Reading

Bengio Y, De Mori R, Flammia G, Kompe R. Global optimization of a neural network hidden Markov model hybrid. *IEEE Transactions on Neural Networks* 1992 Mar 1; 3(2):252–9.

Goodfellow IJ. Piecewise linear multilayer perceptrons and dropout. *arXiv preprint arXiv:1301.5088*. 2013 Jan 22.

Hinton GE. How neural networks learn from experience. *Scientific American*. 1992 Sep 1;267(3):144–51.

Li Y, Zhang Y, Wang H. Partial Parallel Interference Cancellation Multiuser Detection using Recurrent Neural Network Based on Hebb Learning Rule. In 2006 6th World Congress on Intelligent Control and Automation 2006 Jun 21 (Vol. 1, pp. 2989–2992).

Bishop CM. Neural Networks for Pattern Recognition. Oxford: Oxford University Press; 1995. ISBN 978-0-19-853849-3.

Paulsen O, Sejnowski TJ. Natural patterns of activity and long-term synaptic plasticity. *Current Opinion in Neurobiology*. 2000;10(2):172–179.

5

Backpropagation Neural Network

5.1 Backpropagation Neural Network

Cybernetics is a wide-ranging field concerned with circular causal processes, including in ecological, technological, biological, cognitive, and social systems, and also in the context of practical activities, such as designing and learning managing, as shown in Figure 5.1. In the realm of technology, cybernetics delves into the design and control of complex systems such as robotics, automation, and control systems. It investigates how information flows, feedback mechanisms, and control processes can optimize the functioning and efficiency of technological systems. By applying cybernetic principles, engineers and designers can create intelligent and adaptive technologies that learn and adapt to changing conditions.

Overall, cybernetics provides a framework for understanding and managing complex systems across various domains. It offers a unified approach to studying circular causal processes, facilitating advancements in design, learning, management, and decision-making within a wide range of practical activities.

Backpropagation Neural Network (BPNN) is a type of artificial neural network that uses gradient descent and the backpropagation algorithm to learn the weights of the network, as shown in Figure 5.2. The backpropagation algorithm involves computing the gradient of the loss function with respect to the weights of the network. The gradient is then used to update the weights, moving them in the direction of reducing the loss. The mathematical equation for the loss function J for a single training example is given by:

$$J = \frac{1}{2}(\hat{y} - y)^2, \tag{5.1}$$

Cybernetical Intelligence: Engineering Cybernetics with Machine Intelligence, First Edition. Kelvin K. L. Wong.
© 2024 The Institute of Electrical and Electronics Engineers, Inc.
Published 2024 by John Wiley & Sons, Inc.
Companion website: www.wiley.com/go/cyberintel

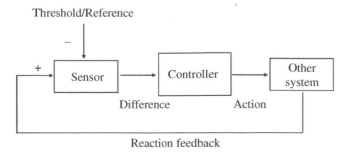

Figure 5.1 Principle diagram of a cybernetic system with a feedback loop.

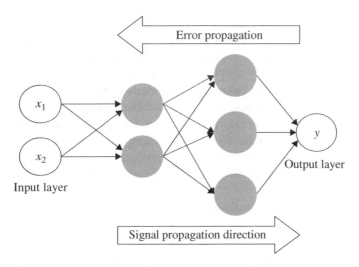

Figure 5.2 Process of Backpropagation Neural Network.

where $\hat{y}$ is the predicted output for the input x, y is the actual output, and $\frac{1}{2}$ is a normalization constant. The gradient of the loss with respect to the weight w_{ij} from the ith neuron in the ith layer to the jth neuron is given by:

$$\frac{dJ}{dw_{ij}} = (\hat{y} - y)a_j(1 - a_j)a_i. \tag{5.2}$$

The weights are updated using the equation:

$$w_i(p + 1) = w_i(p) + \Delta w_i p, \tag{5.3}$$

where $\Delta w_i p$ is the weight correction at iteration p.

5.1.1 Forward Propagation

Forward propagation is the process of computing the output of a neural network based on its input and weights. It starts at the input layer and passes the inputs through each successive layer, computing the weighted sum of inputs at each layer and applying an activation function to generate the output. The output of one layer is used as the input for the next layer until the final layer is reached. The mathematical equation for forward propagation can be represented as:

$$z_i = w_i x + b_i, \tag{5.4}$$

where z_i is the weighted sum of inputs for layer i, w_i is the weight matrix for layer i, x is the input, and b_i is the bias for layer i. The activation function f is then applied to z_i to obtain the output a_i for layer i. Table 5.1 describe the various parameters involved in neural network training.

5.2 Gradient Descent

Gradient descent is an optimization algorithm used to minimize a loss function in machine learning models, such as neural networks. It works by iteratively adjusting the model's parameters in the direction of steepest decrease of the loss function. The algorithm updates the parameters by subtracting the gradient of the loss with respect to the parameters, multiplied by a learning rate. This process is repeated until the loss converges to a minimum value or a stopping criterion is met. The choice of learning rate, the choice of optimization algorithm, and the presence of any regularization techniques can influence the convergence rate and stability of the optimization. Gradient descent is a commonly used optimization algorithm for training neural networks and other machine learning models. It optimizes a model by iteratively adjusting its parameters to minimize a loss function.

5.2.1 Loss Function

The loss function in gradient descent measures the difference between the predicted output and actual output for a single training example, as shown in Figure 5.3. It is used to guide the optimization process of the model by indicating the direction and magnitude of error. The most common loss function used in gradient descent is mean squared error (MSE), represented mathematically as:

$$MSE = \frac{1}{n} \sum_{i=1}^{n} (y_i - \bar{y}_i)^2, \tag{5.5}$$

Table 5.1 Various parameters involved in neural network training.

Property	Forward Propagation Parameters	Backward Propagation Parameters
Input data	The training examples, represented as a matrix of input values.	The training examples, represented as a matrix of input values.
Weights	The weights connecting the neurons in the network.	The weights connecting the neurons in the network.
Biases	The biases added to the weighted inputs of each neuron.	The biases added to the weighted inputs of each neuron.
Activation function	The nonlinear function applied to the output of each neuron.	The derivative of the activation function.
Output	The predicted output of the network given the input.	The gradient of the loss function with respect to the output.
Loss function	Measures the difference between the predicted and actual outputs.	Measures the difference between the predicted and actual outputs and is used to compute the gradient of the loss function.
Error signal	The difference between the predicted and actual outputs.	The gradient of the loss function with respect to the output.
Gradients	The gradients of the loss function with respect to the weights and biases.	The gradients of the loss function with respect to the weights and biases.
Learning rate	A hyperparameter that controls the step size of the weight updates.	A hyperparameter that controls the step size of the weight updates.
Optimization algorithm	A method for finding the optimal weights and biases during training, such as stochastic gradient descent.	A method for finding the optimal weights and biases during training, such as stochastic gradient descent.
Regularization	Techniques used to prevent overfitting of the network during training, such as L1 or L2 regularization.	Techniques used to prevent overfitting of the network during training, such as L1 or L2 regularization.
Dropout	A technique used to prevent overfitting by randomly dropping out some neurons during training.	Not applicable.
Batch size	The number of training examples used in each iteration of training.	The number of training examples used in each iteration of training.
Epochs	The number of times the entire training set is passed through the network during training.	The number of times the entire training set is passed through the network during training.

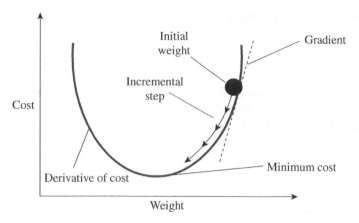

Figure 5.3 Procedure of gradient descent.

where n is the number of samples in the dataset, y_i is the true value of the ith sample, and $\hat{y}_i$ is the predicted value of the ith sample (Figure 5.4).

It is to quantify the discrepancy between predicted and desired outcomes, guiding the learning process toward minimizing this discrepancy for improved model performance. Different loss functions serve specific purposes, such as minimizing deviations in regression tasks with MSE or measuring dissimilarity in classification problems with cross-entropy loss.

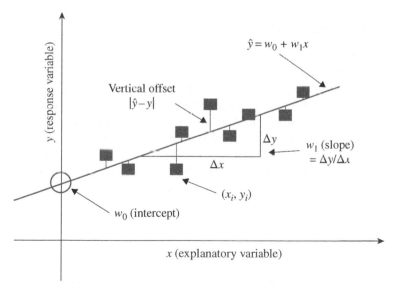

Figure 5.4 Graphical representation for loss function.

5.2.2 Parameters in Gradient Descent

In gradient descent, parameters refer to the variables that are learned by the model in order to minimize the loss function. These parameters are typically represented by weight matrices and bias vectors that are associated with each layer in the neural network. The goal of gradient descent is to iteratively update these parameters in order to minimize the loss function and find the best values that produce the most accurate predictions. The optimization process is performed by computing the gradient of the loss function with respect to the parameters and updating them in the direction of the negative gradient. The size of the update is determined by the learning rate hyperparameter, which controls the step size of the optimization process. The parameters in gradient descent are represented as weights (w) and biases (b) in a neural network model. They can be updated through the following equation during the training process:

$$\theta_{new} = \theta_{old} - \alpha \nabla \theta L(\theta), \tag{5.6}$$

where θ_{old} and θ_{new} are old and updated vectors of parameters, α is the learning rate and $\nabla \theta L(\theta)$ is the gradient of the loss function $L(\theta)$ with respect to the parameters θ. The gradient is calculated using the backpropagation algorithm, which computes the derivative of the loss function with respect to each parameter in the network, and uses this information to update the parameters in a direction that minimizes the loss.

5.2.3 Gradient in Gradient Descent

Gradient in gradient descent refers to the derivative of the loss function with respect to the parameters of the model. It represents the slope of the loss function at a particular point, indicating the direction of the maximum increase in loss. The gradient is used in the gradient descent algorithm to update the parameters in the direction of the minimum loss. The gradient is calculated by taking the partial derivatives of the loss function with respect to each parameter and is used to update the parameters in the direction of the negative gradient, which minimizes the loss. Mathematically, the gradient (∇) is computed by taking the partial derivatives of the function (J) with respect to each parameter (θ), as shown in following equation:

$$\nabla J(\theta) = \left(\frac{\partial J}{\partial \theta_1}, \frac{\partial J}{\partial \theta_2}, \dots, \frac{\partial J}{\partial \theta_n} \right), \tag{5.7}$$

where J represents the cost or loss function, θ represents the vector of parameters or weights.

5.2.4 Learning Rate in Gradient Descent

The learning rate in gradient descent is a hyperparameter that determines the size of the step taken during each iteration of the optimization process. The learning rate controls the speed and convergence of the optimization, with a high learning rate leading to quick but potentially unstable convergence, and a low learning rate leading to slow but stable convergence. The learning rate is multiplied with the gradient calculated at each iteration to update the parameters of the model. A commonly used equation to update the parameters is as follows:

$$\theta_{new} = \theta_{old} - \eta \nabla \theta J(\theta), \tag{5.8}$$

where θ_{old} and θ_{new} are the old and updated model parameters, respectively, η represents the learning rate, $J(\theta)$ represents the loss function, and $\nabla \theta J(\theta)$ represents the gradient of the loss function with respect to the parameters θ.

5.2.5 Update Rule in Gradient Descent

The update rule in gradient descent is a rule that defines how the model parameters are updated based on the gradient of the loss function. The gradient of the loss function with respect to the model parameters provides information about how much the parameters need to be adjusted in order to minimize the loss. The update rule defines the manner in which the model parameters are adjusted using the gradient information. For example, the most commonly used update rule in gradient descent is the gradient descent algorithm, which updates the parameters as follows:

$$\theta_{new} = \theta_{old} - \alpha \nabla \theta L(\theta), \tag{5.9}$$

where θ_{old} and θ_{new} are the old and updated parameters, $L(\theta)$ represents the loss function, $\nabla \theta L(\theta)$ represents the gradient of the loss function with respect to the model parameters, and α represents the learning rate.

5.3 Stopping Criteria

The stopping criteria in gradient descent is a set of conditions that determine when the training process should stop. This is important to prevent overfitting, where the model becomes too complex and starts to memorize the training data rather than generalizing it to new data. Maximum number of iterations: The training process stops after a set number of iterations, regardless of the improvement in the loss function. Threshold on the improvement of the loss function: The training process stops when the improvement in the loss function falls below a certain threshold.

Early stopping: The training process stops when the loss on a validation set stops improving and starts to increase, indicating overfitting. Convergence: The training process stops when the gradient of the loss function approaches zero, indicating that a minimum has been found. The choice of stopping criteria can impact the final performance of the model, so it is important to carefully consider the appropriate criteria for a particular problem.

5.3.1 Convergence and Stopping Criteria

Convergence and stopping criteria in gradient descent refer to the criteria for determining when to end the optimization process. Convergence means that the parameters of the model have reached a stable state and are no longer changing significantly. Stopping criteria are used to determine when the optimization process has converged and should be stopped. There are several common stopping criteria for gradient descent:

The fixed number of iterations stopping criteria for gradient descent is a simple stopping rule in which the optimization algorithm terminates after a predetermined number of iterations have been completed. The mathematical equation for this criteria can be expressed as if (current iteration number >= max iterations) stop optimization, where "current iteration number" is the current iteration of the optimization algorithm and "max iterations" is the maximum number of iterations specified as the stopping criteria. The tolerance on the change in parameters stopping criteria for gradient descent can be defined as follows:

For instance, W be the set of weights in the neural network and W_0 be the initial weights. Then, the stopping criteria can be defined as:

$$|w_t - w_{t-1}| < \varepsilon, \tag{5.10}$$

where t is the iteration number and ε is a small positive number representing the tolerance for change in the parameters. If the difference between the current weights and the previous iteration's weights is less than ε, then the training process stops, and the final weights w_t are used. This stopping criteria helps to prevent overfitting by ensuring that the training process stops when the model has reached a satisfactory level of accuracy, rather than continuing until the model overfits the training data.

In gradient descent optimization, the tolerance on the change in the objective function is a stopping criterion used to determine when to stop the optimization process. This criterion is based on the change in the value of the objective function between two consecutive iterations. If the change in the objective function is below a certain threshold, it can be assumed that the optimization has converged. The threshold is specified as a tolerance parameter. In gradient descent optimization, the tolerance on the gradient can be used as a stopping criterion by checking whether the gradient of the objective function falls below a certain threshold. If the gradient is small enough, it can be assumed that the optimization has reached a local minimum.

The gradient of the objective function J is defined as the vector of its partial derivatives with respect to the parameters θ. The gradient can be computed during each iteration of the optimization and its norm can be used as a measure of the progress of the optimization:

$$\|\nabla J(\theta)\| = \sqrt{\left(\frac{\partial J(\theta)}{\partial \theta_1}\right)^2 + \left(\frac{\partial J(\theta)}{\partial \theta_1}\right)^2 + \dots + \left(\frac{\partial J(\theta)}{\partial \theta_n}\right)^2}. \tag{5.11}$$

A threshold value ε is set for the gradient norm and the optimization stops when $\|\nabla J(\theta)\| < \varepsilon$. So the equation for tolerance on the gradient can be: $\|\nabla J(\theta)\| < \varepsilon$. The choice of stopping criteria depends on the specific problem and the optimization algorithm being used. It is important to choose an appropriate stopping criteria to avoid both underfitting (stopping the optimization too early) and overfitting (continuing the optimization too long).

5.3.2 Local Minimum and Global Minimum

In mathematics, a minimum is a point on a function where the output value is the lowest within a specific range or domain. There are two types of minimums that can be observed in functions: local minimums and global minimums, as shown in Figure 5.5. A local minimum is a point on a function where the output value is the lowest among all the nearby points within a small region. In other words, a local minimum is a point where the function is lower than any other points immediately adjacent to it.

A global minimum, on the other hand, is a point on a function where the output value is the lowest within the entire domain of the function. In other words, a global minimum is the absolute lowest point on the function. In summary, a local minimum is a point on a function where the output value is the lowest among nearby points, while a global minimum is a point on a function where the output value is the lowest within the entire domain of the function.

5.4 Resampling Methods

Resampling methods are techniques for estimating the performance of machine learning algorithms by using different subsets of the available data. They are mainly used to address the problem of overfitting and to provide a more robust assessment of the model's generalization performance (Figure 5.6).

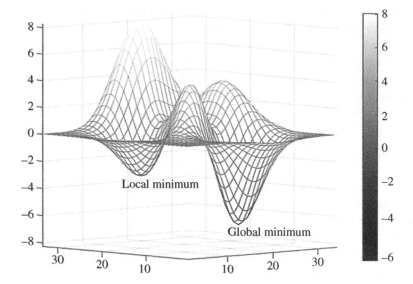

Figure 5.5 Local minimum and global minimum in peaks.

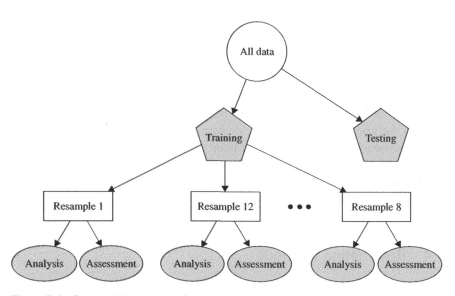

Figure 5.6 Data splitting scheme from the initial data split to resampling.

5.4.1 Cross-Validation

Cross-validation is a technique for evaluating the performance of a model by dividing the dataset into several parts, training the model on a portion of the data, and evaluating it on the remaining portion. The main objective is to prevent overfitting by evaluating the model's ability to generalize to unseen data. There are various types of cross-validation techniques such as k-fold cross-validation, leave-one-out cross-validation, and stratified k-fold cross-validation.

In k-fold cross-validation, the dataset is divided into k parts or folds of roughly equal size and the model is trained on $k-1$ of the folds and evaluated on the remaining fold. This process is repeated k times, with each fold being used as the test set once. The performance metric is then averaged across the k iterations. For instance, one has a dataset with n samples and a model with parameters theta. The x and y be the feature matrix and target vector, respectively. The k-fold cross-validation procedure can be expressed mathematically as:

For each iteration $i = 1, 2, 3, ..., k$:

a. for $i = 1$ to k do

Split data into training set and validation set in the ratio of $(k-1)/k$ and $1/k$, respectively

Train the model on the training set

Evaluate the performance of the model on the validation set using a performance metric (such as MSE, accuracy, or F1-score)

Store the performance metric of the model on the validation set

f. end for

g. Compute the average performance metric across all k iterations

h. Return the average performance metric as the final result of k-fold cross-validation.

5.4.2 Bootstrapping

Bootstrapping is a statistical resampling method used to estimate the distribution of a statistic (e.g. the mean) by generating multiple, independent samples from the original data set with replacement. The goal of bootstrapping is to obtain a more robust estimate of the true population parameters by generating a large number of resamples, each of which provides an estimate of the statistic of interest. Bootstrapping involves randomly selecting samples with replacement from the original dataset to form multiple new datasets (referred to as "bootstrapped" datasets) of the same size as the original dataset.

5.4.3 Monte Carlo Cross-Validation

Monte Carlo cross-validation is a type of cross-validation that uses random sampling to divide a dataset into multiple folds for model validation. It involves repeating the process of training and evaluating the model multiple times with different partitions of the dataset. The performance of the model is estimated by averaging the results of these evaluations. The aim is to reduce the variance of the model evaluation by considering multiple subsets of the data. Monte Carlo cross-validation can be computationally expensive, but it can provide more robust estimates of the model performance compared to other resampling methods. The performance of the model is then evaluated using a metric, such as accuracy, on the validation set. The average of the performance metrics over the K iterations is then taken as the final performance metric for the model. The math equation for Monte Carlo Cross-Validation (MCCV) can be represented as:

$$\text{Performance Metric} = \frac{1}{K} \sum_{i=1}^{K} \text{Performance Metric for fold } i, \qquad (5.12)$$

where performance metric is a metric such as accuracy, precision, recall, or F1-score, and $\sum$ represents the sum of the performance metrics over the K folds.

5.5 Optimizers in Neural Network

Optimizers in neural network are algorithms used to update the model's parameters in order to minimize the loss function. Each optimizer has its own mathematical update rule to adjust the parameters. The choice of optimizer depends on the problem and the desired training speed, stability, and accuracy, and some common optimizers are shown in Figure 5.7.

5.5.1 Stochastic Gradient Descent

Stochastic gradient descent (SGD) is an optimization algorithm in neural networks that updates the parameters in the direction of the negative gradient of the loss function. The equation for SGD update rule is given by:

$$w(t + 1) = wt - \eta \nabla L(wT), \qquad (5.13)$$

where wt is the parameter value at iteration t, η is the learning rate and $\nabla L(w(t))$ is the gradient of the loss function L at wt. In each iteration of SGD, a random sample from the training data is selected and the gradient of the loss function with respect

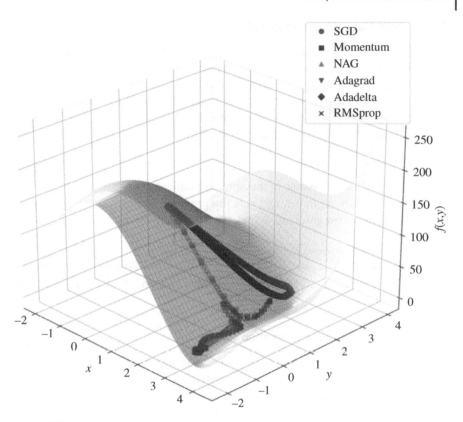

Figure 5.7 Optimizers in neural network.

to the parameters is calculated for that sample. The parameters are then updated according to the following equation:

$$\theta_{new} = \theta_{old} - \alpha \nabla L(\theta x_i, y_i), \tag{5.14}$$

where θ_{old} and θ_{new} are the old and updated vector of parameters to be optimized, respectively. The α is the learning rate, a hyperparameter that determines the step size of the update. The $\nabla L(\theta x_i, y_i)$ is the gradient of the loss function L with respect to the parameters θ, calculated for a single sample (x_i, y_i) from the training data.

The optimization procedure continues until a stopping criteria, such as a fixed number of iterations or a minimum improvement in the loss function, is met. The randomness of SGD provides a regularization effect that helps prevent overfitting and makes it suitable for large-scale datasets. SGD is also computationally effi-cient, as only one sample is used in each iteration and parallel updates can be made for multiple samples.

5.5.2 Root Mean Square Propagation

Root Mean Square Propagation (RMSprop) is a gradient descent optimization algorithm for training deep neural networks. It is similar to SGD, but instead of using a fixed learning rate, it adjusts the learning rate dynamically based on the average of the historical squared gradients of the parameters. This helps to mitigate the issue of fluctuating or diminishing learning rates in SGD, which can slow down or prevent convergence of the optimization process. The update rule is given as:

$$r_t = \gamma r_{t-1} + (1-\gamma)g_t^2, \tag{5.15}$$

where r_t is the moving average of the squared gradient at time step t. The γ is the decay rate, typically set to 0.9, and g_t is the gradient at time step t. The moving average of the squared gradients is updated after each iteration as:

$$\theta_{t+1} = \theta_t - \frac{\eta}{\sqrt{r_t + \varepsilon}}g_t, \tag{5.16}$$

where θ_t is the model parameters, η is the learning rate, and ε is a small constant to avoid division by zero.

5.5.3 Adaptive Moment Estimation

Adaptive Moment Estimation (Adam) is a popular optimization algorithm used in deep learning to update the model parameters. It combines the advantages of RMSprop and SGD with momentum. The Adam algorithm maintains exponential moving averages of the gradient and squared gradient and computes adaptive learning rates for each parameter. The mathematical equation for updating the parameters using Adam is:

$$v_t = \beta_1 v_{t-1} + (1-\beta_1)\left(\nabla_\theta J_\theta\right) \tag{5.17}$$

$$s_t = \beta_2 s_{t-1} + (1-\beta_2)\left(\nabla_\theta J_\theta\right)^2 \tag{5.18}$$

$$\hat{v}_t = \frac{v_t}{1-\beta_1^{\,t}} \tag{5.19}$$

$$\hat{s}_t = \frac{s_t}{1-\beta_2^{\,t}} \tag{5.20}$$

$$\theta_{t+1} = \theta_t + \alpha\,\frac{\hat{v}_t}{\sqrt{\hat{s}_t + \varepsilon}}, \tag{5.21}$$

where θ_{t+1} is the updated parameter at time step $t+1$; θ_t is the parameter at time step t, v_t and s_t are the moving average of the gradient and squared gradient, respectively; $\hat{v}$ and $\hat{s}_t$ are the bias-corrected moving average of v_t and s_t; α is the learning rate; β_1 and β_2 are the hyperparameters for the moving average; and ε is a small constant to avoid division by zero.

The key advantage of the Adam algorithm is that it provides an adaptive learning rate for each parameter, which can help overcome the drawbacks of traditional optimization algorithms, such as a need for manual tuning of the learning rate.

5.5.4 AdaMax

The AdaMax optimizer uses a similar formula to the Adam optimizer, with the difference being in the calculation of the moving average of squared gradient. In AdaMax, the moving average is calculated using the L-infinity norm instead of the $L2$ norm used in Adam. The AdaMax optimizer update rule is given by:

$$
\begin{aligned}
m_t + 1 &= \beta_1 m_t + (1 - \beta_1) g_t, v_t + 1 \\
&= \max(\beta_2 v_t, \varepsilon(g_t)) w_t + 1 \\
&= w_t - l_r \frac{m_t}{\sqrt{v_t + \varepsilon}},
\end{aligned}
\tag{5.22}
$$

where m_t is the moving average of the gradient, v_t is the moving average of the squared gradient, g_t is the gradient at time t, β_1 and β_2 are the decay rates for the moving averages, l_r is the learning rate, w_t is the parameter at time t, and ϵ is a small constant for numerical stability.

5.5.5 Momentum Optimization

Momentum optimization is a gradient descent optimization method that incorporates the information from the past gradients to update the parameters. It works by updating the parameters in the direction of the accumulated past gradients, which helps overcome the oscillations and speed up convergence. The update rule for momentum optimization can be formulated as:

$$
v_t = \beta v_{t-1} + (1 - \beta) g \tag{5.23}
$$

$$
w_t = w_{t-1} - h v_t, \tag{5.24}
$$

where v_t is the velocity, w_t is the weight, β is the momentum term that controls the extent to which past gradients influence the current update, g is the current gradient, and h is the step size (Table 5.2).

Summary

This chapter discussed a wide number of topics that may potentially be connected to either machine learning or artificial neural networks. These topics were spread out throughout the book. In the course of the presentation, a number of

Table 5.2 Summarizing some common optimizers used in neural network training.

Optimizer	Description
Stochastic gradient descent (SGD)	A simple optimization algorithm that updates the weights of the neural network using the gradients of the loss function with respect to the weights.
Adam (adaptive moment estimation)	An optimization algorithm that combines ideas from both momentum-based and RMSprop algorithms. Adam adapts the learning rate based on estimates of the first and second moments of the gradients.
RMSprop (root mean square propagation)	An optimization algorithm that uses a moving average of the squared gradients to adapt the learning rate. It has been shown to work well for nonstationary objectives such as neural network training.
Adagrad (adaptive gradient algorithm)	An optimization algorithm that adapts the learning rate for each weight based on the sum of the squares of past gradients for that weight. It is particularly useful for sparse data problems.
Adadelta	An optimization algorithm that is similar to Adagrad, but adapts the learning rate based on a moving average of the past gradients instead of the sum of the squares of past gradients.
Nesterov accelerated gradient (NAG)	An optimization algorithm that uses a modified gradient that takes into account the current velocity of the weights. This allows the optimizer to "look ahead" and update the weights before computing the gradient.
Momentum-based optimization	An optimization algorithm that uses a momentum term that allows the optimizer to "carry over" some of the previous weight updates when computing the current update. This can help the optimizer avoid getting stuck in local minima.

fundamental concepts were brought up, such as optimizers, backpropagation, gradient descent, overfitting avoidance measures, resampling approaches, and resampling methodologies. These were some of the most significant topics that were to be learned from this chapter. In addition to this, one discussed the mathematical equations that are utilized in the process of explaining these concepts. Some examples of these equations include the update rule in gradient descent, the tolerance on the gradient, cross-validation, bootstrapping, Monte Carlo cross-validation, and the optimizers such as SGD, RMSprop, Adam, AdaMax, and momentum optimization. To be able to comprehend how machine learning algorithms and neural networks function, as well as how to fine-tune them for particular tasks, it is necessary to have knowledge of these elementary concepts, which serve as the fundamental building blocks.

Exercise Questions

Q. 5.1   What is the mathematical expression for the gradient of the loss function with respect to the weights in a neural network, and how is it computed using backpropagation?

Q. 5.2   In a backpropagation neural network, the activation function used in the hidden layer is the rectified linear unit (ReLU), given by:

$$f(x) = \max(0, x)$$

Calculate the output of the ReLU activation function for an input $x = -3$.

Q. 5.3   How do you prevent overfitting in artificial neural networks?

Q. 5.4   Explain the concept of adaptive learning rate methods, such as Adagrad, Adam, and RMSprop, and how they adjust the learning rate dynamically based on the gradient history, and what is the mathematical expression for the update rule of Adagrad?

Q. 5.5   What are some of the popular optimizers used in neural networks?

Q. 5.6   What is the concept of momentum in gradient descent and how it is used to improve the convergence and robustness of the algorithm, and what is the mathematical expression for the update rule with momentum?

Q. 5.7   How does Monte Carlo cross-validation differ from traditional cross-validation?

Q. 5.8   What is the purpose of regularization in neural networks?

Q. 5.9   Can you explain the difference between early stopping and dropout in overfitting prevention?

Q. 5.10 In a backpropagation neural network, the error term for a neuron in the hidden layer is calculated using the following equation:

$$\delta_h = f'(z_h) \times \Sigma\left(\delta_j \times w_{jh}\right)$$

Given the following values:

Derivative of the activation function: $f'(z_h) = 0.5$; Error terms of the neurons in the next layer: $\delta_1 = 0.3$, $\delta_2 = 0.4$; Weights connecting the hidden neuron to the neurons in the next layer: $w_{1h} = 0.6$, $w_{2h} = 0.8$; Calculate the error term δ_h for the hidden neuron.

Further Reading

Cochocki A, Unbehauen R. *Neural networks for optimization and signal processing.* John Wiley & Sons, Inc.; 1993 Jun 1.

Fitrianto A, Linganathan P. Comparisons between resampling techniques in linear regression: a simulation study. *CAUCHY: Jurnal Matematika Murni dan Aplikasi.* 2022 Oct 11;7(3):345–53.

Wythoff BJ. Backpropagation neural networks: a tutorial. *Chemometrics and Intelligent Laboratory Systems.* 1993 Feb 1;18(2):115–55.

6

Application of Neural Network in Learning and Recognition

6.1 Applying Backpropagation to Shape Recognition

The backpropagation algorithm is perhaps the most basic component of a neural network. It was initially presented in 1960s and over 30 years later (1989) popularized by Rumelhart, Hinton, and Williams in a study named "Learning representations by back-propagating mistakes." The program uses a technique called chain rule to efficiently train a neural network. Simply said, backpropagation does a backward pass across a network after each forward pass while modifying the model's parameters (weights and biases). Four neurons make up the input layer of the four-layer neural network, four neurons make up the hidden layers, and one neuron makes up the output layer, as shown in Figure 6.1.

The input neuron can be as simple as scalars or more complex like vectors or multidimensional matrices.

$$y = \sum_{i=1}^{b} w_i x_i + b, \tag{6.1}$$

where y is the output, x_i are the input values, w_i are the weights associated with each input, b is the bias, and n is the number of input neurons.

The final values at the hidden neurons are computed using z^l—weighted inputs in layer 1, and a^l—activations in layer 1. For layer 2, the equations are described below:

$$z^{(2)} = w^{(1)}x + b^{(1)}$$
$$a^{(2)} = f\left(z^{(2)}\right). \tag{6.2}$$

Cybernetical Intelligence: Engineering Cybernetics with Machine Intelligence, First Edition.
Kelvin K. L. Wong.
© 2024 The Institute of Electrical and Electronics Engineers, Inc.
Published 2024 by John Wiley & Sons, Inc.
Companion website: www.wiley.com/go/cyberintel

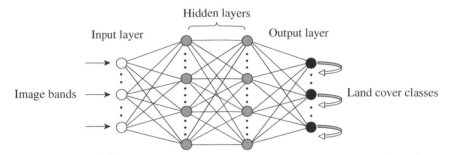

Figure 6.1 Illustration of simple 4-layer neural network.

The final part of a neural network is the output layer which produces the predicted value.

$$y = f(z), \tag{6.3}$$

where y is the output of the output layer, z is the input to the output layer, and f is the activation function applied to z. Backpropagation is a widely used algorithm for training artificial neural networks, including those used in shape recognition. The algorithm works by adjusting the weights of the network in the direction of the negative gradient of the cost function, which measures the difference between the network's output and the desired output. This process is repeated iteratively until the weights converge to a minimum value that corresponds to a good fit for the training data.

The backpropagation algorithm consists of two main phases: the forward phase and the backward phase. In the forward phase, the input is passed through the network, and the output is computed. In the backward phase, the error is propagated back through the network, and the weights are adjusted to reduce the error.

The key equations in the backpropagation algorithm are the gradient of the cost function with respect to the weights, and the update rule for the weights. The gradient is computed using the chain rule of calculus, and the update rule is typically a simple form of stochastic gradient descent.

The general form of the update rule for a weight w_{ij} in a network with L layers is:

$$w_{ij}(t + 1) = w_{ij}(t) - \eta \frac{\partial E}{\partial w_{ij}(t)}, \tag{6.4}$$

where $w_{ij}(t)$ is the weight at time t, η is the learning rate, and $\frac{\partial E}{\partial w_{ij}(t)}$ is the partial derivative of the error E with respect to the weight w_{ij} at time t. This partial derivative is computed using the backpropagation algorithm shown in Equation (6.5), which propagates the error from the output layer back to the input layer, updating the weights in each layer as it goes. The update rule is applied iteratively over a number of epochs or until convergence is achieved.

$$\delta_{ij} = \left(o_j - t_j\right)f'\left(n_j\right)o_i, \tag{6.5}$$

where o_j is the output of neuron j, t_j is the desired output, $f'(n_j)$ is the derivative of the activation function of neuron j with respect to its net input, and $output_i$ is the output of neuron i, which is the input to neuron j.

In shape recognition, the input to the network is typically a set of features that describe the shape of an object, such as its edges or corners. The output is a probability distribution over a set of possible classes, indicating the likelihood that the shape belongs to each class. The cost function used in training is typically the cross-entropy between the network's output and the true class labels.

By adjusting the weights of the network using backpropagation, the network can learn to recognize shapes based on their features. This is a powerful tool for computer vision and other applications that require pattern recognition, the complete process is described below.

- Input data: The first step is to gather and preprocess the input data for the neural network. In the case of shape recognition, this might involve converting an image of a shape into a matrix of pixel values.
- Initialize the network: Next, the neural network is initialized with random weights and biases for each neuron in each layer.
- Forward propagation: The input data is then fed through the network layer by layer using the feedforward process. The inputs are multiplied by the weights and the biases are added to produce the activation of each neuron.
- Compute error: The error between the network's output and the desired output is then computed using a loss function such as mean squared error.
- Backpropagation: The error is then propagated back through the network in reverse order, starting from the output layer and working backward. This is done using the chain rule of calculus to compute the gradient of the error with respect to the weights and biases of each neuron in the network.
- Update weights and biases: The gradients are then used to update the weights and biases of the network using an optimization algorithm such as stochastic gradient descent. The learning rate determines how quickly the weights and biases are updated.
- Repeat: The above steps are repeated for a certain number of epochs or until the error is minimized to an acceptable level.

For instance, one wants to train a neural network to recognize the shape of a triangle. One can represent the triangle as a matrix of pixel values, where each pixel is either "on" or "off." One can also represent the target output as a vector with three elements, each representing one of the three sides of the triangle.

To train the neural network using backpropagation, one would first randomly initialize the weights of the network. One would then feed the pixel values for each triangle in our training set through the network, and compare the output of the network to the target output for that triangle.

Using the difference between the predicted output and the target output, one would calculate the error, and then use the backpropagation algorithm to update the weights of the network in a way that reduces the error. This process is repeated for all triangles in the training set, and typically for many epochs (i.e. iterations through the entire training set).

After the neural network is trained, one can use it to recognize new triangles by feeding their pixel values through the network and observing the output. Here is an example of a small training set with two triangles: Triangle 1 (target output: $[1, 0, 1]$)

$$\begin{bmatrix} 0 & 0 & 1 & 0 & 0 \\ 0 & 1 & 0 & 1 & 0 \\ 1 & 0 & 0 & 0 & 1 \end{bmatrix}. \tag{6.6}$$

Triangle 2 (target output: $[1, 1, 0]$)

$$\begin{bmatrix} 1 & 1 & 0 & 0 & 0 \\ 0 & 1 & 1 & 0 & 0 \\ 0 & 0 & 1 & 1 & 1 \end{bmatrix}. \tag{6.7}$$

One can represent each of these triangles as a matrix with binary pixel values. For example, the first triangle can be represented as:

$$\begin{bmatrix} 0 & 0 & 1 & 0 & 0 \\ 0 & 1 & 0 & 1 & 0 \\ 1 & 0 & 0 & 0 & 1 \end{bmatrix}. \tag{6.8}$$

To train a neural network to recognize these triangles, one would first randomly initialize the weights of the network. One would then feed each triangle through the network and use the difference between the predicted output and the target output to update the weights of the network using the backpropagation algorithm.

After the network is trained, one can use it to recognize new triangles by feeding their pixel values through the network and observing the output. For example, if one had a new triangle with pixel values:

$$\begin{bmatrix} 1 & 0 & 0 & 0 & 1 \\ 0 & 1 & 0 & 1 & 0 \\ 0 & 0 & 1 & 0 & 0 \end{bmatrix}. \tag{6.9}$$

One would feed these pixel values through the network and observe the output to see if the network recognizes the triangle.

6.2 Softmax Regression

Softmax regression, also known as the multinomial logistic regression, is a technique used to perform multi-class classification. It is an extension of logistic regression that allows the classification of multiple classes by outputting a probability distribution over the classes. Ultimately, the algorithm is going to find a boundary line for each class. Softmax regression algorithm produces a set of values that add up to 1, and each value represents the probability of the corresponding class being the correct class. Softmax regression is commonly used in natural language processing, computer vision, and other fields that involve multi-class classification problems.

The softmax function is a generalization of the logistic function to multiple dimensions, and it is used to transform a vector of real numbers into a probability distribution. The softmax function is defined as follows:

$$\sigma\left(\vec{z}\right)j = \frac{e^{z_i}}{\sum_{j=1}^{K} e^{z_j}}, \tag{6.10}$$

where $\vec{z}$ is the input vector to the softmax function, z_i is the element of the input vector to the softmax function, e^{z_i} is the standard exponential function applied to each element of the input vector, and $\sum_{j=1}^{K} e^{z_j}$ is the term on the bottom of the formula, which is the normalization term. It ensures that all the output values of the function will sum to 1 and each will be in the range $(0, 1)$, thus constituting a valid probability distribution, and K is the number of classes. In softmax regression, the goal is to learn the weights and biases of a linear model that maps an input vector x to a vector of scores z. The scores are then passed through the softmax function to obtain a vector of probabilities over the classes. The softmax regression model can be defined as follows:

$$z = wx + b, \tag{6.11}$$

where w is a weight matrix of size $k \times D$, b is a bias vector of size k, x is an input vector of size D, and k is the number of classes. The softmax function is then applied to the scores to obtain the class probabilities:

$$\check{y} = \text{softmax}(z), \tag{6.12}$$

where $\breve{y}$ is a vector of size k that contains the probabilities of the classes. During training, the parameters w and b are learned using the cross-entropy loss function, which measures the difference between the predicted class probabilities and the true class labels. The cross-entropy loss function is defined as follows:

$$L = -\frac{1}{N}\sum_{i=1}^{N}\sum_{j=1}^{k} y_{ij} \log\left(\breve{y}_{ij}\right), \tag{6.13}$$

where N is the number of training examples, y_{ij} is the true label of the ith example for the jth class, and $\breve{y}_{ij}$ is the predicted probability of the ith example for the jth class.

The backpropagation algorithm is then used to compute the gradients of the loss function with respect to the parameters w and b, which are then used to update the parameters using gradient descent. The gradient of the loss function with respect to the weights is given by:

$$\frac{\partial L}{\partial w_{jk}} = \frac{1}{N}\sum_{i=1}^{N} x_{ij}(\breve{y}_{ik} - y_{ik}), \tag{6.14}$$

and the gradient of the loss function with respect to the biases is given by:

$$\frac{\partial L}{\partial b_{k}} = \frac{1}{N}\sum_{i=1}^{N}(\breve{y}_{ik} - y_{ik}). \tag{6.15}$$

In softmax regression, feature importance can be determined by analyzing the magnitude of the learned weights assigned to each feature. These weights are a measure of the contribution of each feature to the prediction of the class labels. The larger the weight, the more important the feature is in the prediction.

The softmax function is commonly used in multi-class classification problems to convert a vector of real numbers into a probability distribution over the classes. To compute the feature importance using softmax regression, one can examine the magnitude of the learned weights. The weight matrix W can be analyzed to identify the most important features by examining the magnitude of the weights for each feature. The features with larger weights are considered more important in the prediction of the class labels.

For instance, assuming a softmax regression model trained on an image classification task with input images of size 32×32 pixels and 10 output classes, the weight matrix W will be of size $(32 \times 32 \times 3, 10)$, where the input images are flattened into a single vector of length 3072. The next step is to the magnitude of the weights in W in order to identify the pixels in the input images that are most important in the classification task. The pixels with larger weights will be considered more important in the prediction of the class labels.

6.3 K-Binary Classifier

A K-binary classifier is a type of classification algorithm used in machine learning to classify data into K classes. The classifier is based on the concept of one-vs-all (OvA) or one-vs-rest (OvR) strategy, in which K classifiers are trained, one for each class. Each classifier is trained to recognize a specific class by comparing the features of the data with the features of the training data for that class. The mathematical formulation for a K-binary classifier can be represented as follows:

For instance, X be the input feature vector of size n, and Y be the output variable representing the class label, which can take one of the K possible values. The K-binary classifier is defined as:

$$P(Y = k|X) = e^{\frac{w_k^T X + b_k}{\sum_e w_j^T X + b_j}}, \tag{6.16}$$

where $P(Y = k|X)$ is the probability of the input feature vector X belonging to class k, e is the exponential function, w_k is the weight vector for class k, b_k is the bias term for class k, and the $\sum$ is overall possible values of j from 1 to K. The output of the classifier is the class label that has the highest probability:

$$\hat{Y} = \text{argmax}_k(P(Y = k|X)), \tag{6.17}$$

where $\hat{Y}$ is the predicted class label for the input feature vector X. The softmax function normalizes the output of the discriminant functions, such that the sum of the probabilities over all classes is equal to one.

The K-binary classifier can be trained using the backpropagation algorithm, which involves minimizing a cost function that measures the difference between the predicted probabilities and the true labels of the training data. The cost function can be represented as the negative log-likelihood of the softmax function:

$$C = -\frac{1}{n} \sum_{i=1}^{N} \log(p(y_i|x_i)) \tag{6.18}$$

where C represents the cost function, N is the total number of training examples, y_i is the true label of the ith training example, and x_i represents the input features of the ith training example.

$p(y_i|x_i)$ represents the predicted probability of the true label y_i given the input features x_i, calculated using the softmax function. The gradient of the cost function with respect to the weights and biases can be calculated using the chain rule of calculus, and the weights and biases can be updated using gradient descent or other optimization algorithms.

The K-binary classifier is widely used in many applications, including image classification, text classification, and speech recognition.

For instance, one has a dataset of flower images and one wants to classify them into K different classes (e.g. daisy, rose, sunflower, etc.). The dataset has N samples, and each sample is represented as a feature vector with D dimensions (e.g. pixel values of the image). For instance, X be the $N \times D$ matrix containing the feature vectors of all samples, and y be the $N \times 1$ vector containing the corresponding labels (i.e. integers from 1 to K).

To perform K-binary classification using Softmax regression, one need to first transform the labels y into K binary indicators (i.e. one-hot encoding). For instance, Y be the $N \times K$ matrix containing the one-hot encoding of y, where each row of Y has a 1 at the index corresponding to the class of the sample and 0 elsewhere.

Then, one need to train a weight matrix W with shape $D \times K$ and a bias vector b with shape $K \times 1$, such that the score of each sample for each class can be computed as:

$$S = wx + b. \tag{6.19}$$

The score S is a $N \times K$ matrix, where each row contains the scores of a sample for all K classes.

6.4 Relational Learning via Neural Network

What will introduce is relational learning by building a neural network, the relational network. To describe it in more detail, a simple neural network module for relational reasoning. It describes how to use relation networks (RNs) as a simple plug-and-play module to solve problems that fundamentally hinge on relational reasoning.

The design philosophy behind RNs is to constrain the functional form of a neural network so that it captures the core common properties of relational reasoning. In other words, the capacity to compute relations is baked into the RN architecture without needing to be learned, just as the capacity to reason about spatial, translation invariant properties is built-in to convolutional neural networks (CNNs), and the capacity to reason about sequential dependencies is built into recurrent neural networks.

For a simple RN, can express as follows:

$$\text{RN}(O) = f_\phi \left(\sum_{i,j} g_\theta \left(o_i, o_j \right) \right), \tag{6.20}$$

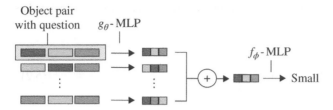

Figure 6.2 Schematic diagram of RNs.

where the input is a set of "objects" $O = \{O_1, O_2, ..., O_n\}$, $O_i \in R^m$ is the ith object, and f_ϕ and g_θ are functions with parameters φ and θ, respectively. For our purposes, f_ϕ and g_θ are multilayer perceptron (MLP), and the parameters are learnable synaptic weights, making RNs end-to-end differentiable. One call the output of g_θ a "relation"; therefore, the role of g_θ is to infer the ways in which two objects are related, or if they are even related at all (Figure 6.2).

The structure of the relational network consists of two parts. One is the embedding module, which is used to extract its features, and the other is the relation module, which is used to compute the relationship.

One popular approach to relational learning via neural networks is the graph neural network (GNN). GNNs operate on graphs, where nodes represent entities and edges represent relationships between entities. They use a message-passing algorithm to propagate information between nodes and update their representations based on the information they receive from neighboring nodes. The output of the GNN can be used for tasks such as link prediction, node classification, and graph classification.

Relational learning via neural networks has a wide range of applications in areas such as social network analysis, recommendation systems, and drug discovery. It allows for more sophisticated modeling of relationships in data and can improve the accuracy of predictions for tasks that involve relational data.

6.4.1 Graph Neural Network

GNNs are a class of neural networks that can operate on graph-structured data, such as social networks, chemical compounds, or protein structures. GNNs aim to learn node-level or graph-level representations by aggregating information from the neighboring nodes and edges in a graph.

One of the popular GNN architectures is the message-passing neural network, which updates the node representations by passing messages between the neighboring nodes. The basic idea of message passing is to combine the feature vectors of the neighboring nodes and edges, apply a neural network function, and produce a new feature vector for the node. The message-passing process can be formalized as follows:

$$h_v^{l+1} = \sigma \left(\sum_{u \in N(v)} W^l h_u^l + W_e^l e_{u,v}^l \right),$$ (6.21)

where h_v^l is the feature vector of node v at layer l, $\sum$ is a nonlinear activation function, $\in N(v)$ is the set of neighboring nodes of v, W^l is a weight matrix for node features, W_e^l is a weight matrix for edge features, and $e_{u,v}^l$ is the feature vector of the edge between nodes u and v at layer l. The superscript $(l+1)$ denotes the next layer.

The message-passing process can be repeated for multiple layers to incorporate information from a larger neighborhood. The final node features can be used for node-level classification, regression, or clustering. For graph-level classification, a readout function can be used to summarize the node features into a graph-level representation, which is then fed to a softmax classifier. The readout function can be a simple summation, mean or max pooling, or a more complex neural network.

GNNs have shown impressive performance on a variety of graph-based tasks, such as node classification, link prediction, and molecular property prediction. They can handle graphs of arbitrary size and structure and can learn meaningful representations even for nodes with no or limited direct connectivity.

With the numerical representation of graphs that we have constructed above (with vectors instead of scalars), one is now ready to build a GNN. One will start with the simplest GNN architecture, one where one learns new embedding for all graph attributes (nodes, edges, global), but where one does not yet use the connectivity of the graph. This GNN uses a separate MLP (or your favorite differentiable model) on each component of a graph; one calls this a GNN layer. For each node vector, one applies the MLP and gets back a learned node vector. One does the same for each edge, learning a per-edge embedding, and also for the global-context vector, learning a single embedding for the entire graph (Figure 6.3).

As is common with neural network modules or layers, one can stack these GNN layers together.

Because a GNN does not update the connectivity of the input graph, one can describe the output graph of a GNN with the same adjacency list and the same number of feature vectors as the input graph. But, the output graph has updated embedding, since the GNN has updated each of the node, edge, and global-context representations.

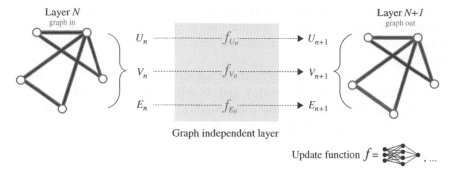

Figure 6.3 A single layer of a simple GNN. A graph is the input, and each component (V, E, U) gets updated by a MLP to produce a new graph. Each function subscript indicates a separate function for a different graph attribute at the nth layer of a GNN model.

6.4.2 Graph Convolutional Network

The majority of GNNs are Graph Convolutional Networks (GCNs), and the convolution in GCN is the same as a convolution in CNNs. It multiplies neurons with weights (filters) to learn from data features. It acts as sliding window on whole images to learn features from neighboring cells.

Now the same functionality to GCNs where a model learns the features from neighboring nodes is transferred. The major difference between GCN and CNN is that it is developed to work on non-Euclidean data structures where the order of nodes and edges can vary (Figure 6.4).

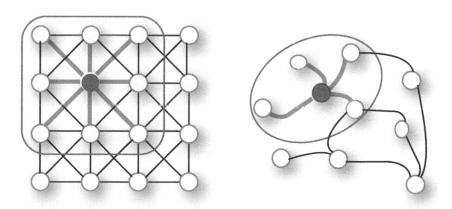

Figure 6.4 The CNN on the left side and GCN on the right side.

GCNs are a type of neural network used for processing data that has a graph structure. The key mathematical equation used in GCNs is the graph convolution, which is a generalization of the traditional convolution operation used in image processing.

For instance, A be the adjacency matrix of a graph with N nodes, where $A_{ij} = 1$ if there is an edge from node i to node j, and $A_{ij} = 0$ otherwise. For instance, X be the feature matrix, where each row corresponds to a node and each column corresponds to a feature. The graph convolution of X with a weight matrix W is given by:

$$H = f(W \times A), \tag{6.22}$$

where f is an activation function, such as ReLU, and H is the output feature matrix.

In a single-layer GCN, the weight matrix W is usually initialized randomly and updated during training using backpropagation. Multiple layers of GCNs can be stacked to form a deeper network, with each layer processing information from the previous layer.

Other mathematical equations used in GCNs include the definition of the Chebyshev polynomial approximation of the graph convolution, which allows for efficient computation, and the definition of the propagation rule, which determines how information is passed between nodes in the graph.

6.5 Cybernetics Using Neural Network

Cybernetics is the study of communication and control in machines and living organisms. One application of cybernetics is in the design and development of neural networks, which are modeled after the structure and function of the human brain. Neural networks are a type of machine learning algorithm that can learn from data, identify patterns, and make predictions based on those patterns.

A neural network is made up of multiple interconnected layers of artificial neurons that process data in a hierarchical manner. The input layer receives data, the hidden layers process the data, and the output layer produces the final result. The activation function is used to transform the output of each neuron in a layer into a usable format for the next layer.

The weights of the connections between neurons are adjusted during training using an optimization algorithm such as backpropagation. This optimization algorithm minimizes the error between the network's prediction and the actual output by adjusting the weights.

The mathematical equation that describes the output of a neuron can be written as:

$$\hat{y} = f\left(\sum_{i=1}^{n} w_i y_i + b\right), \tag{6.23}$$

where $\hat{y}$ is the output of the neuron, f is the activation function, w_i are the weights of the connections between the neuron and the previous layer, y_i are the inputs to the neuron, and b is the bias term. The output of the entire neural network can be written as:

$$y = f(W^L)f(W^{L-1}f(...f(W^1y + b^1)...) + b^{L-1}) + b^L. \tag{6.24}$$

The cybernetical layout of the neuron in artificial intelligence is a conceptual representation of its structure and function, as shown in Figure 6.5. It consists of input connections Y, a processing unit, and an output connection $\hat{Y}$. The input connections receive data or signals from other neurons or external sources, and these inputs are weighted W and combined within the processing unit. The cybernetical layout of the neuron highlights the flow of information and the computational operations performed within the neuron. It demonstrates how inputs are processed and transformed to produce meaningful outputs. This layout, along with the connections and weights between neurons, forms the basis b for learning and decision-making in artificial backpropagation neural networks. The loss which is actually the difference or error rate between actual value and predicted value, is represented as J and calculated when the network makes backpropagation to match the actual input to the network and predicted value, hence thus make a cybernetics loop similar to the backpropagation neural network.

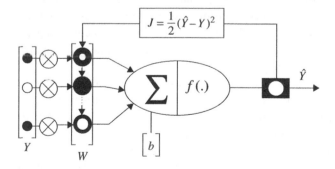

Figure 6.5 Cybernetical layout of the neuron based on perception theory.

By arranging neurons in layers and connecting them in specific ways, more complex computational structures like multilayer perceptrons and deep neural networks can be constructed. These networks leverage the cybernetical layout of neurons to tackle various tasks, such as classification, regression, pattern recognition, and more, in the field of artificial intelligence.

One of the advantages of building neural networks using such a cybernetics concept is their ability to learn and adapt to new information. This makes them useful for applications such as image and speech recognition, natural language processing, and autonomous control systems. Additionally, neural networks are highly parallelizable and can be implemented on hardware such as GPUs or FPGAs for faster processing. Overall, neural networks are a powerful tool for cybernetics and can be used to develop intelligent systems that can learn, adapt, and perform complex tasks.

As presented in Chapters 1 and 2, the field of cybernetics, which is the study of control and communication in machines and living organisms, can be helpful in image recognition tasks by using artificial neural networks and can be understood as a form of cybernetical intelligence. Neural networks can be trained using labeled image data to recognize patterns in images and make predictions about new images that are presented to the network.

In a neural network-based image recognition system, each pixel of an image is treated as an input to the network, and the output of the network is a prediction of the object or class of the image. The network is trained using a set of labeled images, where the correct object or class label is provided for each image. The network learns to recognize patterns in the input image data that are associated with each object or class label.

The network can be designed to have multiple layers of neurons, allowing it to learn more complex representations of the input data. CNNs are a popular type of neural network for image recognition tasks, as they use a series of convolutional layers to extract features from the input image data. These features are then fed into a fully connected neural network layer for classification. Suppose one has a dataset of grayscale images, each with dimensions 28×28 pixels, where each pixel value ranges from 0 to 255. The aim is to build a neural network that can recognize handwritten digits from these images.

A feedforward neural network with two hidden layers, each containing 64 neurons can be implemented. The input layer will have 784 neurons (corresponding to the 28×28 pixel dimensions of the images), and the output layer will have 10 neurons (corresponding to the 10 possible digit classes).

The cross-entropy loss function and the softmax activation function for the output layer can be utilized. The weights and biases of the network can be initialized randomly, and one can use the backpropagation algorithm to adjust them during training.

6.6   Structure of Neural Network for Image Processing

Neural networks can be used for image processing tasks, such as image recognition and classification, by applying the feedforward neural network architecture.

The structure of a neural network for image processing typically consists of an input layer, one or more hidden layers, and an output layer. The input layer receives the pixel values of an image as input, and the output layer produces a probability distribution over the classes of objects that the image may contain.

Each neuron in the hidden layers is connected to all neurons in the previous layer, and the output of each neuron is passed through an activation function to produce a nonlinear transformation of the input. The weights of these connections are adjusted during the training process using backpropagation, a supervised learning algorithm.

The output layer typically uses a softmax activation function, which produces a probability distribution over the possible object classes based on the inputs received from the previous layer. The class with the highest probability is then selected as the predicted class of the image.

An example of the mathematical equations used in a feedforward neural network for image classification can be represented as follows:

For instance x be the input to the network, $a(0)$. Each hidden layer is computed as:

$$z(l) = W(l)a(l-1) + b(l) \tag{6.25}$$

$$a(l) = g(z(l)), \tag{6.26}$$

where $W(l)$ and $b(l)$ are the weight matrix and bias vector for the lth layer, respectively, $z(l)$ is the linear transformation of the input, and g is the activation function.

The output layer uses the softmax function:

$$z(L) = W(L)a(L-1) + b(L) \tag{6.27}$$

$$a(L) = \text{softmax}(z(L)), \tag{6.28}$$

where L is the number of layers in the network, and softmax is the activation function used for the output layer. During the training process, the weights of the connections are updated using backpropagation and gradient descent. The goal is to minimize the difference between the predicted class probabilities and the true class labels using a loss function, such as cross-entropy. Once the network has been trained, it can be used to classify new images by passing them through the network and using the output layer to obtain a probability distribution over the possible object classes.

6.7 Transformer Networks

A type of neural network for natural language processing, transformers use self-attention mechanisms to capture global dependencies between input tokens and enable parallel computation. Transformer networks are complex and involve a number of components, including self-attention, feedforward layers, and residual connections.

- The input to the transformer network is typically a sequence of tokens, such as words in a sentence typically using a lookup table $x_i = E[w_i]$. Where x_i is the embedded representation of the ith token, w_i is the ith token, and E is the embedding matrix.
- The output of the multi-head attention is fed through a feedforward neural network, typically with two fully connected layers and an activation function (e.g. ReLU), $FFN(x) = \max(0, W_1 x + b_1)W_2 + b_2$, where W_1 and b_1 are the weights and biases of the first layer, respectively, and W_2 and b_2 are the weights and biases of the second layer, respectively.
- To improve the flow of information through the network and allow for deeper architectures, the output of each self-attention and feedforward layer is added to the input, resulting in a residual connection, $y = \text{LayerNorm}(x + \text{Multi-Head}(Q, K, V) + FFN(x))$.
- The final output of the transformer network is obtained by applying the same operations multiple times, resulting in a stack of identical layers. The output can be used for various tasks, such as language generation, machine translation, and question answering.

6.8 Attention Mechanisms

A type of mechanism for selectively focusing on relevant input regions, attention mechanisms are used in various types of neural networks such as RNNs and transformers. Here are the main mathematical equations for attention mechanisms:

- The attention score for each position is computed as the dot product of the query, key, and value representations, and then scaled by the square root of the key dimension. Attention $(Q, K, V) = \text{softmax}\left(\frac{(QK^T)}{\sqrt{d_k}}\right)V$, where Q is the query matrix, K is the key matrix, V is the value matrix, and d_k is the key dimension.
- Multi-Head$(Q, K, V) = \text{Concat}(\text{head}_1, \text{head}_2, ..., \text{head}_h)$.

- The attention score is computed as a weighted sum of the query and key representations, using a feedforward neural network, Attention(Q, K, V) = softmax($FFN(Q, K))V$.

where *FFN* is the feedforward neural network, and Q and K are the query and key representations. The feedforward neural network computes the attention score which is given by: $FFN(Q, K) = \tanh(W_1 [Q; K] + b_1)W_2 + b_2$.

6.9 Graph Neural Networks

Designed for graph-structured data such as social networks or molecular structures, GNNs aggregate information from neighboring nodes to make predictions. GNNs are a class of deep learning models that can operate on graph-structured data. Here are some mathematical equations used in GNNs:

- In a message-passing GNN, the representation of a node is updated based on the representations of its neighboring nodes. The message-passing equation can be written as:

$$h_v^{(t)} = \sigma\left(\sum_{u \in N(v)} \frac{1}{N(v)} W^{(t)} h_u^{(t-1)}\right),\tag{6.29}$$

where $h_v^{(t)}$ is the representation of node v at the tth layer, $N(v)$ is the set of neighbors of node v, $|N(v)|$ is the number of neighbors of node v, W^t is the weight matrix for the tth layer, and σ is the activation function.

- Graph Convolutional Network (GCN): In a GCN, the message-passing equation is defined as:

$$h_v^t = \sigma\left(\sum_{u \in N(v)} \frac{1}{\sqrt{deg_u \cdot deg_v}} W^{(t)} h_u^{(t-1)}\right),\tag{6.30}$$

where deg_u and deg_v are the degrees of nodes u and v, respectively. This equation takes into account the sparsity of the graph and helps to prevent over smoothing.

- Graph Attention Network (GAT): In a GAT, the attention mechanism is introduced into the message-passing equation, allowing the model to focus on important neighbors:

$$h_i^{(l+1)} = \sigma\left(\sum_{j\in N_i} \alpha_{i,j}^l W^l h_j^l\right),$$

(6.31)

where h_i^l is the hidden state of node i at layer l, N_i is the set of neighbors of node i, W^l is a learnable weight matrix at layer l, and σ is the activation function.

6.10 Transfer Learning

Transfer learning is a machine learning technique that leverages knowledge learned from one task to improve performance on another related task. In deep learning, transfer learning is often used to fine-tune pretrained models on new data. Here are some mathematical equations that are involved in transfer learning:

- Fine-tuning: In fine-tuning, a pretrained model is further trained on a new task using new data. The objective function for fine-tuning can be written as:

$$L = L_{new} + \lambda L_{old},$$

(6.32)

where L_{new} is the loss function for the new task, L_{old} is the loss function for the original task, and λ is the weighting factor that balances the contribution of the two losses.

- Freeze layers: In some transfer learning scenarios, it may be beneficial to freeze certain layers of the pretrained model and only fine-tune certain layers. The objective function for fine-tuning can be written as:

$$L = L_{new} + \lambda \sum_{i\in F} L_i.$$

(6.33)

- Domain adaptation: In domain adaptation, the goal is to transfer knowledge from a source domain to a target domain, where the source and target domains have different distributions. The objective function for domain adaptation can be written as:

$$L = L_{new} + \lambda D\left(P_{src}, P_{tgt}\right),$$

(6.34)

where D is a distance metric between the source and target domains, such as the maximum mean discrepancy (MMD), P_{src} is the distribution of the source data, and P_{tgt} is the distribution of the target data.

6.11 Generalization of Neural Networks

Figure 6.6 illustrates the overfitting and underfitting compared to the optimum model. The dots represent the data distribution; the curve denotes the predictive model ability. As shown in the graph, overfit gives a minimal error for training data but has a large fluctuation for unseen testing data, whereas underfitting cannot approximate both training and testing data. In machine learning, if the model is not trained well, there will be overfit or underfit.

Both of them will decrease the model's accuracy. In model training, one can use testing and validation data to evaluate the generalization ability of the predictive model. If the model is overfitting, it will catch some detail in training data that does not exist in the whole data space. When this model faces testing data, it cannot find the characters that truly determine the example but handle it with the partial feature. To deal with overfitting, one can expand the dataset with more accurate data samples, use some image processing methods to process the current dataset, choose a more applicable model, and train the algorithm with early stopping.

In a MLP, the input is first passed through the input layer and then sequentially through multiple hidden layers before reaching the final output layer. The hidden layers allow the network to model complex relationships between the inputs and outputs, making it suitable for a broader range of problems than a simple perception. The number of hidden layers and the number of nodes within each layer are hyperparameters that can be adjusted to optimize the model's performance. Adding more hidden layers and nodes can increase the model's capacity, allowing it to model more complex relationships. It also increases the risk of overfitting, where the model becomes too difficult and starts to memorize the training data instead of generalizing to new, unseen data.

Regularization techniques, such as dropout, weight decay, and early stopping, can reduce overfit and improve the model's generalization performance.

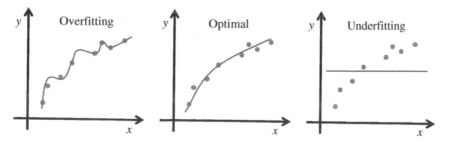

Figure 6.6 Schematic diagram of neural network in overfitting, optimal, and underfitting.

- Dropout: For instance, h_i be the output of node i in a hidden layer. During training, node i is dropped out with probability p, meaning its output is set to zero, i.e. $h_i = 0$ with probability p. The resulting output of the layer, h', is given by $h' = h \times (1-p)$, where $\times$ denotes element-wise multiplication.
- Weight decay: The W is the weights matrix, and λ is the weight decay factor. The cost function J with weight decay is given by $J = J_0 + \lambda \|W\|^2$, where J_0 is the original cost function and $\|W\|^2$ is the $L2$ norm of the weight matrix.
- Early stopping: J_{val} be the cost function evaluated on a validation set, and n_{stop} is the number of epochs after which training will stop if the validation error has not improved. Training stops when the difference between J_{val} and its minimum value over the last n_{stop} epochs is greater than a threshold.

6.12 Performance Measures

Performance measures are used to evaluate the accuracy and effectiveness of a neural network model. Common performance measures for neural networks are described in further subsections.

6.12.1 Confusion Matrix

Confusion matrix is a matrix that compares the predicted class labels with the true class labels in a classification problem. The confusion matrix provides a summary of the correct and incorrect classifications made by the model. It is used to evaluate the accuracy of a binary or multi-class classification model. A typical confusion matrix has the structure, as shown in Figure 6.7. In this Figure, *TP* represents true positives, instances that are positive and classified as positive. *TN* represents true negatives, instances that are negative and classified as negative. *FP* shows the false positives, instances that are negative but classified as positive. *FN* reported the false negatives, instances that are positive but classified as negative.

	Actual values	
	Positive (1)	Negative (0)
Positive (1)	*TP*	*FP*
Negative (0)	*FN*	*TN*

Predicted values

Figure 6.7 Structure of typical confusion matrix.

Using the values in the confusion matrix, various performance measures such as accuracy, precision, recall, F1 score, ROC curve, and *AUC* can be calculated:

$$\text{Accuracy} = \frac{TP + TN}{TP + TN + FP + FN} \tag{6.35}$$

$$\text{Precision} = \frac{TP}{TP + FP} \tag{6.36}$$

$$\text{Recall} = \frac{TP}{TP + FN} \tag{6.37}$$

$$\text{F1 Score} = 2 \cdot \frac{\text{Precision} \times \text{Recall}}{\text{Precision} + \text{Recall}}. \tag{6.38}$$

These performance measures give different insights into the performance of a classifier and are used to evaluate the trade-off between precision and recall.

6.12.2 Receiver Operating Characteristic

The Receiver Operating Characteristic (ROC) is a graphical representation of the performance of a binary classifier. It plots the True Positive Rate (*TPR*) versus the False Positive Rate (*FPR*) at different classification thresholds. The *TPR* and *FPR* are calculated as follows:

$$TPR = \frac{TP}{TP + FN} \tag{6.39}$$

$$FPR = \frac{FP}{TN + FP}, \tag{6.40}$$

where *TP*, *TN*, *FP*, and *FN* are the number of true positives, true negatives, false positives, and false negatives, respectively. ROC curve is used to visualize the trade-off between *TPR* and *FPR* of a binary classifier. The ROC curve is created by plotting the *TPR* against the *FPR* at various threshold settings. The curve represents the relationship between sensitivity (*TPR*) and specificity. The mathematical expression for sensitivity and specificity can be expressed as follows:

$$TPR = \frac{TP}{TP + FN} \tag{6.41}$$

$$\text{Specificity} = \frac{TN}{TN + FP}, \tag{6.42}$$

where *TP*, *TN*, *FP*, and *FN* are the number of true positives, true negatives, false positives, and false negatives, respectively.

The *AUC* of the ROC curve is a scalar value that summarizes the performance of the binary classifier by considering all possible threshold values. The *AUC* can be calculated using the trapezoidal rule or numerical integration methods. $AUC = 1$ represents a perfect classifier, whereas $AUC = 0.5$ represents a random classifier.

For a binary classifier, the optimal threshold is chosen as the threshold that maximizes the difference between *TPR* and *FPR*, or the Youden's *J* statistic. The Youden's *J* statistic is defined as $J = TPR + \text{Specificity} - 1$. The threshold that maximizes *J* provides the best trade-off between *TPR* and *FPR*.

6.12.3 Area Under the ROC Curve

The area under the ROC curve (*AUC*) is a scalar value that represents the performance of a binary classifier system as the discrimination threshold is varied. The *AUC* is calculated by integrating the ROC curve, which is a plot of the *TPR* versus the *FPR* for a binary classifier system. Mathematically, the *AUC* can be calculated as the AUC, which is equivalent to the probability that a randomly selected positive sample will have a higher predicted score than a randomly selected negative sample. The *AUC* ranges from 0 to 1, with values closer to 1 indicating higher performance, and is a commonly used measure to compare different binary classifier models. The mathematical formula for the *AUC* can be calculated as the definite integral of the *TPR* (also known as Sensitivity or Recall) with respect to the *FPR*:

$$AUC = \int_0^1 TPR(FPR) \, dFPR, \tag{6.43}$$

where *TPR* (*FPR*) is the TPR at a specific FPR value, and the integral is calculated over the range of possible *FPR* values, from 0 to 1. In practice, the *AUC* is usually calculated using numerical approximations, such as the trapezoidal rule, rather than analytically solving the integral. These definitions can be used to calculate the *TPR* and *FPR* at different thresholds and plot the resulting values on a ROC curve. Schematic diagram for the understanding of ROC-AUC is shown in Figure 6.8.

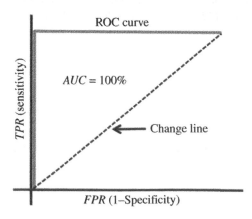

Figure 6.8 Visual representation of schematic diagram for ROC-ACU.

The *AUC* is a scalar summary of the overall performance of a binary classifier and provides a single number that summarizes the trade-off between *TPR* and *FPR*. A perfect classifier will have an *AUC* of 1, while a random classifier will have an *AUC* of 0.5.

Summary

This chapter discussed several topics related to neural networks and their applications in various fields. It began by describing the structure and function of biological neurons and how artificial neural networks mimic these structures. It also discussed the backpropagation algorithm, which is commonly used to train neural networks, and explained how the learning rate can affect training. Softmax regression and its application in multi-class classification problems is explored. The advantages of softmax regression, including feature importance and the ability to handle nonlinearly separable classes, and then described *k*-binary classifiers and their use in multi-class classification problems with more than two classes were also discussed.

Next, relational learning via neural networks and GNNs, which are designed to handle complex relationships between data points, are also discussed. The math equations that underpin these types of neural networks and their applications in fields such as natural language processing and social network analysis are explored. Finally, it discussed the use of neural networks in image processing and how the structure of a neural network can be tailored to handle different types of image recognition problems.

Overall, these topics demonstrate the wide-ranging applications of neural networks and the versatility of this type of machine learning algorithm.

Exercise Questions

Q.6.1   Describe the purpose of the activation function in a neural network, and how is it mathematically defined?

Q.6.2   How does the backpropagation algorithm update the weights and biases of a neural network, and what is the purpose of the learning rate?

Q.6.3   What are the differences between supervised and unsupervised learning, and how are they used in neural networks?

Q.6.4 In a neural network, the activation function is applied to the weighted sum of inputs to introduce nonlinearity. One commonly used activation function is the sigmoid function, given by:

$$\sigma(x) = \frac{1}{1 + e^{-x}}$$

Calculate the activation value for an input $x = 2$.

Q.6.5 Describe transfer learning, and how is it used in neural networks?

Q.6.6 Illustrate the purpose of regularization in neural networks, and how is it achieved mathematically?

Q.6.7 Describe the purpose of batch normalization in neural networks, and how is it achieved mathematically?

Q.6.8 How dropout technique work in neural networks, and how is it achieved mathematically?

Q.6.9 Backpropagation is a key algorithm used to train neural networks. The weight update in backpropagation is calculated using the gradient of the loss function with respect to the weights. For a single neuron, the weight update equation can be written as:

$$\Delta w = \eta \times \delta \times x.$$

Given a learning rate of $\eta = 0.1$, an error gradient of $\delta = 0.5$, and an input $x = 0.8$, calculate the weight update Δw.

Q.6.10 What is the purpose of attention mechanisms in neural networks, and how are they used in natural language processing?

Further Reading

Cruse H. *Neural networks as cybernetic systems*. Thieme, Stuttgart; 1996 Jan.

Getoor L, Taskar B, editors. *Introduction to statistical relational learning*. MIT Press; 2007.

Yoh-Han, Pao. Adaptive Pattern Recognition and Neural Networks. *Addison-Wesle* 12 (1989):113–139.

7

Competitive Learning and Self-Organizing Map

7.1 Principal of Competitive Learning

The self-organizing map (SOM) is one of the most widely used unsupervised artificial neural networks in which the system has no prior knowledge of the input data's properties or qualities, as well as the output data's class labels. The network learns to group sample input patterns into classes or clusters based on their commonalities. A cluster of patterns would have comparable characteristics. There is no prior information of what characteristics are crucial for classification or the number of classes. As the name implies, the network self-organizes to accommodate multiple types of inputs. The weighted layer's number of nodes correlates to the number of various classes. It is founded on the concept of competitive learning.

Competitive learning is a type of Artificial Neural Network (ANN) learning in which various neurons or processing units compete to learn how to represent current input. There are hierarchical groups of units in the network with inhibitory and excitatory connections in a competitive learning model. Individual layers have excitatory connections, while units in layered clusters have inhibitory connections. A cluster's units are either active or inactive. In ANN, competitive learning is a type of unsupervised learning in which nodes fight for the right to respond to a subset of the input data. Competitive learning is a type of Hebbian learning that operates by improving the specialization of each node in the network. It is great for discovering data clusters.

Vector quantization and self-organizing maps are examples of models and algorithms based on the competitive learning concept. The nodes associated with weights compete with each other to win an input pattern in competitive learning (vector). The node with the highest response for each individual input pattern is selected and awarded the winner. Only the weights associated with the winning

Cybernetical Intelligence: Engineering Cybernetics with Machine Intelligence, First Edition.
Kelvin K. L. Wong.
© 2024 The Institute of Electrical and Electronics Engineers, Inc.
Published 2024 by John Wiley & Sons, Inc.
Companion website: www.wiley.com/go/cyberintel

node are trained to be more like the input pattern (vector). The weights of the other nodes remain unchanged. The winner gets everything, while the losers get nothing. As a result, it is known as a Winner Takes All algorithm (Losers gets nothing). For Output Node 1:

$$Y_1 = \sum_{i=1}^{D} X_i W_{i1}, \tag{7.1}$$

where each node is associated with a weight vector having D elements having input vector X_i and associated weight vector of Y_1.

The SOM is a dimensionality reduction approach based on neural networks that is commonly used to represent a high-dimensional dataset as a two-dimensional discretized pattern. The dimensionality of the data is reduced while the topology of the data in the original feature space is preserved. The SOM is one of the most widely used Unsupervised learning ANN, in which the system has no prior knowledge of the input data's properties or qualities, as well as the output data's class labels.

Competitive learning is one of the most commonly used learning strategies in self-organizing networks. First, the basic concept is explained first. Pattern classification, clustering, and similarity in neural network applications, terms such as input samples, input patterns, and input pattern samples are basically equivalent concepts. The concept of common input patterns when it comes to identifying and classifying problems. Patterns are quantitative descriptions or structural descriptions of certain objects of interest, and pattern classes are collections of patterns with certain common characteristics. Classification is under the guidance of class knowledge and other tutor signals, the input patterns to be identified are assigned to the respective pattern classes. The classification of non-tutor guidance is called clustering, and the purpose of clustering is to classify similar pattern samples into a class, and the results are not similar, so that the similarity and inter-class classification of pattern samples are realized. Since there is no expected output in the training sample without a tutor, there is no prior knowledge about which class a sample of the input pattern should belong to. For a set of input patterns, only according to the degree of similarity between them into several classes, so the similarity is the input pattern clustering basis.

- Measurement of similarity comparing the similarities of different patterns can usually be measured by the distance between the two vectors. So, similarity measurements are usually converted to vector distance measurements. The metric between vectors determines the degree of similarity in an application. The two most common classification methods used in traditional pattern recognition are Euclidean distance and angular measurement. The Euclidean distance is usually the L2 norm, whereas the angle measurement uses the cosine theorem.

- Side suppression and competition: When a neuron is excited, it can inhibit nerve cells in the surrounding neurons, causing competition between nerve cells and causing multiple cells to excite, but a nerve cell that is most highly excited can inhibit the surrounding neurons, resulting in a decrease in the excitement of the surrounding neurons, which in turn wins the competition and other neurons fail. The virtual connection line between each neuron in the competition layer represented in the network demonstrates this inhibition. They are the weights in a biological neural network layer that simulate the mutual inhibition of neurons. This kind of inhibitory weight usually satisfies certain distribution relations, such as the inhibition of distance is weak, the inhibition of distance is strong. This weight value is usually fixed in the learning algorithm. The competitive learning method used is the method of "winner is King" in the study of three elements of neural network which is summarized in the basic concept of ANN and principle knowledge (complement).
- Normalization of vectors: Because different modes have nonuniform units, the pattern vectors are normalized, which is the unit length, before data processing, making the similarity metric easier to calculate. Two- and three-dimensional unit vectors, for example, can be visually depicted on units and units of balls. Because most of the time in machine learning, the input patterns are vectors and are usually preprocessed using normalization, this is explained as a distinct section to emphasize the relevance of this.

A competitive learning rule has three main components:

- A group of neurons that are identical except for some randomly distributed synaptic weights and hence respond differentially to a set of input patterns.
- A restriction on each neuron's "strength."
- Only one output neuron (or one neuron per group) is active (i.e. "on") at a time, thanks to a process that allows neurons to compete for the right to respond to a subset of inputs. A "winner-take-all" neuron is the one that wins the competition.

Competitive learning is one of the most commonly used learning strategies in self-organizing networks. The principle of competitive learning is based on the inhibition phenomenon on the side of biological nerve cells. When a biological neuron is in an excited state, the surrounding neurons will be inhibited, and the neuron with the strongest inhibitory effect will be the only winning neuron.

In competitive learning, all units in the network unit group compete with each other for the right to respond to the external stimulus pattern, and the unit that wins the competition inhibits the response of the unit that loses the competition to the stimulus pattern. Competitive learning is a kind of adaptive learning, which makes the network unit have the characteristic of choosing to accept the external stimulus mode. This learning method is applied to the ANN, which can be simply divided into three steps.

7.1.1 Step 1: Normalized Input Vector

Among the best practices for training a Neural Network is to normalize your data to obtain a mean close to 0. Normalizing the data generally speeds up learning and leads to faster convergence. Also, the (logistic) sigmoid function is hardly ever used anymore as an activation function in hidden layers of neural networks, because the tanh function (among others) seems to be strictly superior. As shown in the Equation (7.2), X_i is the ith input pattern vector, W_j is the initial weight vector corresponding to X_i. The input pattern vector and initial weight vector of the network are normalized respectively, where n is the number of input pattern vectors, and N is the number of neurons in the competition layer.

$$\hat{X}_i = \frac{X_i}{\|X_i\|}, i = 1, 2, ..., n \tag{7.2}$$

$$\hat{W}_j = \frac{W_j}{\|w_j\|}, j = 1, 2, ..., N. \tag{7.3}$$

Typically, Euclidean distance of the vector equal to a certain predetermined value, through the transformation below, called min-max normalization:

$$x' = \frac{x - x_{\min}}{x_{\max} - x_{\min}} (u - 1) + 1. \tag{7.4}$$

In Equation (7.4), x is representing the original data, x' is the normalized data, while $x_{\max}$ and $x_{\min}$ are respectively the maximum and minimum values of the original vector, and U, l are respectively the upper and lower values of the new range for normalized data. The Equation (7.4) is a linear transformation that maintains all the distance ratios of the original vector after normalization.

7.1.2 Step 2: Find the Winning Neuron

The similarity between each input pattern vector and the weight vector of each neuron in the competition layer is compared, and the neuron with the highest similarity is defined as the winning neuron. Assuming that the number of neurons in the competition layer is N, the normalized initial weight vector is $\hat{W}_j (j = 1, 2, ..., N)$, and its dimension is the same as the input pattern vector. For the normalized input pattern vector $\hat{X}_i$, denote the neuron most similar to this input pattern vector as c where $c \in \{1, 2, ..., N\}$, then:

$$c = \text{argmin}_j \|\hat{X} - \hat{W}_j\|, \tag{7.5}$$

can be transformed into:

$$\|\hat{X} - \hat{W}_c\| = \min_j \|\hat{X} - \hat{W}_j\|, \tag{7.6}$$

where c is the winning neuron and $\hat{W}_c$ is the weight vector of the winning neuron.

7.1.3 Step 3: Adjust the Network Weight Vector and Output Results

In order for a neural network to learn, weights associated with neuron connections must be updated after forward passes of data through the network. These weights are adjusted to help reconcile the differences between the actual and predicted outcomes for subsequent forward passes.

7.2 Basic Structure of Self-Organizing Map

SOM neural network is an unsupervised neural network, which adopts an unsupervised self-organizing learning training mode. The basic structure of the SOM neural network is shown in Figure 7.1, which mainly includes two layers: the input layer and the competition layer, and the competition layer is also the output layer. The input layer is used to receive the information to be processed and transfer the processing object to the competition layer; the competition layer is used to compare and analyze the received data to find the internal rules between the input information, so as to achieve the purpose of sorting and classification.

SOM were originally mainly used for data presentation, but they have now been utilized to solve a variety of challenges, including the traveling salesman problem.

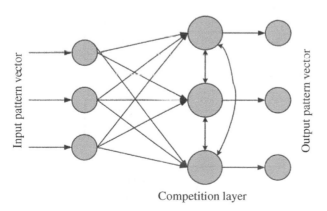

Figure 7.1 SOM network structure diagram.

In most cases, map units or neurons constitute a two-dimensional space, resulting in a mapping from a high-dimensional space to a plane. The computed relative distance between the spots is preserved on the map. In SOM, points in the input space that are closest to each other are mapped to nearby map units. As a result, SOM can be used to analyze clusters in high-dimensional data. SOM are also capable of generalization. The network can detect or classify inputs it has never seen before as data during generalization. New input is taken up with the map unit and is therefore mapped.

The SOM neural network has the competitive classification function of the self-organizing competitive neural network, which can map the topological distribution features of the network input pattern vector to the competitive layer. The algorithm only needs a small amount of sample data, and the data can be automatically clustered by setting the parameters of the clustering algorithm, and the degree of intelligence of the algorithm is good.

The common SOM neural network has two topological structures: one-dimensional linear array and two-dimensional plane lattice. The difference between the SOM network structure is mainly in the competition layer. Figure 7.2 is a schematic diagram of the two-dimensional rectangular plane competition layer, where $\vec{x_1}, \vec{x_2}, ..., \vec{x_n}$ are the input vector of input layer.

Both in construction and algorithmic features, a SOM differs from traditional ANNs. To begin with, rather than a sequence of layers, it is made up of a single-layer linear 2D grid of neurons. All of the nodes on this grid are connected directly to the input vector, but not to one another, implying that the nodes have

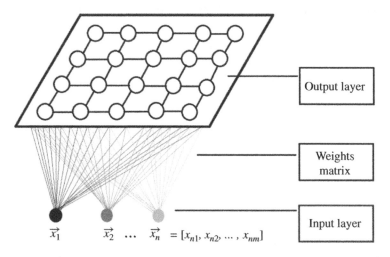

Figure 7.2 Schematic diagram of the two-dimensional rectangular plane SOM.

no knowledge of their neighbor's values and solely update the weight of their connections as a function of the given inputs. The grid is a map that organizes itself based on the input data at each iteration. As such, after clustering, each node has its own (i, j) coordinate, which allows one to calculate the Euclidean distance between two nodes by means of the Pythagorean theorem.

7.2.1 Properties Self-Organizing Map

In addition, a SOM adjusts its weights via competitive learning rather than error-correction learning. As all nodes compete for the right to respond to the input, only a single node is activated at each iteration in which the features of an instance of the input vector are presented to the neural network. The chosen node the Best Matching Unit (BMU) is selected according to the similarity between the current input values and all the nodes in the grid. The node with the least Euclidean difference between the input vector and all other nodes is picked, along with its neighbors within a given radius, to have their positions slightly changed to match the input vector.

The entire grid finally matches the total input dataset by traversing over all of the nodes on the grid, with like nodes grouped together in one area and dissimilar nodes segregated.

7.3 Self-Organizing Mapping Neural Network Algorithm

The SOM is made up of m neurons that are arranged in a regular low-dimensional map, typically a 2-D map. According to topological connections, these neurons are connected to their neighbors as shown in Figure 7.1, for each input data, the neurons are at minimum and maximum distance from among 1-neighborhood. For SOM maps, there are two main topologies: rectangular and hexagonal. Each neuron I have a d-dimensional weight vector $w = (w_{i1}, w_{i2}, ..., w_{id})$ with the same dimension as the input space, where $i = 1, 2 ... m$. One refer to the Figure 7.2 to illustrate the process of the SOM neural network algorithm. This process is repeated for each input vector for a (usually large) number of cycles λ. The network winds up associating output nodes with groups or patterns in the input data set. If these patterns can be named, the names can be attached to the associated nodes in the trained net.

During mapping, there will be one single winning neuron: the neuron whose weight vector lies closest to the input vector. This can be simply determined by calculating the Euclidean distance between input vector and weight vector.

While representing input data as vectors have been emphasized in this article, any kind of object which can be represented digitally, which has an appropriate distance measure associated with it, and in which the necessary operations for training are possible can be used to construct a SOM. This includes matrices, continuous functions, or even other SOM.

7.3.1 Step 1: Initialize Parameter

Consistent with other neural networks, first use random numbers to assign values to each weight vector $W_j (j = 1, 2, ..., N)$ of the output layer, and then normalize the random numbers to obtain $\hat{W}_j (j = 1, 2, ..., N)$.

7.3.2 Step 2: Select Inputs and Determine Winning Nodes

An input pattern X_i^P is selected from the training set, that is, a training sample, and then normalized as an input, that is, the input is $\hat{x}_i^P$. The P refers to the number of features of the input pattern, i.e. the dimension. The number of neurons in the input layer is determined by the dimension of the input vector, and one neuron corresponds to one feature. At this point, there is a need to find the neuron that is most similar to the input pattern as the winning node. Under the premise of normalization, the larger the dot product of two points in the multi-dimensional space, the closer the Euclidean distance is. Therefore, the dot product of the weights $\hat{W}_j$ and $\hat{x}_i^P$ is calculated, and the position of the neuron where the maximum value is located in the calculation result is selected, and the neuron is the winning node:

$$c = \text{argmax} \left(\hat{W}_j \cdot \hat{x}_i^P \right). \tag{7.7}$$

7.3.3 Step 3: Affect Neighboring Neurons

At the beginning of the algorithm, there is also a need to define a parameter: the neighborhood radius, denoted as $N_{j^*}(0)$, which is used to determine the influence range centered on the winning neuron. In the algorithm rules, all neurons located within the radius of the winning neuron's neighborhood should update their weights according to certain rules. This rule is the neighborhood function, which is used to determine the influence of the winning node on its neighbors, that is, the update range of each node in the winning neighborhood. The most common choice is the Gaussian function, which can characterize the relationship between the strength of the influence and the distance in the winning neighborhood. In general, the initial neighborhood $N_{j^*}(0)$ is large, and $N_{j^*}(t)$ will gradually shrink with the training time during the training process.

7.3.4 Step 4: Adjust Weights

Referring to the following equation, adjust the weights for all nodes within the winning neighborhood $N_{j^*}(t)$ calculated from iteration to time t, where $\eta(t, N)$ is a function of the topological distance N between the jth neuron located within the neighborhood radius and the winning neuron j^* when the number of training iterations is t.

$$w_{ij}(t + 1) = w_{ij}(t) + \eta(t, N)\left(x_i^p - w_{ij}(t)\right). \tag{7.8}$$

7.3.5 Step 5: Judging the End Condition

For the judgment of the end condition of the entire algorithm process, it is to determine whether the learning rate in the process of continuously adjusting the value decays to a certain positive number set in advance. If the end condition of the algorithm flow cannot be satisfied, then repeat steps 2–4 in the calculation subprocess.

7.4 Growing Self-Organizing Map

A Growing Self-Organizing Map (GSOM) begins with only two neurons, resulting in a one-dimensional arrangement. Following the standard SOM technique for adapting the two matching weight vectors, either a third neuron is added to make a longer line, alternatively, it is picked to create a 2×2-network by opening up an additional output space dimension. In all following growth phases, the map result space grid is enlarged by one by enhancing the expansion into one of the current dimensions, i.e. $n_i \rightarrow n_i + 1, i \leq d^A(t)$, if a new dimension rises $n_{d^A(t) + 1} = 1 \rightarrow n_{d^A(t) + 1} = 2$, $d^A(t + 1) = d^A(t) + 1$. All the starting nodes of the GSOM are boundary nodes, i.e. each node has the freedom to grow in its own direction at the beginning. The Figure 7.3 shows the three possible node growth options for a rectangular GSOM. The algorithm has a parameter called a spread factor (SF) to decide the level of spreading. It can take values from 0 to 1, where this factor is independent of the data.

The local discrepancies between both the data points and the weight vector onto which they have been mapped are used to decide which direction the grid should be expanded. Take a look at the data points in the cell ω_{rk} (the variety of data points placed on the neuron r_k), as well as the directions $(m_{r_k + e_i} - m_{r + e_i})/(\|m_{r_k + e_i} - m_{r + e_i}\|)$. This is the outcome of local back projection of the directions e_i from the output space to the input space via nearby neurons

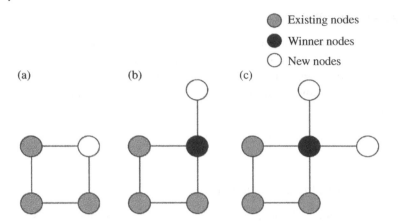

Figure 7.3 Node growth options in GSOM: (a) one new node, (b) two new nodes, and (c) three new nodes.

(with appropriate corrections for neurons at the grid's edge). The discrepancies between data points v and the weight vector m_{r_k} can be decomposed.

$$\theta = \sum_{i=1}^{d^A} a_i(v) \frac{m_{r+e_i} - m_{r+e_i}}{m_{r+e_i} - m_{r+e_i}} + \acute{v}, \tag{7.9}$$

and calculate $a_i(v)$ projection amplitude plus a residual value $\acute{v}$. The residual value is the change in the current output space dimensionality $d^A(t)$ and the nominal input space dimensionality, and it indicates deviations in all remaining dimensions, the residual value represents deviations in all the remaining dimensions. Amplitude of the projection of the $\acute{v}$ is utilized onto the first principal component as an amplitude a $a_{d^A+1}(v)$ to determine the biggest feasible extension of the residuals along one extra dimension after doing a principal component analysis on the $\acute{v}$.

After that, there is a normalization stage.

$$\tilde{a}_i = \sum_v \frac{|a_i(v)|}{\sqrt{\sum_{j=1}^{d^A+1} a_j^2(v)}}, i+1, ..., d^A + 1. \tag{7.10}$$

Growing Phase:

Let $W(i)$ be the weight of node I and X be the input vector. The algorithm will find a BMU when a new input is presented to the network (winner). How can choose the winning node? Calculating the Euclidean distance as shown in Equation (7.11) between the given input and all the nodes in the network identifies the winner BMU node.

$$\text{distance} = |X - W(i)|. \tag{7.11}$$

The node with minimum distance is the Winner (BU). The error value (the difference between BU and the given input) for the winner node is defined as follows:

$$\text{error (BU)} = |X - W(\text{BU})| \tag{7.12}$$

$$E(t + 1) = E(t) + |X - W(\text{BU})|. \tag{7.13}$$

where E is the error function. After calculating the inaccuracy, the algorithm must determine whether or not a new nod should be added to the network. The error distance is used to determine whether the present node network is sufficient. In each iteration, the algorithm keeps adding the incorrect value to the winner node. The algorithm considers the weight initialization under four categories:

Case (a and c):

if $W_2 > W_1 : W_{new} = W_1 - (W_2 - W_1)$

if $W_1 > W_2 : W_{new} = W_1 + (W_1 - W_2)$

Case (b):

$$W_{new} = \frac{W_1 + W_2}{2}$$

Case (d):

There is only one older neighboring node for the new node. This case will occur during the initial stage of the network or when the dummy nodes are removed. $W_{new} = \frac{r_1 + r_2}{2}$, where r_1 and r_2 are upper and lower limits for weights. If W new is not between r_1 and r_2, it will fall under case (d).

Do the weights for the neighborhood nodes need to be adjusted? Yes, it is required to do so. It is time to update the weight vectors. The degree of adaptation (learning rate-LR) will be reduced exponentially over repetition, similar to SOM. Weights of a node before and after updating weights are $W_j(k)$ and $W_j(k+1)$. The input vector is $X(k)$. The winner node's k-neighboring nodes are represented by $N(k+1)$.

if $j \in N(k + 1)$

$\Rightarrow W_j(k + 1) = W_j k + LR(k) \times (X(k) - W_j(k))$

else $\Rightarrow W_j(K + 1) = W_j k.$

When there are no more nodes to create, the smoothing phases begin. The smoothing phase of the method smooths the overall error of the nodes that are grown at the final step or iteration. Even the smoothing phase's initial *LR* is smaller than the growth phases. To converge the error value, the input data is presented multiple times. During the smoothing step, no new nodes are generated.

7.5 Time Adaptive Self-Organizing Map

The time adaptive self-organizing map (TASOM) network is a modified SOM network with adaptive learning rates and neighborhood sizes as its learning parameters. Every neuron in the TASOM has its own learning rate and neighborhood size. TASOM networks are distinguished by their adaptable learning rates and neighborhood sizes. The weights of a TASOM network are continually trained by the input vectors with this feature. As a result, changes in the environment are reflected in the weights and learning without any monitoring. TASOM's parameters TASOM is able to approximate as a result of this. The distribution of input space with a focus on the most important if the input vectors are significantly different, recent input vectors from the ones before it.

For each new input vector, the neighborhood size and learning rate of the winning neuron and the learning rates of its neighboring neurons are updated. The TASOM can be concise in eight steps:

I) Initialization: Choose some values for initial weight vectors $w_j(0)$, where $j = 1, 2, ..., N$;

and N; and N is the no. of neurons in the lattice. Initialize the learning rate parameters $n_j(0)$ with values close to unity. Any value between 0 and 1 can be used for the constant parameters $\alpha, \beta, \alpha_s,$ and β_s. The constant parameters $s_f,$ and s_g should be set to satisfy the need of the application. $R_i(0)$ should be set to include all the neurons. The components $s_k(0)$ of the scaling vectors $s(0) = [s_1(0), ..., s_p(0)]^T$ should be set to random values between 0 and 1, where p is the dimension of input weight vectors. The parameters $E_k(0)$ and $E2_k(0)$ may be initialized with some small random values. Neighboring neurons of any neuron i in a lattice are included in the set. For any neuron i in a one-dimensional lattice N, $NH_i = \{i - 1, i + 1\}$ where $NH_N = \{N - 1\}$ and $NH_1 = \{2\}$. Similarly for any neuron i_1, i_2 in a two-dimensional lattice $N = MxM$, $NH_{(i_1,i_2)} = \{(i_1 - 1, i_2), (i_1 + 1, i_2), (i_1, i_2 - 1), (i_1, i_2 + 1)\}$,

$$NH_{(1,1)} = \{(1,2), (2,1)\}, NH_{(1,M)} = \{(1, M - 1), (2, M)\}, NH_{(M,1)}$$
$$= \{(M, 2)(M - 1)\}, NH_{(M,M)} = \{(M, M - 1), (M - 1, M)\} \quad (7.14)$$

II) Sampling: Draw a sample-input vector x from the input distribution.
III) Similarly matching: To use the maximum-distance Euclidean norm as the matching metric,

pick the ideal matching or winning neuron $i(x)$ at time n:

$$i(x) = \text{argmin} \left\| x(n) - w_j(n) \right\|_s, j = 1, 2, ..., N \tag{7.15}$$

where

$$\left\| x(n) - w_j(n) \right\|_s = \left(\sum_k \left(\frac{x_k n - w_{j,k} n}{s_k n} \right)^2 \right)^{\frac{1}{2}}, \tag{7.16}$$

updating the neighborhood size: Using the following two equations, adjust the winning neuron $i(x)$ neighborhood size $A_i(n)$:

$$A_i(n+1) = \{ j \in N \,|\, d(i,j) \le R_i(n+1) \} \tag{7.17}$$

$$R_i(n+1) = R_i(n) + \beta \left(g \left(\frac{1}{f(NH_i).s_g} \sum_{j \in NH_i} \left\| w_i(n) - w_j(n) \right\|_s \right) - R_i(n) \right),$$
$$\tag{7.18}$$

where the function $f(.)$ gives the cardinality of a set. The neighborhood sizes of the other neurons do not change. $d(i, j)$ is the difference between two neurons i, j in lattice.

- Updating the learning-rate parameters: Adjust the learning-rate parameters in the neighborhood $A_{i(x)}(n+1)$, of the winning neuron $i(x)$ by:

$$n_j(n+1) = n_j(n) + \alpha \left(f \left(\frac{\left\| x(n) - w_j(n) \right\|_s}{s_f} \right) - n_j(n) \right)$$

for $j \in A_{i(x)}(n+1)$.

Updating the Synaptic weights: Using the following update rule, adjust the synaptic weight vectors of all output neurons in the neighborhood of $A_{i(x)}(n+1)$:

$$w_j(n+1) = \begin{cases} w_j(n) + n_j(n+1)(x(n) - w_j(n)), & j \in A_{i(x)}(n+1) \\ w_j(n), & \text{otherwise} \end{cases}, \tag{7.19}$$

where is the neighbor function placed on the winning neuron $n_j(n+1)$ is the learning-rate parameter $i(x)$.

updating the Scaling vector: Adjust the scaling vector $s(n+1)$ with the following equations:

$$s(n+1) = s(n) \frac{\| y(n+1) \|}{\| x(n+1) \|}, \tag{7.20}$$

where $s(n)$ is the scaling vector at time step n, $s(n+1)$ is the updated scaling vector at time step $n+1$ $y(n+1)$ is the output vector at time step $n+1$, $x(n+1)$ is the input vector at time step $n + 1$, $\|.\|$ denotes the Euclidean norm or magnitude of a vector. It should be noted that in this algorithm, the initialization step of the algorithm is used only for once during the lifetime of the network. New versions of TASOM networks were introduced and used for bilevel thresholding of gray-level images, tracking centers or boundaries of moving objects, and adaptive clustering. What makes TASOM interesting is that once the TASOM-based networks are trained in a specific environment, they are able to follow changes of the environment without reinitializing the weight vectors or learning parameters, and without any outside intervention.

7.5.1 TASOM-Based Algorithms for Real Applications

To solve Bilevel thresholding or gray level segmentation TASOM work with two neurons forming a 1-D lattice. The image gray level pixels form the 1-D input values of the TASOM, which are used for training the TASOM. During this network training, the number of neurons is allowed to change. The complete proposed TASOM BTA is specified in the following steps:

- Set the parameter to a positive constant value that is less than 255, which is the image's maximum gray level value. This parameter governs the proposed algorithm's accuracy in determining the threshold value. Lower values yield more precise threshold values.
- Construct a TASOM network with two neurons forming a 1-D lattice.
- Set the two neuron indexes: a and b.
- Create a new neuron between and call it the "virtual valley neuron" or simply "valley neuron" represented as u so that

$$w_u = \frac{w_a + w_b}{2} - \frac{\sigma_a + \sigma_b}{2}, \tag{7.21}$$

$$\eta_u = \eta_a + \eta_b \tag{7.22}$$

- Find the neurons that do not win any competition during the training and delete those of them which are placed at the head or tail of the lattice
- If $\max(\|w_u - w_u - 1\|, \|w_u - w_u + 1\|) < \theta_u$, then goto next step.
- The place that a new neuron is to be inserted next to the current valley neuron is defined:
- If $\|w_u - w_u - 1\| > \|w_u - w_u + 1\|$, then set $a = u$ and $b = u-1$; else set $a = u$ and $b = u+1$.
- The weight of the genuine valley neuron equals the intended threshold. The (virtual) valley neuron u is used to find the true valley neuron, which is detailed below.

The current right neuron is chosen as the left valley neuron. The same process is done for the right direction, and the right valley neuron is found. Now, the real valley neuron is the one having the least winning frequency among the two candidate valley neurons. The desired threshold is then the weight value of the real valley neuron. Now, those pixels of the image having gray levels less than the threshold are set to black, and those pixels with gray levels greater than the threshold are set to white.

7.6 Oriented and Scalable Map

A SOM can be turned into an Oriented and Scalable Map (OS-Map) by generalizing the neighborhood function and the winner selection. The homogeneous Gaussian neighborhood function is replaced with the matrix exponential. Thus, there can specify the orientation either in the map space or in the data space. Moreover, it associates the map's global scale with the locality of winner selection.

SOM's stepwise recursive algorithm is inherited by OS-Map, in which t is representing the current number of iterations, ϕ is a negative constant, and N is the number of nodes of the map. Similarly, d is representing the dimension of the data space while A is the $d \times d$ orientation matrix. Hence, $d \times d$ neighborhood matrix is equal to the $h_{ci}(t)$.

Every model vector should be initialized m_i, $i \in [0, N]$, $m_i \in R^d$. Initialize learning rate $\alpha(t)$ and neighborhood radius $\sigma(t)$.

for T iterations

a) retrieve an input item $x(t)$, $x(t) \in R^d$.

select the winner $m_c(t)$ by $c = \mathrm{argmin}_i \|x(t) - m_i(t)\|$, $i \in \{l \mid s(l) < 0\}$.

b) update the winner and its neighbors:
For each node m_i

$$m_i(t+1) \leftarrow m_l(t) + h_{ci}(t)[x(t) - m_i(t)] \tag{7.23}$$

$$h_{ci}(t) = \alpha(t)e^{-\frac{A}{2\sigma^2(t)}} \tag{7.24}$$

$$\alpha(t) \leftarrow (1-s)\min{}_\alpha + s\max{}_\alpha$$

$$\sigma(t) \leftarrow (1-s) \cdot \min{}_\sigma + s \cdot \max{}_\sigma$$

$$s = \frac{e^{\frac{\varphi t}{T}} - e^\varphi}{1 - e^\varphi}. \tag{7.25}$$

The above algorithm and the original SOM have two major differences. First, rather than choosing the winner from all of the nodes, a contingent subset is chosen. The scaling of the map is directly affected by such local selection. Second, instead of being read as a scalar, the neighborhood function, $h_{ci}(t)$, is treated as a matrix. An anisotropic mapping or, to put it another way, adjusting to the desired direction of the gradient of the model values across the map is possible with such a neighborhood function.

In the regression formula, the term $x(t) - m_i(t)$ is a d-dimensional vector. As a result, it is natural to think of $h_{ci}(t)$ as a matrix (rather than a scalar in SOM), which is useful for orientation control. The increment is represented by three bivariate Gaussian functions in cases when the input term $x(t)$ is three-dimensional (denoted with x, y, and z as subscripts):

$$
h_{ci}(t)[x(t) - m_i(t)] = \alpha(t)
\begin{bmatrix}
e^{-\dfrac{c_x(P_x \cdot D)^2 + \acute{c}_x(\acute{P}_x \cdot D)^2}{2\sigma^2(t)}} & [x(t) - m_i(t)]_x \\[2ex]
e^{-\dfrac{c_y(P_y \cdot D)^2 + \acute{c}_y(\acute{P}_y \cdot D)^2}{2\sigma^2(t)}} & [x(t) - m_i(t)]_y \\[2ex]
e^{-\dfrac{c_z(P_z \cdot D)^2 + \acute{c}_z(\acute{P}_z \cdot D)^2}{2\sigma^2(t)}} & [x(t) - m_i(t)]_z
\end{bmatrix},
\qquad (7.26)
$$

where D is the vector going to the ith node on the map, beginning at the winner c. The horizontal component, D_u represents the horizontal distance between two nodes, while the vertical component, D_v represents the vertical distance between two nodes. P_x indicates the preferred gradient direction for the current winner mc's x-component. For example, if the x-component of model vectors must vary twice as fast in the vertical direction as it does in the horizontal, $P_x = (\pm 1, 0)$ (modulo π) and $cx/c' x = 1/2$ can be used. For the x-component of model mc, P_x represents the first eigenvector of the desired distribution (gradient).

The second eigenvector, P_x, is parallel to the first. As a result, the matrix exponential is the neighborhood function in:

$$
h_{ci}(t) = \alpha(t) \exp\left(
\begin{array}{l}
= \dfrac{1}{2\sigma^2(t)}
\begin{bmatrix}
P_{xu}^2 P_{xv}^2 & 2P_{xu}P_{xv} \\
P_{yu}^2 P_{yv}^2 & 2P_{yu}P_{yv} \\
P_{zu}^2 P_{zv}^2 & 2P_{zu}P_{zv}
\end{bmatrix}
\begin{bmatrix}
D_u^2 D_v^2 \\
D_v^2 D_u^2 \\
D_u D_v - D_u D_v
\end{bmatrix} \times \ldots \\[4ex]
\qquad \ldots \times
\begin{bmatrix}
c_x & c_y & c_z \\
\acute{c}_x & \acute{c}_y & \acute{c}_z
\end{bmatrix} \odot I
\end{array}
\right),
$$

$$(7.27)$$

where identity matrix is I. The Hadamard product yields a diagonal covariance with an exponential that is also a diagonal matrix. Multiple heterogeneous kernels, broaden the notion of neighborhood function. When $P_x = P_y = P_z = \left(\sqrt{\dfrac{1}{2}}, \sqrt{\dfrac{1}{2}}\right)$ and $c_x = \acute{c}_x = c_y = \acute{c}_y = c_z = \acute{c}_z$.

The winner is chosen globally ($s(i) < 0, \forall i$). In data space, the manifold created by the map is expected to be aligned with the torus surface.

The simple and general form of the OS-Map algorithm is suited for mapping from image to image, from image to geometry, from surface to grid, and so forth. From a theoretical point of view, OS-Map still insists on the self-organizing fashion (no formulated global expectation) as the original version of SOM. To find this type of self-organization is ideal for integrating the new notion of orientation and scaling. Self-organization suggests an opportunity to combine the OS-Map with hardware parallel computing.

7.7 Generative Topographic Map

The Generative Topographic Mapping model is a probability density model that depicts the distribution of data in a multi-dimensional space using a fewer number of latent (or hidden) variables. It is possible to employ a nonlinear link between the latent space and the data space while remaining tractable by using a discrete grid of points in latent space, akin to the nodes of the SOM. Generative topographic map (GTM) is a machine learning method that is a probabilistic counterpart of the SOM, is probably convergent, and does not require a shrinking neighborhood or a decreasing step size. It is a generative model: the data is assumed to arise by first probabilistically picking a point in a low-dimensional space, mapping the point to the observed high-dimensional input space (via a smooth function), then adding noise in that space. A latent variable model seeks a D-dimensional representation of the $p(t)$ data $t = (t_1, ..., t_D)$ in terms of a number L of latent variables $x = (x_1, ..., x_L)$. This is accomplished by first considering a function $y(x; W)$ that maps point x in the latent space to points $y(x; W)$ in the data space. The mapping is guided by a matrix of parameters W, which might be a feed-forward neural network with W representing the weights and biases. For example, in the case when the latent-variable space's dimensions L is less than the data space's dimensionality D, since it is needed to capture the fact that the data has an intrinsic dimensionality of less than D. The transformation $y(x, W)$ The latent-variable space is then embedded in an L-dimensional non-Euclidean manifold S. The description of the GTM starts by defining a q-dimensional latent space. Using these basis functions, there define a nonlinear transformation from the latent space to the data space given by a linear combination of the basic functions so that each point u in latent space is mapped to a corresponding point y in the D-dimensional data space given by Equation (7.28).

$$y = W \cdot \phi(u), \tag{7.28}$$

where W is a $D \times M$ matrix of weight parameters.

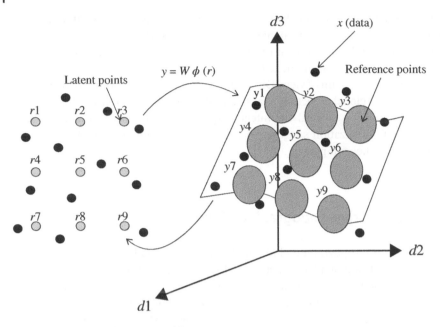

Figure 7.4 Generative topographic map.

In order to formulate a latent variable model which is similar in spirit to the SOM, it considers a prior distribution $p(x)$ consisting of a superposition of delta functions as shown in Figure 7.4, located at the nodes of a regular grid in latent space. Each node is mapped to a point in data space, which forms the center of the corresponding Gaussian distribution.

When a probability distribution $p(x)$ is defined in the latent-variable space, a corresponding distribution $p(y|W)$ is defined in the data space. For reasons that will become evident later, hence refer it to $p(x)$ as the previous distribution of x. Because of $L < D$, the t-space distribution would be conformed to the L-dimensional manifold and so singular. Because the data will only dwell on a lower-dimensional manifold in actuality, it is necessary to add a noise model for the t vector. Here choose a radially-symmetric Gaussian centered on $y(x, W)$ with variance β^{-1} as the t distribution for a given x and W, so that

$$p(t|x, W, \beta) = \left(\frac{\beta}{2\pi}\right)^{D/2} e^{-\frac{\beta}{2}\|y(x; W) - t\|^2}. \tag{7.29}$$

The Bernoulli model for categorical variables (with sigmoid conversion of y) and the multinomial model for two distinct classes are two others $p(t|x)$ models. By integrating the x-distribution, the t-space distribution for a given amount of W is obtained.

$$p(t|x, W, \beta) = \int p(t|x, W, \beta)p(x)\, dx. \tag{7.30}$$

Parameter matrix W and the inverse variance for a data set can be obtained by using maximum likelihood $D = (t_1, ..., t_N)$ containing N data points. In reality, it is more practical to maximize log probability, which is given by

$$L(W, \beta) = \ln \prod_{n=1}^{N} p(t_n|W, \beta). \tag{7.31}$$

Furthermore, once the earlier distribution $p(x)$ is determined and the mapping's functional form $y(x, W)$, then W and β by maximizing $L(W, \beta)$ can be calculated. The integral becomes a convolution of two Gaussians, each of which is a Gaussian, if $y(x, W)$ is a linear function of W and $p(x)$ is Gaussian, the integral becomes a convolution of two Gaussians, each of which is a Gaussian. For a Gaussian noise distributed $p(t\,|\,x)$ with a diagonal covariance matrix, the conventional factor analysis model is built. The model is strongly connected to principal component analysis in the case of the radially symmetric Gaussian provided by Equation (7.29), because the adjusted principal eigenvectors provide columns in the expectation-maximization solution for W. Furthermore, extend this formalism to nonlinear functions $y(x, W)$ and construct a model that is akin to the SOM technique in spirit. As a conclusion, look at a particular version of $p(x)$ that is generated by a summation of delta functions in latent space centered on regular grid nodes.

$$p(x) = \frac{1}{K} \sum_{i=1}^{K} \delta(x - x_i). \tag{7.32}$$

In that case, the integral could be computed once again analytically. The center of a Gaussian density function is formed by mapping each point x_i to a corresponding point $y(x_i, W)$ in data space. The functional form in data space has the following form, as shown below.

$$p(t|x, W, \beta) = \frac{1}{K} \sum_{i=1}^{K} p(t|x_i, W, \beta). \tag{7.33}$$

Then, the log-likelihood function is

$$L(W, \beta) = \sum_{n=1}^{N} \ln \left\{ \frac{1}{K} \sum_{i=1}^{K} p(t_n|x_i, W, \beta) \right\}. \tag{7.34}$$

Since the Gaussians' centers, provided by $p(t|x, W, \beta)$, they are unable to move individually, but are linked by function $y(x_i, W)$, the distribution $p(t|W, \beta)$ For the given noise model, which corresponds to a limited Gaussian mixture model, $y(x, W)$. Note that if the mapping function $y(x, W)$ is smooth and continuous, the projected points $y(x_i, W)$ will need to have a topographic ordering in the sense that any two closes in latent space coordinates x_A and x_B will translate to points y (x_A, W) and $y(x_B, W)$.

In the E-step, it uses the current values of the parameters W and β to evaluate the posterior probability, or responsibility, which each component i takes for every data point x_n, which, using Bayes' theorem, is given by

$$\zeta(W,\beta) = \sum_{n=1}^{N} \ln p(x_n | W, \beta) \tag{7.35}$$

$$R_{ni} = p(i | x_n) = \frac{p(x_n | i)}{\sum_j p(x_n | j)}. \tag{7.36}$$

Then in the M-step, use the responsibilities to re-estimate the weight matrix W by solving the following system of linear equation:

$$\left(\phi^T G \phi + \frac{\alpha}{\beta} I\right) W_{new}^T = \phi^T R X. \tag{7.37}$$

In the Equation (7.37), ϕ represents the design matrix of the input features, G is a matrix that specifies the pairwise similarity between features, α is the regularization parameter, β is the precision parameter, I is the identity matrix, and RX is the target output vector. The equation is used to update the weight vector W in an iterative process, by solving for W_{new}. The regularization term helps to balance the trade-off between the fitting error and the complexity of the model and can improve the generalization performance on unseen data.

By adding a regularization term to the log-likelihood in the standard GTM, one useful modification is to use penalized maximum likelihood. A quadratic regularize of the type is the simplest example:

$$\frac{1}{2} \alpha \|w\|^2, \tag{7.38}$$

where w is a column vector formed by concatenating W's subsequent columns and the hyperparameter α is a fixed constant. The regularized will be interpreted as the logarithm of a Gaussian prior distribution over the weights, and techniques for handling probabilistically will be presented. The regularized is added to the EM algorithm's M-step, resulting in a straightforward modification.

$$\left(\phi^T G \phi + \frac{\alpha}{\beta} I\right) W_{new}^T = \phi^T R X, \tag{7.39}$$

where I is the $M \times M$ unit matrix.

Summary

In this chapter, it is briefly discussed about competitive learning and their principles and also details explanation about self-organized map. The SOM is a general unsupervised technique for grouping comparable instances physically adjacent to one another in high dimensional data. A number of neural processing elements, or units, make up the model. These units are organized using a topology, with the most common option being a two-dimensional grid. Instance presentation and weight vector adaptation can be used to describe the training process of SOM. Each training iteration t starts with the random selection of one instance x, $x \in X$, and $X \subseteq R^n$. The SOM is given with this instance, and each unit chooses whether or not to activate it. The activation of a unit is usually calculated using the Euclidean distance between the weight vector and the instance. A support vector machine (SVM) is a learning algorithm for binary classification (pattern recognition) and real-value function approximation (regression estimate). The goal is to map the n-dimensional input space onto a high-dimensional feature space in a nonlinear way. A linear classifier is built to classify this high-dimensional feature space. The training data is labeled as follows: $S = \{(x_i, y_i) \mid i = 1, 2, ..., N\}, y_i \in \{-1, 1\}, x_i \in R^d$. Consider a hyperplane that separates the positive from the negative examples: w $x + b = 0$ is satisfied from those points x which lie on the hyperplane. Moreover, w is orthogonal to the hyperplane, $|b|/\|w\|$ represents the perpendicular distance from the hyperplane to the origin, and $\|w\|$ is the Euclidean norm of w. Let d^+ and d^- be the two shortest distance from the separating hyperplane to the closest positive (or negative) example. Define the margin of a separating hyperplane to be $d^+ + d^-$. Furthermore, most of the control theory schemes rely on an accurate system model. Writing down the dynamics from basic principles becomes increasingly difficult as these systems become more complicated. In these situations, neural networks are utilized to directly approximate the dynamics using system data. In this sense, neural networks can be regarded as a nonlinear version of linear regression. Without explicitly describing the system dynamics, neural networks can be utilized to develop controllers directly from the state. This problem belongs to the model-free reinforcement learning domain, which is properly titled. Control theory is based on system theory, with a strong emphasis on analyzing the underlying tools and procedures, which are currently mostly unavailable for neural networks. Neural networks are more used within the robotics than in control theory to achieve the above-mentioned goals. A self-organizing map (SOM) or self-organizing feature map (SOFM) is an unsupervised machine learning technique used to produce a low-dimensional (typically two-dimensional) representation of a higher-dimensional data set while preserving the topological structure of the data. The network learns to group sample input patterns into classes or clusters based on their commonalities. A cluster of patterns would have comparable characteristics. There is no prior information of what characteristics are crucial for classification or the number of classes. Unfortunately, the fundamental principles discovered in Cybernetics have been lost in this dark age of AI. Paul Pangaro is one of the last remaining devoted monks of the "old religion" of Cybernetics, and he gives us a detailed definition of cybernetics. In comparison to traditional AI's disembodied and context-free viewpoint, second-order cybernetics, which includes the observer in its discourse, provides a broader foundation for understanding learning. In reality, this second-order concept corresponds to meta-learning concepts. Advances in deep learning reveal a perspective that is more in line with what is found in Cybernetics. This should come as no surprise; after all, cybernetics is influenced by biology, and the artificial neuron is inspired by both. When ideas from related domains like evolutionary biology, nonlinear dynamics, and complexity theory are introduced into the study lexicon, deep learning will advance faster. Norbert Weiner's Cybernetics book is unusual in that it covers a wide range of themes, including groups, statistical mechanics, communication, feedback, oscillation, gestalt, information, language, learning, self-replication, and self-organization.

Exercise Questions

Q.7.1 What is the mathematical expression for the SOM algorithm, and how does it update the weights of the neurons based on the input data?

Q.7.2 Discuss how the Self-Organizing Map (SOM) is biologically inspired?

Q.7.3 What do you mean by competitive learning in machine learning, and what are the basic elements of competitive learning?

Q.7.4 How is the quantization error used to measure the quality of the SOM representation of the input data, and what is the mathematical expression for the quantization error?

Q.7.5 Explain the structure of SOM and differentiate between SOM and PCA.

Q.7.6 Is the self-organized feature map an example of competitive learning?

Q.7.7 How do you apply SOM to handwritten digits recognition?

Q.7.8 Explain how the SOM is analogous to SVM and also applications in robotics, etc.

Q.7.9 How one can use SOM and SVM for email classification?

Q.7.10 Describe and explain the curse of dimensionality in the context of machine learning.

Q.7.11 How can the SOM algorithm be adapted to perform unsupervised clustering of the input data, and what is the mathematical expression for the clustering based on the BMU of each input data point?

Q.7.12 Can cybersemiotics provide an update regarding the design processes in architecture and urbanism?

Q.7.13 What is meant by Cybernetics Protector?

Q.7.14 Explain the concept of the U-matrix in a SOM and visualizes it in the topology of the map and the distance between neighboring neurons, and what is the mathematical expression for the U-matrix?

Further Reading

Bedi J, Toshniwal D. Spark map reduce based framework for seismic facies classification. *Journal of Applied Geophysics*. 2022 Oct 1;1(205):104762.

Boem A. *Norbert Weiner and the origins of cybernetics*. Interface Cultures; 2017.

Dubberly H, Pangaro P. Cybernetics and design: conversations for action. In: *Design cybernetics: navigating the new*; 2019 Jul 31: pp. 85–99. Cham: Springer International Publishing.

Kohonen T, Oja E, Simula O, Visa A, Kangas J. Engineering applications of the self-organizing map. *Proceedings of the IEEE*. 1996 Oct;84(10):1358–84.

8

Support Vector Machine

8.1 The Definition of Data Clustering

Support Vector Machine (SVM) is a type of machine learning algorithm that can be used for classification and regression tasks. While SVMs are typically known for their classification abilities, they can also be used for clustering data. Data clustering is the process of grouping together similar data points into clusters. SVM-based clustering is often referred to as support vector clustering (SVC). SVC is a nonparametric, unsupervised learning algorithm that aims to partition the data into groups such that the points within a group are more similar to each other than to those in other groups.

SVC works by constructing a hyperplane that separates the data into two classes, with the hyperplane being equidistant to the nearest data points of each class. The hyperplane is defined by a set of support vectors, which are the data points closest to the hyperplane. The distance between the hyperplane and the support vectors is maximized, which ensures that the hyperplane is the best possible separator for the given data.

In SVC, the goal is to find a hyperplane that separates the data into groups or clusters. The hyperplane is defined by a weight vector w and a bias term b. Mathematically, the hyperplane can be represented as:

$$W^T x + b = 0, \tag{8.1}$$

where x is a data point. The hyperplane divides the feature space into two regions: one where $W^T x + b > 0$ and one where $W^T x + b < 0$. Data points on either side of the hyperplane are assigned to different clusters.

Cybernetical Intelligence: Engineering Cybernetics with Machine Intelligence, First Edition. Kelvin K. L. Wong.
© 2024 The Institute of Electrical and Electronics Engineers, Inc.
Published 2024 by John Wiley & Sons, Inc.
Companion website: www.wiley.com/go/cyberintel

To find the hyperplane, SVC uses the same optimization problem as SVM for classification. This optimization problem can be formulated as:

$$\text{minimize } \frac{1}{2} ||w||^2 + c \sum_i \xi_i, \tag{8.2}$$

subject to $y_i(w^T x_i + b) \geq 1 - \xi_i$, and $\xi_i \geq 0$ for all $i = 1, ..., N$. Note that $||w||$ is the Euclidean norm of the weight vector, c is a regularization parameter that controls the trade-off between maximizing the margin and minimizing the classification error, y_i is the class label of data point x_i (+1 or −1), and ξ_i is a slack variable that allows for some misclassification of data points.

The objective function of the optimization problem is to minimize the L2 norm of the weight vector, which corresponds to maximizing the margin between the hyperplane and the closest data points of each class. The slack variables ξ_i are added to the objective function to allow for some misclassification of data points. The inequality constraints enforce that the hyperplane separates the data into different classes with a margin of at least 1. To solve the optimization problem, one use the Lagrangian function:

$$L(w, b, \xi, \alpha, \mu) = \frac{1}{2} ||w||^2 + c \sum_i \xi_i - \sum_i \alpha_i [y_i (W^T x + b) - 1 + \xi_i] - \sum_i \mu_i \xi_i, \tag{8.3}$$

where α_i and μ_i are the Lagrange multipliers associated with the inequality and nonnegativity constraints, respectively. One can then obtain the dual form of the optimization problem by maximizing the Lagrangian with respect to the Lagrange multipliers:

$$\text{maximize } L_D(\alpha) = \sum_i \alpha_i - \frac{1}{2} \sum_{i,j} \alpha_i \alpha_j y_i y_j x_i^T x_j, \tag{8.4}$$

subject to $0 \leq \alpha_i \leq c$ for all $i = 1, ..., N$, and $\sum_i \alpha_i y_i = 0$. Where $L_D(\alpha)$ is the dual function, and $x_i^T x_j$ is the dot product between data points x_i and x_j in the feature space. The dual form of the problem is in terms of the Lagrange multipliers α_i, rather than the weight vector w and bias term b.

Once the optimal values of the Lagrange multipliers α_i is found, the weight vector w and bias term b can be found as follows:

$$w = \sum_i \alpha_i y_i x_i \tag{8.5}$$

$$b = y_k \sum_i \alpha_i y_i x_i^T x_K, \tag{8.6}$$

where k is any data point on the margin, i.e. a support vector with $0 < \alpha_i < c$.

There are various distance calculation methods to calculate the distance between a data point x_i and the hyperplane, and for all proposed "distance measure," they need to satisfy:

$$dist(x_i, x_j) \geq 0 \tag{8.7}$$

$$dist(x_i, x_i) = 0 \tag{8.8}$$

$$dist(x_i, x_j) = dist(x_j, x_i) \tag{8.9}$$

$$dist(x_i, x_j) \leq dist(x_i, x_k) + dist(x_k, x_j). \tag{8.10}$$

Next, some common distance measurement methods are given.
(1) Euclidean distance
Figure 8.1 is a schematic diagram of Euclidean distance. Euclidean distance is the easiest-to-understand distance calculation method, which is derived from the distance formula between two points in Euclidean space. Straight-line distance between two points. The Euclidean distance dist (x_i, x_j) of samples x_i and x_j is:

$$dist(x_i, x_j) = \sqrt{\sum_{k=1}^{d} \left(x_i^{(k)} - x_j^{(k)} \right)^2}. \tag{8.11}$$

(2) Manhattan distance
Figure 8.2 is a schematic diagram of Manhattan distance. Manhattan distance, also known as city block distance, is derived from the actual driving distance to drive from one intersection to another intersection in Manhattan. It is mainly used for distance calculation between two points such as chessboard and city. The Manhattan distance $dist(x_i, x_j)$ for samples x_i and x_j is:

$$dist(x_i, x_j) = \sum_{k=1}^{d} \left| x_i^{(k)} - x_j^{(k)} \right|. \tag{8.12}$$

Figure 8.1 Schematic diagram of Euclidean distance.

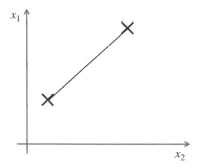

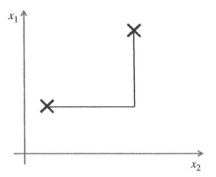

Figure 8.2 Schematic diagram of Manhattan distance.

(3) Minkowski distance

The Minkowski distance is the most commonly used for a given sample. Given sample $x_i = (x_{i1}, x_{i2}, ..., x_{in})$ and $x_j = (x_{j1}, x_{j2}, ..., x_{jn})$, The Minkowski distance $dist(x_i, x_j)$ for samples x_i and x_j is:

$$dist(x_i, x_j) = \left(\sum_{u=1}^{n} |x_{iu} - x_{ju}|^p \right)^{\frac{1}{p}}. \tag{8.13}$$

One can further explore Minkowski distance. When $p = 1$, Minkowski distance is Manhattan distance; when $p = 2$, Minkowski distance is Euclidean distance; when p approaches infinity, Chebyshev distance is achieved.

SVC is a powerful method for clustering data, especially when the data is non-linearly separable. By maximizing the margin between the clusters, SVC can effectively separate the data and assign each point to the appropriate cluster. Additionally, the use of slack variables in the optimization problem allows for some degree of misclassification, making SVC more robust to noisy or imperfect data.

8.2 Support Vector and Margin

SVM is a supervised machine learning algorithm that is used for classification and regression tasks. The goal of SVM is to find a hyperplane in a high-dimensional space that separates the data points into different classes with the largest possible margin as shown in Figure 8.3. The margin is the distance between the hyperplane and the closest data points of each class. SVM is particularly useful for dealing with high-dimensional data and nonlinearly separable data by using kernel functions to transform the input space into a higher-dimensional space where the data points

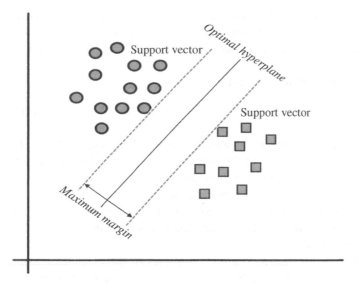

Figure 8.3 Procedure of support vector machine.

are more separable. SVM works by identifying a set of support vectors, which are the data points that lie on the margin boundaries or are misclassified, and using them to define the optimal hyperplane and margin.

Support vectors are the data points that lie on the margin boundaries or are misclassified. These are the most important data points for determining the location of the hyperplane and the margin. The reason for this is that the optimization problem in SVM only depends on the inner product between data points, so the solution depends only on the support vectors.

To see why this is true, consider the dual form of the SVM optimization problem:

$$\text{maximize } L_D(\alpha) = \sum_i \alpha_i - \frac{1}{2} \sum_{i,j} \alpha_i \alpha_j \, y_i \, y_j \, x_i^T x_j, \tag{8.14}$$

subject to $\sum_i \alpha_i y_i = 0$ and $\alpha_i \geq 0$ for all $\iota = 1, ..., N$. Where α_i is the Lagrange multiplier associated with the inequality constraint for data point x_i. The solution to the optimization problem is a weight vector w that can be expressed as a linear combination of the support vectors:

$$w = \sum_i \alpha_i \, x_i y_i, \tag{8.15}$$

where y_i is the class label of the data point. The margin is defined as the distance between the hyperplane and the closest data points of each class. One can define two parallel hyperplanes that pass through the closest data points and have a distance of $2M$ between them. These hyperplanes are called the margin boundaries. The distance between the margin boundaries is $2M$, and the margin is half of this distance or M.

Mathematically, the margin can be represented as:

$$M = \frac{1}{||W||},\qquad(8.16)$$

where $||w||$ is the Euclidean norm of the weight vector w. The margin is therefore inversely proportional to the norm of the weight vector. Maximizing the margin corresponds to minimizing the norm of the weight vector.

The support vectors are the data points for which the equality holds, i.e. the points that are closest to the hyperplane and lie on the margin boundaries. All other data points have a distance greater than the margin and do not affect the location of the hyperplane.

To find the optimal hyperplane and margin, SVM uses an optimization problem that maximizes the margin while minimizing the classification error. The optimization problem can be formulated as:

$$\text{minimize } \frac{1}{2}||w||^2,\qquad(8.17)$$

subject to $y_i(w^T x_i + b) \geq 1$ for all $i = 1, ..., N$, where N is the number of data points. The inequality constraints ensure that all data points are correctly classified and lie on the correct side of the hyperplane. The objective function is to minimize the $L2$ norm of the weight vector, which corresponds to maximizing the margin between the hyperplane and the closest data points of each class. To solve the optimization problem, one use the Lagrangian function:

$$L(w, b, a) = \frac{1}{2}||w||^2 - \sum_i \alpha_i y_i \left(w^T x_i + b\right) - 1,\qquad(8.18)$$

where α_i is the Lagrange multiplier associated with the inequality constraint for data point x_i.

One can then obtain the dual form of the optimization problem by maximizing the Lagrangian with respect to the Lagrange multipliers α_i:

$$\text{maximize } L_D(\alpha) = \sum_i \alpha_i - \frac{1}{2} \sum_{i,j} \alpha_i \alpha_j\, y_i\, y_j\, x_i^T x_j,\qquad(8.19)$$

subject to $\sum_i \alpha_i y_i = 0$ and $\alpha_i \geq 0$ for all $i = 1, ..., N$.

Once the solution has been obtained to the dual problem by maximizing the Lagrangian with respect to the Lagrange multipliers α_i, one can use the values of α_i to compute the weight vector w and the bias term b.

The weight vector w can be computed as:

$$w = \sum_i \alpha_i y_i x_i, \tag{8.20}$$

where x_i is the feature vector of the ith data point. The bias term b can be computed as:

$$b = y_k - \sum_i \alpha_i y_i x_i^T x_k, \tag{8.21}$$

where k is any index for which $0 < \alpha_k < c$, i.e. any index corresponding to a support vector that lies on the margin.

Once one have computed the weight vector w and the bias term b, one can use them to make predictions on new, unseen data points. To classify a new data point x, compute the following decision function:

$$f(x) = w^T x + b. \tag{8.22}$$

If $f(x) > 0$, one classify x as belonging to the positive class, and if $f(x) < 0$, classify x as belonging to the negative class. If $f(x) = 0$, x lies on the decision boundary.

8.3 Kernel Function

In SVM, the kernel function is used to map the input data from the original feature space to a higher-dimensional feature space. This is done to make the data more separable in the transformed space. The kernel function calculates the dot product between the mapped feature vectors without actually computing the mapping. This is known as the kernel trick and allows SVM to work efficiently with high-dimensional data.

A kernel function is a function that takes in two vectors as input and computes a scalar value that represents the similarity or distance between the two vectors. There are many types of kernel functions, but some of the most commonly used ones are:

8.3.1 Linear Kernel

The linear kernel is a common choice for SVMs, especially when the number of features is high relative to the number of training examples. It defines the dot product between two feature vectors as the similarity measure between them:

$$K(x_i, x_j) = x_i^T x_j, \tag{8.23}$$

where x_i and x_j are two feature vectors in the input space. The linear kernel is also known as the inner product kernel because it computes the inner product between the feature vectors.

When one use the linear kernel, the decision function for SVMs takes the form:

$$f(x) = w^T x + b, \tag{8.24}$$

where w is the weight vector and b is the bias term, both learned during training. The weight vector w can be expressed as a linear combination of the training examples:

$$w = \sum_i \alpha_i y_i x_i, \tag{8.25}$$

where α_i is the Lagrange multiplier associated with the ith training example and y^i is its corresponding class label ($+1$ or -1).

To compute the bias term b, one need to find a data point that lies exactly on the hyperplane. One can choose any data point with $\alpha_i > 0$, in this case, one chooses the first data point with $\alpha_1 = 0.324$:

$$\begin{aligned} b &= y_1 - w^T x_1 \\ &= +1 - [0.324(-1)(0.75) + 0.424(1)(1) + 0.288(1)(2) \\ &= -0.564, \end{aligned} \tag{8.26}$$

where $x_1 = [0.75, 1, 2]$ is the feature vector for the first training example. Once one have computed the weight vector w and the bias term b, one can use them to classify new examples using the decision function $f(x)$. If $f(x) > 0$, one classify the example as belonging to the positive class ($+1$); otherwise, one classify it as belonging to the negative class (-1).

8.3.2 Polynomial Kernel

Polynomial kernel is a popular kernel function used in SVMs for nonlinear classification. It transforms the input data into a higher-dimensional feature space, making it easier to separate the classes using a hyperplane.

The polynomial kernel is defined as:

$$K(x, y) = \left(x^T y + c\right)^d, \tag{8.27}$$

where x and y are the input feature vectors, c is a constant, and d is the degree of the polynomial. The degree d controls the degree of nonlinearity of the decision boundary.

When $d = 1$, the polynomial kernel reduces to the linear kernel, and when $d > 1$, it introduces nonlinearity into the decision boundary. The constant c is a regularization parameter that controls the trade-off between the model complexity and the accuracy of the training data. A large value of c will lead to a more complex model, while a small value of c will lead to a simpler model with more regularization. The polynomial kernel is a nonlinear kernel that can handle nonlinearly separable data by transforming the data into a higher dimensional space. The degree parameter d controls the order of the polynomial function, which determines the complexity of the decision boundary. For example, consider a two-dimensional feature space with the polynomial kernel of degree 2:

$$K(x, x') = (\gamma x_1 x_1' + \gamma x_2 x_2' + r)^2, \tag{8.28}$$

where $x = [x_1, x_2]$ and $x' = [x_1', x_2']$. To classify a new example y, one can compute the kernel function between y and each support vector in the training set. Then, one can use the support vectors and their corresponding weights to predict the class of the new example:

$$f(y) = \text{sign}\left(\sum_{i=1}^{n} \alpha_i y_i K(y, x_i) + b\right). \tag{8.29}$$

8.3.3 Radial Basis Function

The Radial Basis Function (RBF) kernel is a popular kernel used in SVMs for nonlinear classification and regression tasks. It is also known as the Gaussian kernel due to its Gaussian-like shape. The RBF kernel measures the similarity between two feature vectors by computing the distance between them in a high-dimensional space, where the distance is weighted by the kernel's parameter gamma.

The RBF kernel function can be defined as:

$$K(x_i, x_j) = e^{-\gamma \|x_i - x_j\|^2}, \tag{8.30}$$

where x_i and x_j are the feature vectors for two data points i and j, $\|\cdot\|$ represents the Euclidean distance between the two feature vectors, and γ is a hyperparameter that controls the shape of the kernel function.

The RBF kernel maps the input data to an infinite-dimensional space, where the distance between two points is given by the kernel function. The kernel function assigns high values to data points that are close to each other in the input space, and low values to points that are far apart. This allows the SVM to capture complex nonlinear decision boundaries between the different classes.

The kernel matrix K is an $N \times N$ symmetric matrix where each element $K_{ij} = K(x_i, x_j)$ represents the similarity between data points x_i, x_j. The kernel matrix is used in the dual optimization problem to compute the Lagrange multipliers α_i and the decision function.

To classify a new data point x, one compute its distance from the support vectors in the feature space using the kernel function:

$$f(x) = \text{sign}\left(\sum_i \alpha_i y_i K(y, x_i) + b\right),$$

(8.31)

where the sign function returns $+1$ if the sum is positive, and -1 if the sum is negative. The decision function $f(x)$ computes the predicted class label for the new data point x.

The bias term b is computed using the support vectors, which are the data points that have nonzero Lagrange multipliers α_i. The bias term can be computed as:

$$b = \frac{1}{N_s}\sum_i\left(y_i - \sum_j \alpha_j y_j K(x_j, x_i)\right),$$

(8.32)

where N_s is the number of support vectors, and the sum is over all support vectors. This equation ensures that the decision function $f(x)$ satisfies the constraint that the output is $+1$ for the most positive support vector and -1 for the most negative support vector. In summary, the input to an SVM consists of a matrix X of feature vectors, a vector y of class labels, and optionally a kernel function that maps the original feature space into a higher-dimensional space. The SVM algorithm uses this input to learn a decision boundary that separates the positive and negative examples in the transformed feature space. Once the SVM has learned this decision boundary, it can be used to classify new, unlabeled examples by mapping their feature vectors into the same transformed feature space and determining which side of the decision boundary they lie on.

The output of a SVM depends on the classification task. In a binary classification problem, the output is a predicted class label ($+1$ or -1) for a given input vector x.

To predict the class label for a new input vector x, one compute the following function:

$$f(x) = \text{sign}\left(w^T x + b\right),$$

(8.33)

where sign() is the sign function that returns $+1$ for positive values and -1 for negative values. The weight vector w and the bias term b are learned during the training phase of the SVM. The function $f(x)$ represents the distance of the input vector x from the decision boundary (i.e. hyperplane) that separates the positive and negative classes. If the value of $f(x)$ is positive, then the predicted class label is $+1$, and if the value of $f(x)$ is negative, then the predicted class label is -1. The magnitude of $f(x)$ represents the confidence of the prediction. In some cases, it may be useful to obtain a probabilistic output from the SVM, which represents the probability of the input vector x belonging to each of the classes. This can be achieved using the plat scaling method, which involves fitting a sigmoid function to the SVM output scores.

The probability of the input vector x belonging to the positive class can be computed as follows:

$$P(y = 1|x) = \frac{1}{1 + e^{A \cdot f(x) + B}},$$ (8.34)

where A and B are constants that are learned during the calibration phase of the SVM. Overall, the output of an SVM can be either a predicted class label or a probability estimate, depending on the task and the method used for calibration.

8.3.4 Laplace Kernel

Overall, the output of an SVM can be either a predicted class label or a probability estimate, depending on the task and the method used for calibration. The Laplace kernel is a similarity measure between two data points that is less sensitive to small variations than the Gaussian kernel. The Laplace kernel function is defined as:

$$K(x, y) = e^{-\frac{\|x - y\|}{\sigma}},$$ (8.35)

where x and y are the input vectors, $|\cdot|$ denotes the Euclidean distance, and σ is the bandwidth parameter. The Laplace kernel function decreases exponentially as the distance between the input vectors increases, making it suitable for tasks where a robust similarity measure is required.

8.3.5 Sigmoid Kernel

The Sigmoid kernel, also known as the hyperbolic tangent kernel, is inspired by neural networks and can be interpreted as a two-layer perceptron. The Sigmoid kernel function is defined as:

$$K(x, y) = \tanh(\alpha x^T y + \beta),$$ (8.36)

where x and y are the input vectors, and α and β are the parameters of the kernel. The Sigmoid kernel is useful for problems where the decision boundaries are nonlinear and can be approximated by hyperbolic tangent functions. This kernel is particularly popular in kernel-based learning algorithms for classification tasks. Both Laplace and Sigmoid kernels can be used in SVMs and other kernel-based learning algorithms to handle nonlinearly separable data and find appropriate decision boundaries in the higher-dimensional feature space. Moreover, various kernels and their parameters details are shown in Table 8.1.

Table 8.1 Various kernels used in SVM.

Name	Equation	Parameter
Linear kernel	$x_i^T x_j$	Null
Polynomial kernel	$\left(x_i^T x_j\right)^d$	$d \geq 1$, degree of the polynomial
Gaussian kernel	$e^{-\frac{\|x_i - x_j\|^2}{2\sigma^2}}$	$\sigma > 0$, bandwidth
Laplace kernel	$e^{-\frac{\|x_i - x_j\|}{2\sigma^2}}$	$\sigma > 0$, bandwidth
Sigmoid kernel	$\tanh\left(\beta x_i^T x_j + 0\right)$	$\beta > 0, \theta > 0$

8.4 Linear and Nonlinear Support Vector Machine

Linear SVM is a type of binary classification algorithm that works well for linearly separable data. The basic idea of linear SVM is to find the optimal hyperplane that separates the two classes of data with the maximum margin. The margin is the distance between the hyperplane and the closest data points of each class. The intuition behind the margin is that the larger the margin, the more robust the classification model is to noise and outliers.

The hyperplane can be expressed as a linear function of the input features:

$$w^T x + b = 0, \tag{8.37}$$

where w is the weight vector and b is the bias term. The decision boundary is the hyperplane that separates the two classes of data. The sign of the output of the decision function $f(x) = w^T x + b$ determines the predicted class label of the input feature x:

$$f(x) = w^T x + b \geq 0, \Rightarrow \text{predict class} + 1 \tag{8.38}$$

$$f(x) = w^T x + b < 0, \Rightarrow \text{predict class} - 1. \tag{8.39}$$

To find the optimal hyperplane, one need to solve an optimization problem that involves minimizing the norm of the weight vector w subject to the constraints that all data points are classified correctly. The optimization problem can be written as:

$$\text{minimize } \frac{\|w\|^2}{2}. \tag{8.40}$$

Subject to $y_i(w^T x + b) \geq 1$ for all $i = 1, ..., N$, where N is the total number of data points, x_i is the feature vector of the ith data point, y_i is the class label of the ith data point (+1 or −1). The objective function $\dfrac{||w||^2}{2}$ represents the norm of the weight vector w, which measures the complexity of the decision boundary. The larger the norm of w, the more complex the decision boundary is, and the more likely it is to overfit the training data. The constraints ensure that all data points are classified correctly, and the margin is at least 1. The margin is defined as the distance between the hyperplane and the closest data points of each class.

The optimization problem can be solved using Lagrange multipliers. The Lagrangian can be written as:

$$L(w, b, a) = \frac{||w||^2}{2} - \sum_i \alpha_i y_i \left(w^T x_i + b\right) - 1, \qquad (8.41)$$

where α_i are the Lagrange multipliers. The solution to the optimization problem is given by:

$$w = \sum_i \alpha_i y_i x_i, \qquad (8.42)$$

where $\alpha_i > 0$ are the nonzero Lagrange multipliers. The bias term b can be computed from the Karush–Kuhn–Tucker (KKT) conditions; $y_i(w^T x + b) = 1$ for all i such that $\alpha_i > 0$.

Once one have computed the weight vector w and the bias term b, one can use them to predict the class label of new data points by computing the decision function $f(x) = (w^T x + b)$ and checking its sign. If $f(x)$ is positive, one predict class +1, otherwise one predict class −1.

Suppose one have a dataset with two classes, +1 and −1, and two features, x_1 and x_2. The dataset is shown in Figure 8.4.

Figure 8.4 Sample dataset for Linear SVM.

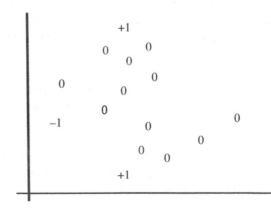

The objective of the linear SVM is to find the optimal hyperplane that separates the two classes of data with the maximum margin. The hyperplane can be expressed as a linear function of the input features; $w^T x + b = 0$, where w is the weight vector and b is the bias term.

To find the optimal hyperplane, one need to solve an optimization problem that involves minimizing the norm of the weight vector w subject to the constraints that all data points are classified correctly. One can minimize $L(w, b, \alpha)$ by taking the partial derivatives of L with respect to w and b, setting them to zero, and solving for w and b:

$$\frac{\partial L}{\partial w} \ w - \sum_i \alpha_i y_i x_i = 0 \Rightarrow w = \sum_i \alpha_i y_i x_i \tag{8.43}$$

$$\frac{\partial L}{\partial b} - \sum_i \alpha_i y_i = 0 \Rightarrow \sum_i \alpha_i y_i = 0. \tag{8.44}$$

Substituting w into L, one get the dual form of the optimization problem:

$$\text{maximize } L_D(\alpha) = \sum_i \alpha_i - \frac{1}{2} \sum_{i,j} \alpha_i \alpha_j \, y_i \, y_j \, x_i^T x_j, \tag{8.45}$$

subject to $\sum_i \alpha_i y_i = 0$ and $\alpha_i \geq 0$ for all $i = 1, \ldots, N$.

One can solve the dual problem using any standard quadratic programming solver. The solution to the dual problem gives us the Lagrange multipliers α_i, which one can use to compute the weight vector w and the bias term b.

Suppose one obtain the following Lagrange multipliers for our dataset: $\alpha =$ [0.324, 0, 0.297, 0.003, 0.000, 0.625, 0.000, 0.000, and 0.000].

Only the nonzero Lagrange multipliers contribute to the weight vector w and the bias term b; $w = \sum_i \alpha_i y_i x_i = [0.021, -0.526]$. To compute the bias term b, one need to find a data point that lies exactly on the hyperplane. One can choose any data point with $\alpha_i > 0$, in this case, one choose the first data point with $\alpha_1 = 0.324$; $b = y_1 - w^T x_1 = 1.486$. So the equation of the hyperplane is:

$$w^T x + b = 0. \tag{8.46}$$

This equation can be used to make predictions on new data points. If the value of the left-hand side is positive, then the data point is classified as +1, and if it is negative, then the data point is classified as −1.

Nonlinear SVMs are used when the data cannot be separated by a linear hyperplane in the input space. In such cases, one need to map the input data to a higher-dimensional feature space where it becomes separable by a linear hyperplane. This is known as the kernel trick.

The idea behind the kernel trick is to replace the inner product of the input vectors with a nonlinear function called a kernel function. The kernel function computes the similarity between the input vectors in the higher-dimensional feature space without explicitly computing the coordinates of the vectors in that space.

There are several types of kernel functions that can be used in SVMs, including:

- Polynomial kernel: $K(x, y) = (x^T y + c)^d$, where d is the degree of the polynomial and c is a constant.
- Gaussian RBF kernel: $K(x, y) = e(-\gamma \ ||x-y||^2)$, where γ is a parameter that controls the width of the kernel.
- Sigmoid kernel: $K(x, y) = \tanh(ax^T y + c)$, where a and c are constants.

The optimization problem for nonlinear SVMs is similar to that for linear SVMs, except that the input vectors are mapped to a higher-dimensional feature space using a kernel function. The decision boundary is still a hyperplane, but it is now represented in the feature space instead of the input space. For instance, start with the nonlinear SVM optimization problem:

$$\text{minimize} \ \frac{1}{2}||w||^2 + c\sum_i \xi_i, \tag{8.47}$$

subject to $y_i(w^T \varphi(x_i) + b) \geq 1 - \zeta_i$, for all $i = 1, ..., N$ and $\xi_l \geq 0$, for all $l = 1, ..., N$.

Here, φ is a function that maps the input x_i to a higher-dimensional feature space, and c is a hyperparameter that controls the trade-off between maximizing the margin and minimizing the classification error. ξ_i are slack variables that allow for some misclassification of the training examples. The dual form of the optimization problem is:

$$\text{maximize} \ L_D(\alpha) = \sum_i \alpha_i - \frac{1}{2}\sum_{i,j}\alpha_i\alpha_j \, y_i \, y_j \, K(x_i, x_j), \tag{8.48}$$

subject to $\sum_i \alpha_i y_i = 0$ and $0 \leq \alpha_i \leq c$ for all $i = 1, ..., N$.

Here, $K(x_i, x_j)$ is the kernel function that computes the dot product of the transformed feature vectors $\varphi(x_i)$ and $\varphi(x_j)$ without explicitly computing the coordinates of the vectors in the feature space.

Once the optimal values of α_i is obtained from the dual problem, then can compute the weight vector w and the bias term b as:

$$w = \sum_i \alpha_i \, y_i \varphi x_i \tag{8.49}$$

$$b = y_i - \sum_i \alpha_i y_i K(x_i, x_j), \tag{8.50}$$

where i is any index such that $0 < \alpha_i < c$.

To make predictions on a new data point x, its transformed feature vector $\varphi(x)$ is computed using the kernel function, and then the equation is utilized as follows:

$$f(x) = w^T \varphi(x) + b. \tag{8.51}$$

If $f(x)$ is positive, the data point is classified as $+1$, and if it is negative, the data point is classified as -1. One advantage of SVMs is that the kernel trick allows us to work with high-dimensional feature spaces without explicitly computing the coordinates of the vectors in that space, which can be computationally expensive or even impossible in some cases.

Another advantage is that SVMs are less prone to overfitting than other classification algorithms, especially when the number of features is large compared to the number of training examples. However, one disadvantage of SVMs is that they can be sensitive to the choice of kernel function and its parameters. Choosing the right kernel function and its parameters can be a difficult task that requires trial and error or even domain knowledge.

8.5 Hard Margin and Soft Margin in Support Vector Machine

For instance, start with a set of data points that one want to classify into two groups. One can consider two cases for these data: either they are linearly separable, or the separating hyperplane is nonlinear. When the data is linearly separable, and one do not want to have any misclassifications, one use SVM with a hard margin. However, when a linear boundary is not feasible or need to allow some misclassifications in the hope of achieving better generality.

For instance, assume that the hyperplane separating our two classes is defined as $w^T x + b = 0$

Then, the margin by two parallel hyperplanes can be defined as:

$$w^T x + \alpha = 0. \tag{8.52}$$

$$w^T x + \beta = 0. \tag{8.53}$$

They are the green and purple lines in the Figure 8.5. Without allowing any misclassifications in the hard margin SVM, one want to maximize the distance between the two hyperplanes. To find this distance, one can use the formula for the distance of a point from a plane. So the distance of the blue points and the red point from the black line would respectively be:

$$\frac{\left|w^T x + \alpha\right|}{\|w\|} \text{ and } \frac{\left|w^T x + \beta\right|}{\|w\|}. \tag{8.54}$$

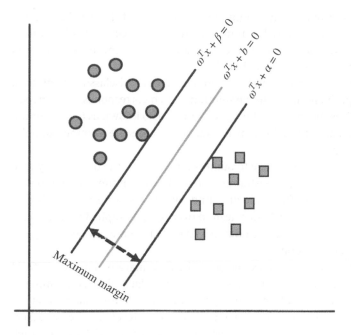

Figure 8.5 Hard margin in support vector machine.

As a result, the total margin would become:

$$\frac{|\alpha - \beta|}{||w||},$$ (8.55)

if there is a need to maximize this margin, without the loss of generality, consider $\alpha = b + 1$ and $\beta = b - 1$. Subsequently, the problem would be to maximize $\frac{2}{||w||}$ or minimize $\frac{||w||}{2}$.

In SVM, the hard margin is a concept used to describe the condition when the training data is linearly separable without any errors or misclassifications. In other words, the hard margin is a strict condition that requires the SVM to find a hyperplane that perfectly separates the two classes in the training data. The hard margin is defined by the following optimization problem:

$$\text{minimize } \frac{1}{2}||w||^2,$$ (8.56)

subject to $y_i(W^T x_i + b) \geq 1$ for $i = 1, ..., N$, where N is the number of training examples, x_i is the ith example, y_i is its corresponding label ($+1$ or -1), w is the weight vector, and b is the bias term.

The optimization problem aims to minimize the norm of the weight vector w subject to the constraint that each training example is correctly classified with a margin of at least 1. The margin is the distance between the hyperplane and the closest training example from either class.

If the training data is linearly separable and there are no misclassifications, then the optimization problem has a unique solution, which corresponds to the hyperplane that maximizes the margin. This hyperplane is also known as the maximum margin hyperplane, and it is defined by the support vectors the training examples that lie on the margin.

The hard margin SVM is sensitive to outliers and noise in the data, as any misclassification will violate the constraints and make the optimization problem infeasible. In practice, it is often difficult to find data that is perfectly linearly separable, and the hard margin SVM may lead to overfitting if applied to noisy data. Therefore, soft margin SVM was introduced to handle the case of linearly separable data with misclassifications.

The soft margin approach is an extension of the hard margin approach in SVM that allows for some misclassifications in the training data while still aiming to maximize the margin. The soft margin approach is suitable for datasets that are not perfectly linearly separable, or when one expect some level of noise or outliers in the data. In the soft margin approach, one introduce slack variables ξ_i for each training example, which measure how much the example violates the margin. One modify the optimization problem by penalizing the misclassifications with a term that is proportional to the slack variables and adding a hyperparameter c that controls the trade-off between maximizing the margin and allowing some misclassifications.

To derive the soft margin optimization problem, one need to allow for some misclassifications of the training data. One can introduce slack variables ξ_i for each data point to represent the amount by which it violates the margin or is misclassified:

$$y_i\left(w^T x_i + b\right) \geq 1 - \xi_i \tag{8.57}$$

$$\xi_i \geq 0 \, \xi_i \in i, ..., N. \tag{8.58}$$

The optimization problem for soft margin SVM can be written as:

$$\text{minimize } \frac{1}{2}||w||^2 + c \sum_i \xi_i, \tag{8.59}$$

subject to $y_i(W^T x_i + b) \geq 1 - \xi_i$ and $\xi_i \geq 0$ for $i = 1, ..., N$, where c is a hyperparameter that controls the trade-off between maximizing the margin and minimizing the sum of slack variables. The term $c \sum_i \xi_i$ is known as the "slack penalty" and represents the cost of misclassifying a data point.

Similar to the hard margin case, one can solve the optimization problem using Lagrange multipliers. The Lagrangian (L) for the soft margin SVM is:

$$L(w, b, \xi, \alpha, \mu) = \frac{1}{2}||w||^2 + c\sum_i \xi_i - \sum_i \alpha_i[y_i(w^T x_i + b) - 1 + \xi_i] - \sum_i \mu_i \xi_i,$$

$$(8.60)$$

where α_i and μ_i are Lagrange multipliers. One can then obtain the dual form of the optimization problem by maximizing the Lagrangian with respect to the Lagrange multipliers α_i and μ_i:

$$\text{maximize } L_D(\alpha, \mu) = \sum_i \alpha_i - \frac{1}{2}\sum_{i,j} \alpha_i \alpha_j \, y_i \, y_j x_i^T x_j, \qquad (8.61)$$

subject to $\sum_i \alpha_i y_i = 0$, $0 \leq \alpha_i \leq c$ for all i, and $\sum_i \mu_i = 0$. The solution to the dual problem gives us the Lagrange multipliers α_i and μ_i, which one can use to compute the weight vector w and the bias term b. The support vectors are the data points with nonzero Lagrange multipliers. Similar to the hard margin case, the decision boundary is given by:

$$w^T x + b = \sum_i \alpha_i y_i x_i^T x + b. \qquad (8.62)$$

The soft margin allows for some degree of misclassification and is more robust to noisy data. However, the choice of the hyperparameter c is important and can affect the performance of the model. A smaller value of c results in a wider margin and more misclassifications, while a larger value of c results in a narrower margin and fewer misclassifications.

8.6 I/O of Support Vector Machine

The input to a SVM is a set of training examples represented as a matrix X with dimensions $N \times M$, where N is the number of examples and M is the number of features. Each row of the matrix X corresponds to a single example, and each column corresponds to a single feature.

8.6.1 Training Data

The input to a SVM is a set of training examples represented as a matrix X with dimensions $N \times M$, where N is the number of examples and M is the number of features. Each row of the matrix X corresponds to a single example, and each column corresponds to a single feature. The SVM algorithm learns from a set of labeled training examples, where each example represents an observation of the problem. For instance, in a binary classification problem, each training example consists of a feature vector and a corresponding class label that indicates whether the example belongs to the positive or negative class. In a binary classification problem, for instance $x_i \in R^d$ be the feature vector for the ith training example and $x_i \in \{+1, -1\}$ be its class label. Assume that the training examples are linearly separable, which means that there exists a hyperplane that separates the positive examples from the negative examples. The hyperplane is defined by:

$$w^T x + b = 0, \tag{8.63}$$

where $w \in R^d$ is the weight vector that determines the orientation of the hyperplane, and $b \in R$ is the bias term that determines its position. The decision function of the SVM is:

$$f(x) = \text{sign}(w^T x + b), \tag{8.64}$$

where $\text{sign}(x)$ is the sign function that returns $+1$ if $x > 0$, -1 if $x < 0$, and 0 if $x = 0$.

The SVM algorithm learns the weight vector w and the bias term b from the training examples, by solving the following optimization problem: minimize $1/2$ $\|w\|^2$. Where $\|w\|$ is the Euclidean norm of the weight vector, and n is the number of training examples. The optimization problem can be solved using a variety of methods, such as quadratic programming or gradient descent. The solution w^* and b^* of the optimization problem determine the hyperplane that maximizes the margin between the positive and negative examples. The margin is defined as the distance between the hyperplane and the closest positive and negative examples, as shown in the previous example.

8.6.2 Feature Matrix and Label Vector

The set of feature vectors for all the training examples are collected into a matrix X, where each row corresponds to a single example and each column corresponds to a single feature. Each element of the matrix X is a real-valued number that represents a feature of the example. For instance, if one are trying to classify images of handwritten digits, each feature might represent the intensity of a particular pixel in the image. The set of class labels for all the training examples are collected into a vector y, which has length N (the number of training examples). Each element of the vector y is a binary value that indicates whether the corresponding example belongs to the positive or negative class. Specifically, $y_i = +1$ if the ith example is a positive example and $y_i = -1$ if the ith example is a negative example.

8.7   Hyperparameters of Support Vector Machine

SVM have several hyperparameters that need to be set before training the model. These hyperparameters control the behavior of the SVM algorithm and can significantly affect the performance of the model. In this answer, one will discuss some of the most important hyperparameters of SVM.

8.7.1   The C Hyperparameter

The C hyperparameter in SVMs controls the trade-off between maximizing the margin and minimizing the classification error on the training data. It is a regularization parameter that balances the bias-variance trade-off in the model.

The C hyperparameter is introduced in the optimization problem as a constraint on the Lagrange multipliers α_i. Specifically, the C parameter controls the upper bound on the value of α_i, which in turn controls the amount of slack allowed in the optimization problem.

The optimization problem with the C hyperparameter can be expressed as minimize $1/2 \, \|w\|^2 + c \sum_i \xi_i$. Where ξ_i is the slack variable that measures the distance of the ith data point from the correct margin. The C parameter determines how much one penalize misclassification errors and violations of the margin. A larger value of C leads to a stricter margin, which may result in overfitting, while a smaller value of C allows for more errors and a wider margin, which may result in underfitting. The choice of C should be based on cross-validation or other model selection techniques to find the value that provides the best trade-off between bias and variance in the validation data.

8.7.2   Kernel Coefficient

The kernel coefficient, denoted as γ, is a hyperparameter in the kernel function of the SVM that controls the shape of the decision boundary. In particular, it determines how far the influence of a single training example reaches, with low values meaning "far" and high values meaning "close."

The RBF kernel is a commonly used kernel function that depends on the kernel coefficient. In the RBF kernel, a small value of γ makes the decision boundary more flexible, allowing more points to be classified as part of the positive or negative class. Conversely, a large value of γ makes the decision boundary less flexible, resulting in a smaller number of support vectors and a more strict classification.

The appropriate value of γ depends on the problem being solved and can be chosen using cross-validation or other techniques. In general, larger values of γ are suitable for problems with fewer training examples and simpler decision boundaries, while smaller values of γ are suitable for problems with more training examples and more complex decision boundaries.

8.7.3 Class Weights

Class weights are used to address the issue of imbalanced classes in a binary classification problem. In such problems, one class (the minority class) may have significantly fewer examples than the other class (the majority class), which can lead to biased predictions.

The class weight hyperparameter in SVM assigns a weight to each class, which affects the penalty for misclassifying a sample from that class. The weight assigned to the positive class is typically set to be smaller than that of the negative class, which gives more importance to correctly classifying positive examples.

The objective function becomes:

$$\text{minimize } \frac{1}{2}\|w\|^2 + c_{pos}\, \Sigma[i : y_i = +1]\, \xi_i + c_{neg}\, \Sigma[i : y_i = -1]\, \xi_i, \qquad (8.65)$$

where ξ_i is the slack variable for the ith sample. The weights assigned to each class can be calculated using weight_{pos} = (total samples)/($2 \times$ number of positive samples) weight_{neg} = (total samples)/($2 \times$ number of negative samples). Where total samples is the total number of training samples, and number of positive/negative samples is the number of samples in the positive/negative class, respectively.

8.7.4 Convergence Criteria

In SVM, the convergence criterion determines when to stop the training process. SVM algorithms typically use the KKT conditions to check for convergence. The KKT conditions state that for a given optimization problem with constraints, a feasible solution is optimal if the gradient of the objective function with respect to the variables is proportional to the constraints, and the constraints are satisfied.

The convergence criterion for SVM can be defined in terms of the KKT conditions. Specifically, the training algorithm can be terminated when the following conditions are met:

- The difference between the current objective value and the previous objective value is less than a certain tolerance ε.
- The norm of the gradient of the objective function with respect to the parameters is less than a certain tolerance δ.
- All constraints are satisfied within a certain tolerance η.

Mathematically, the convergence criterion can be written as:

$$|L(w) - L(w_{prev})| \le \varepsilon$$
$$\|\nabla L(w)\| \le \delta \tag{8.66}$$
$$|y_i(w^T x_i + b) - 1| \le \eta,$$

where $L(w)$ is the objective function, w is the weight vector, w_{prev} is the weight vector in the previous iteration, $\nabla L(w)$ is the gradient of the objective function with respect to w, y_i is the ith class label, x_i is the ith feature vector, and b is the bias term.

The values of ε, δ, and η are typically chosen empirically based on the specific problem and the desired level of accuracy. A smaller value for these tolerances will result in a more accurate solution but will also require more computational resources and may result in slower training.

8.7.5 Regularization

Regularization is a technique used to prevent overfitting in machine learning models. In the context of SVMs, regularization is achieved through the C hyperparameter, which controls the trade-off between maximizing the margin and minimizing the classification error.

The regularization parameter C can be thought of as a penalty for misclassifications. As C increases, the penalty for misclassifications becomes larger, and the algorithm will prioritize correctly classifying as many examples as possible. On the other hand, as C decreases, the algorithm will prioritize maximizing the margin even if this means making more misclassifications. The hyperparameters of support vector machine are summarized in Table 8.2.

8.8 Application of Support Vector Machine

SVM is a versatile machine learning algorithm that has various applications in different fields.

8.8.1 Classification

SVM can be used for binary and multi-class classification problems, where the goal is to classify data points into one of several categories. In this case, the output of the SVM is a binary or multi-class label indicating the predicted class of each input data point. For binary classification, the output of the SVM is a binary label that indicates the predicted class of each input data point. Given a new input data point x, the predicted class label y_{pred} is determined as follows:

$$y_{pred} = \text{sign}(w^T + b), \tag{8.67}$$

Table 8.2 Summarizing the hyperparameters of support vector machine.

Hyperparameter	Description
Kernel	SVM uses a kernel function to transform the input data into a higher-dimensional feature space where it can be separated more easily. Common kernel functions include linear, polynomial, RBF, and sigmoid.
Regularization parameter (C)	This parameter controls the trade-off between maximizing the margin and minimizing the classification error. A larger value of C allows for more flexible decision boundaries, while a smaller value of C encourages the classifier to have a wider margin.
Gamma	This parameter is used in the RBF kernel to control the width of the Gaussian function used to transform the data into the higher-dimensional feature space. A larger value of gamma leads to a narrower peak of the Gaussian function, resulting in a more complex decision boundary.
Degree	This parameter is used in the polynomial kernel to specify the degree of the polynomial function used to transform the data into the higher-dimensional feature space. A higher degree leads to a more complex decision boundary.
Coefficient (coef0)	This parameter is used in the polynomial and sigmoid kernels to control the influence of high-degree polynomials. A larger value of coef0 allows for higher-degree polynomials to have a larger influence on the decision boundary.
Shrinking	This parameter controls whether the algorithm will use a shrinking heuristic to speed up the optimization process by removing support vectors that are unlikely to affect the decision boundary. Enabling shrinking can speed up training, but may slightly degrade the performance of the model.
Cache size	This parameter controls the amount of memory allocated to caching the kernel matrix during training. A larger cache size can speed up training but may require more memory.
Class weight	This parameter can be used to adjust the penalty assigned to misclassifications of different classes. It can be useful in cases where the classes are imbalanced or where misclassifying one class is more costly than misclassifying another.

where sign () is the sign function that returns -1 for negative values and $+1$ for positive values. The w is the weight vector learned by the SVM algorithm, and b is the bias term. The SVM algorithm learns these parameters based on the training data.

For multi-class classification, the SVM can be used in several ways. One common approach is to use the one-vs-all (OVA) method, where one train one

SVM for each class and classify a new data point based on the highest SVM score. Given a new input data point x, the predicted class label y_{pred} is determined as follows:

$$y_{pred} = \text{argmax}_j \left(w_j^T x + b_j \right), \qquad (8.68)$$

where j is the index of the SVM for the jth class, w_j is the weight vector learned by the SVM for the jth class, and b_j is the bias term for the jth class. The argmax function returns the index of the SVM with the highest score.

Another approach for multi-class classification is to use the one-vs-one (OVO) method, where one train one SVM for each pair of classes and classify a new data point based on the majority vote of the SVMs.

8.8.2 Regression

SVM can also be used for regression problems, where the goal is to predict a continuous numerical value, rather than a class label. This is known as Support Vector Regression (SVR). The idea behind SVR is to find a hyperplane that best fits the training data, while still allowing some margin of error or tolerance. The margin of error is controlled by a hyperparameter called epsilon. The solution to the SVR problem involves finding the optimal values of w and b that satisfy the constraints and minimize the objective function. This can be done using various optimization techniques, such as quadratic programming or gradient descent.

Once the SVM model is trained, it can be used to predict the output value for a new input data point x_test using the equation:

$$y_{test} = w^T x_{test} + b, \qquad (8.69)$$

where y_{test} is the predicted output value for the input x_{test}, w and b are the learned weight vector and bias term, respectively, and the superscript T denotes the transpose operation.

8.8.3 Image Classification

Image classification using SVM involves using SVM to train a model that can classify images into different categories based on their features. One popular approach is to use a variant of SVM called "Support Vector Machines for Image Classification" (SVMIC).

In SVMIC, the input to the SVM is a feature vector that describes the image, such as a vector of pixel intensities. The SVM is trained on a labeled set of such feature vectors, where each label corresponds to a particular category or class. Once the SVM is trained, it can be used to predict the category of new, unlabeled images based on their feature vectors.

The mathematical equations involved in image classification using SVMIC are similar to those for binary classification in SVM. However, the feature vectors in image classification are typically much larger, as they may include thousands or even millions of features. The SVMIC algorithm is designed to handle such large feature vectors efficiently.

8.8.4 Text Classification

SVM can be used for text classification tasks, where the goal is to classify text documents into different categories based on their content. In this case, the input to the SVM is a feature vector extracted from the text, and the output is a predicted class label. For instance, a binary classification problem is where one wants to classify a text document into one of two classes, either positive ($+1$) or negative (-1). One represent each document as a bag-of-words, which is a vector of word frequencies. Let x_i be the feature vector for the ith document, and y_i be its corresponding class label.

One can use a linear kernel for this problem, where the kernel function is defined as:

$$K\left(x_i, x_j\right) = x_i^T x_j, \tag{8.70}$$

where x_i^T is the transpose of the feature vector for the ith document and K represents a kernel function that takes as input two data points.

To predict the class of a new document, one compute the sign of the decision function $f(x) = w^T x + b$. If $f(x) > 0$, one classify the document as positive ($+1$), and if $f(x) < 0$, one classify it as negative (-1).

Summary

This chapter described about SVM, a powerful machine learning algorithm used for classification and regression tasks. SVM finds a hyperplane that maximally separates the two classes in the feature space. The hard-margin SVM aims to separate the classes perfectly with a linear decision boundary, while the soft-margin SVM allows some misclassifications to handle nonlinearly separable data.

This chapter discussed the mathematics behind SVM, including the optimization problem, the Lagrange multipliers, and the dual problem. One also explored the different types of kernel functions used in SVM, such as the linear kernel, polynomial kernel, and RBF kernel. Furthermore, one discussed hyperparameters, including the regularization parameter (C), kernel coefficient (γ), and class weights, which affect the performance of the SVM algorithm. One also discussed different convergence criteria and regularization techniques.

Finally, the discussion about the applications of SVM in image and text classification, as well as regression problems are described. SVM is particularly useful in high-dimensional data analysis, where it can handle large feature spaces effectively. Overall, SVM provide an effective and efficient approach for solving a wide range of machine learning problems.

Exercise Questions

Q.8.1 Describe the difference between a hard margin and a soft margin in SVM?

Q.8.2 What is the mathematical expression for the decision boundary in a linear SVM, and how is it determined based on the margin and the support vectors?

Q.8.3 In support vector machines (SVM), the decision boundary is determined by maximizing the margin between the support vectors. The margin can be calculated using the equation:

$$\text{Margin} = \frac{1}{2} \|w\|,$$

where $\|w\|$ represents the Euclidean norm of the weight vector w. Calculate the margin for a given weight vector $w = [0.5, -0.8, 0.2]$.

Q.8.4 How is the kernel trick used to extend the SVM to nonlinear decision boundaries, and what is the mathematical expression for the kernel function?

Q.8.5 In which way does SVM handle imbalanced datasets?

Q.8.6 Describe the role of hyperparameters in SVM?

Q.8.7 The objective of support vector machines (SVM) is to find the hyperplane that maximizes the margin while minimizing the classification error. The optimization problem for SVM can be formulated as:

Minimize $: \frac{1}{2} \times \|w\|^2$ Subject to: $y_i \times (w^T \times x_i + b) > = 1$ for all training examples.

Given a set of training examples and their corresponding labels, determine the Lagrangian dual form of the SVM optimization problem.

Q.8.8 How does SVM handle large datasets?

Q.8.9 Explain the difference between binary and multi-class SVM?

Q.8.10 In support vector machines (SVM), the decision function is defined as the sign of the linear combination of support vectors and their corresponding weights. It can be expressed as:

$$f(x) = \text{sign}\left(\sum (\alpha_i \times y_i \times K(x_i, x) + b)\right).$$

Where α_i represents the Lagrange multipliers, y_i is the label of the ith training example, $K(x_i, x)$ is the kernel function, and b is the bias term. Calculate the decision function value for a given test example $x = [1.2, -0.5]$ using the linear kernel $K(x_i, x) = x_i^T \times x$.

Further Reading

Lessmann S, Stahlbock R, Crone SF. Optimizing hyperparameters of support vector machines by genetic algorithms. In IC-AI 2005 Jan (Vol. 74, p. 82).

Pontil M, Verri A. Properties of support vector machines. *Neural Computation*. 1998 May 15;10(4):955–74.

Thomas J, Maszczyk T, Sinha N, Kluge T, Dauwels J. Deep learning-based classification for brain-computer interfaces. In 2017 IEEE International Conference on Systems, Man, and Cybernetics (SMC) 2017 Oct 5 (pp. 234–239).

9

Bio-Inspired Cybernetical Intelligence

Bio-inspired artificial intelligence is an emerging field of research that draws inspiration from biological systems and their self-regulating properties to develop new bio-inspired computational models and algorithms for solving complex problems. The form of intelligence is a combination of two fields: cybernetics and biomimetics.

As mentioned in our previous chapters, cybernetics is the study of the control and communication processes in both biological and artificial systems. Cybernetics seeks to understand how systems can be designed to maintain stability and adapt to changes in their environment. Bio-inspired computing, on the other hand, draws inspiration from biological systems to develop new bio-inspired computational algorithm. Bio-inspired computing techniques include evolutionary algorithms, swarm intelligence, and artificial neural networks. In the machine learning context, bio-Inspired machine intelligence combines these two fields to develop new approaches to problem-solving. The goal is to create systems that can self-regulate and adapt to changes in their environment, much like biological systems and biomimetics do. By using the principles of cybernetics and bio-characterized algorithms, researchers can create systems that are more robust, flexible, and efficient than traditional computational methods.

One of the key areas of research is in developing new algorithms for machine intelligence and data analysis. By drawing inspirational concepts from biological systems such as the brain, researchers can develop artificial neural networks that are more efficient and accurate than traditional machine learning algorithms. For example, deep learning algorithms that are based on neurons have been developed to recognize patterns in images and speech. Another area of artificial intelligence development is to conceptualize new optimization methodologies. Bio-inspired optimization algorithms such as evolutionary algorithms and swarm intelligence algorithms have been developed to solve complex optimization problems in a wide

Cybernetical Intelligence: Engineering Cybernetics with Machine Intelligence, First Edition.
Kelvin K. L. Wong.
© 2024 The Institute of Electrical and Electronics Engineers, Inc.
Published 2024 by John Wiley & Sons, Inc.
Companion website: www.wiley.com/go/cyberintel

range of fields, including engineering, cybernetic intelligence, etc. Overall, it is a promising field of research that has the potential to revolutionize the way one approach complex problems. By drawing inspiration from biological systems, researchers can develop new bio-inspired computational models and algorithms that are more efficient, accurate, and adaptable than traditional methods. As the field continues to grow, one can expect to see many exciting new developments in bio-inspired machine learning, optimization, and other applications of computer science.

9.1 Genetic Algorithm

Genetic Algorithm (GA) is a popular biomimetics algorithm used to solve optimization problems. The process of natural selection inspires it, and it works by evolving a population of potential solutions over generations. In relation to bio-characterized algorithms, it is a concept to develop intelligent systems by taking inspiration from biological and cybernetic principles, which includes approaches such as neural networks, swarm intelligence, and evolutionary algorithm. By using the above-mentioned machine intelligence techniques such as GA, AI researchers can create intelligent systems that are adaptable, robust, and capable of learning and evolving over time. In this way, GA is one of the many tools that can be used to develop bio-inspired cybernetical intelligence, enabling machines to mimic and learn from the complex and dynamic systems found in nature. In the Initialization step, GA creates an initial population of potential solutions, where each solution is represented as a chromosome. The chromosome is a string of genes that represent the solution's parameters. The initial population is created randomly, or it can be based on some prior knowledge of the problem. In a GA, the set of genes of an individual is represented using a string, in terms of an alphabet. Usually, binary values are used (strings of 1 s and 0 s). Hence can say that genes in a chromosome have encoded (Figure 9.1).

After the population is initialized, the fitness of each solution in the population is evaluated. The fitness function determines how well each solution solves the problem. It is assumed that there has a minimization problem, and need to look for a solution that minimizes the objective function $f(x)$. The fitness function for each solution can be represented as follows:

$$\text{Fitness}(x) = \frac{1}{f(x)}. \tag{9.1}$$

Note that the fitness function is higher for better solutions (i.e. lower values of $f(x)$). In this step, it is required to select the fittest individuals from the population in order to create a new generation of potential solutions. The selection process is

Figure 9.1 Initialization of genetic algorithm.

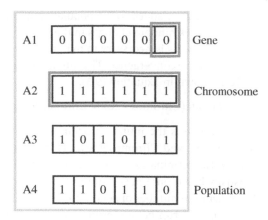

based on the fitness function. The idea is to select individuals with a higher fitness value so that their genes can be passed on to the next generation. There are various selection methods, including roulette wheel selection, tournament selection, rank-based selection, and others. In crossover step, creating a new generation of potential solutions by combining the genes of the selected individuals. The idea is to create a new solution that inherits the desirable characteristics of its parents. The crossover process can be represented mathematically as follows:

$$\text{Chromosome}_{new} = \text{Crossover}(\text{Parent}_1, \text{Parent}_2), \tag{9.2}$$

where Chromosome_{new} is the chromosome of the new solution, and Crossover is the crossover operator that combines the genes of the two parents (Parent_1 and Parent_2). For example, consider the crossover point to be three as shown in Figure 9.2a.

Offsprings are created by exchanging the genes of parents among themselves until the crossover point is reached as described in Figure 9.2b and finally, the

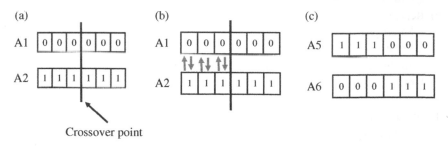

Figure 9.2 Example of genetic algorithm. (a) represents the crossover point, while (b) and (c) represents exchanging genes among parents and new offspring respectively.

new offspring are added to the population as shown in Figure 9.2c. The mutation step introduces random changes in the new generation of potential solutions. The mutation process is necessary to maintain diversity in the population and to prevent premature convergence. The mutation process can be represented mathematically as shown in Equation (9.3).

$$\text{Mutate}(\text{Chromosome}) = \text{Chromosome}_{new}, \tag{9.3}$$

where Mutate is the mutation operator that introduces random changes in the chromosome, and Chromosome$_{new}$ is the resulting chromosome after mutation. Finally, GA terminates when a stopping criterion is met. The stopping criterion is usually based on a maximum number of generations or a target fitness value. The maximum number of generations is the number of iterations that the genetic algorithm will run before terminating. The target fitness value is the minimum acceptable fitness value for the solution to be considered as acceptable. Where x_i is the ith individual in the population, f is the objective function being optimized, fitness$_i$ is the fitness of the ith individual, and the selection, crossover, mutation, and survivor selection operators are applied to create the offspring and select the next generation.

The termination condition is checked at the end of each generation. If the maximum number of generations is reached or the target fitness value is achieved, the GA terminates and returns the best individual found so far as the solution to the optimization problem. Otherwise, the GA continues to the next generation until the termination condition is met. If the stopping criterion is not met, there is a need to repeat the selection, crossover, and mutation steps until the algorithm converges to a satisfactory solution. Overall, the GA can be summarized in the following pseudocode (Algorithm 9.1):

Algorithm 9.1   Pseudocode for Genetic Algorithm

---

a) Initialize the population
b) Evaluate fitness of each individual
c) Repeat
   Select parents based on fitness
   Perform crossover and mutation
   Evaluate fitness of each individual in new population
d) Until stopping criterion met
e) Return the best solution found
f) Initialize the population
g) Evaluate fitness of each individual

h) Repeat
    Select parents based on fitness
    Perform crossover and mutation
    Evaluate fitness of each individual in new population
i) Until stopping criterion met
j) Return the best solution found
k) Initialize the population
l) Evaluate fitness of each individual
m) Repeat
    Select parents based on fitness
    Perform crossover and mutation
    Evaluate fitness of each individual in new population
n) Until stopping criterion met
o) Return the best solution found

The GA can offer several advantages and benefits in solving complex problems. It can lead to the development of highly adaptive and robust biomimetics systems. By mimicking the principles of natural selection, GA can help to evolve and adapt to changing environments, making them more resilient and capable of handling unpredictable situations. It also can be used to develop bio-inspired computing models that are more autonomous and require less human input. By incorporating feedback mechanisms and self-learning capabilities, biological inspired systems can become more self-sufficient, reducing the need for constant human supervision and intervention.

9.2 Ant Colony Optimization

Ant Colony Optimization (ACO) is a bio-characterized algorithm that is inspired by the foraging behavior of ants. It is used to solve optimization problems that involve finding the shortest path in a graph, such as the Traveling Salesman Problem (TSP).

In ACO, a set of artificial ants are used to explore the graph, and each ant builds a solution by selecting edges in a probabilistic manner. The probability of selecting an edge is determined by the amount of pheromone deposited on the edge by previous ants, as well as the distance between the two nodes connected by the edge. The pheromone trail represents the collective knowledge of the ants and is used to guide the search toward better solutions. The typical example of the algorithm is shown in Figure 9.3.

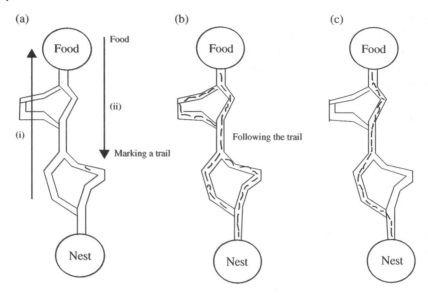

Figure 9.3 Example of the procedural steps from (a) to (b), and then to (c) of the ant colony optimization.

The ACO is an example of a biomimetical algorithm that falls under the broader umbrella of bio-characterized algorithms, which aims to develop bio-inspired intelligent systems that draw inspiration from the principles of bio-inspired computing and cybernetics, and ACO is a prime example of how the behavior of animals can be used to solve complex optimization problems. By mimicking the behavior of ants and their ability to find efficient paths, ACO can be used to solve a wide range of optimization problems, including those in logistics, transportation, and telecommunications and the algorithm consists of the following steps. A set of artificial ants are placed at a starting node. The pheromone trail on all edges is initialized to a small value. Each ant selects an edge to move to the next node based on a probabilistic rule. The probability of selecting an edge is given by:

$$
p_{ij}^k = \frac{\tau_{ij}^\alpha \, \eta_{ij}^\beta}{\sum_{l \in N_i^k} \tau_{ij}^\alpha \, \eta_{ij}^\beta},
\tag{9.4}
$$

where p_{ij}^k is the probability of selecting edge (i, j) for ant k. Here τ_{ij} is the amount of pheromone on edge (i, j), and the η_{ij} is the inverse of the distance between nodes i and j. The α and β are parameters that control the importance of pheromone and distance, respectively. The N_i^k is the set of neighboring nodes of node i that have not been visited by ant k. After an ant has selected an edge, it moves to the next node and repeats the process until it has visited all nodes. After all ants have completed their tours, the amount of pheromone on each edge is updated according to the Equation (9.5):

$$\tau_{ij} \leftarrow (1 - \rho)\tau_{ij} + \sum_{k=1}^{m} \Delta\tau_{ij}^k, \tag{9.5}$$

where ρ is the evaporation rate of the pheromone. By definition m is the number of ants.

$\Delta\tau_{ij}^k$ is the amount of pheromone deposited on edge edge (i, j) by ant k, which is given by:

$$\Delta\tau_{ij}^k = \begin{cases} \dfrac{Q}{L_k}, & \text{edge } (i,j) \text{ is used in ant } k's \text{ tour} \\ 0, & \text{otherwise} \end{cases}, \tag{9.6}$$

where Q is a constant that controls the amount of pheromone deposited. The L_k is the length of ant $k's$ tour. The algorithm terminates when a stopping criterion is met, such as reaching a maximum number of iterations or a satisfactory solution. One common stopping criterion in ACO is to terminate the algorithm after a maximum number of iterations, $T_{\max}$, has been reached. This can be expressed as:

$$t \geq T_{\max}, \tag{9.7}$$

where t is the current iteration of the algorithm. Another stopping criterion is to terminate the algorithm when a satisfactory solution has been found. This is often based on a threshold value, ϵ, that determines how close the current best solution is to the optimal solution. Specifically, the algorithm can terminate if the relative difference between the current best solution, f_{best}, and the optimal solution, f_{opt}, is less than or equal to ε. This can be expressed as Equation (9.8).

$$\frac{f_{opt} - f_{best}}{f_{opt}} \leq \varepsilon, \tag{9.8}$$

where f_{opt} is the optimal solution and f_{best} is the current best solution found by the algorithm. In practice, these stopping criteria can be combined or used individually depending on the specific problem and computational resources available. The choice of stopping criterion can have a significant impact on the performance of the algorithm, as it affects the balance between exploration and exploitation in the search process. For instance, see the pseudocode for applying the ACO algorithm. An artificial ant is made for finding the optimal solution. In the first step of solving a problem, each ant generates a solution. In the second step, paths found by different ants are compared, and in the third step, paths value or pheromone is updated (Algorithm 9.2).

Algorithm 9.2   Pseudocode for ACO Algorithm

---

a) Procedure ACO_MetaHeuristic
b) While not_termination do
    generateSolutions()
    daemonActions()
    PheromoneUpdate()
    Repeat
c) End procedure

Overall, ACO is an effective method for solving optimization problems that involve finding the shortest path in a graph. The algorithm is robust and can handle large and complex biomimetics problems. In the context of biologically characterized algorithms, ACO can be combined with other bio-inspired algorithms such as neural networks or swarm intelligence. For example, a biological system that uses ACO and neural networks might include the Equation (9.9).

$$y = f(w_1 x_1 + w_2 x_2 + \ldots + w_n x_n), \tag{9.9}$$

where y is the output of the neural network, x_i is the input, w_i is the weight associated with input x_i, and f is the activation function. These equations demonstrate how ACO can be combined with other bio-inspired algorithms within a biological-inspired system to create a more powerful optimization algorithm that is inspired by the principles of biology and cybernetics.

9.3   Bees Algorithm

The Bees Algorithm (BA) is a biologically characterized optimization technique that is based on the behavior of bees as they search for nectar. The BA is a swarm intelligence optimization algorithm that was inspired by the foraging behavior of honeybees. The algorithm has been applied to a wide range of optimization problems in engineering cybernetics.

The BA works by simulating the behavior of bees in a hive. In the algorithm, a population of bees is used to explore the search space and find the optimal solution to a given optimization problem. The population is divided into three groups of bees: employed bees, onlooker bees, and scout bees.

The employed bees represent the solutions that are currently being exploited, while the onlooker bees select a solution from the employed bees based on its fitness value. The scout bees are responsible for introducing new solutions into the

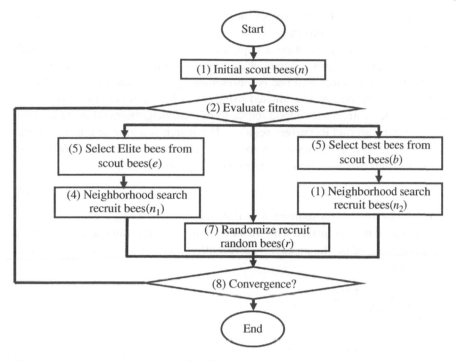

Figure 9.4 Flowchart of the bees algorithm.

population by randomly exploring the solution space. The complete flowchart of the algorithm is shown in Figure 9.4.

During each iteration of the BA, the employed bees and onlooker bees collaborate to generate new solutions, and the best solutions are updated in the population. The scout bees also randomly search the solution space, and if they find a better solution than the current solutions in the population, they replace the worst solution in the population. The aim of this algorithm is to develop bio-related computing systems that draw inspiration from the principles of biology and cybernetics. The BA is a prime example of how the behavior of animals can be used to solve complex optimization problems, and it can be used in a wide range of applications, including engineering, cybernetic intelligence and also in biomimetics to solve problems. One of the strengths of the BA is its ability to balance exploration and exploitation. The algorithm uses a combination of random search and exploitation of the best solutions found so far, which allows it to efficiently search the solution space and find high-quality solutions. Overall, the BA is a powerful biometric intelligence optimization algorithm that is inspired by the behavior of bees in a hive. By using a combination of local search and global search strategies, the

algorithm is able to efficiently search the solution space and find high-quality solutions to optimization problems.

The BA starts by generating a population of n employed bees, where each
employed bee represents a potential solution to the optimization problem. The
position of the ith employed bee is represented by the vector x_i, and the fitness
of the ith employed bee is evaluated using the objective function(s), $f(x_i)$. Each
employed bee searches for a food source in its local neighborhood by performing
a local search around its current position. The search is performed using a mutation operator that generates a new solution, v_i, based on the current position, x_i,
and a random perturbation r as described in Equation (9.10).

$$v_i = x_i + r. \tag{9.10}$$

The fitness of the new solution, $f(v_i)$, is then evaluated. If $f(v_i)$ is better than $f(x_i)$,
the employed bee is replaced with the new solution, v_i. The onlooker bees select a
food source based on the probability distribution function, p_i, which is calculated
as follows:

$$p_i = \frac{\text{fitness}_i}{\sum\limits_{j=1}^{n} \text{fitness}_j}, \tag{9.11}$$

where fitness$_i$ is the fitness of the ith employed bee, and n is the total number of
employed bees. The onlooker bee then performs a local search around the selected
food source using the mutation operator. The fitness of the new solution is evaluated, and if it is better than the current solution, the employed bee is replaced
with the new solution. The scout bees search for new food sources by randomly
generating new solutions, x_i, and evaluating their fitness, $f(x_i)$. If a new solution
is better than any of the current solutions, the employed bee is replaced with
the new solution.

The BA continues to iterate through the employed bee, onlooker bee, and scout
bee phases until a stopping criterion is met, such as a maximum number of iterations or a minimum improvement in the objective function(s). Overall, the BA is a
powerful bio-inspired computational intelligence algorithm that combines global
search and local search strategies to efficiently search the solution space and find
high-quality solutions to optimization problems.

9.4 Artificial Bee Colony Algorithm

The Artificial Bee Colony (ABC) algorithm is a bio-related computing algorithm
that mimics the foraging behavior of honeybees. It widely used in machine learning applications to solve complex biomimetics problems. The algorithm is based on

the principles of swarm intelligence, which is a collective behavior exhibited by groups of animals that emerge from the interactions between individual members of the group. The ABC algorithm takes advantage of the collective behavior of bees to efficiently search for the best solution in a large search space. The complete pseudocode for ABC is described below (Algorithm 9.3):

Algorithm 9.3   Pseudocode for ABC Algorithm

---

a) Initialize the colony of bees
b) Set the number of iterations
c) Set the number of trials
d) Set the limit of the number of trials for each food source
e) Set the abandonment limit for each food source

- For each iteration:
- For each employed bee:
  - Select a random food source
  - Generate a new solution using the neighborhood search
  - Evaluate the new solution
  - If the new solution is better than the old one:
    - Replace the old solution with the new one
  - Else:
    - Increment the number of trials for the food source
    - If the number of trials exceeds the limit:

- Abandon the food source
- Generate a new solution randomly
- Evaluate the new solution
- Assign the new solution to the abandoned food source
  - For each onlooker bee:
    - Select a food source based on its fitness
    - Generate a new solution using the neighborhood search
    - Evaluate the new solution
    - If the new solution is better than the old one:
  - Replace the old solution with the new one
- Select the best solution found so far as the global best

a) For each scout bee:
  - If the number of trials for a food source exceeds the abandonment limit:
  - Generate a new solution randomly
  - Evaluate the new solution
  - Assign the new solution to the abandoned food source

b) Return the global best solution

During each iteration of the algorithm, the employed bees and onlooker bees collaborate to generate new solutions, and the best solutions are updated in the population. The scout bees also randomly search the solution space, and if they find a better solution than the current solutions in the population, they replace the worst solution in the population. In the Figure 9.5, the flowchart to employed bees generates new solutions and onlooker bees observe employed bees and generate their own solutions. The algorithm keeps track of the best solution found so far and continues to search for a better solution until a convergence condition is met.

The ABC technique starts by generating a population of n employed bees, where each employed bee represents a potential solution to the optimization problem. The position of the ith employed bee is represented by the vector x_i, and the fitness of the ith employed bee is evaluated using the objective function(s). Each employed bee searches for a food source in its local neighborhood by performing a local search around its current position. The search is performed using a mutation

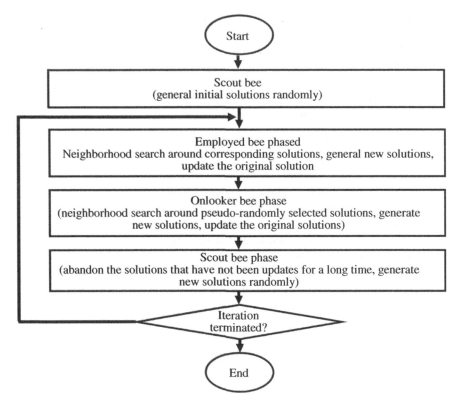

Figure 9.5 The flowchart for the artificial bee colony.

operator that generates a new solution v_i, based on the current position x_i, and a random perturbation r as shown in Equation (9.12).

$$v_i = x_i + r. \tag{9.12}$$

The fitness of the new solution $f(v_i)$, is then evaluated. If $f(v_i)$ is better than $f(x_i)$, the employed bee is replaced with the new solution v_i. The onlooker bees select a food source based on the probability distribution function p, which is calculated as shown in Equation (9.13).

$$p_i = \frac{\text{fitness}_i}{\sum\limits_{j=1}^{n} \text{fitness}_j}, \tag{9.13}$$

where fitness$_i$ is the fitness of the ith employed bee, and n is the total number of employed bees. The onlooker bee then performs a local search around the selected food source using a mutation operator, similar to the employed bees. The onlooker bee generates a new solution v_i, based on the selected food source x_i, and a random perturbation r. The ABC methodology continues to iterate through the employed bee, onlooker bee, and scout bee phases until a stopping criterion is met. This can be a maximum number of iterations, a minimum improvement in the objective function(s), or any other criterion specified by the user. Overall, the ABC method ology is a powerful bio-characterized machine intelligence algorithm that balances local search and global search strategies to efficiently search the solution space and find high-quality solutions to optimization problems.

9.5 Cuckoo Search

Cuckoo Search is an example of bio-related machine intelligence algorithm, which involves using insights from biological systems to develop computational algorithms that can solve complex problems. By mimicking the behavior of cuckoo birds, this algorithm provides a novel approach to optimization that is both efficient and effective. Other examples of bio-inspired computing intelligence include GAs, particle swarm optimization, and ACO, among others. The complete workflow of the algorithm is shown in Figure 9.6.

The algorithm starts by randomly generating a set of solutions, or nests, to represent potential solutions to the optimization problem. Each nest is represented by a vector x_i, where i is the index of the nest. After the initial solutions are generated, the fitness of each solution is evaluated using the objective function(s) of the optimization problem. The objective function(s) map each solution to a scalar value representing its fitness or quality. The goal of the optimization problem is typically

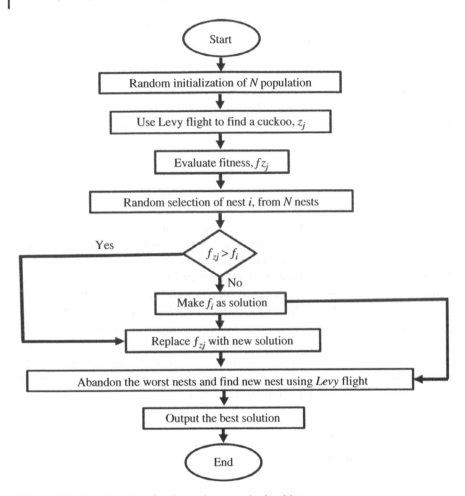

Figure 9.6 The flowchart for the cuckoo search algorithm.

to minimize or maximize the objective function(s), depending on the problem. The pseudocode of the algorithm is given below (Algorithm 9.4).

Algorithm 9.4   Pseudocode for the Cuckoo Search Algorithm

---

a) Initialize the population of cuckoos
b) Set the number of iterations
c) Set the fraction of nests to be replaced each iteration
d) Set the lower and upper bounds of the search space
e) Set the step size scaling factor

f) For each iteration:
- Evaluate the fitness of each cuckoo
- Sort the cuckoos based on their fitness
- Select the fraction of nests to be replaced
- For each new cuckoo:
  - Choose a random cuckoo from the population
  - Generate a new cuckoo solution by Lévy flight
  - Evaluate the fitness of the new cuckoo
  - If the new cuckoo's fitness is better than the old one:
  - Replace the old cuckoo with the new one
- Apply Levy flight to some of the existing cuckoos
- Replace some of the worst cuckoos with new ones
- Clip the cuckoo population to the lower and upper bounds of the search space

g) Return the best solution found so far

The initial population of solutions can be represented as a matrix X of size $n \times d$, where n is the number of solutions, and d is the dimensionality of each solution. Each row of the matrix X represents a solution vector x_i. The fitness of each solution can be evaluated using the objective function(s) $f(x_i)$, which takes the solution vector x_i as input and returns a scalar value representing its fitness. Therefore, the fitness of the initial population can be represented as a vector F of size $n \times 1$, where each element i corresponds to the fitness of the ith solution as described in Equation (9.14).

$$F = (f(x_1), f(x_2), ..., f(x_n))^T. \tag{9.14}$$

The goal of the optimization problem is typically to minimize or maximize the fitness function(s) F. In the case of minimization, the algorithm seeks to find a solution vector x_i such that:

$$\text{minimize } F = f(x_i), \tag{9.15}$$

in the case of maximization, the algorithm seeks to find a solution vector x_i such that:

$$\text{maximize } F = f(x_i), \tag{9.16}$$

the new solution v_i is generated based on the current solution, x_i, and a random perturbation, u, using the following equation:

$$v_i = x_i + \alpha L(u)(x_i - x_j), \tag{9.17}$$

where α is a step size factor, $L(u)$ is the Lévy distribution function, and x_j is a randomly selected solution from the population. The Lévy distribution function is a probability distribution used in stochastic processes and mathematical finance as shown in Equation (9.18).

$$L(u) = \frac{e^{-u}}{\sqrt{2\pi u}} \int_0^\infty e^{-\frac{l^2}{2u}} dt, \tag{9.18}$$

where Γ is the gamma function, β is a parameter that controls the shape of the distribution, and $|u|$ is the Euclidean norm of the perturbation vector u. The gamma function is defined as shown in Equation (9.19).

$$\Gamma(x) = \int_0^\infty [0, \infty] t^{(x-1)} e^{-t} dt, \tag{9.19}$$

the Lévy distribution function is used to generate a random perturbation vector u of length d, where d is the dimensionality of the solution vectors:

$$u = [u_1, u_2, ..., u_d]. \tag{9.20}$$

Each element of the perturbation vector u_i is generated independently from the others, according to the Lévy distribution function. The new solution vector v_i is then generated using the following equation:

$$v_i = x_i + \alpha L(u)(x_i - x_j), \tag{9.21}$$

where α is a step size factor, $L(u)$ is the Lévy distribution function evaluated at the perturbation vector u, and x_j is a randomly selected solution vector from the population.

The Lévy distribution function introduces a degree of randomness into the search process, which allows the algorithm to explore different regions of the search space. The step size factor controls the magnitude of the change between x_i and v_i and can be adjusted during the course of the optimization to balance exploration and exploitation. The selection of a random solution vector x_j promotes diversity in the search process and helps to prevent the algorithm from becoming trapped in local optima. Once a new solution, v_i, is generated, it is compared with the solutions in the population. If the fitness of v_i is better than the fitness of the ith solution in the population, the cuckoo bird replaces the host egg (solution) with its own egg (new solution).

The following procedures present the operational principles of the algorithm. Generate New Solution: A new solution vector v_i is generated using the Lévy Flight step, as described previously. Evaluate Fitness: The fitness of the new solution v_i is evaluated by applying the objective function to v_i. The objective function is a mathematical function that defines the problem being optimized. Replace Host Egg: The fitness of the new solution v_i is compared with the fitness of the solution in the population that is being replaced, which is typically the worst solution. If the fitness of v_i is better than the fitness of the solution being replaced, then the cuckoo bird replaces the host egg (solution) with its own egg (new solution) by updating the solution vector and its fitness value. For instance, f_i be the fitness of the ith solution in the population, and let f_{vi} be the fitness of the new solution v_i. If f_{v_i} is better than f_i, then the cuckoo bird replaces the ith solution with its own egg (new solution) v_i as shown in Equation (9.22).

$$\text{if } f_{v_i} > f_i \Rightarrow x_i = v_i$$
$$f(x_i) = f(v_i),$$

(9.22)

where x_i is the solution vector of the ith solution, and f_i is its fitness value. The replacement process ensures that the population always contains the best solutions found so far in the search process. The Egg Laying step ensures that the population of solutions is constantly being updated with new, potentially better solutions. By comparing the fitness of the new solution with the fitness of the worst solution in the population, the algorithm ensures that only solutions that improve the overall quality of the population are retained. This helps to prevent the algorithm from getting stuck in local optima and promotes convergence toward the global optimum.

9.6 Particle Swarm Optimization

Particle Swarm Optimization (PSO) is a popular bio-inspired optimization algorithm that is based on the collective behavior of swarms of birds. This bio-characterized algorithm aims to develop bio-related intelligent systems that draw inspiration from the principles of biology and cybernetics. By using the principles of PSO within a biomimetics system, researchers can develop more efficient and effective optimization algorithms that are inspired by the behavior of birds and other animals. Therefore, the integration of the PSO algorithm into a biologically characterized system can lead to the development of novel optimization techniques that can help address complex problems in different domains.

The PSO algorithm starts by initializing a population of particles, each of which represents a potential solution to the optimization problem. The particles move through the search space, adjusting their position based on their current velocity and their distance from the best-known solution. The velocity of each particle is determined by the particle's previous velocity, the distance to the particle's personal best solution, and the distance to the global best solution found so far by any particle in the population. At each iteration of the algorithm, the particles evaluate their fitness based on the objective function of the optimization problem. The personal best solution and the global best solution are updated based on the fitness of the particles. The personal best solution is the best solution found by each particle so far, while the global best solution is the best solution found by any particle in the population.

The PSO algorithm uses a stochastic search strategy that allows it to effectively explore the solution space and converge to the global optimum solution. The algorithm is also able to balance exploration and exploitation, which helps to avoid getting stuck in local optima. One of the strengths of the PSO algorithm is its simplicity and ease of implementation. The algorithm has relatively few parameters, which makes it easy to use and adapt to different optimization problems. Another strength of the PSO algorithm is its ability to handle nonlinear, non-convex, and multimodal optimization problems. However, like all optimization algorithms, the PSO algorithm has its limitations. It can sometimes suffer from premature convergence or slow convergence, particularly when the search space is large or the objective function is noisy. The complete flowchart for the working of the algorithm is shown in Figure 9.7.

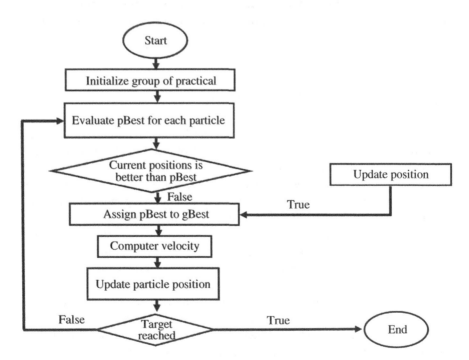

Figure 9.7 Flowchart for the particle swarm optimization.

Here are the main steps of the PSO method. The algorithm starts by randomly initializing a population of particles, where each particle is represented by a vector of positions and velocities in the search space. The positions represent the candidate solutions, and the velocities represent the direction and magnitude of the movement of the particle. The fitness value of each particle is evaluated by applying the objective function to its position vector. Each particle updates its personal best position, which is the position that has the best fitness value among all the positions it has visited so far. The particle with the best fitness value among all the personal best positions in the population is selected as the global best position. Each particle updates its velocity based on its current velocity, its personal best position, and the global best position. The new velocity is calculated using the following Equation (9.23).

$$v_i^{t+1} = \omega V_i^t + c_1 r_1 \left(P_i^t - X_i^t\right) + c_2 r_2 \left(P_g^t - X_i^t\right),$$ (9.23)

where $v_i^{t+1} = \omega V_i^t$ is the velocity of particle i at time t, X_i^t is the position of particle i at time t, P_i^t is the personal best position of particle i up to time t, P_g^t is the global best position of the swarm up to time t, ω is the inertia weight, c_1 and c_2 are the acceleration coefficients, and r_1 and r_2 are random numbers uniformly distributed in the range [0, 1]. Each particle updates its position using the new velocity vector calculated in step 5. The new position is calculated using the Equation (9.24).

$$x_i(t+1) = x_i(t) + v_i(t+1),$$ (9.24)

where $x_i(t)$ is the current position of the particle at time t. The algorithm terminates when a stopping criterion is met, such as reaching a maximum number of iterations, or when the fitness value of the global best position meets a predefined threshold. The inertia weight, w, is a parameter that controls the balance between the global and local search capabilities of the PSO algorithm. It determines how much the particle maintains its current velocity. The inertia weight is usually initialized to a high value and decreased over time to balance the exploration and exploitation abilities of the algorithm. The updated value of the inertia weight, $w(t)$, can be computed as shown in Equation (9.25).

$$w(t) = w_{\max} - (w_{\max} - w_{mix}) \frac{t}{T},$$ (9.25)

where $w_{\max}$ and $w_{\min}$ are the maximum and minimum values of the inertia weight, t is the current iteration, and T is the maximum number of iterations.

The acceleration constants, c_1 and c_2, are parameters that control the influence of the personal and global best positions on the velocity update equation. They determine how much the particle is attracted to its own best solution and the best solution found by the swarm, respectively. The values of c_1 and c_2 are usually set to be equal and within the range of $[0, 2]$. The PSO algorithm starts by randomly initializing a population of particles in the search space. Each particle represents a candidate solution to the optimization problem and is defined by its position and velocity vectors. The position vector x_i of each particle represents a potential solution to the problem and is initialized randomly within the search space. The velocity vector v_i of each particle represents the direction and magnitude of the particle's movement in the search space. It is also initialized randomly within a specified range.

9.7 Bacterial Foraging Optimization

Bacterial foraging optimization (BFO) is a bio-related algorithm that is modeled after the foraging behavior of bacteria. The algorithm simulates the process by which bacteria search for food sources in their environment, and use chemical signaling to communicate with each other to coordinate their movements. BFO has been applied to a variety of optimization problems, including parameter optimization, function optimization, and feature selection. The complete workflow of the algorithm is shown in Figure 9.8.

In BFO, movement refers to the displacement of bacteria in the search space. Bacteria move by changing their position through a process called chemotaxis,

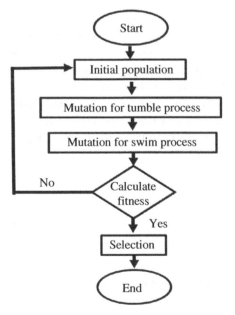

Figure 9.8 Flowchart for the bacterial foraging optimization.

which is influenced by attractant and repellent signals in their environment. The movement of bacteria is modeled using a movement equation as shown in Equation (9.26), which updates the position of each bacteria based on its current position and its swimming speed.

$$x_i(t + 1) = x_i(t) + \eta |(t) \times rand(\,), \tag{9.26}$$

where $x_i(t)$ is the position of the ith bacteria at time t, $x_i(t + 1)$ is its new position at time $t+1$, η is the step size or swimming speed of the bacteria, $|(t)$ is the tumble probability or the probability of the bacteria changing its direction at time t, and $rand(\,)$ is a random number between -1 and 1.

The swimming speed of bacteria is also updated using a chemotaxis equation as shown in Equation (9.27), which takes into account the attractant and repellent signals at their current position. By adjusting their swimming speed and direction, bacteria can explore the search space and search for food sources more efficiently. The movement of bacteria in BFO is inspired by the behavior of bacteria in nature, where they move toward areas with high concentrations of nutrients and avoid areas with high concentrations of toxins.

$$w_i(t + 1) = w_i(t) + c_1(Attract_i - Repel_i) - c_2\,w_i(t), \tag{9.27}$$

where $w_i(t)$ is the swimming speed of bacteria i at time t, $Attract_i$ and $Repel_i$ are the attractant and repellent signals at the current position of bacteria i, respectively, and c_1 and c_2 are the scaling coefficients. The update equation for the attractant and repellent signals is described in Equation (9.28).

$$A(x_i(t)) = A(x_i(t)) + P_i(t) - D_i(t),$$
$$R(x_i(t)) = R(x_i(t)) + P_i(t). \tag{9.28}$$

9.8 Gray Wolf Optimizer

Gray Wolf Optimizer (GWO) is a metaheuristic optimization algorithm inspired by the social hierarchy and hunting behavior of gray wolves in the wild and the complete workflow of the algorithm is shown in Figure 9.9, where ct represents in correct number of iterations.

In GWO, the positions of the α, β, and δ wolves are updated iteratively to find the optimal solution of an optimization problem as shown in Equations (9.29), (9.30) and (9.31) respectively.

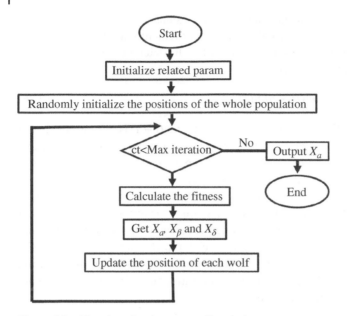

Figure 9.9 Flowchart for the gray wolf optimizer.

$$\vec{D}_a = \left| \vec{C}_a . \vec{X}_a - X_a \right|$$
$$\vec{X}_a = \vec{X}_a - \vec{A}_1 \vec{D}_a$$
(9.29)

$$\vec{D}_\beta = \left| \vec{C}_\beta \vec{X}_\beta - X_\beta \right|$$
$$\vec{X}_\beta = \vec{X}_\beta - \vec{A}_2 \vec{D}_\beta$$
(9.30)

$$\vec{D}_\delta = \left| \vec{C}_\delta \vec{X}_\delta - X_\delta \right|$$
$$\vec{X}_\delta = \vec{X}_\delta - \vec{A}_3 \vec{D}_\delta,$$
(9.31)

where $\vec{X}$ is the position vector of the current search agent, $\vec{X}_a, \vec{X}_\beta$, and $\vec{X}_\delta$ are the position vectors of the α, β, and δ wolves, respectively. The $\vec{C}_a, \vec{C}_\beta$, and $\vec{C}_\delta$ are the position vectors of the prey for the α, β, and δ wolves, respectively. The $\vec{A}_1, \vec{A}_2$, and $\vec{A}_3$ are the updated coefficients. The step size is updated using the Equation (9.32).

$$\vec{\alpha} = 2 \cdot \frac{\vec{A}}{\|\vec{C}\|} \left(1 - \frac{t}{T_{max}}\right) - \vec{A},$$
(9.32)

where $\vec{A}$ is the initial step size, $\vec{C}$ is the average distance between the search agents, t is the current iteration, and T_{max} is the maximum number of iterations. In GWO, the fitness function of the optimization problem is used to evaluate the quality of the solutions. The algorithm starts with an initial population of search agents and iteratively updates their positions using the Equation (9.32) until the stopping criterion is met.

9.9 Firefly Algorithm

The Firefly Algorithm (FA) is a metaheuristic algorithm inspired by the flashing behavior of fireflies. In FA, each firefly is attracted to other fireflies with higher brightness, leading to the formation of clusters of fireflies around the global optimum. The complete workflow of the algorithm is shown in Figure 9.10.

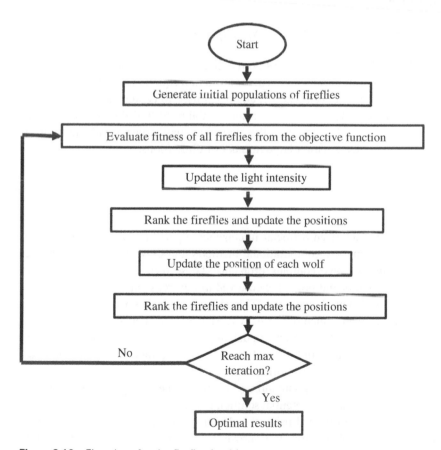

Figure 9.10 Flowchart for the firefly algorithm.

The algorithm starts by initializing the population of fireflies with random solutions. Objective function is used to evaluate the fitness of each firefly. Fireflies are attracted to each other based on their relative brightness. The brightness of each firefly is proportional to its fitness value. The attraction between fireflies is described by the Equation (9.33).

$$F_{ij} = \beta_0 e^{-\gamma r_{ij}^2} \left(X_j - X_i \right), \tag{9.33}$$

where F_{ij} is the attractiveness of firefly i to firefly j, β_0 is the initial attractiveness, γ is the light absorption coefficient, r_{ij} is the Euclidean distance between fireflies i and j, and X_j and X_i are the positions of fireflies j and i, respectively. The movement of each firefly is determined by the attractiveness of the other fireflies in the population. The firefly moves toward the brightest firefly in its vicinity, while also incorporating some random movement. The movement of firefly i is described by Equation (9.34).

$$X_i(t + 1) = X_i(t) + \beta_0 e^{-\gamma r_{ij}^2} \left(X_j - X_i \right) + \alpha(\varepsilon - 0.5), \tag{9.34}$$

where $X_i(t)$ and $X_i(t + 1)$ are the positions of firefly i at time t and $t+1$, respectively, β_0 and γ are the same parameters as in the attraction equation, α is the step size, ε is a random number between 0 and 1, and 0.5 is used to center the random movement around zero. The FA is known for its ability to find the global optimum quickly and efficiently. However, the algorithm may struggle with multimodal problems or problems with a large number of dimensions.

Summary

Biologically characterized artificial intelligence algorithms, also known as bio-inspired algorithms, are computational methods that draw inspiration from biological systems to solve complex problems. These techniques are designed to mimic the behaviors and processes observed in nature, such as evolution, swarm intelligence, and neural networks. This chapter describes various bio-inspired optimization concepts, including BA, ABC Algorithm, Cuckoo Search, and PSO. In addition, the initialization and update equations for the population, as well as the objective function and fitness function, are examined as the mathematical underpinnings of these frameworks.

For example, in BA, a population of employed bees is generated and each employed bee represents a potential solution to the optimization problem. The fitness of each bee is evaluated using the objective function, and the bees perform local search and global search to improve their solutions. In PSO, a population of particles is initialized with random positions and velocities, and each particle represents a potential solution. The velocity of each particle is updated based on its personal best position and the global best position, and the position of each particle is updated based on its velocity. The importance of stopping criteria in these optimization algorithms also discussed. Both ABC Algorithm and PSO are powerful optimization techniques, but they have some limitations. One common limitation of both algorithms is that they may converge to local optima when dealing with problems that have multiple local optima. Additionally, PSO may suffer from premature convergence, while ABC Algorithm requires a large number of function evaluations to converge. Future research for both algorithms focuses on developing hybrid algorithms that combine them with other optimization techniques to overcome their limitations, improving their scalability, and making them more robust to noisy and dynamic environments by incorporating adaptive mechanisms. They have been shown to be effective and efficient in many applications and have inspired the development of new algorithms and computational models. BFO and GWO are two popular biological-inspired optimization algorithms used to solve complex optimization problems. Additionally, combining BFO and GWO with biologically characterized algorithms can lead to the development of hybrid optimization techniques that leverage the strengths of each algorithm for more effective optimization. As future perspective, the bio-inspired algorithms are expected to play an increasingly important role in developing advanced cybernetical technologies, such as autonomous systems, smart cities, and personalized medicine. The future perspective of bio-inspired algorithms is therefore highly promising and holds great potential for solving some of the most pressing challenges of our time.

Exercise Questions

Q.9.1   How does the Artificial Bee Colony Algorithm handle constraints in optimization problems?

Q.9.2   Describe the main idea behind the Particle Swarm Optimization algorithm.

Q.9.3   Explain how does the topology of the Particle Swarm Optimization affect its performance.

Q.9.4   What is the role of the inertia weight parameter in Particle Swarm Optimization?

Q.9.5 Describe the difference between a global best position and a personal best position in Particle Swarm Optimization.

Q.9.6 How can the convergence speed of the Artificial Bee Colony Algorithm be improved?

Q.9.7 Explain the difference between the Bees Algorithm and the Artificial Bee Colony Algorithm.

Q.9.8 What is the Lévy flight in the Cuckoo Search algorithm?

Q.9.9 Which challenges do Artificial Bee Colony Algorithm and Particle Swarm Optimization face when dealing with multi-objective optimization problems?

Q.9.10 How can Particle Swarm Optimization be modified to handle dynamic environments?

Q.9.11 Which factors should be considered when selecting a suitable optimization algorithm for a specific problem?

Q.9.12 Illustrate the main components of the BFO algorithm.

Q.9.13 How does the Gray Wolf Optimizer algorithm handle constraints in optimization problems?

Further Reading

Aydin E, Purlu M, Turkay BE. Economic dispatch of multi-microgrid systems by using particle swarm optimization. In 2021 13th International Conference on Electrical and Electronics Engineering (ELECO) 2021 Nov 25 (pp. 268–272).

Edin BB, Beccai L, Ascari L, Roccella S, Cabibihan JJ, Carrozza MC. Bio-inspired approach for the design and characterization of a tactile sensory system for a cybernetic prosthetic hand. In Proceedings 2006 IEEE International Conference on Robotics and Automation, 2006. ICRA 2006 May 15 (pp. 1354–1358).

Holland JH. *Adaptation in natural and artificial systems: an introductory analysis with applications to biology, control, and artificial intelligence.* MIT press; 1992 Apr 29.

Ruiz-Cruz R, Sanchez EN, Ornelas-Tellez F, Loukianov AG, Harley RG. Particle swarm optimization for discrete-time inverse optimal control of a doubly fed induction generator. *IEEE Transactions on Cybernetics.* 2012 Dec 13;43(6):1698–709.

10

Life-Inspired Machine Intelligence and Cybernetics

Bio-inspired and life-inspired machine intelligence demonstrate a major breakthrough in artificial intelligence and in the history of computing and technological development. Both terminologies seem to be similar, but in fact, differ in their ultimate objectives and functionality to serve mankind. Bio-inspired machine intelligence involves the study of biological processes, systems, and structures to create algorithms and optimization models that can be applied to machine learning. For example, scientists may study the way neurons in the brain work to develop artificial neural networks for deep learning, which uses insights from biology to create efficient and effective algorithms for solving complex problems. In contrast, life-inspired machine intelligence is focused on simulating living organisms and biological phenomena using computer technology. This approach aims to create digital models of biological systems that can be used to study their behavior and predict how they will react to different stimuli. For example, scientists may use computer simulations to study the behavior of complex microbial communities or to model the behavior of individual cells and tissues. In essence, there is some form of machine intelligence inherent. Overall, life-inspired artificial intelligence is an exciting and rapidly growing field that has the potential to transform the way one live and work. By harnessing the power of natural intelligence and applying it to automated cellular machines, one can create more efficient, adaptive, and intelligent systems than ever before.

10.1 Multi-Agent AI Systems

Multi-agent AI systems are computational systems composed of multiple intelligent agents that interact with each other and with the environment to achieve a common goal as shown in Figure 10.1. These systems have a broad range of

Cybernetical Intelligence: Engineering Cybernetics with Machine Intelligence, First Edition.
Kelvin K. L. Wong.
© 2024 The Institute of Electrical and Electronics Engineers, Inc.
Published 2024 by John Wiley & Sons, Inc.
Companion website: www.wiley.com/go/cyberintel

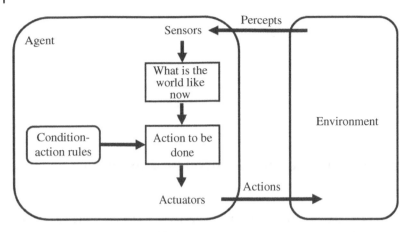

Figure 10.1 Workflow of multi-agent system.

applications, such as in robotics, economics, and social networks. In this context, multi-agent systems are modeled using mathematical frameworks that capture agent interactions.

Mathematically, a multi-agent AI system can be represented as a tuple $M = <A, S, T, R>$ where A is the set of agents, S is the set of states, T is the transition function, and R is the reward function. Each agent $a_i \in A$ has its own set of actions A_i, state space S_i, and policy π_i. The state space S is the set of possible configurations of the environment that the agents perceive. The transition function $T : S \times A \rightarrow S$ determines how the environment changes in response to the actions of the agents. The reward function $R : S \times A \rightarrow R$ is a function that associates a reward or penalty with each state-action pair. The goal of each agent is to maximize its expected cumulative reward over time.

The behavior of the multi-agent AI system can be studied by simulating the interactions between the agents over time. This can be represented mathematically as a sequence of states $s_1, s_2, ..., s_T$, where T represents the number of time steps. At each time step, each agent i observes the current state s_t, selects an action $a_i(t)$ from its action space A_i based on its policy $\pi_i(s_t)$, and receives a reward or payoff $u_i(s_t, a_1(t), a_2(t), ..., a_n(t))$ based on the joint action of all agents. The interactions between agents can be modeled using game-theoretic approaches, such as the prisoner's dilemma or the Nash equilibrium. In these models, each agent's utility or payoff is determined by the actions of all agents, and the goal of each agent is to maximize its own utility given the actions of the other agents.

A popular approach for modeling multi-agent AI systems is reinforcement learning, which is a machine learning technique that allows agents to learn from their interactions with the environment. In reinforcement learning, agents learn to select actions that maximize their expected cumulative reward over time. This is achieved through an iterative process of trial and error, where the agents adjust their policies based on the feedback they receive from the environment. Multi-agent AI systems and cybernetics are closely related fields that have emerged from the study of complex systems. Cybernetics provides a theoretical framework for understanding how these multi-agent systems can operate and adapt in a complex environment. The principles of feedback and control, which are central to cybernetics, can be applied to designing and implementing multi-agent systems. By incorporating feedback loops and control mechanisms into the system, the agents can adjust their behavior and coordination in response to changes in the environment and the behavior of other agents.

10.1.1 Game Theory

Game theory is a mathematical framework used to analyze the strategic behavior of decision-makers, or "players," in situations where their choices are interdependent. The primary assumption in game theory is that players are rational, meaning that they act in their own self-interest, attempting to maximize their expected utility.

A game in game theory consists of four elements: the set of players, the set of possible strategies for each player, the payoff function that maps each combination of strategies to the payoff for each player, and the information available to each player. To illustrate, consider a simple game between two players, player 1 and player 2, where each player can choose to cooperate (C) or defect (D). The payoff for each player depends on the combination of strategies played by both players and can be represented in a payoff matrix. Game theory provides several tools and concepts to analyze games, including Nash equilibrium as shown in Equation (10.1), dominance, and iterated games. Nash equilibrium is a set of strategies, one for each player, where no player can improve their payoff by unilaterally changing their strategy.

$$(A^*, B^*) \text{ such that } \forall A, B, u_1(A^*, B) \geq u_1(A, B^*) \text{ and } u_2(A^*, B) \geq u_2(A, B^*).$$
$$(10.1)$$

Dominance is a situation where one strategy is always better than another, regardless of the other player's choice. Iterated games allow for repeated rounds of play and can lead to the development of more complex strategies such as tit-for-tat, which involves cooperating initially and then mimicking the other player's previous choice. Dominant strategy is a strategy that is always better than any other strategy, regardless of the other player's strategy. Mathematically, a dominant strategy can be represented as Equation (10.2).

$$A \text{ is a dominant strategy if } \forall B, U_1(A, B) \geq u_1(B', B) \forall B'! = A$$
$$B \text{ is a dominant strategy if } \forall A, U_2(A, B) \geq u_2(A, B') \forall B'! = B. \tag{10.2}$$

Game theory has numerous applications in various fields such as economics, political science, psychology, biology, and computer science. It can help to understand social interactions, predict behavior, and develop optimal strategies in complex situations. Overall, game theory is a powerful tool that provides a structured and quantitative approach to analyzing strategic decision-making. In addition to game theory, multi-agent systems can be modeled using other mathematical frameworks such as reinforcement learning and swarm intelligence. These frameworks provide alternative approaches to modeling the interaction between agents and can be used to design multi-agent systems for specific applications. Game theory and cybernetics are closely linked disciplines that share several commonalities. Game theory provides a framework for analyzing strategic decision-making in multi-agent systems, which is a central problem in cybernetics. By using game-theoretic models, cyberneticists can design control systems that optimize the behavior of multiple agents in complex environments. Conversely, cybernetics provides a framework for understanding the dynamics of feedback systems, which is used to inform the development of game-theoretic models. Together, game theory and cybernetics offer powerful tools for analyzing and controlling complex systems in a variety of domains, from economics and politics to engineering and biology.

10.1.2 Distributed Multi-Agent Systems

Distributed multi-agent systems are a type of multi-agent AI system in which the agents are distributed across a network or a physical space and interact with each other in a decentralized manner. These systems have many applications, such as in robotics, sensor networks, and distributed computing. A distributed multi-agent system can be represented mathematically as a tuple $M = <A, S, T, R>$, where A is the set of agents, S is the set of states, T is the transition function, and R is the reward function. Each agent $a_i \in A$ has its own set of actions A_i, state space S_i, and policy π_i. At each time step t, each agent i observes the current state $s_i(t)$, selects an action $a_i(t)$ from its action space A_i based on its policy $\pi_i(s_i(t))$, and receives a reward or payoff $u_i(s_1(t), a_1(t), a_2(t), ..., a_n(t))$ based on the joint action of all agents. The transition function $T: S \times A \rightarrow S$ determines how the environment changes in response to the actions of the agents as shown in Equation (10.3).

$$T(s_1(t + 1), s_2(t + 1), ..., s_n(t + 1) | s_1(t), s_2(t), ..., s_n(t), a_1(t), a_2(t), ..., a_n(t)), \tag{10.3}$$

where $s_1(t + 1)$ represents the next state of agent i, given the current state $s_1(t)$ and the joint action $a_1(t)$, $a_2(t)$, ..., $a_n(t)$ of all agents.

The reward function $R{:}S \times A \to R$ is a function that associates a reward or penalty with each state-action pair. In a distributed multi-agent system, the reward function may depend on the joint actions of the agents as shown in Equation (10.4).

$$R(s_1(t), a_1(t), a_2(t), ..., a_n(t)), \tag{10.4}$$

which gives the reward or penalty for the joint action of all agents at time t. The behavior of the distributed multi-agent system can be studied by simulating the interactions between the agents over time. This can be represented mathematically as a sequence of states $s_1(0)$, $s_2(0)$, ..., $s_n(0)$, $s_1(1)$, $s_2(1)$, ..., $s_n(1)$, ..., $s_1(T)$, $s_2(T)$, ..., $s_n(T)$.

The interactions between agents in a distributed multi-agent system can be modeled using various approaches, such as message passing, gossip protocols, and swarm intelligence. In message passing, each agent communicates with a subset of other agents to exchange information and coordinate their actions. In gossip protocols, agents randomly select other agents to exchange information with, which can help spread information quickly and efficiently. In swarm intelligence, agents interact with each other using simple rules to achieve complex collective behavior, such as flocking, foraging, or pattern formation.

Distributed multi-agent systems can be analyzed using various mathematical tools, such as graph theory, game theory, and control theory. Graph theory can be used to model the network topology of the agents and study the connectivity and communication patterns of the system. Game theory can be used to model the strategic interactions between the agents and study the equilibria of the system. Control theory can be used to design controllers for the agents that achieve certain performance objectives, such as stability, robustness, or optimality.

10.1.3 Multi-Agent Reinforcement Learning

Multi-agent reinforcement learning (MARL) is a subfield of life-inspired machine learning that focuses on learning policies for multiple agents that interact with each other and with a shared environment. MARL can be represented mathematically as a Markov game, which is an extension of the Markov decision process (MDP) to multiple agents. In MARL, the agents interact with each other and with the environment and receive a joint reward signal that depends on the joint action they take. The goal is to learn a policy for each agent that maximizes its expected cumulative reward over time. In a MARL system, agents learn to cooperate or compete with each other to maximize a shared or individual reward signal, while also adapting to changes in the environment and the behavior of other agents.

This mirrors the cybernetic concept of feedback and control, where agents continually adjust their actions based on the feedback received from the environment and other agents. MARL has many practical applications in areas such as robotics, game AI, and transportation systems, where decentralized decision-making is critical to achieving efficient and robust performance.

For instance, a simple case of two agents, i and j, that interact with each other and with the environment. The state of the environment at time t is denoted by s (t), and the actions of the agents are denoted by $a_i(t)$ and $a_j(t)$, respectively. The joint action of the agents is denoted by $a(t) = (a_i(t), a_j(t))$, and the joint state-action pair is denoted by $(s(t), a(t))$. The transition function $T(s(t+1)|s(t), a(t))$ specifies the probability of transitioning from state $s(t)$ to state $s(t+1)$ when the joint action $a(t)$ is taken. This can be modeled as a probability distribution over the next state $s(t+1)$ given the current state $s(t)$ and joint action $a(t)$. The reward function $R(s(t), a(t))$ specifies the joint reward that the agents receive for taking the joint action $a(t)$ in state $s(t)$. This can be a function of the current state and action or a function of the current state and the resulting next state. The value function $V_i(s(t))$ represents the expected cumulative reward that agent i can achieve starting from state $s(t)$ and following its policy π_i. This can be defined mathematically as:

$$V_i(s(t)) = E\left[\sum_{k=0}^{\infty} \gamma^k r_i(t + k + 1)|s(t), \pi_i\right], \tag{10.5}$$

where γ is the discount factor, $r_i(t + k + 1)$ is the reward that agent i receives at time $t + k + 1$, and the expectation is taken over the possible future trajectories of the environment and the policies of the agents. The action-value function $Q_i(s(t), a_i(t))$ represents the expected cumulative reward that agent i can achieve starting from state $s(t)$, taking action $a_i(t)$, and following its policy π_i. This can be defined mathematically as:

$$Q_i(s(t), a_i(t)) = E\left[\sum_{k=0}^{\infty} \gamma^k r_i(t + k + 1)|s(t), a_i(t), \pi_i\right], \tag{10.6}$$

where $r_i(t + k + 1)$ is the reward that agent i receives at time $t + k + 1$, and the expectation is taken over the possible future trajectories of the environment and the policies of the agents. The optimal value function $V^{s(t)}$ represents the maximum expected cumulative reward that can be achieved from state $s(t)$ by following the optimal policies of all agents. Similarly, the optimal action-value function $Q^{s(t),a_i(t)}$ represents the maximum expected cumulative reward that can be achieved by taking action $a_i(t)$ in state $s(t)$ and following the optimal policies of all agents.

The optimal value function $V^{s(t)}$ and optimal action-value function $Q^{s(t),a_i(t)}$ can be obtained by solving the Bellman optimality equations as shown in Equations (10.7) and (10.8).

$$V_\pi(s) = \mathbb{E}_\pi[G_t | s = s_t] = \mathbb{E}_\pi\left[\sum_{j=0}^{T} \gamma^j r_{t+j+1} | s = s_t\right] \qquad (10.7)$$

$$V_\pi(s,a) = \mathbb{E}_\pi[G_t | S_t = s, A_t = a] = \mathbb{E}_\pi\left[\sum_{j=0}^{N} \gamma^j r_{t+j+1} | S_t = s, A_t = a\right].$$

$$(10.8)$$

Another approach to MARL is to use communication and coordination between the agents to improve their performance. This can be achieved by adding a communication channel between the agents, or by using a centralized critic that observes the joint state and action space and provides feedback to the agents. In summary, MARL is a subfield of machine learning that focuses on learning policies for multiple agents that interact with each other and with a shared environment. It can be formulated mathematically as a Markov game and can be addressed using various approaches such as Q-learning, actor-critic methods, and policy gradient methods.

10.1.4 Evolutionary Computation and Multi-Agent Systems

Evolutionary computation (EC) is a subfield of bio-inspired machine intelligence that is based on the principle of natural selection. It is a powerful optimization technique that can be used to solve complex problems that are difficult to solve using traditional optimization methods. EC is often used in conjunction with multi-agent systems (MAS) to solve complex problems that require the collaboration of multiple agents. In this context, EC can be used to evolve the behavior of individual agents, while MAS can be used to coordinate the behavior of multiple agents toward a common goal. One of the most popular EC algorithms is the genetic algorithm (GA), which is inspired by the process of natural selection. In GA, a population of candidate solutions is evolved over a number of generations. Each candidate solution is represented as a chromosome, which is a string of bits that encode the solution. The fitness of each chromosome is evaluated based on how well it solves the problem at hand. The fittest chromosomes are then selected for reproduction, while the less fit chromosomes are discarded. The process of selection, crossover, and mutation is repeated over multiple generations, with the hope that the population will evolve toward a better solution.

In the context of MAS, EC can be used to evolve the behavior of individual agents toward a common goal. Each agent is represented as a chromosome, and its behavior is encoded in the chromosome. The fitness of each agent is evaluated based on how well it contributes toward the common goal. The fittest agents are then selected for reproduction, while the less fit agents are discarded. The process of selection, crossover, and mutation is repeated over multiple generations, with the hope that the population of agents will evolve toward a better solution.

GA:

- Initialization: Generate an initial population of N chromosomes
- Evaluation: Evaluate the fitness of each chromosome in the population
- Selection: Select the fittest chromosomes for reproduction
- Crossover: Perform crossover between pairs of selected chromosomes to create offspring
- Mutation: Mutate the offspring to introduce new genetic material
- Termination: Check if termination criteria are met, otherwise go to step 2

MAS-EC:

- Initialization: Generate an initial population of N chromosomes, each representing an agent
- Evaluation: Evaluate the fitness of each agent in the population based on its behavior in the multi-agent system
- Selection: Select the fittest agents for reproduction
- Crossover: Perform crossover between pairs of selected agents to create offspring
- Mutation: Mutate the offspring to introduce new behavior
- Update: Update the behavior of the agents in the multi-agent system based on the evolved chromosomes
- Termination: Check if termination criteria are met, otherwise go to step 2

Evolutionary computation can be used to optimize control strategies for cybernetic systems, while multi-agent systems can provide a distributed control approach that is robust to failures and can adapt to changing conditions. Furthermore, the study of emergent behaviors in multi-agent systems can inform the design of cybernetic systems that exhibit desired emergent properties. The EC and MAS are powerful techniques that can be used in combination to solve complex problems that require the collaboration of multiple agents. The use of EC allows the behavior of individual agents to be evolved toward a common goal, while MAS allows the coordination of multiple agents toward the same goal. The mathematical equations that govern EC and MAS provide a framework for implementing these techniques in a systematic and efficient manner.

10.2 Cellular Automata

Cellular automata are often used in the context of biomimetic intelligence to simulate and study complex biological systems. The behavior of a cellular automaton can be used to model the behavior of individual cells in a tissue or organ, and the emergent patterns that arise from the interactions between these cells can be used to model the behavior of the system as a whole. The basic mathematical equation for a one-dimensional cellular automaton with n cells is:

$$S(t + 1, i) = f(S(t, i - 1), S(t, i), S(t, i + 1)), \tag{10.9}$$

where $S(t, i)$ represents the state of cell i at time t, and f is a local rule that determines the state of the cell at the next time step based on its own state and the states of its two neighbors. This local rule is often represented as a lookup table or a Boolean function. In a one-dimensional CA, the cells are arranged in a line, and the state of each cell is updated based on the states of its two neighbors. In a two-dimensional CA, the cells are arranged in a grid, and the state of each cell is updated based on the states of its eight neighbors.

Cellular automata can exhibit a wide range of behaviors, including simple periodic patterns, chaotic patterns, and complex emergent patterns. The behavior of a cellular automaton can be analyzed using techniques from dynamical systems theory and statistical physics. One of the most well-known examples of a cellular automaton is Conway's Game of Life, which is a two-dimensional CA with four states: dead, alive, dying, and birthing. The local rule for the Game of Life is as follows:

- A dead cell with exactly three live neighbors becomes a live cell (birth).
- A live cell with two or three live neighbors stays alive (survival).
- All other live cells die, and all other dead cells remain dead.

The Game of Life exhibits a wide range of interesting and complex patterns, including gliders, oscillators, and spaceships, which have been studied extensively in the field of cellular automata. Cellular automata have many applications, including in physics, computer science, and biology. They are particularly useful for simulating complex systems that exhibit emergent behavior, such as traffic flow, population dynamics, and pattern formation. Bacterial biofilms are complex communities of microorganisms that adhere to surfaces and communicate with each other through chemical signals. In the context of bio-inspired machine intelligence, cellular automata can be used to model the behavior of bacterial biofilms and their interactions with the surrounding environment. Consider a biofilm be represented as a grid of cells, where each cell i, j represents an individual bacterium at position (i, j) in the biofilm. The state of each cell can be represented as $S(i, j)$, which can take on different values depending on the behavior of the bacterium. For example, $S(i, j) = 0$ can represent a dead cell, while $S(i, j) = 1$ can represent a live cell.

The behavior of each cell is determined by a set of rules that depend on the local environment. For example, a cell may secrete a chemical signal if it is surrounded by a certain number of other cells, or it may move to an adjacent location if it detects a nutrient gradient. These rules can be represented mathematically as a set of functions $f(S(i, j), S(i−1, j), S(i+1, j), S(i, j−1), S(i, j+1))$ that determine the new state of the cell based on its current state and the states of its neighboring cells. The emergent behavior of the biofilm can be studied by simulating the behavior of the cellular automaton over time. This can be represented mathematically as a set of update rules that determine the new state of each cell at each time step.

By studying the emergent behavior of the cellular automaton, researchers can gain insights into the behavior of bacterial biofilms and develop new strategies for controlling their growth and spread. This approach can be used to design new antimicrobial agents or to engineer surfaces that are resistant to biofilm formation. Cellular automata models can be seen as a type of cybernetic system, where each cell represents a simple computational unit that interacts with its local environment based on a set of rules. This concept of decentralized decision-making and information processing is a key principle in cybernetics. Moreover, the study of cellular automata has contributed to the development of cybernetic theories and methods, such as self-organization and emergence. Cellular automata have been used to model a wide range of phenomena in various fields, such as biology, physics, and social sciences. By studying the behavior of cellular automata, researchers have gained insights into the emergence of complex patterns and structures, which can be applied to design cybernetic systems that are capable of adaptive and intelligent behavior. Thus, cellular automata provide a valuable tool for understanding and designing cybernetic systems.

10.3 Discrete Element Method

The DEM is a numerical technique used to study the behavior of a system of discrete particles subjected to external forces as shown in Figure 10.2. It is widely used in various fields, including physics, chemistry, engineering, and material science. DEM treats each particle as an individual entity and takes into account the interactions between particles, such as contact forces, friction, and collisions.

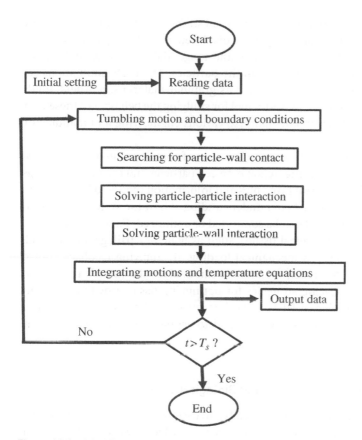

Figure 10.2 Workflow of discrete element method.

The equations used in DEM can be divided into two main categories: particle motion equations and force equations. The particle motion equations are used to calculate the position and velocity of each particle at each time step. The force equations are used to calculate the forces acting on each particle due to the interactions with other particles and external forces. The force acting on particle i can be written as the sum of all the forces acting on it:

$$F_i = F_{contact} + F_{external},\tag{10.10}$$

where $F_{contact}$ is the contact force acting on particle i due to its interaction with neighboring particles, and $F_{external}$ is any external force acting on particle i, such as gravity. The contact force between two particles i and j can be calculated using the Hertzian contact model:

$$F_{contact} = k_n \delta_n^{\frac{3}{2}} n_{ij} - k_t \delta_t v_{ij} t_{ij},\tag{10.11}$$

where k_n and k_t are the normal and tangential stiffness coefficients, respectively, δ_n and δ_t are the normal and tangential displacements of the particles at their contact point, n_{ij} and t_{ij} are the normal and tangential contact normal vectors, and v_{ij} is the relative velocity between the particles. The DEM simulations can be used to model various systems, such as granular materials, powders, fluids, and biological tissues. It is a powerful tool for studying the behavior of these complex systems used to design and optimize various engineering and manufacturing processes.

The cybernetics used to analyze the behavior of complex systems that involve feedback loops, such as the interaction between particles and their surroundings. By applying feedback control principles and information theory to DEM simulations, researchers can gain a better understanding of how the system responds to different stimuli and how it can be controlled or optimized. For example, to simulate the behavior of biological tissues, such as bone or cartilage, and to study how the tissue responds to mechanical loading. By applying feedback control principles to the DEM model, researchers can analyze the tissue's response to different loads and develop strategies for optimizing tissue growth and repair. Overall, the combination of DEM and cybernetics has the potential to advance our understanding of complex systems and to enable the development of new technologies in various fields.

10.3.1 Particle-Based Simulation of Biological Cells and Tissues

Particle-based simulation of biological cells and tissues using DEM is a widely used technique for studying the mechanical behavior of biological materials. In this approach, cells and tissues are modeled as discrete particles that interact with each other through contact forces. The goal is to simulate the mechanical response of the system to external stimuli and to study the effects of various parameters, such as cell shape, size, and stiffness.

The equations used in particle-based simulations of biological cells and tissues are similar to those used in traditional DEM simulations. However, additional equations are needed to account for the biological properties of the system. One of the key parameters in cell mechanics is the cytoskeleton, which is a network of protein filaments that gives the cell its mechanical stability and shape. To model the cytoskeleton, the cell is divided into discrete particles that represent the nodes of the cytoskeletal network. The cytoskeletal particles are connected by springs, which represent the cytoskeletal filaments. The stiffness of the springs depends on the properties of the cytoskeletal filaments, such as their length, diameter, and cross-linking density. The contact force between two cells is calculated using the Hertzian contact model as described earlier.

The motion of the particles in the system is governed by the equations of motion, which are given by:

$$m_i \frac{d^2 r_i}{dt^2} = F_i, \tag{10.12}$$

where m_i is the mass of particle i, r_i is the position vector of particle i, and F_i is the net force acting on particle i. The force acting on particle i can be written as the sum of all the forces acting on it:

$$F_i = F_{contact} + F_{cytoskeleton} + F_{external}, \tag{10.13}$$

where $F_{contact}$ is the contact force acting on particle i due to its interaction with neighboring particles, $F_{cytoskeleton}$ is the force acting on particle i due to the cytoskeleton, and $F_{external}$ is any external force acting on particle i, such as gravity or a magnetic field.

Particle-based simulations of biological cells and tissues using DEM have been used to study a wide range of biological processes, such as cell division, migration, and differentiation. These simulations have also been used to design and optimize tissue engineering and regenerative medicine strategies. Overall, life-inspired machine intelligence techniques can help improve the accuracy and efficiency of particle-based simulations of biological cells and tissues, leading to a better understanding of the mechanical behavior of biological materials and the development of more effective biomedical applications.

10.3.2 Simulation of Microbial Communities and Their Interactions

Simulation of microbial communities and their interactions involves modeling the behavior of multiple species of microorganisms in a shared environment. This field of research is important for understanding the dynamics of microbial ecosystems and how they respond to different environmental conditions. There are various mathematical models and computational tools that can be used to simulate microbial communities and their interactions. In agent-based models, the behavior of individual microorganisms is represented by a set of rules or algorithms. The interactions between microorganisms and their environment can be represented mathematically using functions or equations. For example, the behavior of bacterial populations can be modeled using the following equation:

$$N_i(t+1) = N_i(t) + r_i(t)N_i(t)\left(1 - \left(\frac{N_i(t)}{k_i}\right)\right) - D_i(t)N_i(t), \tag{10.14}$$

where $N_i(t)$ is the population size of bacterial species i at time t, $r_i(t)$ is the growth rate of species i at time t, k_i is the carrying capacity of the environment for species I,

$D_i(t)$ is the death rate of species i at time t. In Dynamic Flux Balance Analysis, metabolic network models are used to predict the metabolic fluxes of microorganisms under different environmental conditions. These models can be represented mathematically using a set of equations that describe the mass balance and reaction kinetics of the different metabolites in the network. For example, the following equation can be used to describe the rate of change of the concentration of a metabolite x in a microbial community:

$$\frac{dx}{dt} = \sum v_j s_{ji}, \tag{10.15}$$

where $\dfrac{dx}{dt}$ is the rate of change of the concentration of metabolite x, v_j is the rate of reaction j in the metabolic network and s_{ji} is the stoichiometric coefficient of metabolite i in reaction j. Game theory models can be used to simulate the interactions between different microorganisms in a microbial community. These models can be represented mathematically using a set of equations that describe the costs and benefits of different strategies. For example, Table 10.1 can be used to represent the payoff matrix for a two-player game:

Here, S_A and S_B are the two strategies being played, R is the reward for playing strategy S_A against strategy S_A, S is the sucker's payoff for playing strategy S_B against strategy S_A, T is the temptation for playing strategy S_A against strategy S_B, and P is the punishment for playing strategy S_B against strategy S_B.

10.3.3 Discrete Element Method-Based Modeling of Biological Fluids and Soft Materials

DEM is a numerical technique used for modeling complex systems composed of many interacting particles. In the context of bio-inspired machine intelligence, DEM is used for simulating biological fluids and soft materials such as blood, mucus, and tissues. The basic idea is to represent these materials as a collection of particles that interact with each other through contact and frictional forces. The behavior of the particles is determined by solving the equations of motion and contact mechanics using numerical methods.

Table 10.1 Representation of the payoff matrix.

Strategies	S_A	S_B
S_A	R	S
S_B	T	P

One of the key challenges in modeling biological fluids and soft materials is the complex interplay between the particles and the surrounding fluid. This is typically modeled using a combination of fluid dynamics equations and particle-based models such as DEM. The fluid flow is modeled using the Navier-Stokes equations, while the particle-based model is used to simulate the mechanical interactions between the particles. DEM is a powerful computational technique for simulating the mechanical behavior of discrete elements in a system. In the context of bio-inspired machine intelligence, DEM has been used to model the behavior of biological fluids and soft materials, such as blood, mucus, and tissues. The basic idea is to represent the fluid or soft material as a collection of discrete particles, and then use Newton's laws of motion to simulate their interactions. The equations of motion for each particle in the system are given by:

$$m_i \frac{d^2 r_i}{dt^2} = \sum_{J=1} j \neq i^N F_{ij}, \tag{10.16}$$

where m_i is the mass of the ith particle, r_i is its position, F_{ij} is the force on particle i due to particle j, and N is the total number of particles in the system. The force between two particles i and j is modeled as a sum of elastic and dissipative forces:

$$F_{ij} = F_{ij}^{elastic} + F_{ij}^{dissipative}. \tag{10.17}$$

The elastic force represents the deformation of the particles due to their interaction and is given by:

$$F_{ij}^{elastic} = F_{ij}^{repulsive} + F_{ij}^{adhesive}, \tag{10.18}$$

where $F_{ij}^{repulsive}$ is the repulsive force between the particles, and $F_{ij}^{adhesive}$ is the adhesive force between them. The dissipative force represents the dissipation of energy due to the deformation of the particles and is given by:

$$F_{ij}^{adhesive} = -\eta v_{ij}, \tag{10.19}$$

where η is the coefficient of friction, and v_{ij} is the relative velocity between the particles. By solving these equations of motion numerically, one can simulate the behavior of biological fluids and soft materials, and study their properties and interactions in detail. This has important applications in fields such as bioengineering, where the behavior of biological materials must be understood in order to design effective treatments and therapies.

10.4   Smoothed Particle Hydrodynamics

Smoothed Particle Hydrodynamics (SPH) is a numerical technique used for simulating fluid flows and other physical phenomena. In the context of bio-inspired machine intelligence, SPH is used for modeling biological fluids such as blood, mucus, and cerebrospinal fluid. The basic idea is to represent the fluid as a collection of particles that interact with each other through pairwise forces. The motion of each particle is then determined by solving the equations of motion and the continuity equation. SPH is a numerical technique used for simulating fluid flows and other physical phenomena. The complete workflow of the SPH is shown in Figure 10.3.

The basic equations of SPH involve the calculation of the density and pressure at each particle location. Consider a fluid particle located at position r_i with mass m_i, velocity v_i, and density ρ_i. The density at this particle location is calculated as:

$$w_{ij} = \frac{1}{h^d} e^{-\frac{(r_i - r_j)^2}{2h^2}}, \tag{10.20}$$

where h is the smoothing length, which controls the size of the smoothing kernel, and d is the dimensionality of the simulation. The pressure at each particle location is calculated using an equation of state, which relates the pressure p_i to the density ρ_i and other fluid properties. A commonly used equation of state is the ideal gas law:

$$p_i = \gamma - \rho_i e_i, \tag{10.21}$$

where γ is the ratio of specific heats, which is typically set to 1.4 for air, and e_i is the internal energy of the fluid. The velocity of each particle is updated based on the forces acting on it, which include the pressure and viscosity forces. The pressure force f_i^p on particle i is given by:

$$f_i^p = -\sum_j m_j \frac{p_i}{p_i^2} + \frac{p_j}{p_j^2} \nabla_i w_{ij}, \tag{10.22}$$

where $\nabla_i w_{ij}$ is the gradient of the smoothing kernel with respect to the position of particle i. The viscosity force f_i^v on particle i is given by:

$$f_i^v = \mu \sum_j m_j \frac{v_j - v_i}{\rho_j} \nabla_i^2 w_{ij}. \tag{10.23}$$

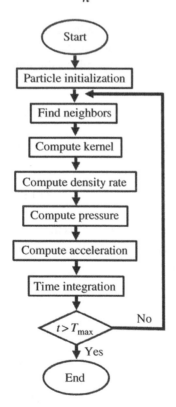

Figure 10.3   Workflow of SPH.

In addition, the use of SPH in cybernetics can also aid in the development of control systems for bio-inspired engineering applications. By modeling the behavior of fluids through SPH and incorporating feedback mechanisms, researchers can design control systems that adjust the behavior of the fluid in real-time to achieve a desired outcome. This has potential applications in fields such as robotics, where bio-inspired systems are used to improve the performance of robots in various tasks. The combination of SPH and cybernetics provides a powerful tool for studying and designing bio-inspired systems with complex fluid dynamics. By understanding the behavior of these systems and their interactions with the environment, researchers can develop more advanced and efficient technologies that mimic the natural world.

10.4.1 SPH-Based Simulations of Biomimetic Fluid Dynamic

SPH is a Lagrangian method for simulating fluid dynamics. In SPH, the fluid is discretized into particles and each particle represents a certain volume of fluid. The equations of motion for each particle are solved based on the interactions between neighboring particles, which are calculated using a smoothing kernel function. This approach allows for the simulation of complex fluid phenomena, including turbulence and multiphase flows.

In the context of biomimetic fluid dynamics, SPH has been used to simulate the fluid dynamics of swimming organisms, such as fish and jellyfish. These simulations can provide insights into the underlying mechanisms of swimming, as well as the hydrodynamic forces and energy expenditure involved. SPH has also been used to simulate the flow of blood through vessels and the movement of cilia in the respiratory system. The equations of motion for each particle in SPH are given by:

$$\frac{dv_i}{dt} = \sum_{j \neq i}^{N} m_j \left(\frac{p_i}{p_i^2} + \frac{p_j}{p_j^2} + \prod_{ij} \right) \nabla_i w_{ij} \tag{10.24}$$

$$\frac{d\rho_i}{dt} = \sum_{j \neq i}^{N} m_j \left(v_i - v_j \right) \nabla_i w_{ij}, \tag{10.25}$$

where v_i is the velocity of particle i, m_j is its mass, p_i and ρ_i are its pressure and density, respectively, and w_{ij} is the smoothing kernel function between particles i and j. The smoothing kernel function w_{ij} is typically a Gaussian or cubic spline function and is used to calculate the influence of neighboring particles on each particle's properties. The choice of smoothing kernel function can have a significant impact on the accuracy and stability of the simulation. Overall, SPH-based simulations of biomimetic fluid dynamics have shown promise in providing insights into the complex fluid dynamics of biological systems.

10.4.2 SPH-Based Simulations of Bio-Inspired Engineering Applications

SPH is a popular method for simulating fluid dynamics in bio-inspired engineering applications. One of the key advantages of SPH is its ability to handle complex geometries and boundary conditions. In bio-inspired engineering, SPH has been used to model fluid flow in various systems, such as blood flow in the cardiovascular system, fish swimming, and insect flight. SPH-based simulations of these applications involve the use of SPH particles to represent the fluid or fluid-like substances. These particles interact with each other based on a smoothing kernel function that determines the strength and range of the interaction. The governing equations for SPH-based simulations of fluid dynamics are the continuity equation and the Navier-Stokes equations. These equations can be discretized using the SPH method, resulting in a set of equations for the motion of SPH particles. The continuity equation in SPH form can be expressed as:

$$\frac{d\rho_i}{dt} = \sum_j m_j v_{ij} \nabla_i w_{ij}, \tag{10.26}$$

where ρ_i is the density of particle i, m_j is the mass of particle j, v_{ij} is the velocity difference between particles i and j, and w_{ij} is the smoothing kernel function. The momentum equation in SPH form can be expressed as:

$$\frac{dv_i}{dt} = \sum_j m_j \left(\frac{p_i}{p_i^2} + \frac{p_j}{p_j^2} + \prod_{ij} \right) \nabla_i w_{ij}, \tag{10.27}$$

where v_i is the velocity of particle i, p_i is the pressure of particle i, and p_{iij} is the viscous stress tensor. SPH-based simulations can also incorporate particle interactions with solid surfaces. This is achieved by introducing boundary particles that interact with fluid particles through boundary conditions. Overall, SPH-based simulations of bio-inspired engineering applications provide a powerful tool for understanding fluid dynamics and optimizing the design of biomimetic devices.

Summary

The chapter provides an overview of life-inspired machine intelligence, which aims to simulate living organisms and biological phenomena using computer technology. This approach creates digital models of biological systems to study their behavior and predict their reactions. Examples of life-inspired machine intelligence include computer simulations of microbial communities and models of individual cells and tissues. While, bio-inspired machine intelligence involves studying biological processes, systems, and structures to create machine learning algorithms and optimization models, the life-inspired approach uses insights from living organisms to simulate life. Every cell or element in the framework is perceived to be alive and functionally active in interacting with neighboring cell elements. This provides a concept of a living thing that may be programmed to be alive in the computational environment. It also discusses several subtopics, such as evolutionary computation and multi-agent systems, particle-based simulation of biological cells and tissues, and SPH-based simulations of biomimetic fluid dynamics and life-inspired engineering applications. Each element's functionality and interaction states are programmed based on equations often relating to cybernetics, which is basically control theory. The overall integration gives rise to a system form of machine intelligence. Some schools of thought termed this cellular automaton, while others relate this to DEMs. The systematic framework based on such concepts can generate a version of intelligent life beings from the cellular to the organism perspective. This may be termed as life-inspired machine intelligence from a broader perspective.

One potential future research direction for biomimetic intelligence is the development of more advanced multi-agent systems that can effectively collaborate and communicate with each other. Another area of interest is the use of DEM-based models to simulate more complex living biological systems, such as tissues and organs. Furthermore, there is potential for the use of life-inspired machine intelligence models in personalized medicine and drug discovery. By leveraging insights from biology, these models can aid in the development of intelligent targeted therapies and more efficient drug discovery processes. In summary, the field of biomimetic intelligence has significant potential for driving innovation and advancing various fields. Future research in this area can lead to the development of more advanced and sophisticated living models that can have a significant impact on healthcare, biotechnology, robotics, and other AI-related fields.

Exercise Questions

Q.10.1 In what ways can life-inspired machine intelligence be used to improve cybernetic systems and processes, and how can it be incorporated into existing technologies?

Q.10.2 How can multi-agent AI systems be designed to effectively coordinate and collaborate in complex environments, and what are some examples of successful applications of these systems?

Q.10.3 Describe the role of game theory in the development of intelligent systems, and how can it be used to optimize decision-making in multi-agent scenarios.

Q.10.4 How can distributed multi-agent systems be designed to enable efficient communication and coordination between agents, and what are some challenges associated with implementing these systems?

Q.10.5 Illustrate the key principles of evolutionary computation, and how can they be applied to the design of multi-agent systems to improve their adaptability and robustness.

Q.10.6 Explain how cellular automata can be used to model complex biological systems, and what are some examples of successful applications of this approach?

Q.10.7 What is the discrete element method, and how can it be used to simulate the behavior of complex materials and structures?

Q.10.8 Describe how particle-based simulations can be used to model the behavior of biological cells and tissues, and what are some of the challenges associated with implementing these simulations?

Q.10.9 How can the principles of Smoothed Particle Hydrodynamics be applied to bio-inspired engineering applications?

Q.10.10 Describe some future directions for research in bio-inspired machine intelligence.

Q.10.11 How can bio-inspired machine intelligence models be applied in real-world applications, such as robotics and biotechnology?

Further Reading

Barresi J. Prospects for the cyberiad: certain limits on human self-knowledge in the cybernetic age. *Journal for the Theory of Social Behaviour.* 1987 Mar;17(1):19–46

Byrski A, Dreżewski R, Siwik L, Kisiel-Dorohinicki M. Evolutionary multi-agent systems. *The Knowledge Engineering Review.* 2015 Mar;30(2):171–86.

Jozwiak L. Life-inspired systems: assuring quality in the era of complexity. In 5th International Workshop on System-on-Chip for Real-Time Applications (IWSOC'05) 2005 Jul 20 (pp. 139–142).

Monaghan JJ. Smoothed particle hydrodynamics. *Annual Review of Astronomy and Astrophysics.* 1992 Sep;30(1):543–74.

11

Revisiting Cybernetics and Relation to Cybernetical Intelligence

11.1 The Concept and Development of Cybernetics

In 1948, American mathematician Norbert Wiener titled his book *Cybernetics*. This simple and ancient name was given a new meaning and became a synonym for a brand new discipline, which has been used since then. Cybernetics has since been spread and applied rapidly and has spurred the intense interest of mathematicians, engineers, biologists, psychologists, and even scholars in philosophy and social sciences. At the same time, this theory quickly spread to the world and has influenced many disciplines. Today, its influence has a far-reaching impact: the words "control," "feedback," "information," and "communication" have been integrated into people's daily life, just as the evolution of "natural selection," "competition for survival," "survival of the fittest"—are familiar and understood by the public. The conceptualized structure for the development of cybernetics is shown in Figure 11.1.

11.1.1 Attributes of Control Concepts

There seems to be little debate on the attributes of control concepts for cybernetics, and it is generally agreed that "the essence of control lies in enabling the system to achieve stable and purposeful action." First of all, "control" and "behavior" are closely related and mutually causal. Lerner described control as "the effects imposed on an object or objects, selected based on the information that is required to be obtained and used to 'improve' the function or development of that object." Its meanings are as follows:

- The purpose of exerting this effect is to improve the object and achieve the desired goal.

Cybernetical Intelligence: Engineering Cybernetics with Machine Intelligence, First Edition.
Kelvin K. L. Wong.
© 2024 The Institute of Electrical and Electronics Engineers, Inc.
Published 2024 by John Wiley & Sons, Inc.
Companion website: www.wiley.com/go/cyberintel

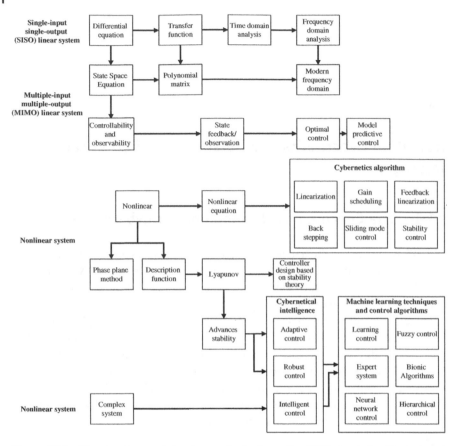

Figure 11.1 The structure and development of cybernetics. SISO stands for Single Input Single Output and MIMO is the abbreviation of Multiple Input Multiple Output. The difference lies on the number of inputs and outputs, which means SISO systems are often less complex than MIMO systems.

- Control is an action imposed on an object.
- This function is realized through the selection and use of information.

It can be reduced to the following simplistic understanding: the so-called control is the regulation of the system itself to achieve stability.

11.1.2 Research Objects and Characteristics of Cybernetics

The discussion on the research object of cybernetics has not been interrupted until now, and academia has not formed a unified view. The more consistent basic view is that the research object of cybernetics is wide, and the purpose is to explore these systems' regulation and control rules.

Since there is feedback, there must be a related communication problem, which is the reception, processing, and transmission of information. Wiener often demonstrated that communication and control are the same things, that control requires communication, and that it (the communication between the agent and the controlled body in a cybernetic system) must be bidirectional. Wiener pointed out that control is communication. In the field of control systems, there are several mathematical equations that are commonly used to model and analyze the communication and control in cybernetic systems such as transfer function of a system, which describes the relationship between the input and output of a system in the frequency domain represented by the Equation (11.1).

$$G(s) = \frac{\text{Output}(s)}{\text{Input}(s)}. \tag{11.1}$$

The PID controller, which is a control algorithm commonly used in control systems. The PID controller uses three types of control, proportional, integral, and derivative control, represented mathematically as represented by Equation (11.2).

$$u(t) = K_p e(t) + K_i \int e(t) \mathrm{d}_t + K_d \frac{d_e(t)}{d_t}. \tag{11.2}$$

11.1.3 Development of Cybernetical Intelligence

Cybernetics has had an important influence on the development of the following modern disciplines: control theory, computer science, information theory, automata theory, artificial intelligence, artificial neural networks, cognitive science, computer simulation science, dynamical systems, and artificial life. In the 1940s and 1950s, cybernetics first explored the core concepts of these fields, such as complexity, self-organization, self-reproduction, autonomy, networks, connectionism, and adaptability. For example, von Neumann's computer architecture, game theory, cellular automata; Ashby and von Forester's self-organizing analysis; Braitenberg's autonomous robots; McCulloch's artificial neural networks, perceptron, and classifiers, etc.

11.2 The Fundamental Ideas of Cybernetics

11.2.1 System Idea

The object of cybernetics is system. The cybernetic methodology is a prerequisite to treating the object as a system. This mainly refers to system thinking, which distinguishes it from the two main ways of thinking in human history—holistic and reductive thinking. System thinking is the inheritance development of these two ways of thinking. It is based on the system concept, system relationship, and structural properties. Objects are organized from the model to study the function and behavior of the system. Focusing on the holistic and integrated properties of things reveals the diversity of contact, system, structure, and function. System thinking comprises four pillars: "One is the organic nature of life, that is, the living organism is placed in the center of the conceptual system for investigation; the second is wholeness, which regards the living organism as an orderly, open, self-regulating and purposeful organic whole and focuses on its wholeness and non-additively. Third, the model is used to describe the object. It is not to decompose the whole into parts but to simulate the object's behavior in the way of the model after forming the concept of the object. The fourth is to emphasize sufficient knowledge of the whole, rather than precise knowledge because precise knowledge of a complex system is elusive." The system idea corresponds to the black box approach. The black box approach opens up a new way to recognize and study complex systems. A cybernetic approach that uses external observations and tests to study black box's functional characteristics and behavior and explore their possible internal structures and mechanisms through input and output information. "Several alternative structures are enclosed in 'closed boxes,' and the one way to study them is by using the inputs and outputs of the closed boxes," Wiener wrote in the role of models in science. Classical control is based on the mathematical model of the transfer function for linear time-invariant (LTI) system analysis and design. A linear system is one that linear differential equations can describe. LTI system is a special kind of linear system which inherits the characteristics of the superposition of linear systems. When solving the response of the LTI system, the unit's short rectangular impulse response $h_\Delta(t)$ of the system at time 0 is assumed. The unit short rectangular pulse is Δ in width and $1/\Delta$ in amplitude. Now the magnitude of the short matrix impulse near time 0 is $u(0)$, and the impulse response to the system is $\Delta u(0)h_\Delta(t)$. The output y in the time domain becomes as shown in Equation (11.3):

$$y(t) = \int_0^\infty u(\tau)h(t-\tau)d\tau, \ t \geq 0. \tag{11.3}$$

Laplace transform is an important mathematical transformation and plays an important role in classical control theory. However, it is related to Fourier transform for a long time which is essentially the projection of the time domain signal $f(t)$ onto an orthogonal basis $e^{j\omega t}$, and the orthogonal basis $e^{j\omega t}$ here according to Euler's formula as shown in Equation (11.4).

$$e^{jwt} = \cos(\omega t) + j\sin(\omega t), \tag{11.4}$$

the Fourier transform is defined by the integral as shown in Equation (11.5):

$$F(\omega) = \int_{-\infty}^{\infty} f(t)e^{-j\omega t}dt. \tag{11.5}$$

The Laplace transform transforms the signal from the time domain to the frequency domain, which is the same as the Fourier transform, except that the Laplace transform adds a decay factor t which guarantees convergence of the Fourier integral. The concept of transfer function from the Laplace transform is derived to solve the response of LTI system.

11.2.2 Information Idea

Information theory is one of the essential contents of cybernetics. The primary research method of cybernetics is the feedback control method, and the feedback here is mainly from the perspective of information. In other words, feedback in the cybernetic system mainly refers to information feedback, and the process of feedback control is the process of information generation, maintenance, transmission, and acceptance. Each control link is the information source and the information acceptor. The process of control and the achievement of the purpose of the system is carried out around information. Therefore, the communication process is central to the whole feedback control method. The excellent communication process between each link of the system determines the efficiency of the system. Information ideas correspond to information methods, which belong to the most important contents of cybernetics methodology. In cybernetics, the concept of information has an expansive meaning. As a new idea, the function of the control system is studied from an information aspect. It uses the concept of information as the basis for analyzing and processing problems and abstracts the movement process of the system as an information transformation process, leaving aside all the concrete movement forms of objects. It focuses on studying the system's information process from the perspective of connection and transformation. Therefore, it does not need to deconstruct and analyze the whole structure of things but to consider the flow of its information comprehensively. It may be expressed by information input and output functions to achieve a sense of the whole system. The concept of information makes it possible to study different natural or social phenomena from a wholly new and unified point of view. Norbert Wiener looked at control systems from the point of view of information; the essence of discovery control is communication. The feedback control process of adequate action in different material systems is regarded as obtaining, using, maintaining, and transmitting information to maintain its internal stability. In information theory, there are several mathematical equations that are commonly used to quantify and analyze the amount of information in a system. Some examples include:

- Shannon's entropy, which measures the amount of uncertainty or randomness in a system. It is represented mathematically as:

$$H(x) = -\sum p(x) \log_2 p(x), \tag{11.6}$$

where x is the random variable, $p(x)$ is the probability of x, and $H(x)$ is the entropy of x.

- The mutual information between two random variables x and y, which measures the amount of information that x provides about y. It is represented mathematically as:

$$I(x,y) = \sum p(x,y) \log_2 \left(\frac{p(x,y)}{p(x)p(y)} \right), \tag{11.7}$$

where $p(x, y)$ is the joint probability of x and y, $p(x)$ is the marginal probability of x and $p(y)$ is the marginal probability of y.

11.2.3 Behavioral Idea

Cybernetic behavior thoughts are divided into two parts: the first is the definition and classification of behavior, and the second is the concept of adaptive behavior. From the cybernetic perspective, behavior is any change that occurs ontogeny concerning the external environment. The basis of this definition is a pair of concepts, "individual" and "environment." The individual is an entity that can be felt, while the environment is everything that exists outside that entity. In general, behavior is any change in an individual that the outside world can detect. Cybernetics categorizes behavior in a typical dichotomy. The primary criterion for classifying behavior as passive or dynamic is whether all the energy involved in ontogenetic change is directly imported from the outside world. The second criterion is whether the dynamic behavior serves a function, making it purposeful or aimless. There are two types of dynamic behavior: one, in which people supply this energy to accomplish a goal, and another, in which people provide this energy for no apparent reason. The third criterion of cybernetic behavior classification is: Does purposeful behavior have feedback? If there is, there is feedback behavior; if not, there is no feedback behavior. The fourth criterion of cybernetic behavior classification is where it is negative feedback behavior predicted, which defines it as predictive behavior or non-predictive behavior. The whole cybernetic behavior definition and classification can be briefly summarized in Figure 11.2.

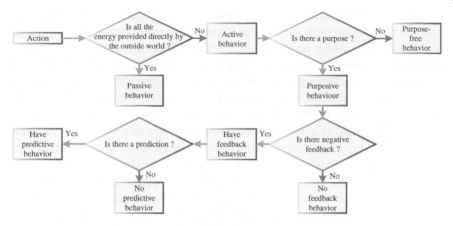

Figure 11.2 Cybernetic dichotomies of behavior.

11.2.4 Cybernetical Intelligence Neural Network

Artificial intelligence (AI) is built on the pillars of a few major branches of science and engineering, namely, systematology, information theory, and cybernetics, which is typically based on control theory that was derived from the studies of Norbert Wiener, the world-renowned father of cybernetics. In 1954, Hsue-sen Tsien founded engineering cybernetics by publishing the famous "Engineering Cybernetics" in the United States. On the basis of cybernetics, a predictive system may be regarded as a multiple feedback system. The framework of multilayer perceptron as well as that of a backpropagation neural network (BP) can be based on the theoretic of system control in modern cybernetics. With this type of thinking, perceptron theory offers a cohesive approach to the statistical mechanics and principles of cybernetics as a basis for successful neural network modeling.

A feedback controller's operation is to change the behavior of a system fundamentally. Feedback control systems sample a system's outputs, compare them to a set of desired outputs, and then utilize the resulting error signals to compute the system's control inputs in such a way that the errors are minimized. Artificially built feedback control systems, which are utilized to govern industrial, automotive, and aeronautical systems, are responsible for today's aerospace achievements. Although neural network controllers are adaptive learning systems, they do not need the conventional assumptions of adaptive control theory, such as parameter linearity and the presence of a regression matrix. It is demonstrated in detail how to create neural network controllers for cybernetical systems, a general category of nonlinear systems, complicated industrial systems with vibrations and flexibility effects, force control, motor dynamics control, and other applications. These strategies are given for both continuous-time and discrete-time weight tuning.

Cybernetical intelligence is introduced based on the integration of AI and cybernetics, which can produce applications in predictive control, pattern recognition, and classification, which essentially are based on the same fundamentals. The key concept of cybernetical intelligence grew from a desire to understand and build systems that can achieve goals, whether complex human goals or just goals. It is an even deeper underlying conceptual term. Cybernetics holds the world sufficiently to gain feedback in order to correct the actions to achieve goals. It is a mutual combination of automated communication and control systems between artificially intelligent machines and the environment with subsequent strong support from machine learning, the concepts of systems thinking and systems theory became integral parts of the established scientific language of cybernetical intelligence and can lead to numerous new methodologies and applications. The various influencing factors in the neural network control system are complicated, and the internal interaction cannot be directly observed, so it can be considered a gray or even black system. One can fit the model by system identification or statistical regression. However, it can only make a preliminary analysis from the rough development curve, unable to accurately analyze the role of the influencing factors. The appropriate neural network can simulate any curve and select specific samples through deep learning to get more accurate results, more suitable for analyzing the network control system. Inspired by "Re3 Writer" and other works in neural networks, conceptualize the design scheme of the neural network as "Re8 analytics" as given by: Read, Refine, Reflect, Review, Rectify, Response, Reason, and Report as shown in Figure 11.3.

Specific description of each operator is as follows:

1) Read: Collecting the data required for training and validation. It is necessary to preprocess the data before training the neural network. The data should be unified into one order of magnitude. The appropriate data preprocessing, including normalization, can achieve better training results. This operator can also be termed as Retrieve if the perceptual information is obtained from a sensor via data acquisition.

2) Refine: Building and defining the structure of the neural network. In the design of network layers, the more layers of the neural network, the higher the accuracy of the obtained data and the lower the error, but at the same time, the more layers, the more complex the network structure, which may significantly increase the training time.

3) Reflect: Specifically evaluating the errors of the neural network. Error analysis is performed after training to quantify the performance of the neural network via the designed loss function.

4) Rectify: Adjusting the parameters of the neural network. Many works choose the classical BP neural network for training, which updates the parameters

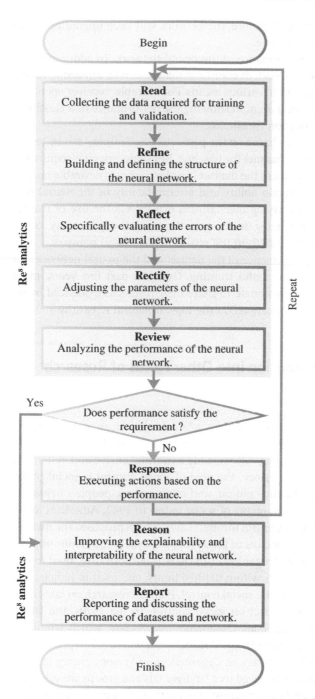

Figure 11.3 The flow chart of Re[8] analysis for cybernetical intelligence neural networks.

based on the loss function. Therefore, the network will keep upgrading in the way that reducing the loss value.

5) Review: Analyzing the performance of the neural network. In addition to the loss function, other metrics, such as confusion matrix, can be utilized to reflect the capability of the network in various means. For example, receiver operating characteristic (ROC) curve is a graph showing the performance of a classification model at all classification thresholds.

6) Response: Executing actions based on the performance. Training can be terminated if the neural network has met the baseline. But sometimes it is required to rebuild the network or augment the dataset in order to obtain desirable results.

7) Reason: Improving the explain ability and interpretability of the neural network. By making the underlying mechanisms explicit via the use of mathematical formulae or visualizing features in the model, experts may better comprehend and have more faith in the results of the neural network.

8) Report: Reporting the performance of the dataset and the neural network and discuss techniques for a successful training. Over the past few years, more researchers have become passionate to share their results as evidenced by on the growing number of publications on the topic of neural networks.

11.3 Cybernetic Expansion into Other Fields of Research

11.3.1 Social Cybernetics

In the history of social cybernetics, E.A. Ross, a famous American sociologist, and social psychologist, first mentioned the concept of "social control" in his 1896 article "American Journal of Sociology." Ross made a comprehensive and systematic study of social control. In his theory, the goal of social control is social order. Through the law, religion, public opinion, and other means, people's behaviors are restricted to meet the requirements of social order. In 1942, American jurist, Ezra Pound, published "Social Control through Law," which proposed the method of social control from the perspective of law. From the cybernetics point of view, the nature and tasks of law and regarded its decrees as authoritative, used to recognize and protect those interests within defined limits, and used in judicial and administrative processes to exercise social control. Pound's research on law-based control has had a profound impact on social control. In the 1970s, the Dutch scholar, Hanken, published the book *Cybernetics and Society*, which stipulated social control from the perspective of individual behavior with a micro perspective. In the *Fourth International Conference on Cybernetics and Systems Theory* in 1978, Baumgatler and other scholars believed that "individuals and groups are subject to material, social structure, and cultural constraints in their actions, but at the same time, they are also locally creating their own, historical, creative and active forces." The development of social control theory is closely connected with cybernetics, system theory, and information theory, which are intercrossing and supporting each other. Therefore, the social control theory should be integrated with relevant theories instead of being independent and static.

1) **The Definition of Cybernetics in the Social System**

   Cybernetics was formed in the 1940s and was first used by Wiener in his book *Cybernetics: or Control and Communication in the Animal and the Machine*, marking the birth of cybernetics. In the social system, to conduct economic, political, and other social activities orderly, it is necessary to restrict human behavior and implement social control through norms. Social control refers to anti-deviant, anti-immoral, anti-criminal, and other behaviors for the safety and interests of individuals and society so that society can achieve a stable state of order. Social cybernetics is a branch that can use the theory of cybernetics, take the system as the research object, and use the communication of information to achieve the purpose of control.

2) **Social Cybernetics and Systems Theory**

   In 1968, Bertalanffy L, an Austrian-American biologist, took systems as the object of scientific research in his book *General System Theory: Foundations, Development, Applications* and gave a comprehensive exposition of the dynamic, open systems theory. In his theory, there will be some similarity or isomorphism between different systems, which is the basis of general systems theory. In the theory of social systems, social organizations are composed of people, and people coordinate their activities to form a system. In this system, the internal departments or subsystems are the lower-level system, and the social system, composed of multiple subsystems, belongs to the higher-level system. In social cybernetics, the control object is also a part of the social system. It is necessary to use the theory and method of system theory to coordinate the relationship between individual elements to realize the optimal control of the system.

   In systems theory, there are several mathematical models and equations that are commonly used to represent and analyze social systems. Some examples include:

   - The Lotka-Volterra equation, which is used to model the dynamics of predator-prey systems. It is represented mathematically as shown in Equation (11.8).

$$\frac{dx}{dy} = ax - bxy$$
$$\frac{dy}{dt} = -cy + dxy$$

(11.8)

where x and y are the populations of the predator and prey, respectively, and a, b, c, and d are parameters that describe the interaction between the predator and prey.

- The DeGroot model, which is used to model the dynamics of opinion formation in a social system. It is represented mathematically as shown in Equation (11.9).

$$x(i, t+1) = (1-a)x(i, t) + a\left(\frac{1}{n}\right) \sum x\,(j, t),\tag{11.9}$$

where $x(i, t)$ is the opinion of agent i at time t, a is the weight of the influence of others, and the summation is over all agents.

3) **Social Cybernetics and Information Theory**

In 1948, Shannon published *A Mathematical Theory of Communication*, which marked the birth of information theory. According to information theory, a system realizes its purposeful movement by acquiring, transmitting, processing, and processing information. In social cybernetics, the purposeful movement of the system is abstracted as a process of information transformation. The system contains a tremendous amount of information. In order to control the system with less information, the theoretical basis is information theory, which studies the laws of information transmission and transformation.

In information theory, there are several mathematical equations that are commonly used to quantify and analyze the amount of information in a system. Some examples include:

- The Shannon entropy, which measures the amount of uncertainty or randomness in a system. It is represented mathematically as represented by Equation (11.10).

$$H(x) = -\sum p(x) \log_2 p(x),\tag{11.10}$$

where x is the random variable, $p(x)$ is the probability of x, and $H(x)$ is the entropy of x.

- The mutual information between two random variables X and Y, which measures the amount of information that X provides about Y. It is represented mathematically as:

$$I(X, Y) = \sum p(x, y) \log_2\left(\frac{p(x, y)}{p(x)p(y)}\right),\tag{11.11}$$

where $p(x, y)$ is the joint probability of x and y, $p(x)$ is the marginal probability of x and $p(y)$ is the marginal probability of y.

11.3.2 Internal Control-Related Theories

Internal control can be interpreted from both accounting and management directions. The Committee of Sponsoring Organizations of the Treadway Commission (COSO) defines internal control as follows: internal control by the enterprise's board of directors, managers, and other employees, to the efficiency of operational management effect, reliability of financial reporting, abide by the relevant laws and regulations such as the achievement of goals and provide reasonable assurance of the process. It also stipulates the five elements of internal control: control environment, risk assessment, control activities, information communication, and monitoring. In 2008, the enterprise internal control is defined as a basic norm of middle management, which is a process for implementing the subject's board of directors, supervisors, and management staff. The target is for the enterprise operation and legal management compliance, asset security, financial report, and related information to provide reasonable assurance and improve management efficiency and effectiveness through this process. The strategy promotes the enterprise to realize development.

In the current internal control theory, ensuring the safety of assets and the truth of accounting information should be regarded as the main task of internal control. Moreover, one cannot ignore the connection between internal control and accounting. The improvement of the accounting system needs the guarantee of internal control. On the other hand, internal control should use the information provided by accounting to complete their tasks. The development of internal control theory is bound to require accounting theory in this aspect. Throughout the whole development process of internal control, it can be found that accounting control is a primary means to ensure the smooth implementation of internal control. Accounting control is using the information provided by accounting to manage the production and operation of the enterprise, which is the ultimate value maximization of the enterprise. Although the internal control theory mentioned above is diversifying, the core of its accounting control is still unshaken. Management power and internal control should interact and influence each other, including positive guidance and harmful restraint. From the perspective of informatics, management power, and internal control are transmitted to each other in the form of information. The information room has energy and value, which allows the decision and choices of both sides affect each other. At the same time, both sides will use their function to choose "favorable information" and avoid "unfavorable information."

11.3.3 Software Control Theory

Software cybernetics has been an emerging research direction in software engineering recently. It mainly discusses the cross-application of software engineering

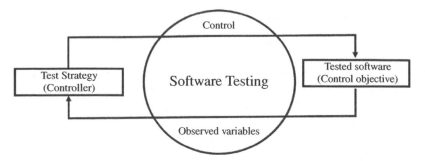

Figure 11.4 Software testing as a control problem in cybernetics.

and feedback cybernetics, aiming to apply the cybernetics method to the practice of software engineering, take the software process as the controlled object, and quantitatively analyze its various feedback mechanisms. It optimizes the control of software behavior so that the software process becomes rule-based to ensure better and improve the reliability of software. The research of software control theory comes from a core problem in software engineering: whether the highly complex software behavior can be controlled or how to control it effectively. There are two main research backgrounds. The first is to deal with the problem of software trustworthiness. In order to deal with various software trustworthiness problems, it is required to carry out real-time, practical, and quantitative monitoring and control of software behavior. The second is dealing with the problem of software adaptability: the software system is required to have adaptability under the open network environment, and the dynamic changes of user behavior and user needs to ensure the quality of service, providing different forms of services.

By harnessing cybernetics, which is based on control theory to solve the problem of how to design an effective test strategy. The studies on the selection strategy of test cases from the perspective of the testing process, transformed the software testing process into a control problem according to the control theory, and finally proposed a Markov control method for software testing. A closed-loop feedback control system is constructed by taking the software under test as a controlled object and using Markov chain to model it mathematically. And the testing strategy is treated as the corresponding controller, as shown in Figure 11.4.

11.3.4 Perceptual Cybernetics

There is one overwhelming truth about life: for any living thing that faces the troubles of turbulence from its external environment, its survival requires stabilizing its vital internal chemistry in some way. Every creature has instinctive behaviors that allow its stable internal chemicals to spread its genes long enough. Preventing instability in the outside world can take two forms. Life also uses both methods to maintain stability: the first is to develop passive armor (such as membranes, skin, or shells), which is not a perfect shield against outside organisms, however. The second way that a creature can actively and forcefully defend itself against the world to which it is subjected is more critical. The organism must be able to sense the critical state of the external world; it must be possible to compare perceived states with the desired conditions of those states and take action to influence them to achieve and maintain the desired conditions. "Sensing" means changing an internal state (such as a chemical concentration or the activity frequency of a neuron) in response to changes in the external world. In PCT, such an internal state is called a "sensing signal," and the signal value is "sensing." Perception refers to a signal value with unconscious meaning. It may be directly related to the current state of an attribute in the external world, but most of the time, the correlation is indirect. In most cases, the value of the perceptual signal depends not only on the current state of the physical variables affecting the perceptron but also on the current value of the internal variables. The external variables that affect the perceived signal value can be very complex and depend on the external environment. Comparing the value (reference or goal) expected to perceive some state to it, and keeping it there, is the strict engineering sense of the word "control." The perception of the external state is unstable, but the external state itself can be stable. The organism still uses fewer actions to influence its external state, hence perceptual cybernetics. For this reason, the PCT has a core principle: all actions are perceived controls. The behavior of stabilizing perception may vary with changing environmental influences, but a sound control system will change when its reference value changes.

As for PCT, there is a ubiquitous example in daily life. For example, when the external temperature is high, humans will perceive heat and sweat, which is not a cognitive level behavior, but a PCT behavior: no matter what the external temperature is, the human body constantly regulates and controls its body temperature to maintain an average temperature by sensing it and comparing it with the normal body temperature. Therefore, one can define perceived control as a negative feedback process. The Laplace Transform, which is a mathematical method that can be used to transform a time domain function into a frequency domain function. It is commonly used to analyze the stability of negative feedback systems. The Laplace transform of a function $f(t)$ is represented mathematically as shown in Equation (11.12).

$$F(s) = L(f(t))$$
$$= \int_0^\infty e^{-st} f(t) \mathrm{d}t, \tag{11.12}$$

where s is the complex frequency variable and $F(s)$ is the Laplace transform of $f(t)$.

11.4 Practical Application of Cybernetics

11.4.1 Research on the Control Mechanism of Neural Networks

The cyber financial crime control system aims to control the number of cyber financial crimes. At present, analyzing the influencing factors of network financial crimes mainly starts from different angles of law, society, economy, and other aspects. Therefore, the "man-machine-property-law-ring" is used to analyze network financial crime as an influencing factor.

11.4.2 Balance Between Internal Control and Management Power Relations

Organizations with a high cost of internal control implementation usually have the problem of the greater power of the management. The excessive power of the management will affect the establishment of the internal control system, and internal control can restrain the excessive "expansion" of the power of the management. The characteristics, alternative strategies, utility functions, and information structures of the internal control involved in the game and the management are different. Therefore, one can study from two different angles: the incomplete information dynamic game model and the incomplete information static game model, trying to find a refined Bayesian Nash equilibrium. In this state, the game should be the ideal state (incentive compatibility constraint), that is, the internal control to achieve the optimal state of management power at the same time, to get the maximum benefit.

1) **Dynamic Game with Incomplete Information**
Assume that x_1 is the utility that the enterprise achieves the expectation of the owner and the internal control executive, and then the revenue available to the management is s_1. x_2 is the utility that the enterprise fails to achieve the expectation of the owner and the internal control executive, and the income that the management can obtain is denoted by s_2. D is the failure to conclude the contract, and the management will find jobs again to get their benefits. d_1 and d_2 are the negative benefits at a_1 and a_2, respectively. There are only two kinds of information in the information system: Good News (GN) and Bad News (BN). There are also two situations: Good Situation (GS) and Bad Situation (BS). Therefore, the benefit function that internal control executive and management can obtain is shown in Table 11.1.

If the internal control is expected to achieve the expected and achievable state, starting from the rational assumption, the benefit obtained by the management in this state is bound to be greater than or equal to the benefit obtained by the internal

Table 11.1 The yarns of game theory.

	α_1 (Internal Control Meets Expectations)	α_2 (Internal Control Fails to Meet Expectations)
Management	$f(s_1) - d_1$	$f(s_2) - d_2$
Internal control execution	$x_1 - s_1$	$x_2 - s_2$

control when it fails to achieve the expected and achievable state, which can be expressed in a mathematical formula as shown in Equations (11.13) and (11.14):

$$f(s_1)P\left(\frac{GN}{GS}\right) + f(s_2)P\left(\frac{BN}{GS}\right) \geq f(s_1)P\left(\frac{GN}{BS}\right) + f(s_2)P\left(\frac{BN}{BS}\right) \tag{11.13}$$

$$\frac{P\left(\frac{GN}{GS}\right)}{P\left(\frac{GN}{BS}\right)} \geq \frac{P\left(\frac{BN}{GS}\right)}{P\left(\frac{BN}{BS}\right)}. \tag{11.14}$$

Furthermore, in order to meet the regular progress of the game, it is necessary to ensure that the management will accept the policies proposed by the internal control executive and the constraints on the power of his management, which can be expressed in a mathematical expression as shown in Equation (11.15).

$$f(s_1)P\left(\frac{GN}{GS}\right) + f(s_2)P\left(\frac{BN}{GS}\right) - d_1 \geq D. \tag{11.15}$$

Finally, in order to enable the management to promote the smooth progress of internal control from a positive perspective, according to the rational assumption, the model must ensure that the benefit function of the executor in the case of a_1 (internal control meets expectations) is greater than or equal to the case of a_2 (internal control fails to meet expectations). Mathematical terms can be expressed as in Equations (11.16) and (11.17).

$$(x_1 - s_1)P\left(\frac{GN}{GS}\right) + (x_2 - s_2)P\left(\frac{BN}{GS}\right) \geq (x_1 - s_1)P\left(\frac{GN}{BS}\right) + (x_2 - s_2)P\left(\frac{BN}{BS}\right) \tag{11.16}$$

$$((x_1 - s_1) - (x_2 - s_2))\left(P\left(\frac{GN}{GS}\right) - P\left(\frac{BN}{GS}\right)\right) \geq 0. \tag{11.17}$$

For the purpose of generalization, one can assume that the behavior of the management is entirely observable and that the asymmetric information phenomenon has wholly disappeared. The extraordinary situation must send out good news, and the lousy situation must send out bad news, namely, $P(GN/GS) = P(BN/BS) = 1$, $P(BN/GS) = P(GN/BS) = 0$. Therefore, the following can be obtained from the above three expressions.

$$f(s_1)P\left(\frac{GN}{GS}\right) - f(s_2)P\left(\frac{BN}{GS}\right) - d_1 \geq 0 \tag{11.18}$$

$$f(s^*) = d_1 + D. \tag{11.19}$$

2) Static Game with Incomplete Information

Assume that the internal control is executed in order to guarantee the regular operation of the internal control. The cost of system supply is C, the probability that internal control implementation can achieve the desired effect is P. Internal control execution party bring overall enterprise yields w. The stringency of executive party or penalties for violation of the internal control is b. The influence degree of management power on internal control is e.

The optimal decision of the management is:

$$\max E(S_1) = f(s^*) - bPf^2(s^*). \tag{11.20}$$

Take $f(s^*)$ as the independent variable, make the derivative of the above equation and make it equal to 0, one can achieve this as shown in following expressions.

$$\frac{dE(S_1)}{df(s^*)} = 1 - 2bPf(s^*) = 0 \tag{11.21}$$

$$f(s^*) = \frac{1}{2bP}. \tag{11.22}$$

11.4.3 Software Markov Adaptive Testing Strategy

In order to apply the Markov decision process to optimize the software testing process without loss of generality, the following assumptions are made for the software under test.

1) There are N defects in the system at time 0;
2) Only one decision is selected at any time, and at most, one defect is found;
3) When a defect is detected, it is considered that the defect has been eliminated. The system state is transferred immediately, and no new defects will be introduced. If $S_t = j$, $Z_t = 1$, then $S_{t+1} = j - 1$. Then $j = 0, 1, ..., N, t = 0, 1, 2, ...,$ indicates that there are j software defects in the system under test at time t;
4) If the system does not detect the defect, it will keep the original state: If $S_t = j$, $Z_t = 0$, $S_t + 1 = j$;

5) $S_t = 0$ is the convergence state, namely the target state;
6) There are m alternative decisions in each state, whose set is $A = \{1, 2, ..., m\}$;
7) The value of Z_t is only related to the value of S and A_t at time t;
8) After the decision A_t is selected and executed at time t, if a defect is detected, a cost of size $W_{St}(A_t)$ will be generated if the defect is detected;
9) The cost of defect removal is ignored. Order $\theta = \{0, 1, ..., N-1\}$ represents the set of state stages, the state of the dynamic system is denoted by $x(n)$, $n \in \theta$. The evolution process of it is described by the Equation (11.23).

$$x(n + 1) = Ax(n) + B_1(n)u(n) + B_2(n)v(n) + w(n), \quad x_0 \in R^r \quad (11.23)$$

The utility functions of the front and rear states are defined by Equation (11.24).

$$J_1(N, 0; u, v; x_0) = E\left[\sum_{n=0}^{N-1}\left(|x(n)|^2_{Q_{1(n)}} + |u(n)|^2_{R_{11(n)}} + |v(n)|^2_{R_{12(n)}}\right) + |x(n)|^2_{Q_{1(n)}}\right]$$

$$(11.24)$$

$$J_2(N, 0; u, v; x_0) = E\left[\sum_{n=0}^{N-1}\left(|x(n)|^2_{Q_{2(n)}} + |u(n)|^2_{R_{21(n)}} + |v(n)|^2_{R_{22(n)}}\right) + |x(n)|^2_{Q_{2(n)}}\right].$$

$$(11.25)$$

The policy spaces corresponding to the front and back states are defined by Equation (11.26).

$$\tau_{2,n} = \{y_{2,n}: R^r \to V, \text{such as } E\{\langle y_2(\varphi(n)), y_2(\varphi(n))\rangle_v\}\} < \infty. \quad (11.26)$$

The so-called game problem is to find a specific leader strategy to meet:

$$J_1\left(y_1^*, R(y_1^*)\right) = \min J_1(y_1, R(y_1)) \quad (11.27)$$

$$R(y_1) = \text{argmin} J_2(y_1, y_2). \quad (11.28)$$

According to the above assumptions, if τ is used to represent the time taken by the system to reach the target state (all defects are detected), there are shown in Equation (11.29).

$$J_\omega(N) = E_\omega \sum_{t=0}^{\tau} W_{S_t}(A_t), \quad (11.29)$$

where ω represents the software testing strategy, which determines the selection of test cases during the testing process; E_ω is the expected value relative to the testing strategy; $J_\omega(N)$ denotes the expected testing cost caused by all defects detected.

11.4.4 Task Analysis Model

Perceptual Control Based Task Analysis (PCBTA) model mainly focuses on the state transition during the execution of the system rather than the sequence of operations. The process by which users adjust the system's state according to their intentions is the process of controlling display variables according to task objectives. Unlike traditional task analysis models or methods, which focus on providing users with a practical working set, PCBTA models provide users with the correct system state determined by display variables. Combined with the basic process of software development, the primary process and steps of this model modeling are given, as shown in Figure 11.5.

In order to introduce the user's viewpoint and model the dynamic external environment, the PCBTA model uses task analysis based on perceptual cybernetics, which is used to represent the relationship between user goals and display variables. Perceived control refers to the behavior people adopt to achieve their goals in the face of a dynamic, complex, and uncertain external environment. A premise for introducing perceptual cybernetics into task modeling is that the way one think humans process things in this dynamic, complex world is essentially based on the theory. PCT takes the user's point of view and models interaction abstractions in a

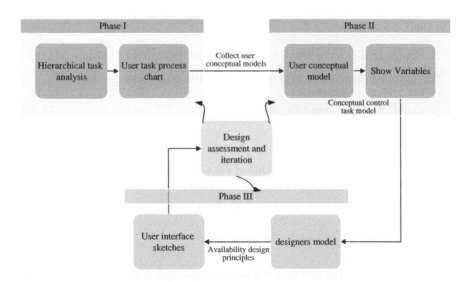

Figure 11.5 PCBTA modeling process.

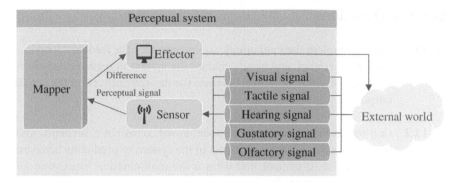

Figure 11.6 The relationship between perceptual control system and environment.

dynamic environment. The relationship between the perceptual control system and the environment is shown in Figure 11.6.

Summary

Cybernetics, along with relativity and quantum theory, has been identified as the three major leaps in the development of science in the first half of the 20th century. The research on cybernetics has basic practical significance, and with the development of cybernetics, it is more deeply connected with other fields. They keep crossing each other and play a crucial role in solving problems in other fields. This chapter mainly presents the theoretical content and application of cybernetics. After half a century of development, the application of control theory has greatly broken the limits of human beings and become an indispensable basic means for humans to understand and transform the natural process. In the future, the development of control theory will enable people to deal with the complex system control problems in people's life, social economy, ecological environment, industrial production, and other fields in a more scientific way, and benefit mankind in a wider range of aspects. The novel perspective of machine intelligence with cybernetics, which is termed as cybernetical intelligence, will have extensive and practical applications in combinatorial optimization problems and pattern recognition, data mining, and other related machine intelligence-based cybernetics problems. The ingenious Re[8] series of operators is summarized as a general investigation scheme for cybernetical intelligence neural networks.

Exercise Questions

Q.11.1 Can you explain the mathematical expression for the feedback loop in a cybernetic system, and how it enables the system to regulate its behavior based on the comparison between the desired output and the actual output?

Q.11.2 Can you explain the concept of model-based control in cybernetics, and how it uses a mathematical model of the system to predict its behavior and optimize its control, and what is the mathematical expression for the model-based feedback control system?

Q.11.3 Describe the new term, cybernetical intelligence, defined as in the paper.

Q.11.4 Demonstrate the Re8 analytics and how is it used in the development of cybernetical intelligent neural networks.

Q.11.5 How does the paper present the new perspectives of social control theory, internal control-related theory, and perceptual theory?

Q.11.6 Examine and explain how cybernetics is connected to other fields and what role does it play in solving problems in other fields.

Q.11.7 How does the concept of adaptive control in cybernetics enable a system to adjust its control parameters based on its changing environment or dynamics, and what is the mathematical expression for the adaptive feedback control system?

Q.11.8 Illustrate the application of control theory broken the limits of human beings.

Q.11.9 How will the development of control theory benefit mankind in the future?

Q.11.10 What are the extensive and practical applications of cybernetical intelligence in machine intelligence?

Q.11.11 Explain how does the Re^8 series of operators function as a general investigation scheme for cybernetical intelligence neural networks.

Q.11.12 How does cybernetics compare to relativity and quantum theory in terms of its significance in the development of science?

Q.11.13 What is the concept of homeostasis in cybernetics, and how does it relate to the goal of maintaining a stable internal state in a system, and what is the mathematical expression for the feedback control system that achieves homeostasis?

Q.11.14 Explain the concept of cybernetical intelligence and how it can be used in combinatorial optimization problems and pattern recognition, data mining, and other related machine intelligence-based cybernetics problems.

Further Reading

Bertalanffy LV. *General system theory: foundations, development, applications.* G. Braziller; 1968.

Breiman L. The individual ergodic theorem of information theory. *The Annals of Mathematical Statistics.* 1957 Sep 1;28(3):809–11.

Clemson B. *Cybernetics: a new management tool.* CRC Press; 1991.

Dahling RL. Shannon's information theory: the spread of an idea. *Studies of Innovation and of Communication to the Public.* II 1962;118–39.

Dimirovski GM. An overview of fastcinating ideas on complexity and complex networks and systems in computational cybernetics: Dedicated to Prof. Rudoplh E. Kalman, a giant of systems and control sciences, who past away on July 3, 2016: Jean Jacques Russeaux:"Who dares to say—this far man can go but not a step further." In IEEE EUROCON 2017-17th International Conference on Smart Technologies 2017 Jul 6 (pp. 650–664). IEEE.

Nee V, Ingram P. Embeddedness and beyond: institutions, exchange, and social structure. *The New Institutionalism in Sociology.* 1998 Feb 1;19:45.

Pias C, editor. Cybernetics-the Macy conferences 1946 1953: the complete transactions. In *Macy conferences 2016.* Chicago University Press.

Ross EA. Social control. *American Journal of Sociology.* 1896 Mar 1;1(5):513–35.

Wiener N. *Cybernetics or control and communication in the animal and the machine.* MIT Press; 2019 Oct 8.

Wiener N, Polatin P, Philtine EC, Hiltner S, Hirsh J, Doerr Hallenbeck P, Brozek J, Louis PA, Schafer R. *Cybernetics or control and com-munication in the animal and the machine Norbert Wiener.* MIT Press; 1948.

12

Turing Machine

The Turing machine is a theoretical model of computation that was first introduced by the British mathematician and computer scientist Alan Turing in the 1930s. A simple abstract machine is capable of performing any computation that can be carried out by any computer or algorithm.

The Turing machine consists of an infinite tape divided into squares, each of which can contain a symbol from a finite set of possible symbols. The machine also has a read/write head that can move left or right along the tape and can read and write symbols on the tape. The machine has a set of states and a transition function that determines how the machine should behave based on the current symbol on the tape and the current state of the machine. The operation of the Turing machine proceeds as follows:

- The machine starts in an initial state and the read/write head is positioned over a square on the tape.
- The machine reads the symbol on the tape at the current position.
- Based on the current state of the machine and the symbol on the tape, the machine consults its transition function to determine the next state of the machine and the symbol to write on the tape.
- The machine writes the symbol on the tape at the current position and moves the read/write head left or right as instructed by the transition function.
- The machine continues to perform steps 2–4 until it reaches a halting state, at which point the computation is complete.

The Turing machine is a powerful theoretical concept that has been used to prove fundamental results in computer science and mathematics. For example, Turing used the concept of the Turing machine to show that there are some problems that are fundamentally unsolvable by any algorithm, a concept known as

Cybernetical Intelligence: Engineering Cybernetics with Machine Intelligence, First Edition.
Kelvin K. L. Wong.
© 2024 The Institute of Electrical and Electronics Engineers, Inc.
Published 2024 by John Wiley & Sons, Inc.
Companion website: www.wiley.com/go/cyberintel

Table 12.1 Table summarizing the parameters of a Turing machine.

Parameter	Description
States	A Turing machine has a finite set of states that it can be in. When the machine is in a particular state, it performs a particular action (e.g. read a symbol, write a symbol, and move the tape head).
Tape	The tape of a Turing machine is divided into discrete cells, each of which can contain a symbol from a finite set of symbols. The tape is initially blank except for a finite sequence of symbols that represent the input.
Tape head	The tape head of a Turing machine is a read/write head that can move left or right along the tape one cell at a time.
Alphabet	The alphabet of a Turing machine is the set of symbols that can be written to or read from the tape.
Transition function	The transition function specifies the behavior of the Turing machine. Given the current state and symbol read from the tape, it specifies the next state of the machine, the symbol to write to the tape, and the direction for the tape head to move (left or right).
Halting state	The halting state is a special state that indicates that the Turing machine has finished its computation. Once the machine enters the halting state, it stops and outputs the contents of the tape.

the "halting problem." Additionally, the Turing machine has been used to define the notion of computability, which is the ability to solve a problem using an algorithm. The parameters of a Turing machine are summarized in Table 12.1.

12.1 Behavior of a Turing Machine

A Turing machine is a theoretical computing machine that operates on an infinite tape of symbols. The behavior of a Turing machine is described by its transition function, which specifies how the machine moves and changes the symbol on the tape based on its current state and the symbol that it is currently reading.

To describe the behavior of a Turing machine, one start with an initial tape configuration, which consists of a finite sequence of input symbols followed by an infinite sequence of blank symbols. The machine starts in the initial state $q0$, with the tape head positioned on the leftmost input symbol.

At each step, the machine reads the symbol on the tape under the tape head, looks up its current state in the transition function, and performs the transition specified by the function. This involves writing a new symbol on the tape, moving the tape head in one position to the left or right, and changing the state of the machine. The behavior of a Turing machine can be modeled using a mathematical notation called a transition table. The table lists each possible combination of current state and current symbol, along with the new state, new symbol, and direction (left or right) of the head movement for that combination. The table also specifies a halting state, which indicates that the machine has reached the end of its computation and should stop. The behavior of a Turing machine can also be described using a mathematical formalism known as a Turing machine program. The program consists of a set of rules that specify the behavior of the machine at each step of its computation. The program can be used to simulate the behavior of the machine on a given input, and can also be used to prove theoretical results about the capabilities of Turing machines. Formally, a Turing machine can be defined as a 7-tuple $(Q, \Sigma, \Gamma, \delta, q0, B, F)$, where Q is a finite set of states, Σ is a finite set of input symbols, Γ is a finite set of tape symbols, where $\Sigma \subseteq \Gamma$. $\delta : Q \times \Gamma \rightarrow Q \times \Gamma \times \{L, R\}$ is the transition function, which describes how the machine transitions between states, $q0 \in Q$ is the initial state of the machine, $B \in \Gamma$ is the blank symbol, which is used to represent empty cells on the tape. $F \subseteq Q$ is the set of final states, which represent the acceptance states of the machine. The transition function $\delta(q, a) = (p, b, d)$ specifies that if the machine is in state q and is reading symbol a, it should transition to state p, write symbol b on the tape, and move the head in direction d (either left or right).

12.1.1 Computing with Turing Machines

- Computing with Turing Machines involves specifying a set of rules that the machine will follow to perform a computation. The rules describe how the machine will read and write symbols on its tape, move its head left or right on the tape, and change its internal state. A Turing machine can be thought of as having an infinite tape divided into cells, each of which can hold a symbol from a finite set of possible symbols. The machine also has a head that can read and write symbols on the tape and move left or right along the tape. The state of the machine is determined by its internal state and the symbol currently being read by the head. The basic steps involved in computing with a Turing machine are:
- Start in an initial state with the head positioned over the first cell of the tape.
- Read the symbol on the current cell and look up the corresponding transition rule in the machine's rule table.
- Write the new symbol on the current cell, move the head left or right on the tape, and transition to a new state as specified by the rule.
- Repeat steps 2 and 3 until the machine enters a final state, indicating that the computation is complete.

The rules for a Turing machine are typically specified using a transition function that maps the current state and input symbol to a new state, output symbol, and head movement direction. The transition function can be written as:

$$\delta(q, a) = (p, b, d),\tag{12.1}$$

where q is the current state, a is the input symbol, p is the new state, b is the symbol to be written on the tape, and d is the direction in which the head should move (either L for left or R for right). The transition function for a Turing Machine can be expressed as:

$$\delta : Q \times \sum \to Q \times \sum \times \{L, R\},\tag{12.2}$$

where Q is the set of states, Σ is the tape alphabet, and L and R indicate the direction to move the tape head (left or right). The function that describes the behavior of a Turing Machine can be written as:

$$f : \sum{}^{*} \to \sum{}^{*},\tag{12.3}$$

where $\sum^{*}$ is the set of all possible strings over the tape alphabet Σ. The universal Turing Machine can simulate the behavior of any other Turing Machine. The transition function for the universal machine is:

$$\delta : Q \times \sum \times \tau \to Q \times \sum \times \tau \times \{L, R, S\},\tag{12.4}$$

where Γ is the set of all symbols that can appear on the tape. The halting problem, which asks whether a given Turing Machine will eventually halt or run forever, can be expressed as: $H = \{\langle M, w \rangle \mid M$ is a Turing Machine that halts on input $w\}$.

Where $\langle M, w \rangle$ is a string encoding the Turing Machine M and its input string w. It can be shown that there is no algorithm that can solve the halting problem for all possible Turing Machines and input strings.

Turing machines can simulate any algorithm or computer program, which makes them a powerful tool for studying computability and complexity theory. They are also the theoretical basis for modern digital computers and programming languages.

12.2 Basic Operations of a Turing Machine

A Turing Machine operates on a tape that is divided into discrete cells, each containing a symbol from a finite alphabet. The machine has a tape head that can read and write symbols on the tape, and move back and forth along the tape. The basic operations of a Turing Machine can be described as follows:

- Reading a symbol from the tape: The current symbol under the tape head is read and stored in the machine's memory.
- Writing a symbol on the tape: The Turing Machine can write a new symbol to the current cell under the tape head.
- Moving the tape head: The tape head can move one cell to the left or right.
- Changing states: The Turing Machine can change its state according to its transition function, which takes as input the current state and the symbol under the tape head, and outputs a new state and a set of instructions for how to manipulate the tape and move the tape head.

These basic operations can be combined to perform any computation that a Turing Machine is capable of. By reading symbols from the tape, writing new symbols, moving the tape head, and changing states according to its transition function, a Turing Machine can simulate any algorithm that can be expressed in terms of these operations.

12.2.1 Reading and Writing to the Tape

A Turing Machine operates on a tape that is divided into discrete cells, each containing a symbol from a finite alphabet. The machine has a tape head that can read and write symbols on the tape, and move back and forth along the tape. To read a symbol from the tape, the Turing Machine moves the tape head to the cell that it wants to read and then reads the symbol that is stored in that cell. The symbol is then temporarily stored in the machine's memory. To write a symbol to the tape, the Turing Machine moves the tape head to the cell that it wants to write to and then writes the symbol to that cell. The previous symbol that was stored in that cell is overwritten.

Consider the tape to be represented as an infinite sequence of cells, indexed by integers: $T = (..., T[-2], T[-1], T[0], T[1], T[2], ...)$.

Each cell in the tape contains a symbol from a finite alphabet Σ, which may include a special blank symbol to indicate unused cells. To read a symbol from the tape, the Turing Machine reads the symbol in the current cell under the tape head and stores it in a temporary variable:

$$\omega = T[h], \tag{12.5}$$

where, h represents the current position of the tape head on the tape. To write a symbol to the tape, the Turing Machine writes the new symbol σ to the current cell under the tape head, overwriting the previous symbol:

$$T[h] = \sigma, \tag{12.6}$$

where, σ is a symbol from the tape alphabet Σ. To move the tape head to the left or right, the Turing Machine updates the position variable h accordingly:

$$h = h + d, \tag{12.7}$$

where, d is either -1 (to move the tape head one cell to the left) or 1 (to move the tape head one cell to the right). The above operations of reading, writing, and moving the tape head can be combined to perform any computation that a Turing Machine is capable of. By reading symbols from the tape, writing new symbols, moving the tape head, and changing states according to its transition function, a Turing Machine can simulate any algorithm that can be expressed in terms of these operations. Note that the tape is infinite in both directions, so the Turing Machine can access any cell on the tape by moving the tape head left or right. However, in practice, a physical Turing Machine would have a finite amount of memory to store the tape, and so would be limited in the number of cells it could access.

12.2.2 Moving the Tape Head

A Turing Machine operates on a tape that is divided into discrete cells, each containing a symbol from a finite alphabet. The machine has a tape head that can read and write symbols on the tape, and move back and forth along the tape. To move the tape head, the Turing Machine can either move it to the left or to the right by one cell at a time. This is done by changing the position of the tape head on the tape. Consider h be the current position of the tape head on the tape. To move the tape head to the left, the Turing Machine subtracts 1 from h:

$$h = h - 1. \tag{12.8}$$

To move the tape head to the right, the Turing Machine adds 1–h:

$$h = h + 1. \tag{12.9}$$

In practice, the Turing Machine would also need to check whether the tape head has reached the end of the tape and take appropriate action (such as moving to a new blank cell or halting the computation). Note that the tape is infinite in both directions, so the Turing Machine can move the tape head left or right by any finite number of cells. However, in practice, a physical Turing Machine would have a finite amount of memory to store the tape, and so would be limited in the number of cells it could access.

12.2.3 Changing States

In a Turing Machine, the machine's state describes the current condition of the machine, including the position of tape head, the contents of the tape, and the machine's internal memory. The machine's state can change during computation, allowing the Turing Machine to perform different operations depending on its current state. To change states, the Turing Machine can transition from one state to another based on a set of predefined rules called the transition function.

The transition function is defined by a set of rules that describe what action the Turing Machine should take based on its current state and the symbol it reads from the tape. These rules define the next state of the machine, the symbol to write to the tape, and the direction to move the tape head (left or right). The rules are typically written in the form:

$$(q, a) \rightarrow (p, b, d), \tag{12.10}$$

where q is the current state, a is the symbol being read from the tape, p is the next state, b is the symbol to write to the tape, and d is the direction to move the tape head (either left or right). For example, suppose there is a Turing Machine that operates on a tape with the alphabet $\{0, 1, \text{blank}\}$, and the machine is currently in state q_0. The transition function for the machine might include a rule that says:

$$(q_0, 1) \rightarrow (q_1, 0, R). \tag{12.11}$$

This rule means that if the machine is in state q_0 and reads a "1" from the tape, it should transition to state q_1, write a "0" to the tape, and move the tape head one cell to the right.

The ability to change states based on the contents of the tape allows the Turing Machine to perform complex computations and is the basis for its computational power.

12.3 Interchangeability of Program and Behavior

The interchangeability of program and behavior is a fundamental concept in the field of computer science, particularly in the study of Turing machines and other computational models.

At a basic level, the idea is that any computation that can be performed by a particular program can also be performed by a particular behavior, and vice versa. In other words, its program can define the behavior of a machine, and the program of a machine can be inferred from its behavior. This concept has important implications for the development of software and computer systems, as it suggests that different implementations of the same program can have the same behavior, and different programs can achieve different behaviors. One of the key insights behind this concept is that the behavior of a machine is determined by its state and its input, and the transition between states is determined by the program. This can be represented mathematically using a transition function that maps the current state and input to a new state and output.

For example, consider a simple Turing machine that accepts the binary input "101" and outputs the binary number "3" in decimal. A program that specifies the transition function for each state and input combination can define the behavior of the machine.

By examining the behavior of the machine, it is possible to infer the program that generates that behavior. In this way, the program and behavior are interchangeable, and different programs can be used to achieve the same behavior, or different behaviors can be achieved with different programs.

Overall, the interchangeability of program and behavior is a powerful concept that has important implications for the design and analysis of computer systems and the development of new computing technologies.

12.4 Computability Theory

Computability theory, also known as recursion theory, is a branch of theoretical computer science and mathematical logic that studies the concept of computability. It deals with the fundamental question of what can be computed and what cannot be computed.

Intelligent control, on the other hand, is a field of study that deals with the design and analysis of control systems that can operate autonomously and make decisions based on the available data. It involves the use of machine learning, artificial intelligence, and other advanced techniques to develop control systems that are more efficient and effective than traditional control systems.

The intersection of computability theory and intelligent control lies in the development of algorithms and decision-making processes that are based on the principles of computability. These algorithms and decision-making processes can be used to design and optimize intelligent control systems. Some key concepts in computability theory are summarized in Table 12.2.

One example of the application of computability theory in intelligent control is the use of machine learning algorithms to learn patterns in data and make predictions based on those patterns. The computability theory provides the theoretical framework for understanding the limits of what can be learned and predicted.

Another example is the use of feedback control systems, which are based on the principles of computability and control theory, to regulate the behavior of intelligent systems. Feedback control systems use sensors to measure the output of the system and adjust the input based on the difference between the desired output and the actual output.

Table 12.2 Summarizing some key concepts in computability theory.

Concept	Description
Decision problem	A problem that has a yes-or-no answer, such as "is this number prime?" or "does this program terminate?"
Turing machine	A mathematical model of a computer that consists of a tape, a tape head, and a set of rules for moving the tape head and reading/writing symbols to the tape.
Halting problem	The decision problem of determining, given a Turing machine and an input, whether the machine will eventually halt or run forever. It has been proven to be undecidable, meaning there is no algorithm that can solve it for all possible inputs.
Church-Turing thesis	The informal claim that any problem that can be solved by an algorithm (i.e. a step-by-step procedure) can be solved by a Turing machine. This thesis has not been proven or disproven, but it is widely believed to be true.
Recursively enumerable set	A set of numbers that can be generated by a Turing machine (i.e. the machine can eventually halt and output the number).
Recursive set	A set of numbers for which there exists a Turing machine that can decide whether a given number is a member of the set (i.e. the machine will always halt and output either "yes" or "no").
Undecidable problem	A decision problem for which no algorithm exists that can solve it for all possible inputs. Examples include the halting problem and the problem of determining whether two given Turing machines compute the same function.

In summary, the concepts and principles of computability theory can be used to develop and optimize intelligent control systems that are more efficient and effective than traditional control systems. The integration of these two fields can lead to the development of more advanced and sophisticated intelligent control systems that can operate autonomously and adapt to changing conditions.

12.4.1 Complexity Theory

Complexity theory is a field of study that seeks to understand the inherent complexity of computational problems and algorithms, and the resources required to solve them. It is an important area of research in intelligent control, as it helps to determine the efficiency and scalability of algorithms used in intelligent control systems. One of the main measures of complexity in computational problems is time complexity, which measures the amount of time required to solve a problem as a function of the size of the input. Another important measure is space complexity, which measures the amount of memory required to solve a problem. One of the most famous problems in complexity theory is the P versus NP problem, which asks whether or not problems that can be verified in polynomial time can also be solved in polynomial time. If $P = NP$, it would have significant implications for the efficiency of algorithms used in intelligent control systems.

Another important concept in complexity theory is the notion of completeness. A problem is said to be NP-complete if it is in the set of NP problems and every problem in NP can be reduced to it in polynomial time. NP-complete problems are believed to be inherently difficult to solve efficiently, and their study has led to the development of important algorithms such as the traveling salesman problem. In intelligent control, complexity theory is used to determine the efficiency and scalability of algorithms used in various applications such as machine learning and optimization. For example, the time complexity of an algorithm used for training a neural network is an important factor in determining the feasibility of using that algorithm for real-time applications. The time complexity of a neural network training algorithm can be expressed in terms of the number of iterations required to converge to a solution. Let n be the number of iterations and $T(n)$ be the time complexity of the algorithm.

$$T(n) = O(f(n)), \tag{12.12}$$

where $O(f(n))$ denotes the upper bound of the time complexity in terms of a function $f(n)$. The overall time complexity of training a neural network can be expressed as the product of the number of iterations required to converge and the time complexity of computing the gradient for one mini-batch:

$$T = n \times O(k \times m), \tag{12.13}$$

where n is the number of iterations required to converge, k is the size of the mini-batch, and m is the number of parameters in the network. Overall, complexity theory is a critical field of study in intelligent control as it helps to ensure that algorithms used in intelligent control systems are efficient and scalable, leading to better performance and more successful applications.

12.5 Automata Theory

Automata theory is a branch of computer science that studies the properties of abstract computing devices called automata. These devices are mathematical models of machines that can perform a finite number of operations, or transitions, on inputs from a finite set of symbols. Automata theory is closely related to the study of formal languages, which are sets of strings of symbols that can be generated by a particular set of rules. The theory provides a formal framework for describing and analyzing the properties of languages, including regular, context-free, and context-sensitive languages.

In the context of intelligent control, automata theory can be used to model and analyze the behavior of control systems. For example, a finite-state machine can be used to represent the behavior of a system that has a finite number of states and transitions between those states. This machine can then be used to design a control system that achieves a desired behavior.

Formally, an automaton can be defined as a 5-tuple $(Q, \Sigma, \delta, q_0, F)$, where Q is a finite set of states

Σ is a finite set of input symbols, also known as the alphabet. The $\delta : Q \times \Sigma \rightarrow Q$ is a transition function that maps a state and an input symbol to a new state $q_0 \in Q$ is the initial state

$F \subseteq Q$ is the set of accepting states.

An automaton can be visualized as a directed graph, where each state is represented by a node and each transition is represented by an edge labeled with an input symbol. The initial state is usually marked with an arrow pointing to it, and the accepting states are typically denoted by double circles. Automata theory includes several types of automata, such as:

- Finite-state automata (FSAs), which have a finite number of states and can recognize regular languages
- Pushdown automata (PDAs), which have a stack that allows them to recognize context-free languages
- Turing machines, which have an infinite tape and can recognize recursively enumerable languages

In the context of intelligent control, automata theory can be used to analyze the behavior of a control system and determine whether it satisfies certain properties, such as safety or liveness. It can also be used to design a control system that achieves a desired behavior, based on a formal specification of that behavior in terms of a formal language.

12.6 Philosophical Issues Related to Turing Machines

The concept of Turing machines raises several philosophical issues, including the nature of computation, the limits of knowledge, and the relationship between mind and machine.

One of the most significant philosophical issues raised by Turing machines is the question of whether they provide a complete model of computation. Some theorists argue that there may be forms of computation that cannot be carried out by

Turing machines, and that therefore, the Turing machine model is incomplete. This has led to the development of alternative models of computation, such as quantum computing and hypercomputation.

Another philosophical issue related to Turing machines is the question of whether they have any relevance to the study of the mind. Some theorists argue that the Turing machine model is limited in its ability to capture the complexities of mental processes, and that therefore, it cannot be used to fully understand the nature of human thought and consciousness. However, others argue that Turing machines provide a useful framework for studying the mind and that they can be used to develop intelligent systems that simulate human thought processes. Finally, Turing machines raise questions about the nature of knowledge and understanding. Since Turing machines are purely formal systems, some philosophers argue that they cannot provide genuine knowledge or understanding of the world. Others argue that Turing machines can provide genuine knowledge and understanding and that they are useful tools for exploring the limits of knowledge and understanding. Overall, the philosophical issues raised by Turing machines highlight the need for interdisciplinary approaches to understanding the nature of computation, mind, and knowledge.

12.7   Human and Machine Computations

Human and machine computations are two different approaches to solving problems, and they differ in the way they process information. Human computations rely on the use of biological neurons and are typically more flexible and adaptable to new situations. Machine computations, on the other hand, rely on algorithms and digital circuits, which are programmed to perform specific tasks.

Mathematically, human and machine computations can be described in different ways. For human computations, researchers often use models of biological neurons, such as the McCulloch-Pitts model, to describe how the brain processes information. These models use mathematical equations to represent the behavior of individual neurons and the connections between them. For example, the McCulloch–Pitts model describes the behavior of a neuron as a function of its inputs, which are weighted according to the strength of the connections between neurons. The output of the neuron is then compared to a threshold value, and if the output exceeds this value, the neuron fires, sending a signal to other neurons in the network.

Machine computations, on the other hand, are typically described using formal languages and algorithms. Formal languages are sets of symbols and rules for manipulating those symbols, and they are used to define the syntax and semantics of programming languages. Algorithms are sets of instructions for solving a specific problem or performing a specific task, and they can be described using pseudocode or flowcharts. Pseudocode is a high-level description of an algorithm that uses plain language to describe the steps involved, while flowcharts use graphical symbols to represent the steps of the algorithm. Overall, while human and machine computations are different approaches to problem-solving, both can be described using mathematical and computational models, and both have contributed to the development of modern computing and artificial intelligence.

12.8 Historical Models of Computability

Historical models of computability refer to the different theoretical frameworks that have been proposed to capture the notion of computation. Some of the most significant models of computability include:

- Turing machines: Turing machines were first proposed by Alan Turing in 1936 as a way of formalizing the concept of computation. A Turing machine consists of a tape divided into cells, a read/write head that can move back and forth along the tape and a set of states that define the machine's behavior. The machine starts in an initial state and reads the symbol on the current cell of the tape. Based on the current state and the symbol read, the machine can write a new symbol to the tape, move the read/write head left or right, and transition to a new state. A Turing machine can compute any function that is computable by an algorithm.
- Lambda calculus: Lambda calculus was first proposed by Alonzo Church in the 1930s as an alternative model of computation. Lambda calculus is based on the idea of applying functions to arguments. A lambda expression consists of a variable, a body that specifies how the variable is used, and an abstraction operator that binds the variable to the body. Lambda calculus can be used to compute any function that is computable by an algorithm.
- Recursive functions: Recursive functions were first proposed by Kurt Gödel and Jacques Herbrand in the 1930s as a way of formalizing the concept of computability. A recursive function is a function that can be defined in terms of itself. Recursive functions can be used to compute any function that is computable by an algorithm.
- Post-Turing machines: Post-Turing machines were proposed by Emil Post as an alternative to Turing machines. Post-Turing machines are similar to Turing machines but have a slightly different set of operations. Post-Turing machines can compute any function that is computable by a Turing machine.

- Register machines: Register machines were first proposed by Marvin Minsky in the 1960s as a way of modeling computer architectures. A register machine consists of a set of registers that can hold values, a set of operations that can be performed on the registers, and a program that specifies the sequence of operations to be performed. Register machines can compute any function that is computable by an algorithm.

These models of computability have had a significant impact on the development of computer science and the study of algorithms. They have also helped to establish the theoretical limits of computation and have provided a framework for understanding the nature of computation and its relationship to other areas of mathematics and science.

12.9 Recursive Functions

Recursive functions, also known as computable functions, are a class of functions that can be calculated by an algorithm. In other words, these are functions that can be computed by a Turing machine. Recursive functions can be thought of as a set of rules that generate an output for each input.

The basic building blocks of recursive functions are primitive recursive functions, which include constants, successor functions, and projection functions. From these, more complex functions can be built using operations such as composition, recursion, and minimization. Composition is the process of combining two or more functions to create a new function. For example, if $f(x) = 2x$ and $g(x) = x + 1$, then the composite function $h(x) = f(g(x))$ is equal to $h(x) = 2(x + 1) = 2x + 2$.

Consider a base case $f(0) = c$, where c is a constant value. Inductive step for all positive integers n, define $f(n)$ recursively in terms of $f(n-1)$ and other mathematical operations. For example, as defined below:

$$f(n) = g(n, f(n-1)), \tag{12.14}$$

where $g()$ is mathematical function that takes n and x as input and returns a new value. This allows us to build up complex functions by defining them in terms of simpler functions.

If there is a need to define a function that cannot be expressed using only primitive recursion, one can use the minimization operator. For example, define a function $h(x)$ that computes the smallest integer y such that $f(y) > x$ as follows:

$$h(x) = \mu y \, [f(y) > x], \tag{12.15}$$

where μ is the minimization operator, and $[f(y) > x]$ is an indicator function that evaluates to 1 if $f(y)$ is greater than x and 0 otherwise. Recursion is the process of defining a function in terms of itself. This allows for the creation of functions that can repeat a process a certain number of times or perform an operation until a certain condition is met. For example, the factorial function can be defined recursively as follows:

$$n! = n!(n-1) \quad \text{if } n > 0$$
$$n! = 1 \quad \text{if } n = 0,$$

$$(12.16)$$

using recursion, this function can be called repeatedly until the base case ($n = 0$ or $n = 1$) is reached, at which point the function terminates. Minimization is a process of finding the minimum value of a function. In the context of recursive functions, this involves finding the smallest value of n for which a certain condition is met. For example, the smallest natural number that is not the sum of two squares can be found using a minimization function.

Recursive functions can also be used to solve problems in various fields such as computer science, mathematics, and physics. For example, they can be used in the design of algorithms for searching, sorting, and data analysis. They can also be used in the development of mathematical models for complex systems. Overall, recursive functions are an important concept in the field of computability and have a wide range of applications in various fields.

12.10 Turing Machine and Intelligent Control

Turing machine is a fundamental concept in intelligent control and artificial intelligence. It serves as a theoretical framework for understanding the limits and capabilities of computing systems. In intelligent control, Turing machines are used to model various computational processes and to analyze the complexity of algorithms.

Turing machines consist of a tape, a head that can read and write symbols on the tape, and a control unit that determines the machine's behavior. The tape is divided into cells, each of which can hold a symbol from a finite alphabet. The head can move back and forth along the tape and can read and write symbols on the tape. The control unit of a Turing machine is a finite-state machine that determines the machine's behavior based on the current state of the machine and the symbol on the tape under the head. The control unit can change the state of the machine, move the head left or right along the tape, and write a new symbol on the tape. Turing machines can compute any computable function, which includes all functions that can be computed by a digital computer.

This is known as the Church-Turing thesis, which states that any function that can be computed by an algorithm can be computed by a Turing machine, and vice versa.

In intelligent control, Turing machines are used to analyze the computational complexity of algorithms and to design algorithms for solving complex problems. They are also used as a theoretical framework for understanding the limits and capabilities of intelligent systems, including artificial neural networks and other machine learning algorithms. The inputs to a Turing machine can be represented as a string of symbols, and the machine operates by reading these symbols one at a time, using its set of rules to determine what action to take based on each symbol. The machine can also write new symbols to a tape, allowing it to store information and perform calculations. One application of Turing machines in intelligent control is in the development of artificial intelligence algorithms. For example, a machine learning algorithm can be represented as a Turing machine that has been trained to recognize patterns in data and make predictions based on those patterns. The machine can read in new data and use its set of rules to make predictions about future outcomes.

Turing machines can also be used to model and analyze the behavior of complex control systems, such as those used in manufacturing or transportation. By representing these systems as Turing machines, researchers can study their behavior and develop more efficient and effective control strategies. Overall, the concept of Turing machine has played a significant role in the development of intelligent control and artificial intelligence and continues to be an important tool for analyzing and designing computational systems.

Summary

This chapter has described the concept of Turing machines, their behavior, and the interchangeability of program and behavior. Philosophical issues related to Turing machines were also discussed. Additionally, the use of Turing machines in intelligent control systems was explored.

In the future, the development of more advanced computing technologies will likely have a significant impact on the field of intelligent control. The use of Turing machines and other computational models will continue to evolve, and new applications of these models will be discovered. The use of intelligent control systems will become more widespread, as they have the potential to improve the efficiency and effectiveness of a wide range of processes and systems. As these technologies continue to evolve, it will be important to consider their ethical implications and ensure that they are being used in a responsible and beneficial way.

Exercise Questions

Q.12.1 What is the relationship between the Halting problem and the limits of computation?

Q.12.2 How does the concept of undecidability relate to computability theory?

Q.12.3 Can a modern computer compute all functions that can be computed by a Turing machine?

Q.12.4 What is the mathematical expression for the transition function in a Turing machine, and how does it determine the next state and tape symbol based on the current state and tape symbol?

Q.12.5 How do finite state machines differ from Turing machines in terms of computational power?

Q.12.6 How can Turing machines be used to model and prove the computability of functions and languages, such as the Church-Turing thesis and the Universal Turing machine, and what is the mathematical expression for the computation of a Turing machine?

Q.12.7 How does the concept of complexity relate to the analysis of algorithms?

Q.12.8 How can Turing machines be used to define and study complexity classes, such as *P, NP,* and *NP*-complete, and what is the mathematical expression for the time and space complexity of a Turing machine computation?

Q.12.9 What is the role of randomness in computation, and how is it related to complexity?

Q.12.10 Can machines ever achieve true artificial intelligence?

Further Reading

Conti M, De Gaspari F, Mancini LV. A novel stealthy attack to gather SDN configuration-information. *IEEE Transactions on Emerging Topics in Computing.* 2018 Feb 16;8(2):328–40.

Cooper SB. *Computability theory*. CRC Press; 2003 Nov 17.

Hodges A. Did church and turing have a thesis about machines. *Church's Thesis After*. 2006;70:242–52.

Nakao Y. *Precision control of single point diamond turning machine using intelligent controller*. LMA. 1998 Oct:71.

13

Entropy Concepts in Machine Intelligence

Entropy is a fundamental concept in information theory, and it plays an important role in machine intelligence. In simple terms, entropy refers to the degree of disorder or randomness in a system. In machine intelligence, entropy is often used as a measure of uncertainty or information content. One of the most common uses of entropy in machine intelligence is in decision trees, where it is used to determine the optimal split for a given dataset. In this context, entropy is used to measure the impurity of a given dataset, with lower entropy indicating a more homogeneous dataset. By minimizing entropy, decision trees can efficiently split the data into smaller and more homogeneous subsets, ultimately leading to predictions that are more accurate.

Entropy is also used in the field of natural language processing, where it can be used to measure the degree of uncertainty or ambiguity in a given sentence or text. This can be useful in tasks such as machine translation or sentiment analysis, where understanding the meaning and context of a given text is essential. In addition to its uses in decision trees and natural language processing, entropy is also used in a variety of other machine learning algorithms, such as clustering and anomaly detection. In clustering, for example, entropy can be used to determine the optimal number of clusters, with lower entropy indicating a more clearly defined set of clusters.

Overall, entropy is a powerful and versatile tool in machine intelligence, providing a way to measure uncertainty and information content across a wide range of applications. By understanding the concept of entropy and its uses in machine intelligence, researchers and practitioners can develop more accurate and efficient machine learning algorithms that can help to solve a wide range of real-world problems.

Cybernetical Intelligence: Engineering Cybernetics with Machine Intelligence, First Edition.
Kelvin K. L. Wong.
© 2024 The Institute of Electrical and Electronics Engineers, Inc.
Published 2024 by John Wiley & Sons, Inc.
Companion website: www.wiley.com/go/cyberintel

13.1 Relative Entropy of Distributions

Relative entropy, also known as Kullback–Leibler divergence, is a measure of how different two probability distributions are from each other. It is commonly used in statistics and information theory to quantify the distance between two probability distributions. Relative entropy is defined as follows:

Given two probability distributions P and Q over the same sample space X, the relative entropy of P with respect to Q, denoted by $D(P\|Q)$, is defined as:

$$D(P\|Q) = \sum_x P(x) \log \frac{P(x)}{Q(x)}, \tag{13.1}$$

where $\sum_x$ denotes the sum over all values of x in the sample space X, and $P(x)$ and $Q(x)$ are the probabilities assigned to x by the distributions P and Q, respectively.

The relative entropy can be interpreted as the amount of additional information required to encode data generated from P using an optimal code designed for Q. In other words, it measures the inefficiency of using a code designed for Q to encode data generated from P. Some key properties of relative entropy include:

- $D(P\|Q) \geq 0$ for all probability distributions P and Q, and $D(P\|Q) = 0$ if and only if $P = Q$.
- Relative entropy is not a symmetric measure, that is, $D(P\|Q)$ is not necessarily equal to $D(Q\|P)$.
- Relative entropy is not a metric, since it violates the triangle inequality.
- Relative entropy is additive over independent random variables.
- Relative entropy can be extended to continuous probability distributions by replacing the summation with an integral.

Relative entropy has many important applications in machine learning, including model selection, clustering, and data compression. For example, in model selection, relative entropy can be used to compare the performance of different models by measuring the difference between the predicted and actual probability distributions.

Overall, relative entropy is a powerful and versatile tool in information theory and machine learning, providing a way to measure the difference between probability distributions and quantify the amount of information required to encode data generated from one distribution using a code designed for another distribution.

13.2 Relative Entropy and Mutual Information

Relative entropy and mutual information are both important concepts in information theory, and they are closely related to each other. In this response, one will describe each concept in detail and explain their relationship. Relative entropy, also known as Kullback–Leibler divergence, is a measure of how different two probability distributions are from each other. Given two probability distributions P and Q over the same sample space X, the relative entropy of P with respect to Q, denoted by $D(P\|Q)$, is defined as shown in Equation (13.2).

The relative entropy can be interpreted as the amount of additional information required to encode data generated from P using an optimal code designed for Q. In other words, it measures the inefficiency of using a code designed for Q to encode data generated from P. Mutual information, on the other hand, measures the amount of information that two random variables share. It is defined as:

$$I(X, Y) = D(P(X, Y)\|P(X)P(Y)), \tag{13.2}$$

where $P(X, Y)$ is the joint probability distribution of X and Y, and $P(X)$ and $P(Y)$ are the marginal probability distributions of X and Y, respectively.

The mutual information can be interpreted as the reduction in uncertainty of one random variable when the value of the other variable is known. It measures the degree to which two random variables are dependent on each other. The relationship between relative entropy and mutual information is given by:

$$I(X, Y) = D(P(X, Y)\|P(X)P$$
$$= D(P(X, Y)\|P(X)Q(Y)) - D(P(X, Y)\|Q(X)Q(Y)), \tag{13.3}$$

where $Q(X)$ and $Q(Y)$ are any other probability distributions over X and Y, respectively.

This equation shows that mutual information can be expressed as the difference between two relative entropies. The first term measures the difference between the joint distribution and the product of the marginal under the true distribution, while the second term measures the difference between the joint distribution and the product of the marginal under an alternative distribution.

Overall, relative entropy and mutual information are both important concepts in information theory, providing a way to measure the difference between probability distributions and quantify the amount of information shared between random variables. The relationship between the two concepts highlights the fundamental connections between information theory and probability theory, and their appli cations in fields such as machine learning, data compression, and signal processing.

13.3 Entropy in Performance Evaluation

Entropy can be used as a metric to evaluate the performance of a classification model. It measures the degree of uncertainty or disorder in the system, and in the context of classification, it represents the uncertainty in the classification decision. Consider there is a classification model that assigns a label y to an input x. One also have a true label t for each input x. If one consider the set of all possible labels Y, the entropy of the classification model is defined as:

$$H = -\sum_{y} p(y) \log_2(p(y)),\tag{13.4}$$

where py is the proportion of inputs that are classified as label y by the model, and $\log_2$ is the base-2 logarithm.

In this equation, one can see that the entropy H is a function of the distribution of the labels assigned by the model. If the model assigns the correct label to all inputs, the entropy will be 0, indicating that there is no uncertainty in the classification decision. On the other hand, if the model assigns different labels to different inputs with equal probability, the entropy will be maximal, indicating maximum uncertainty. To evaluate the performance of a classification model, one can use the concept of cross-entropy. Cross-entropy measures the difference between the predicted distribution and the true distribution of the labels. Assume to represent the true distribution of the labels as $p'(y)$. The cross-entropy $H(p', p)$ between the predicted distribution $p(y)$ and the true distribution $p'(y)$ is defined as:

$$H(p', p) = -\sum_{y} p'(y) \log_2(p(y)),\tag{13.5}$$

In this equation, one can see that the cross-entropy is a function of both the predicted distribution and the true distribution. If the predicted distribution is identical to the true distribution, the cross-entropy will be 0, indicating that the model is perfectly accurate. On the other hand, if the predicted distribution is different from the true distribution, the cross-entropy will be positive, indicating that the model is less accurate.

Finally, one can use the concept of information gain to evaluate the contribution of each feature to the classification performance. Information gain measures the reduction in entropy achieved by splitting the dataset based on a particular feature. Assume that one have a dataset consisting of input-output pairs (x, y). The entropy of the dataset is $H(y)$, as defined above. If one split the dataset based on a particular feature f, one obtain two subsets of the data: one subset with inputs that have feature f, and another subset with inputs that do not have feature f. The information gain $IG(f)$ achieved by splitting the dataset based on feature f is defined as:

$$IG(f) = H(y) - H(y|f),\tag{13.6}$$

where $H(y|f)$ is the entropy of the output labels given the feature f. This equation represents the information gain is a function of both the dataset entropy and the entropy of the output labels given the feature. If the feature is highly informative, the entropy of the output labels given the feature will be low, resulting in a high information gain. On the other hand, if the feature is not informative, the entropy of the output labels given the feature will be high, resulting in a low information gain.

13.4 Cross-Entropy Softmax

Cross-entropy Softmax is a commonly used method for multi-class classification problems. It is a variant of the Softmax function that maps the output of a neural network to a probability distribution over multiple classes. The cross-entropy Softmax loss function measures the difference between the predicted probability distribution and the true probability distribution of the classes. Consider there is a neural network with K output nodes, where each node represents a class. Denote the output of the network for input x and class k as $z_k(x)$. The Softmax function is defined as:

$$\sigma\left(\vec{z}\right)j = \frac{e^{z_i}}{\sum_{j=1}^{K} e^{z_j}},$$ (13.7)

where $\vec{z}$ is the input vector to the softmax function, z_i is the elements of the input vector to the softmax function, e^{z_i} is the standard exponential function applied to each element of the input vector, $\sum_{j=1}^{K} e^{z_j}$ is the term on the bottom of the formula: the normalization term. It ensures that all the output values of the function will sum to 1 and each be in the range (0, 1), thus constituting a valid probability distribution, and K is the number of classes. In softmax regression, the goal is The cross-entropy SoftMax loss function measures the difference between the predicted probability distribution and the true probability distribution of the classes. Denote the true probability distribution of the classes for input x as $y_k(x)$, where $y_k(x) = 1$ if input x belongs to class k, and $y_k(x) = 0$ otherwise. The cross-entropy SoftMax loss function L is defined as:

$$L = -\sum k y_k(x) \log_2\left(\text{softmax}(z_k(x))\right),$$ (13.8)

where log is the natural logarithm, and the summation is: taken over all classes k. This equation shows the cross-entropy softmax loss function is a function of both the predicted probability distribution and the true probability distribution. If the predicted probability distribution is identical to the true probability distribution, the cross-entropy softmax loss function will be 0, indicating that the network is perfectly accurate. On the other hand, if the predicted probability distribution is different from the true probability distribution, the cross-entropy softmax loss function will be positive, indicating that the network is less accurate.

The cross-entropy softmax loss function is commonly used as the objective function for training neural networks for multi-class classification problems. The goal of training is to minimize the cross-entropy softmax loss function with respect to the network weights, using methods such as gradient descent. By minimizing the cross-entropy softmax loss function, the network learns to output probabilities that are close to the true probabilities of the classes, and hence achieve high accuracy on the classification task.

13.5 Calculating Cross-Entropy

Cross-entropy is a measure of the difference between two probability distributions. It is commonly used in machine learning as a loss function for classification tasks. The formula for calculating cross-entropy between two probability distributions P and Q is:

$$H(P, Q) = -\sum_{x} P(x) \log(Q(x)), \tag{13.9}$$

where x represents the possible outcomes, $P(x)$ is the probability of outcome x in distribution P, and $Q(x)$ is the probability of outcome x in distribution Q.

Intuitively, the cross-entropy measures the average number of bits required to encode outcomes from distribution P using a code optimized for distribution Q. If the two distributions are the same, the cross-entropy will be 0. Otherwise, the cross-entropy will be positive. In the context of machine learning, the cross-entropy is used to measure the difference between the predicted probability distribution and the true probability distribution of the classes. Consider there is a neural network with K output nodes, where each node represents a class. Let's denote the predicted probability distribution over classes for input x as $Q_k(x)$, and the true probability distribution over classes for input x as $P_k(x)$. The cross-entropy loss function L is defined as:

$$L = -\sum_{k} P_k(x) \log_2(Q_k(x)), \tag{13.10}$$

where the summation is taken over all classes k. In this equation, one can see that the cross-entropy loss function is a function of both the predicted probability distribution and the true probability distribution. If the predicted probability distribution is identical to the true probability distribution, the cross-entropy loss function will be 0, indicating that the network is perfectly accurate. On the other hand, if the predicted probability distribution is different from the true probability distribution, the cross-entropy loss function will be positive, indicating that the network is less accurate. The goal of training a neural network for classification tasks is to minimize the cross-entropy loss function with respect to the network weights, using methods such as gradient descent. By minimizing the cross-entropy loss function, the network learns to output probabilities that are close to the true probabilities of the classes, and hence achieve high accuracy on the classification task.

13.6 Cross-Entropy as a Loss Function

Cross-entropy is a commonly used loss function in machine learning, particularly in classification tasks. It is a measure of the difference between the predicted probability distribution and the true probability distribution of the classes. The cross-entropy loss function measures how well the predicted distribution matches the true distribution and is used as a guide for adjusting the model parameters during the training process.

In the context of classification tasks, one can assume that one have a neural network with K output nodes, where each node represents a class. Assume to denote the predicted probability distribution over classes for input x as $Q_k(x)$, and the true probability distribution over classes for input x as $P_k(x)$. The cross-entropy loss function L is defined as:

$$L = -\sum_k P_k(x) \log(Q_k(x)),\tag{13.11}$$

where the summation is taken over all classes k. The cross-entropy loss function has several desirable properties as a loss function for classification tasks:

- A continuous and differentiable function can be used with gradient-based optimization algorithms.
- It penalizes heavily for incorrect predictions with high confidence, encouraging the network to output probabilities that are close to the true probabilities.
- It is a convex function, which means that the optimization problem is well-behaved and can be efficiently solved using standard optimization techniques.

During the training process, the goal is to minimize the cross-entropy loss function with respect to the network weights, using methods such as gradient descent. The gradients of the loss function with respect to the network weights are computed using the chain rule of calculus and are used to update the weights in the direction that minimizes the loss function. This process is repeated iteratively until the network converges to a set of weights that achieve high accuracy on the classification task.

In summary, cross-entropy loss function is a widely used loss function for classification tasks in machine learning. It is a measure of the difference between the predicted and true probability distributions and is used as a guide for adjusting the model parameters during the training process to achieve high accuracy.

13.7 Cross-Entropy and Log Loss

Cross-entropy and log loss are two commonly used loss functions in machine learning, particularly in binary classification tasks. While they are mathematically similar, there are some differences between the two that are important to understand.

Cross-entropy is a more general loss function that can be used for multi-class classification tasks as well as binary classification tasks. It measures the difference between the predicted probability distribution and the true probability distribution of the classes and is defined as:

$$L = -\sum_k P_k(x) \log_2(Q_k(x)), \tag{13.12}$$

where the summation is taken over all classes k, and $P_k(x)$ and $Q_k(x)$ represent the true and predicted probability distributions over the classes, respectively. In the binary classification case, there are only two classes, and the cross-entropy loss reduces to:

$$L = -y \log_2(p) - (1-y) \log_2(1-p), \tag{13.13}$$

where y is the true label (either 0 or 1) and p is the predicted probability of the positive class.

While cross-entropy and log loss are mathematically similar, there are some differences between the two that are worth noting. First, cross-entropy is a more general loss function that can be used for multi-class classification tasks as well as binary classification tasks, while log loss is only used for binary classification tasks. Second, while both loss functions penalize heavily for incorrect predictions with high confidence, cross-entropy is more sensitive to the difference between the predicted and true probabilities, particularly when the true probability is close to zero or one. Finally, cross-entropy tends to be more stable numerically than log loss, particularly when the predicted probability is close to zero or one.

In practice, both cross-entropy and log loss are commonly used as loss functions in binary classification tasks. The choice between the two often depends on the specific problem at hand, and the performance of the model using each loss function should be evaluated empirically.

13.8 Application of Entropy in Intelligent Control

Entropy has various applications in the field of intelligent control, particularly in the context of optimizing control systems. In this context, entropy can be used to quantify the level of disorder or uncertainty in a system and to help control systems make decisions based on the available information.

One application of entropy in intelligent control is in the area of adaptive control. In adaptive control, the control parameters of a system are adjusted based on the observed behavior of the system, with the goal of optimizing its performance. Entropy can be used in this context to measure the degree of uncertainty or unpredictability in the system and to guide the adaptation process. Specifically, entropy can be used to estimate the information content of the system, which can be used to adjust the control parameters in a way that maximizes the system's information content.

Another application of entropy in intelligent control is in the area of feedback control. In feedback control, the behavior of the system is monitored and adjusted based on feedback signals, with the goal of achieving a desired output. Entropy can be used in this context to measure the degree of uncertainty or unpredictability in the feedback signals and to adjust the control parameters accordingly. Specifically, entropy can be used to estimate the information content of the feedback signals, which can be used to adjust the control parameters in a way that maximizes the system's information content. Entropy can also be used in the context of control systems that operate in environments with high levels of noise or uncertainty. In these systems, entropy can be used to quantify the level of uncertainty or unpredictability in the environment and to adjust the control parameters accordingly. Specifically, entropy can be used to estimate the information content of the environment, which can be used to adjust the control parameters in a way that maximizes the system's information content.

Overall, entropy has a variety of applications in intelligent control, particularly in the areas of adaptive control, feedback control, and control in uncertain or noisy environments. By quantifying the level of uncertainty or unpredictability in a system or environment, entropy can help control systems make decisions based on the available information, and optimize their performance accordingly.

13.8.1 Entropy-Based Control

Entropy-based intelligent control is a control strategy that uses the concept of entropy to design and optimize control systems. The basic idea behind entropy-based control is to use the amount of entropy in a system as a measure of its complexity or disorder and to use this measure to guide the control of the system.

Entropy-based control can be used in a variety of control systems, including industrial process control, robotics, and environmental control systems. The basic approach involves three main steps:

- Entropy measurement: The first step is to measure the entropy of the system being controlled. This can be done using a variety of techniques, depending on the system being controlled. For example, in a temperature control system, the entropy might be measured by monitoring the fluctuations in temperature over time.
- Control design: Once the entropy has been measured, the next step is to design a control system that is able to regulate the entropy within the desired range. This might involve designing a feedback controller that adjusts the control inputs in response to changes in the entropy, or it might involve designing a model-based controller that uses a mathematical model of the system to predict how the entropy will change in response to different control inputs.
- Optimization: Finally, the control system can be optimized to improve its performance. This might involve adjusting the control parameters to minimize the entropy of the system, or it might involve using a reinforcement learning algorithm to find the optimal control policy.

Entropy-based control has several advantages over traditional control approaches. One advantage is that it can be used to control systems that are difficult to model or that have complex, nonlinear dynamics. Another advantage is that it can be used to optimize the performance of the system, rather than simply regulating a single variable such as temperature or pressure. Overall, entropy-based intelligent control is a powerful and flexible approach to control system design and optimization, and has applications in a wide range of fields.

13.8.2 Fuzzy Entropy

Fuzzy entropy is a measure of the degree of uncertainty or fuzziness of a fuzzy set. Fuzzy sets are a generalization of classical sets that allow for the representation of vague or imprecise concepts. In a fuzzy set, each element has a degree of membership in the set, rather than being either a member or a nonmember as in a classical set. Fuzzy entropy is a measure of the amount of uncertainty in the degree of membership of the elements of a fuzzy set.

The concept of fuzzy entropy was first introduced by Yager in 1984. It has since been used in a variety of applications, including fuzzy clustering, pattern recognition, and decision-making.

There are several different measures of fuzzy entropy, including Tsallis entropy, Renyi entropy, and Shannon entropy. Each of these measures has its own advantages and disadvantages, and the choice of measure depends on the specific application. One of the main advantages of fuzzy entropy is that it provides a way to quantify the degree of uncertainty or fuzziness in a fuzzy set. This can be useful in a variety of applications, such as decision-making or pattern recognition, where it is important to have a measure of the degree of uncertainty in the data.

Another advantage of fuzzy entropy is that it can be used to guide the design of fuzzy systems. For example, in a fuzzy control system, the entropy of the fuzzy sets can be used as a measure of their complexity, and the control system can be optimized to minimize the entropy. Overall, fuzzy entropy is a useful concept in fuzzy set theory and has a wide range of applications in decision-making, pattern recognition, and control system design.

13.8.3 Entropy-Based Control Strategies

Entropy-based control strategies involve using entropy as a control variable to regulate the behavior of a system. The basic idea is to use entropy as a measure of the level of disorder or uncertainty in the system and to use this measure to adjust the control inputs in order to achieve a desired level of performance.

The entropy-based control approach is particularly useful in situations where the behavior of the system is complex and difficult to model accurately. By using entropy as a measure of the system's behavior, the controller can adapt to changes in the system and maintain a desired level of performance, even in the presence of disturbances and uncertainties. The most common entropy-based control strategy is based on the principle of maximum entropy. This principle states that, given a set of constraints, the most likely distribution is the one that maximizes the entropy. This principle can be used to design a control strategy that maximizes the entropy of the system, subject to constraints on the control inputs and the desired level of performance. Mathematically, the entropy-based control strategy can be formulated as follows:

- Define the system state variables $X(t)$, the control inputs $U(t)$, and the desired level of performance $Y(t)$.
- Calculate the entropy of the system at time t, given by the entropy $H(X(t))$.
- Define a cost function $J(U(t))$ that measures the performance of the system as a function of the control inputs.
- Design a control law that maximizes the entropy of the system subject to the constraints on the control inputs and the desired level of performance, i.e.
- Implement the control law in real time, using feedback from the system to adjust the control inputs as necessary to maintain the desired level of performance.

The entropy-based control strategy can be applied to a wide range of systems, including industrial processes, environmental control systems, and robotics.

It is particularly useful in situations where the behavior of the system is highly nonlinear or uncertain, and where traditional control strategies may not be effective.

13.8.4 Entropy-Based Decision-Making

Entropy-based decision-making is a method for making decisions in situations where the available information is uncertain or incomplete. The basic idea is to use entropy as a measure of the uncertainty or randomness of the available information and to use this measure to guide the decision-making process.

The entropy-based decision-making process can be broken down into the following steps:

- Define the decision problem: This involves identifying the decision variables, the possible outcomes, and the criteria for evaluating the outcomes.
- Collect information: This involves gathering information about the relevant variables and their relationships, as well as any available data.
- Calculate entropy: This involves calculating the entropy of the available information using the formula: $H(X) = -\Sigma p(x)\log_2 p(x)$, where X is the set of possible outcomes, $p(x)$ is the probability of outcome x, and $\log_2$ is the base-2 logarithm.
- Calculate conditional entropy: This involves calculating the entropy of the available information given a particular decision variable using the formula: $H(Y|X) = -\Sigma p(x, y) \log_2 p(y|x)$, where Y is the decision variable, X is the set of possible outcomes, $p(x, y)$ is the joint probability of outcome x and decision y, and $p(y|x)$ is the conditional probability of decision y given outcome x.
- Calculate mutual information: This involves calculating the mutual information between the available information and the decision variable using the formula: $I(Y; X) = H(Y) - H(Y|X)$, where $I(Y; X)$ is the mutual information between Y and X, $H(Y)$ is the entropy of the decision variable, and $H(Y|X)$ is the conditional entropy of the decision variable given the available information.
- Make the decision: The decision is made based on the mutual information. The decision variable with the highest mutual information is selected as the optimal decision.

The entropy-based decision-making method can be applied to a wide range of decision problems, including resource allocation, risk management, and product design. It is particularly useful in situations where the available information is incomplete or uncertain, and where traditional decision-making methods may not be effective.

Summary

Entropy is a concept that is used in various fields, including information theory, physics, statistics, and machine learning. In information theory, entropy is a measure of the uncertainty or randomness of a system; while in physics, it is a measure of the disorder or randomness of a system. In statistics, entropy is used to measure the amount of information in a probability distribution. In machine learning, entropy is used to measure the impurity of a set of training data in decision tree algorithms. In intelligent control, entropy-based methods are used to make decisions and control systems in situations where the available information is uncertain or incomplete. Entropy-based intelligent control methods include entropy-based control strategies and entropy-based decision-making. Entropy-based control strategies involve using entropy to guide the control process, while entropy-based decision-making involves using entropy to make decisions based on the available information. These methods are particularly useful in situations where traditional control methods may not be effective, such as in complex systems with multiple variables and uncertain outcomes.

As entropy-based methods continue to evolve and be refined, they hold great promise for a wide range of applications in intelligent control. One area where these methods may prove particularly useful is in the development of autonomous systems and robots, where the ability to make decisions and navigate complex environments is critical. Another potential area for future research is the integration of entropy-based methods with other techniques from machine learning and artificial intelligence. For example, combining entropy-based decision-making with deep learning algorithms could lead to more robust and effective decision-making processes.

There is also a need for further exploration of the practical applications of entropy-based control strategies and decision-making methods in real-world scenarios. While these methods have shown promise in research settings, more work is needed to determine how well they perform in complex and dynamic systems with uncertain and changing conditions.

Exercise Questions

Q.13.1 Can you explain the concept of entropy in the context of decision trees and information gain, and what is the mathematical expression for the entropy of a random variable?

Q.13.2 What is the mathematical equation for Shannon entropy, and how is it used to measure the uncertainty or randomness of a discrete probability distribution?

Q.13.3 In a multi-class classification problem, you have a dataset with four classes: $A, B, C,$ and $D.$ The class distribution in the dataset is as follows: $p(A) = 0.5,\ p(B) = 0.2,\ p(C) = 0.15,$ and $p(D) = 0.15.$ Calculate the entropy of the dataset using the Gini impurity formula: Gini Impurity $= 1 - \sum (p(c)^2)$

Q.13.4 Can you provide the mathematical equation for the entropy-based regularization term in logistic regression, and how does it help to prevent overfitting of the model?

Q.13.5 How does the concept of entropy relate to the performance evaluation of machine learning models?

Q.13.6 How can entropy-based methods be used to improve the efficiency of renewable energy systems?

Q.13.7 Consider a dataset with five possible classes: $A, B, C, D,$ and $E.$ The class distribution in the dataset is as follows: $p(A) = 0.2,\ p(B) = 0.3,$ $p(C) = 0.25,\ p(D) = 0.1,$ and $p(E) = 0.15.$ Calculate the entropy of the dataset using the Shannon entropy formula:

$$\text{Entropy}(S) = -\sum (p(c) \times \log 2(p(c)))$$

What is the entropy of the dataset?

Q.13.8 Can entropy-based methods be used to improve the performance of financial trading systems?

Q.13.9 How can entropy-based decision-making methods be used to optimize supply chain management?

Q.13.10 What is the mathematical equation for the entropy of a continuous probability distribution, such as the Gaussian distribution, and how is it related to the differential entropy measure?

Further Reading

Abbas AE. *Wiley encyclopedia of biomedical engineering*. Entropy;2006 Apr 14.

Bulut F. Different mathematical models for entropy in information theory. *Bilge International Journal of Science and Technology Research*. 2017;1(2):167–74.

Dubois D, Prade H, Yager R. Merging fuzzy information. In: *Fuzzy sets in approximate reasoning and information systems*. Springer; 1999:pp. 335–401.

Karmeshu J, editor. *Entropy measures, maximum entropy principle and emerging applications*. Springer; 2003.

Saridis GN. Entropy formulation of optimal and adaptive control. *IEEE Transactions on Automatic Control*. 1988 Aug;33(8):713–21.

Weber S. Measures of fuzzy sets and measures of fuzziness. *Fuzzy Sets and Systems*. 1984 Aug 1;13(3):247–71.

14

Sampling Methods in Cybernetical Intelligence

14.1 Introduction to Sampling Methods

The sampling methods in cybernetical intelligence (CI) involve the use of statistical techniques to obtain information about a population from a sample. The sampling methods are used to select a subset of data from a larger dataset, which can then be analyzed and used to make predictions or decisions. Sampling methods can be classified into two broad categories: probabilistic sampling and non-probabilistic sampling. Probabilistic sampling methods involve selecting samples randomly from a population, while non-probability sampling methods do not involve random selection. Common probability sampling methods used in machine learning include simple random sampling, systematic sampling, stratified sampling, and cluster sampling. The characteristics chart for the categories of sampling methods is shown in Figure 14.1. Simple random sampling involves randomly selecting samples from the entire population. Systematic sampling involves selecting samples based on a specific interval or pattern. Stratified sampling involves dividing the population into strata or subgroups and then selecting samples from each stratum based on a predetermined criterion. Cluster sampling involves dividing the population into clusters and then randomly selecting clusters to sample from.

Non-probability sampling methods used in CI include convenience sampling, snowball sampling, and purposive sampling. Convenience sampling involves selecting samples based on their accessibility and availability. Snowball sampling involves selecting samples based on referrals from other participants. Purposive sampling involves selecting samples based on a predetermined criterion, such as their expertise or experience. Sampling methods in CI play a crucial role in

Cybernetical Intelligence: Engineering Cybernetics with Machine Intelligence, First Edition.
Kelvin K. L. Wong.
© 2024 The Institute of Electrical and Electronics Engineers, Inc.
Published 2024 by John Wiley & Sons, Inc.
Companion website: www.wiley.com/go/cyberintel

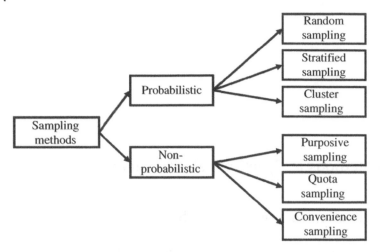

Figure 14.1 Categories of sampling methods.

ensuring the accuracy and reliability of data analysis and decision-making. By using appropriate sampling methods, researchers and practitioners can obtain representative samples that accurately reflect the characteristics of the population being studied.

14.2 Basic Sampling Algorithms

In the context of sampling methods, standard distributions refer to the probability distributions that are commonly used as a basis for generating random samples. Some of the most common standard distributions used in sampling methods include:

- Uniform distribution: A probability distribution where all values within a given range are equally likely to be selected. It can be denoted by the following equation:

$$P(x) = \begin{cases} \dfrac{1}{b-a} & \text{if } a \leq x \leq b, \\ 0 & \text{otherwise} \end{cases} \tag{14.1}$$

where a and b are the lower and upper bounds of the distribution.

- Normal distribution: A continuous probability distribution that is often used to model real-world phenomena. It is characterized by its mean and standard deviation, and can be denoted by the following equation:

$$P(x) = \frac{1}{\sigma\sqrt{2\pi}}e^{-\frac{(x-\mu)^2}{2\sigma^2}}, \tag{14.2}$$

where μ is the mean and σ is the standard deviation of the distribution.

- Poisson distribution: A discrete probability distribution that is often used to model count data. If X is the number of events in the given interval, then the probability of observing x events in the given interval is shown in Equation (14.3).

$$P(X = x) = e^{-\lambda}\frac{\lambda^x}{x!} \quad x = 0, 1, 2, ...N, \tag{14.3}$$

where e is the mathematical constant and λ is the mean number of events per interval. These are just a few examples of standard distributions that are commonly used in sampling methods. Other distributions include the beta distribution, gamma distribution, and t-distribution, among others. Geometrical interpretation of the transformation method for generating non uniformly distributed random numbers is shown in Figure 14.2, where $h(x)$ is the indefinite integral of the desired distribution $P(x)$. If a uniformly distributed random variable y is transformed using $x = h^{-1}(y)$, then x will be distributed according to $P(x)$.

Figure 14.2 Geometrical interpretation of the transformation method for generating non uniformly distributed random numbers.

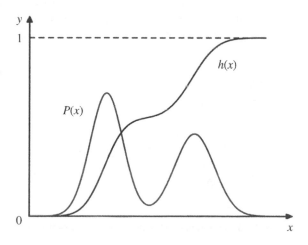

14.2.1 Importance of Sampling Methods in Machine Intelligence

Sampling methods play a critical role in machine intelligence as they enable us to learn from large datasets efficiently. When dealing with high-dimensional data, the computational cost of evaluating the objective function for every possible data point can be prohibitively high. Sampling methods provide an effective solution to this problem by allowing us to estimate the objective function from a small subset of the data, as shown in Figure 14.3. Sampling methods are important in machine intelligence because they allow us to make accurate predictions and decisions based on incomplete or limited data. In many real-world scenarios, collecting data on the entire population is impossible or impractical, and one has to rely on a sample of the population to make inferences about the population as a whole. By using various sampling methods, we can ensure that the collected sample is representative of the population, which increases the accuracy of our predictions and decisions.

In addition, sampling methods are also used in machine learning and data analysis to train models and make predictions. These methods are used to divide the available data into training, validation, and testing sets, which are then used to train and evaluate machine learning models. Proper sampling techniques ensure that the data used for training and testing is representative of the population and reduce the risk of overfitting or underfitting the model. Sampling methods are also important in addressing issues related to bias and fairness in machine learning models. Biases can arise due to differences in the representation of different subgroups in the data, and sampling methods can be used to ensure that the data used to train the model is representative of the population and does not favor any particular subgroup. This is important for ensuring fairness in decision-making systems and reducing the risk of discrimination.

In summary, sampling methods are essential in machine intelligence as they enable us to make accurate predictions and decisions based on incomplete or limited data, ensure fairness and reduce biases in decision-making systems, and improve the accuracy of machine learning models.

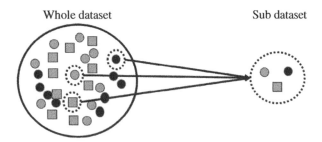

Figure 14.3 Difference between original and sample data.

14.3   Machine Learning Sampling Methods

Machine learning sampling methods are techniques used to select and analyze a representative subset of data from a larger dataset. In machine learning, data is the foundation for training models, and the accuracy and reliability of the models depend on the quality of data used for training. However, the amount of data available for analysis is often large, and the cost of obtaining more data can be prohibitively expensive. Sampling methods provide a solution by enabling researchers to analyze smaller subsets of data that still provide accurate insights into the larger dataset.

There are different types of sampling methods in machine learning, such as random sampling, stratified sampling, systematic sampling, and cluster sampling. Random sampling is the simplest form of sampling, where data is randomly selected from the larger dataset. Stratified sampling involves dividing the dataset into subgroups based on certain characteristics and then selecting a sample from each subgroup. Systematic sampling involves selecting data at regular intervals from the larger dataset. Cluster sampling involves selecting data from subgroups or clusters within the larger dataset. The widely used sampling method is stratified sampling, which involves dividing the population into strata and then selecting samples from each stratum in proportion to the size of the stratum. The equation for stratified sampling can be expressed as shown in Equation (14.4).

$$x_s = \bigcup_{h=1}^{H} x_h, \tag{14.4}$$

where x_s represents the sample selected from the population, x_h represents the elements of the hth stratum, H is the number of strata in the population, and $\bigcup$ represents the union of sets. The union of sets refers to the collection of all elements that are members of any of the sets in the collection. In stratified sampling, the union of the strata forms the entire population being sampled. Additionally, importance sampling is a technique used to generate samples from a probability distribution that is difficult to sample directly. Consider there is a need to compute the expected value $E[g(X)]$ of a function of a random vector x by Monte Carlo integration. The standard way to proceed is to produce a computer-generated sample of realizations of n independent random vectors $x_1, ..., x_n$ having the same distribution as x.

$$\bar{g}_{X,n} = \frac{1}{n} \sum_{i=1}^{n} g(x_i). \tag{14.5}$$

The importance of sampling methods in machine learning lies in their ability to reduce the cost and time required for data collection and analysis, while still providing accurate insights into the larger dataset. By analyzing a representative

Table 14.1 Comparing different sampling methods used in machine learning.

Sampling Method	Description	Equation
Random sampling	Each data point in the dataset has an equal chance of being selected for the sample.	$P(x_i) = \dfrac{1}{N}$
Stratified sampling	Samples are drawn from each stratum in the dataset, where each stratum represents a different category or class.	$P(x_i) = \dfrac{n_i}{N}$ where n_i is the number of data points in stratum i and N is the total number of data points in the dataset.
Cluster sampling	The dataset is divided into clusters, and a random sample of clusters is selected. All data points within the selected clusters are included in the sample.	$P(x_i) = \dfrac{1}{k}$ where k is the number of clusters in the dataset.
Systematic sampling	Every k^{th} data point in the dataset is selected for the sample.	$P(x_i) = \begin{cases} \dfrac{1}{k} & \text{if } i = 0 \\ 0 & \text{otherwise} \end{cases}$

subset of data, researchers can identify patterns, trends, and correlations that can inform the development of machine learning models. Additionally, sampling methods can help to identify outliers or anomalies in the data, which can improve the accuracy of machine learning models. The choice of sampling method will depend on the specific research question, the size and nature of the dataset, and the desired level of precision and accuracy. Sampling methods play a crucial role in machine learning, as they can help to reduce the amount of data needed for analysis, improve the efficiency of algorithms, and minimize bias in the results. Table 14.1 compares different sampling methods used in machine learning, along with their mathematical equations.

14.3.1 Random Oversampling

Random oversampling is a popular technique used in machine learning to address the problem of imbalanced datasets, where one class has significantly fewer samples than the other(s). This technique involves randomly duplicating instances from the minority class until they are balanced with the majority class. The generic overview of the sampling technique applied to the dataset is shown in Figure 14.4.

Figure 14.4 The generic overview of the sampling technique applied to the dataset.

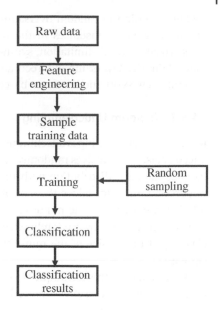

In the case of binary classification, consider there is a dataset with two classes, positive (*P*) and negative (*N*), and there is a need to oversample the minority class (*P*) using random oversampling.

- First, count the number of instances in each class, N_P for positive and N_N for negative.
- Next, calculate the λ, which is the ratio of the number of samples in the majority class to the number of samples in the minority class.

$$\lambda = \frac{N_N}{N_P}.$$

(14.6)

- Randomly select instances from the positive class and duplicate them until the number of instances in the positive class equals that of the negative class.
- After oversampling, the new imbalance ratio is 1.

Random oversampling can be done with or without replacement. In the case of replacement, instances from the minority class are randomly selected and duplicated with replacement until the number of instances in the minority class equals that of the majority class. In the case of without replacement, instances from the minority class are randomly selected without replacement until the number of instances in the minority class equals that of the majority class.

One limitation of random oversampling is that it can lead to overfitting, as it duplicates existing instances in the minority class rather than generating new ones. To address this limitation, synthetic oversampling techniques such as Synthetic Minority Oversampling Technique (SMOTE) have been developed, which generate new synthetic instances based on existing ones.

14.3.2 Random Undersampling

Random undersampling is a technique used in machine learning to handle imbalanced datasets. It involves randomly removing instances from the majority class to balance the class distribution with the minority class. The idea behind random undersampling is to reduce the size of the majority class, thereby increasing the relative importance of the minority class in the dataset. Random undersampling can be implemented by randomly selecting a subset of instances from the majority class equal to the size of the minority class. This can be expressed mathematically as:

The idea behind this technique is to randomly remove examples from the majority class until the dataset is balanced.

The process of random undersampling involves the following steps:

- Determine the ratio of the minority class to the majority class.
- Randomly select a subset of the majority class samples.
- Combine the minority class samples with the randomly selected subset of the majority class samples to form a new, balanced dataset.

One potential problem with random undersampling is that it can discard useful information from the majority class, leading to a reduction in overall accuracy. To mitigate this issue, researchers have developed more sophisticated undersampling techniques. Overall, random undersampling is a simple and computationally efficient way to address the class imbalance problem in machine learning. However, it should be used judiciously and in conjunction with other techniques, such as oversampling or generating synthetic examples. The process of randomly selecting a subset of instances from the majority class can be repeated multiple times to obtain multiple balanced datasets, which can then be used to train and evaluate machine learning models. However, it is important to note that random undersampling can lead to loss of information from the majority class and may not be effective for highly imbalanced datasets. The overview and difference between undersampling and oversampling can be seen in Figure 14.5.

14.3.3 Synthetic Minority Oversampling Technique

SMOTE is a popular oversampling technique used in machine learning to handle imbalanced datasets. In SMOTE, synthetic samples are generated for the minority class by interpolating between existing minority class samples. The algorithm

Under sampling   Over sampling

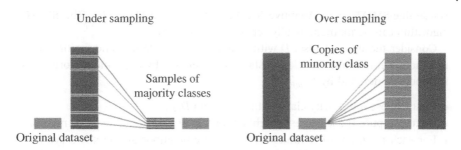

Figure 14.5 Overview and difference between undersampling and oversampling.

works by selecting a minority class sample at random and then finding its k nearest neighbors. The synthetic sample is then generated by taking a linear combination of the feature values of the minority sample and one of its k nearest neighbors. This synthetic sample is added to the dataset, and the process is repeated until the desired level of oversampling is achieved.

$$x_i' = x_i + \gamma(x_j - x_i), \tag{14.7}$$

where x_i' is the newly generated synthetic sample, x_i is the original minority sample, x_j is one of the k nearest neighbors of x_i randomly selected, and γ is a random value representing the proportion of the distance between x_i and x_j to add to x_i to create x_i'. This equation ensures that the synthetic samples are not identical to the original minority samples, but rather lie on the line segment between x_i and x_i' in the feature space. The basic principle of SMOTE is shown in Figure 14.6.

SMOTE has been shown to be effective in balancing datasets while also avoiding overfitting. However, it can sometimes generate synthetic samples that are too similar to existing samples, leading to reduced model generalization. There are several variations of SMOTE that aim to address this issue, such as

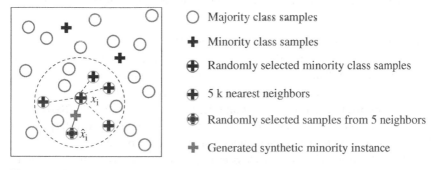

Figure 14.6 Basic principle of synthetic minority oversampling technique.

Borderline-SMOTE and Adaptive Synthetic Sampling (ADASYN). The SMOTE algorithm can be mathematically represented as follows:

Consider there is a dataset D with minority class instances and majority class instances. Let the minority class instances be denoted by D_{min} and majority class instances be denoted by D_{maj}.

- First, choose a minority class instance x from D_{maj}.
- Next, compute the k nearest neighbors of x in D_{min} using a distance metric.
- For each neighbor of x, randomly select one neighbor and create a synthetic instance as a linear combination of x and the selected neighbor. The synthetic instance is added to the dataset D_{min}.

This process is repeated until the desired level of oversampling is achieved. SMOTE is often combined with random undersampling to balance the class distribution.

14.3.4 Adaptive Synthetic Sampling

ADASYN is a variant of the SMOTE algorithm that was proposed to address the issue of class imbalance in binary classification problems. It generates synthetic samples of the minority class by interpolating between existing minority class instances. The algorithm first calculates the density distribution of the minority class instances, which is then used to calculate the number of synthetic instances that need to be generated for each minority class instance. The Generic working of ADASYN algorithm is shown in Figure 14.7.

ADASYN generates more synthetic instances for minority class instances that are in areas of higher density and fewer synthetic instances for minority class instances that are in areas of lower density. This makes it possible to balance the class distribution in a dataset while still preserving the underlying distribution of the data. The ADASYN algorithm can be represented mathematically as follows:

Consider X to be the input feature matrix and y to be the corresponding class labels, where $y = \{0, 1\}$ for a binary classification problem. Let N be the total number of examples in the dataset, and let n be the number of examples in the minority class.

- Calculate the class imbalance ratio (CIR) as n/N.
- For each example x_i in the minority class, compute its K nearest neighbors from the majority class. The K is a user-defined hyperparameter.
- For each minority example x_i, calculate the density ratio (DR).
- For each minority example x_i, calculate the synthetic sample ratio (SSR).
- Generate synthetic samples for each minority example x_i by interpolating between x_i and its K nearest neighbors from the majority class.
- Combine the original minority class examples with the synthetic samples to obtain a new balanced dataset.

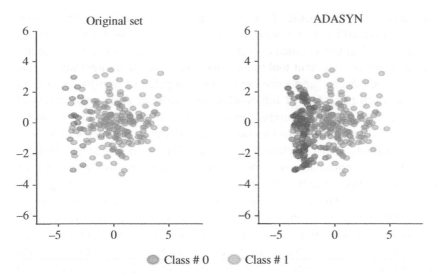

Figure 14.7 Generic working of ADASYN algorithm.

The ADASYN algorithm is an iterative process that can be repeated until the desired level of balance is achieved. It is a computationally efficient method for handling imbalanced datasets and has been shown to improve the performance of classifiers on imbalanced data.

14.4 Advantages and Disadvantages of Machine Learning Sampling Methods

Machine learning sampling methods have several advantages that make them important in improving the performance of machine learning models. One of the primary advantages of these methods is their ability to address the class imbalance problem, which is a common issue in many real-world machine learning applications. By balancing the class distribution of the data, these methods can improve the model's accuracy and reduce bias toward the majority class. Another advantage of CI sampling methods is their ability to reduce the variance of the model, which helps to improve the generalization ability of the model. This is particularly important when working with small datasets or datasets that are noisy or contain outliers. Sampling methods can help to reduce the impact of these factors on the model's performance and make it more robust. Furthermore, sampling methods can help to reduce the computational cost of training a machine learning model. By reducing the size of the training data, these methods can speed up the training process and enable the use of more complex models that would otherwise be computationally infeasible. This can be particularly useful in applications where speed is a critical factor, such as real-time prediction or decision-making.

Overall, the advantages of such artificial intelligence (AI)-based sampling methods make them an important tool in its toolkit. However, it is important to note that these methods also have some limitations and potential drawbacks, such as the risk of overfitting, loss of information, and reduced representativeness of the original data. Therefore, careful consideration and evaluation of the specific problem and data at hand are necessary when deciding whether and how to use these methods. While machine learning sampling methods can be beneficial in improving the performance of models, they also have some disadvantages. One of the main drawbacks is that oversampling methods can result in overfitting of the model to the training data. This means that the model may perform well on the training data but fail to generalize to new, unseen data. Additionally, oversampling can lead to a biased representation of the minority class, which may not accurately reflect the true distribution of the data. Undersampling methods, on the other hand, can result in loss of information and underfitting of the model. This means that the model may not capture the full complexity of the data and may perform poorly on both the training and testing data. Synthetic sampling techniques, such as SMOTE and ADASYN, may also introduce noise into the data, particularly when the minority class is highly variable. This can lead to incorrect decision boundaries and reduced performance of the model. Moreover, the choice of sampling method can have a significant impact on the final model's performance, and there is no one-size-fits-all solution. The optimal sampling method may depend on the specific dataset and the problem at hand. Another disadvantage of CI sampling methods is that they can be computationally expensive, particularly when dealing with large datasets or high-dimensional feature spaces. This can make it difficult to scale the models for real-world applications.

Finally, it is important to note that sampling methods are just one approach to address class imbalance in machine learning. Other techniques, such as cost-sensitive learning, anomaly detection, and one-class classification, may also be effective in certain scenarios.

14.5 Advanced Sampling Methods in Cybernetical Intelligence

Advanced sampling methods in CI refer to techniques that go beyond the traditional oversampling and undersampling methods used in machine learning. These techniques are used to overcome the limitations of conventional sampling methods and improve the accuracy and efficiency of machine learning algorithms.

One advanced sampling method is the ensemble method, which combines multiple learning algorithms to improve the accuracy of predictions. This method uses a combination of diverse models and data sets to create a more robust and accurate model. Another advanced sampling method is the cost-sensitive learning approach, which takes into account the cost of misclassification errors. This approach assigns different weights to different samples based on their relative importance and helps to reduce the overall cost of classification errors. Another advanced sampling method is the active learning approach, which involves selecting the most informative samples for labeling rather than labeling all samples in the data set. This approach reduces the cost of labeling and improves the efficiency of machine learning algorithms. Another advanced sampling method is the semi-supervised learning approach, which uses a small labeled data set and a large unlabeled data set to improve the accuracy of CI algorithms.

However, advanced sampling methods also have their limitations. These methods are often computationally expensive and require large amounts of training data to work effectively. They also require a high level of expertise in machine learning and data science to implement correctly. Despite these limitations, advanced sampling methods have shown great potential in improving the accuracy and efficiency of machine learning algorithms in CI. These methods are essential for the development of intelligent systems that can learn and adapt to new situations and data.

14.5.1 Ensemble Sampling Method

Ensemble sampling is a type of advanced sampling method in machine learning, which combines multiple models or algorithms to improve the overall predictive performance, as shown in Figure 14.8. In other words, it is a technique that aggregates the predictions of multiple models to arrive at a more accurate and reliable prediction. The idea behind ensemble sampling is that combining multiple models with different strengths and weaknesses can produce a more accurate and robust prediction than any individual model on its own.

One popular ensemble sampling technique is the random forest algorithm, which combines multiple decision trees to create a forest of trees. Each tree in the forest is trained on a randomly selected subset of the data, and the final prediction is made by aggregating the predictions of all the trees. Another ensemble sampling technique is gradient boosting, which involves iteratively adding models to the ensemble and adjusting the weights of the training data to improve the accuracy of the predictions.

Assume there is a dataset $D = \{(x_1, y_1), (x_2, y_2), ..., (x_n, y_n)\}$, where x_i is the ith input data and y_i is the corresponding output label.

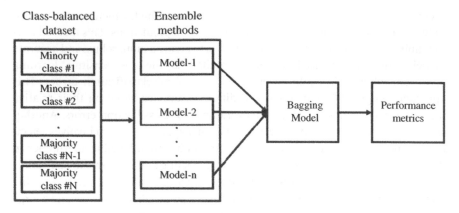

Figure 14.8 Workflow of ensemble sampling technique.

- Bagging: For bagging, randomly sample the dataset with replacement to generate B new datasets. In Bagging, the bootstrapped samples are first created. Then, either a regression or classification algorithm is applied to each sample. Finally, in the case of regression, an average is taken over all the outputs predicted by the individual learners. Mathematically, Bagging is represented by the following formula:

$$\widehat{f_{bag}} = \widehat{f_1}(X) + \dots + \widehat{f_b}(X). \tag{14.8}$$

The term on the left-hand side is the bagged prediction, and the terms on the right-hand side are the individual learners.

- Boosting: For boosting, sequentially train a series of models on the same dataset D, where each model focuses on the samples that the previous model misclassified. The final prediction is a weighted sum of the predictions from each model (Figure 14.9).

- Stacking: For stacking, train several base models on the original dataset and then use the predictions from the base models as input features to train a meta-model. The final prediction is the prediction from the meta-model. The equation is as follows:

$$y_{ens} = f_{meta}(y_1, y_2, \dots, y_m), \tag{14.9}$$

where y_{ens} is the ensemble prediction, f_{meta} is the meta-model that combines the predictions of the base models, and ($y_1, y_2, \dots, y_m$) are the predictions of the base models.

Ensemble sampling has several advantages over traditional sampling methods. Firstly, it can improve the accuracy of predictions by combining the strengths of

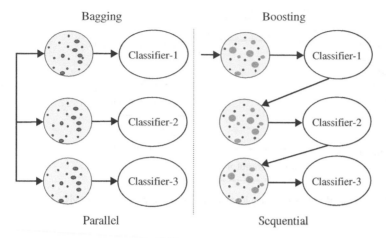

Figure 14.9 Ensemble learning bagging vs boosting.

multiple models. Secondly, it can reduce overfitting by combining multiple models with different biases. Thirdly, it can provide more reliable predictions by using the predictions of multiple models rather than relying on a single model.

However, there are also some disadvantages to ensemble sampling. One potential drawback is that it can be computationally expensive and time-consuming, particularly when dealing with large datasets. Additionally, the performance of the ensemble is dependent on the quality of the individual models, so if the models are poorly constructed or trained, the performance of the ensemble will suffer. Finally, ensemble sampling can be more difficult to interpret and explain than individual models, which can be a challenge in some applications where transparency is important.

14.5.2 Active Learning

Active learning is an approach in which an AI algorithm selects the most informative data points to be labeled by an expert to improve the performance of the model, as shown in Figure 14.10. In active learning, the algorithm interacts with the expert to obtain the most relevant and useful data points for training.

The main idea behind active learning is to select the most informative data points that can help the model learn better. This is done by selecting the data points that are the most uncertain or where the model has the highest prediction error. By selecting these data points for labeling, the model can improve its accuracy by reducing the error rate. The equation used in active learning is the query function, which is used to select the most informative data points. The query

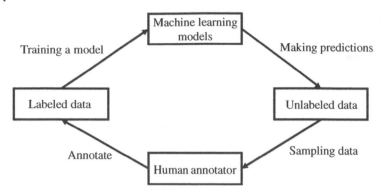

Figure 14.10 Process of active learning in machine learning and computer vision.

function selects data points that are the most uncertain or where the model has the highest prediction error. The query function is defined as:

$$x_q = \text{argmax}\, x_i \in U f(x_i), \tag{14.10}$$

where x_q is the data point selected by the query function, U is the set of unlabeled data points, and $f(x_i)$ is the function used to measure the uncertainty of the model at the data point x_i. The query function can be designed using different methods, such as entropy-based methods, margin-based methods, and confidence-based methods. After selecting the most informative data points, the model is trained on this data, and the process is repeated until the model achieves the desired level of accuracy. Active learning can significantly reduce the amount of labeled data required for training, making it a powerful tool in machine learning.

The selection of informative samples is based on the uncertainty of the model's predictions. For example, the model may be more uncertain about the classification of certain data points and therefore would select those points for labeling to improve the model's accuracy. There are several methods for measuring uncertainty, such as margin sampling, entropy sampling, and querying by committee. One advantage of active learning is that it reduces the labeling effort, as the model only selects the most informative samples for labeling. This can lead to significant cost savings, particularly when labeling is expensive or time-consuming. Additionally, active learning can improve the performance of the model as it focuses on the most informative samples for learning. One common strategy in active learning is uncertainty sampling, which selects instances for annotation that are predicted to be uncertain or difficult for the current model to classify. This can be formalized using the following equation:

$$x_t = \text{argmax}_{x_i \in U}\, p(x_i y_i, D_t), \tag{14.11}$$

where x_t is the instance selected for annotation at time t, U is the set of unanno-
tated instances, $p(x_i y_i, D_t)$ is the predictive distribution of the model at time t given
the training data D_t, and argmax selects the instance with the highest uncertainty.
Another popular active learning strategy is query by committee, which maintains
an ensemble of models and selects instances that cause disagreement or uncertainty among the models, as shown in Equation (14.12).

$$x_t = \text{argmax}_{x_i \in U} \frac{1}{K} \sum_{j=1}^{k} p\left(x_i y_i, D_t^j\right), \tag{14.12}$$

where k is the number of models in the committee, D_t^j is the training data for the jth
model at time t, and the argmax selects the instance with the highest disagreement
or entropy. However, one disadvantage of active learning is that it requires an
expert to label the selected samples, which may not always be available or reliable.
Additionally, the performance of the active learning model can be sensitive to the
selection of the initial labeled set and the selection of the active learning algorithm.

14.5.3 Bayesian Optimization in Sampling

Bayesian optimization is an advanced sampling method in machine learning that
is used to optimize expensive black-box functions, as shown in Figure 14.11. It is
particularly useful in cases where evaluating the objective function is computationally expensive and time-consuming. Bayesian optimization is a sequential
approach that uses a surrogate model to approximate the true objective function
and an acquisition function to guide the search for the optimum. The algorithm
maintains a probabilistic model, called a surrogate or a proxy model, which predicts the value of the objective function at any point x in the search space. The surrogate model is constructed based on the samples collected so far and is used to
guide the search for the next sample. The overall schematic of Bayesian optimization is shown in Figure 14.12.

The acquisition function, often denoted by $\alpha(x)$, is a measure of the utility of
sampling the function at a given point x. The most commonly used acquisition
function is the expected improvement (EI) function, which is defined as:

$$EI(x) = E[\max(f(x') - f(x^*))], \tag{14.13}$$

where x' is the point at which the function is sampled next, and x^* is the current
best point found so far $E[\ ]$, denotes the expected value operator, and max( ) returns
the maximum value between its arguments. The expected improvement is the
expected value of the maximum improvement in the objective function that can
be achieved by sampling at x'.

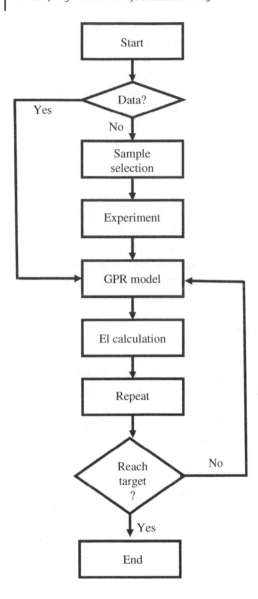

Figure 14.11 Workflow of Bayesian optimization.

The surrogate model and the acquisition function are updated iteratively based on the samples collected so far. At each iteration, the algorithm chooses the point that maximizes the acquisition function and samples the objective function at that point. The sample is then used to update the surrogate model and the acquisition function for the next iteration. Bayesian optimization is particularly useful in

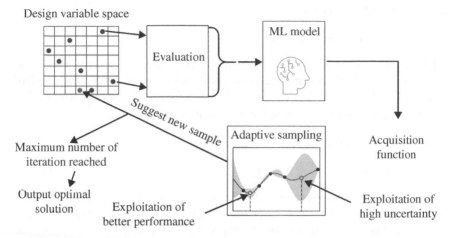

Figure 14.12 Schematic of Bayesian optimization framework.

settings where the objective function is expensive to evaluate since it can minimize the number of function evaluations required to find the optimum.

- Gaussian process regression:

$$f(x) \sim GP(m(x), k(x, x')),\qquad(14.14)$$

where $m(x)$ is the mean function and $k(x, x')$ is the covariance function. *GP* stands for Gaussian process, which is a flexible probabilistic model that can be used to model the unknown function $f(x)$ in Bayesian optimization.

- Acquisition function:

$$A(x) = E[I(f(x) > f(x^*))],\qquad(14.15)$$

where I is the indicator function, $f(x)$ is the predicted value of the unknown function at point x, and $f(x^*)$ is the best-observed value so far. The acquisition function measures the potential usefulness of evaluating the unknown function at a new point x.

- Expected improvement:

$$EI(x) = E[\max(f(x) - f(x^*), 0)],\qquad(14.16)$$

where $EI(x)$ is the expected improvement in the best-observed value if the unknown function is evaluated at point x. $EI(x)$ is a popular acquisition function in Bayesian optimization.

- Upper confidence bound:

$$UCB(x) = m(x) + \beta\sigma(x), \tag{14.17}$$

where $UCB(x)$ is the upper confidence bound at point x, β is a hyperparameter that controls the balance between exploration and exploitation, and $\sigma(x)$ is the standard deviation of the predicted value of the unknown function at point x. The UCB is another popular acquisition function in Bayesian optimization.

- Posterior distribution update:

$$p(f|X, Y, X^*) = p(Y|X, f)\, p(f|X, X^*), \tag{14.18}$$

where $p(f|X, Y, X^*)$ is the posterior distribution of the unknown function given the observed data Y at points X and the best-observed value so far at points X^*, $p(Y|X, f)$ is the likelihood function, and $p(f|X, X^*)$ is the prior distribution. The posterior distribution is updated after each evaluation of the unknown function.

14.6 Applications of Sampling Methods in Cybernetical Intelligence

Sampling methods in CI have a wide range of applications. One of the main applications is in the field of image recognition and processing. By using various sampling methods, images can be resized, compressed, and enhanced. Moreover, these methods are used to balance class distribution in machine learning algorithms, which is particularly useful in medical diagnosis and fraud detection.

Sampling methods also have applications in data mining, where they are used to explore and extract patterns from large datasets. In addition, sampling methods are used in process control, where they are applied to monitor and control industrial processes. They can also be used in robotics and autonomous systems, where they are applied to decision-making and control tasks. Overall, the applications of sampling methods in CI are diverse and span across different domains, including image processing, natural language processing (NLP), recommendation systems, data mining, process control, and robotics. By using appropriate sampling techniques, the data can be optimized for a particular application, leading to improved performance and accuracy of machine learning algorithms.

14.6.1 Image Processing and Computer Vision

Sampling methods are commonly used in image processing and computer vision to address the issue of imbalanced datasets. In image classification, datasets often have an uneven distribution of samples across different classes, making it challenging for machine learning models to accurately classify new images. Image processing and computer vision are broad fields that involve various techniques and algorithms. However, in general, the following equations provide a high-level overview of how image processing and computer vision work:

- Image acquisition: An image is first acquired using a camera or other sensors and represented as a matrix of pixels.
- Preprocessing: The acquired image is then preprocessed to remove noise, enhance contrast, and perform other operations that make the image more suitable for subsequent analysis. A commonly used preprocessing technique is the convolution operation and the Gaussian filter, as shown in Equations (14.20) and (14.21), respectively.

$$x(f,g) = \int_{-\infty}^{\infty} f(t)g(x-t)dt \tag{14.19}$$

$$G(x,y) = \frac{1}{2\pi\sigma^2} e^{-\frac{x^2+y^2}{2\sigma^2}}. \tag{14.20}$$

- Feature extraction: Next, features are extracted from the preprocessed image. Features can be edges, corners, blobs, or any other characteristic that can help distinguish one image from another. The popular feature extraction technique is Sobel operator for edge detection, as shown in Equations (14.22) and (14.23).

$$G_x = \begin{bmatrix} -1 & 0 & 1 \\ -2 & 0 & 2 \\ -1 & 0 & 1 \end{bmatrix} f \tag{14.21}$$

$$G_y = \begin{bmatrix} -1 & -2 & -1 \\ 0 & 0 & 0 \\ 1 & 2 & 1 \end{bmatrix} f. \tag{14.22}$$

- Object recognition: The extracted features are then used for object recognition, where the goal is to identify objects or regions of interest in the image. One widely used algorithm for object recognition is the Convolutional Neural Network (CNN), which involves training a deep neural network on a large dataset of labeled images.
- Classification: Once objects or regions of interest are identified, they are classified into different categories. The classification algorithm used depends on the

specific task at hand. For example, for facial recognition, a Support Vector Machine (SVM) classifier may be used.

- Post-processing: Finally, the results of the analysis are post-processed, which can involve further filtering, thresholding, or other operations to improve the accuracy of the analysis.
- Sampling methods have been widely applied in image processing and computer vision applications. One of the key challenges in these fields is to efficiently and accurately extract useful features from large datasets of images. The use of sampling techniques such as random oversampling and undersampling, SMOTE, and adaptive synthetic sampling has been proven effective in addressing the problem of imbalanced data in image classification tasks.
- Moreover, ensemble sampling methods such as bagging and boosting have also been used to improve the accuracy and robustness of image classifiers by combining multiple base classifiers. In addition, active learning approaches using uncertainty sampling and query-by-committee have been employed to minimize the annotation cost and improve the performance of image classification tasks.
- Bayesian optimization has also been applied in image processing and computer vision tasks such as image segmentation and object detection. Bayesian optimization can help efficiently search the high-dimensional parameter space of complex models and algorithms and find the optimal parameter settings for achieving the best performance.
- The use of sampling methods can be described mathematically using techniques from statistics and machine learning. For example, the probability distribution of the sample can be represented using equations such as the Gaussian distribution or the multinomial distribution. The oversampling and undersampling techniques can be described using equations for generating new samples based on the original samples. Ensemble methods such as bagging and boosting can be described using equations for combining the outputs of multiple classifiers. Bayesian optimization can be formulated using equations for the acquisition function and the posterior distribution over the model parameters.

14.6.2 Natural Language Processing

NLP is a branch of AI that deals with the interaction between computers and human language. It focuses on developing algorithms and techniques that enable computers to understand, interpret, and generate human language.

One of the fundamental tasks in NLP is language modeling, which involves predicting the likelihood of a sequence of words. Language models are typically trained on large datasets of text, and the most common approach is to use a neural network-based architecture, such as a Recurrent Neural Network (RNN) or a

Transformer. In addition to language modeling, NLP involves a range of other tasks, including:

- Part-of-Speech Tagging (POS Tagging): This involves labeling each word in a sentence with its corresponding part of speech, such as noun, verb, adjective, etc. This task is typically performed using statistical models or machine learning algorithms, such as Hidden Markov Models (HMMs) or Conditional Random Fields (CRFs).
- Named Entity Recognition (NER): This involves identifying and extracting named entities, such as people, places, organizations, etc., from text. This task is typically performed using machine learning algorithms, such as SVMs or CRFs.
- Sentiment Analysis: This involves analyzing the emotional tone of a piece of text, such as positive, negative, or neutral. This task is typically performed using machine learning algorithms, such as Naive Bayes or SVMs.

A common approach to language modeling is to use a neural network-based architecture, such as a RNN or a Transformer. The probability of a sequence of words, given a previous sequence, can be calculated using the following equation:

$$P(w_1, w_2, ..., w_n) = \prod_{i=1}^{n} P(w_i | w_1, w_2, ..., w_{i-1}), \tag{14.23}$$

where w_i represents the ith word in the sequence, and $P(w_i | w_1, w_2, ..., w_{i-1})$ represents the conditional probability of the ith word given the previous words in the sequence. Another example of a mathematical equation used in NLP is in Part-of-Speech (POS) tagging. A common approach to POS tagging is to use HMMs, where the probability of a particular tag sequence, given a sequence of words, can be calculated using the following equation:

$$P(T_1, T_2, ...T_n | w_1, w_2, ..., w_n) = \prod_{i=1}^{n} P(T_i | T_{i-1}) P(w_i | T_i), \tag{14.24}$$

where T_i represents the ith tag in the sequence, and w_i represents the ith word in the sequence. In the context of NLP, sampling methods are commonly used in generative models such as language models and machine translation models. These methods are used to estimate the conditional probability distribution of the next word or sequence of words given the previous words in the text.

One of the most widely used sampling methods in NLP is the Markov chain Monte Carlo (MCMC) method. In this method, a chain of samples is generated by iteratively proposing a new sample and accepting or rejecting it based on a probability criterion. The chain converges on the target distribution, which is the distribution of interest. The Metropolis–Hastings algorithm is one of the most widely used MCMC algorithms. It works by proposing a new state, accepting it with a certain probability, and rejecting it otherwise. The acceptance probability ensures that the Markov chain converges to the target distribution, as the ratio of the target distribution probabilities cancels out in the acceptance probability. The algorithm generates a sequence of samples that converge to the target distribution as the number of samples approaches infinity. In NLP, MCMC methods are used to estimate the parameters of probabilistic models, such as HMMs and Bayesian networks, and to generate samples from the models. MCMC is also used in topic modeling, where it is used to estimate the topic distributions of a corpus of text. Another popular sampling method in NLP is the Gibbs sampling method, which is a special case of the MCMC method. In Gibbs sampling, a new sample is generated by sampling each variable from its conditional distribution, given the current values of the other variables.

Given a joint probability distribution $P(X)$, the conditional probability distribution of each variable given the current values of the other variables can be denoted as $P(X_i|X_{-i})$. The Gibbs sampling method iteratively updates the value of each variable by sampling from its conditional distribution given the current values of the other variables. The equations for one iteration of Gibbs sampling for a binary variable X_i, given its neighbors X_{-i} are:

$$p(X_i = 0|X_{-i}) = \frac{P(x_i = 0, X_{-i})}{P(X_i = 0, X_{-i}) + P(X_i = 1, X_{-i})} \tag{14.25}$$

$$p(X_i = 0|X_{-i}) = \frac{P(x_i = 1, X_{-i})}{P(X_i = 0, X_{-i}) + P(X_i = 1, X_{-i})}, \tag{14.26}$$

where X_{-i} represents all variables except X_i. These equations calculate the probability of X_i being 0 or 1, given the current values of all other variables. The new value of X_i is then sampled from this distribution. The process is repeated for all variables until convergence is reached.

Importance sampling is another sampling method used in NLP. In this method, a set of samples is generated from a proposal distribution, which is a distribution that is easy to sample from, but may not be similar to the target distribution. The importance of each sample is then estimated by a weight function, and the final estimate is computed as a weighted sum of the samples. Finally, annealed importance sampling is a variant of importance sampling that can be used to sample from complex distributions. In this method, a sequence of intermediate distributions is constructed between the proposal distribution and the target distribution, and samples are generated from each intermediate distribution using importance sampling. Overall, sampling methods play an important role in NLP by enabling the estimation of complex probability distributions and facilitating the development of generative models for natural language generation, machine translation, and other NLP applications.

14.6.3 Robotics and Autonomous Systems

One important concept in robotics is kinematics, which describes the motion of objects without considering the forces that cause that motion. In the case of robots, kinematics is used to describe the position, orientation, and velocity of the robot's end-effector (the tool or hand of the robot) relative to its base. The kinematics equations for a robotic manipulator can be derived using the Denavit–Hartenberg (DH) convention, which provides a systematic method for assigning coordinate frames to each link of the manipulator. The DH parameters are used to transform between adjacent frames and calculate the position and orientation of the end-effector in terms of the joint angles. For autonomous systems, the main challenge is to develop algorithms that enable the system to perceive and interpret its environment, plan and execute actions, and learn from its experience. A key approach in autonomous systems is reinforcement learning (RL), which involves the use of mathematical models to learn from trial-and-error experience.

The RL problem can be formulated as a Markov Decision Process (MDP), which is a mathematical framework that models the interaction between an agent and its environment. The goal of RL is to learn a policy that maps states to actions that maximize the expected cumulative reward. The equations for the MDP can be written as follows:

- S: set of states
- A: set of actions
- $P(s'|s, a)$: transition probability function from state s to state s' given action a
- $R(s, a, s')$: reward function for transitioning from state s to state s' with action a
- τ: discount factor
- $\pi(s)$: policy function that maps states to actions

The state-value function $V(s)$ and action-value function $Q(s, a)$ are defined as follows:

$$V(s) = E\left[R(t + 1) + \tau R(t + 2) + \tau^2 R(t + 3) + ... \big| S_t = s\right] \tag{14.27}$$

$$Q(s, a) = E\left[R(t + 1) + \tau R(t + 2) + \tau^2 R(t + 3) + ... \big| S_t = s, A_t = a\right]. \tag{14.28}$$

The optimal value function V^* and Q^* are defined as the maximum expected cumulative reward achievable from any given state or state-action pair, respectively:

$$V^*(s) = \max_a Q^*(s, a) \tag{14.29}$$

$$Q^*(s, a) = R(s, a, s') + \tau \max_a Q^*(s', a'). \tag{14.30}$$

The Bellman equation is used to compute the optimal value function:

$$V(s) = \max_a \sum_{s'} P(s'|s, a)[R(s, a, s') + \gamma V(s')] \tag{14.31}$$

The policy improvement theorem states that if the value function of a policy π is improved by changing the policy in one or more states, then the new policy is better than or equal to the old policy.

Sampling methods are widely used in CI in robotics and autonomous systems for a range of applications, including state estimation, control, and planning. These methods aim to approximate the distribution of a set of random variables, which represent the state of the system, by generating a set of samples that are drawn from this distribution. One commonly used method is MCMC, which is based on generating a Markov chain that has the desired distribution as its equilibrium distribution. In robotics and autonomous systems, MCMC methods are often used for state estimation and localization, where the goal is to estimate the robot's state based on noisy sensor measurements. Both MCMC and particle filtering can be formulated as a recursive Bayes filter, where the posterior distribution over the state variables is updated based on the sensor measurements and the system dynamics.

14.7 Challenges and Future Directions

CI, which combines the fields of control theory, AI, and cognitive science, has made significant progress in recent years. However, there are still many challenges to be addressed in this field. One major challenge is the lack of robustness and reliability in many existing cybernetical systems. These systems can be vulnerable to various types of attacks, such as adversarial attacks or system failures, which can have serious consequences in safety-critical applications.

Another challenge is the need for more efficient and scalable algorithms for decision-making and control. Many existing cybernetical systems rely on hand-crafted or heuristic-based control strategies, which may not be optimal or adaptable to different scenarios. More research is needed to develop data-driven approaches that can learn from experience and adapt to changing environments. Furthermore, there is a need for better integration between cybernetical systems and human operators. Many existing systems are designed to operate autonomously, without considering the potential impact on human users or stakeholders. Future directions in CI should focus on developing more transparent, explainable, and human-centered systems that can work collaboratively with humans in a safe and efficient manner.

Overall, it is promising, but there are still many challenges and opportunities for research and development. By addressing these challenges and focusing on human-centered design principles, cybernetical systems can be more reliable, efficient, and useful in a wide range of applications.

14.8 Challenges and Limitations of Sampling Methods

Sampling methods have been widely used in CI to solve various problems, including NLP, robotics, and autonomous systems. However, these methods also face some challenges and limitations that need to be addressed.

One of the main challenges with sampling methods in CI is the trade-off between exploration and exploitation. Sampling methods need to explore the search space to find a good solution while also exploiting the current knowledge to improve the search efficiency. The balance between these two can be difficult to achieve, leading to either slow convergence or premature convergence to a suboptimal solution. Another challenge is the curse of dimensionality. As the dimensionality of the search space increases, the number of samples required to obtain a representative sample increases exponentially. This can make the sampling process computationally expensive and impractical for high-dimensional problems. Furthermore, sampling methods rely on the choice of the proposal distribution, which can significantly affect the performance of the sampling algorithm. Designing an effective proposal distribution can be challenging, especially for complex and high-dimensional problems.

Finally, sampling methods are prone to getting stuck in local optima, leading to suboptimal solutions. Overcoming this limitation requires developing more sophisticated sampling methods that can escape from local optima and explore the search space more efficiently. In the future, addressing these challenges and limitations will be crucial for the advancement of sampling methods in cybernetical machine intelligence (CMI). Developing new algorithms that can balance exploration and exploitation, overcome the curse of dimensionality, and efficiently explore complex search spaces will be essential. Additionally, incorporating deep learning techniques and other machine learning approaches into sampling methods can also lead to improved performance and more efficient search.

14.9 Emerging Trends and Innovations in Sampling Methods

Sampling methods are essential tools in CI that enable efficient and effective learning in various applications. As technology advances, there are emerging trends and innovations in sampling methods that improve their effectiveness and applicability. Some of the emerging trends and innovations in sampling methods in CI include:

- Variational Inference: A recent development in sampling methods that allows the efficient approximation of intractable posterior distributions. It provides a computationally efficient alternative to traditional methods such as Gibbs sampling and Metropolis–Hastings algorithms.

- Deep Generative Models: Models, such as variational autoencoders and generative adversarial networks, provide a powerful framework for sampling methods. They allow for the generation of complex, high-dimensional data that can be used in various applications, including image and speech recognition.
- Importance Sampling: An efficient technique that allows for the estimation of rare events that occur in complex systems. It enables efficient sampling of distributions that have low probability regions, which are difficult to sample using traditional sampling methods.
- Bayesian Optimization: A powerful sampling method that can be used to optimize complex systems. It uses a probabilistic model to explore the parameter space of a system and determine the best possible parameters to achieve the desired outcome.
- Parallel and Distributed Sampling: With the availability of large-scale computing resources, parallel and distributed sampling has emerged as a popular trend in CI. It enables efficient sampling of large datasets and complex systems, which are difficult to handle using traditional sampling methods.

These emerging trends and innovations in sampling methods are expected to have a significant impact on their development. They will enable the efficient and effective processing of large and complex datasets, leading to improved performance and accuracy in various applications.

Summary

CI-based sampling methods involve the process of selecting representative samples from a population in order to estimate the characteristics of the entire population. In machine learning, sampling methods are used to train and evaluate models, and various advanced sampling techniques have been developed in the field of CI, such as MCMC and importance sampling. These methods are widely applied in NLP, robotics, and other areas of AI. Despite their usefulness, there are also challenges and limitations associated with sampling methods, such as bias and inefficiency. Future directions in this field may involve the development of new sampling methods that address these limitations, as well as the integration of sampling techniques with other areas of AI research.

However, there are also challenges and limitations associated with sampling methods, such as the need for large amounts of data, the computational cost of generating samples, and the difficulty in choosing appropriate sampling methods for a given problem. Future directions in sampling methods may include developing more efficient and scalable algorithms, combining sampling methods with other techniques such as RL, and exploring applications in new domains such as healthcare and finance. Overall, sampling methods are an important tool in machine learning and CI, with potential for a wide range of applications and continued innovation.

Exercise Questions

Q.14.1 Explain the difference between random sampling and stratified sampling in the context of machine learning.

Q.14.2 Describe the difference between importance sampling and rejection sampling?

Q.14.3 Based on the following equation,

$$p(x) = \frac{1}{N}\sum_{i=1}^{N}\delta(x - x_i)$$

How does the Monte Carlo method utilize random samples to estimate the probability density function (PDF) of a continuous random variable?

Q.14.4 What is the difference between deterministic and stochastic sampling methods?

Q.14.5 Provide an example of an advanced sampling method used in cybernetical intelligence?

Q.14.6 How can importance sampling be used to estimate the properties of a target distribution?

Q.14.7 Explain an example of an application of sampling methods in cybernetical intelligence?

Q.14.8 How do sampling methods help in data augmentation and improve the performance of machine learning models?

Q.14.9 Explain the role of the acceptance probability in the Metropolis–Hastings algorithm and how it ensures the convergence of the Markov chain to the desired target distribution.

$$\propto (x, x') = \min\left(1, \frac{p(x')q(x|x')}{p(x)q(x'|x)}\right).$$

Q.14.10   Describe the challenges in implementing sampling methods in large-scale distributed systems and how can they be addressed?

Further Reading

Tippets WE, Moyle PB. Epibenthic feeding by rainbow trout (*Salmo gairdneri*) in the Mccloud River, California. *The Journal of Animal Ecology*. 1978 Jun; 1:549–59.

Batista GE, Prati RC, Monard MC. A study of the behavior of several methods for balancing machine learning training data. *ACM SIGKDD Explorations Newsletter*. 2004 Jun 1;6(1):20–9.

Lewis DD, Catlett J. Heterogeneous uncertainty sampling for supervised learning. In Machine Learning Proceedings 1994 1994 Jan 1 (pp. 148–156). Morgan Kaufmann.

Schaffer C. Overfitting avoidance as bias. *Machine Learning*. 1993 Feb;10:153–78.

Meek C, Thiesson B, Heckerman D. The learning-curve sampling method applied to model-based clustering. *Journal of Machine Learning Research*. 2002 Feb;2:397–418.

15

Dynamic System Control

Dynamic system control is the use of control theory and algorithms to regulate the behavior of a dynamic system over time. A dynamic system is a system that changes over time in response to its inputs and environment. Examples of dynamic systems include robots, aircraft, chemical processes, and biological systems.

The goal of dynamic system control is to design a control system that can maintain stability, track reference signals, and reject disturbances in the face of uncertainty and variability. This is achieved by using feedback control, which involves measuring the output of the system and comparing it to a desired reference signal. The difference between the measured output and the reference signal is called the error, and it is used to adjust the inputs to the system to reduce the error and maintain stability. The design of a control system for a dynamic system involves several steps. First, the system must be modeled mathematically, either using analytical equations or numerical simulations. The model must be able to capture the essential dynamics of the system and the interactions between its components.

Next, a control strategy must be selected, such as proportional-integral-derivative (PID) control, model predictive control (MPC), or adaptive control. The choice of control strategy depends on the complexity of the system, the level of uncertainty and variability, and the desired performance criteria. Once the control strategy is selected, the controller parameters must be tuned to achieve the desired performance. This involves adjusting the gains of the controller to balance the tradeoff between stability, tracking, and disturbance rejection.

Finally, the control system must be implemented and tested on the real system. This involves verifying that the control system can maintain stability and achieve the desired performance in the face of uncertainty and variability. Dynamic system control has many applications in engineering, science, and technology. It is used to

Cybernetical Intelligence: Engineering Cybernetics with Machine Intelligence, First Edition.
Kelvin K. L. Wong.
© 2024 The Institute of Electrical and Electronics Engineers, Inc.
Published 2024 by John Wiley & Sons, Inc.
Companion website: www.wiley.com/go/cyberintel

regulate the behavior of complex systems, such as robots, autonomous vehicles, and chemical processes, and to optimize their performance. It is also used in biological systems, such as the control of insulin secretion in the human body, and in social systems, such as the regulation of traffic flow in a city.

15.1 Linear Systems

A linear system is a mathematical model that describes the relationship between inputs and outputs of a physical or abstract system. The basic principle of a linear system is that the response of the system to a linear combination of inputs is the same as the linear combination of the individual responses to each input. In other words, the output of a linear system is a linear function of its input. Mathematically, a linear system can be represented by a set of linear equations, which relate the inputs and outputs of the system.

$$y = Ax, \tag{15.1}$$

where y is the output vector, x is the input vector, and A is the system matrix. The system matrix is a square matrix of coefficients that represents the relationship between the inputs and outputs of the system.

The behavior of a linear system can be analyzed using various tools and techniques from linear algebra and calculus. For example, the eigenvalues and eigenvectors of the matrix A can be used to determine the stability and frequency response of the system. The stability of a linear system is determined by the eigenvalues of the matrix A, and the frequency response of a linear system is determined by the transfer function, which is the ratio of the output to the input in the frequency domain. Linear systems have many important properties that make them useful for modeling and control. They can be easily analyzed using mathematical tools, and their behavior can be predicted and controlled with high accuracy. However, linear systems also have limitations since many physical systems are nonlinear and cannot be accurately represented by linear models. Therefore, nonlinear systems and control techniques are also important for many applications. Linear systems are used in many areas of science and engineering, such as electrical engineering, mechanical engineering, control theory, signal processing, and communications. They are used to model a wide range of physical systems, such as circuits, mechanical systems, chemical processes, and biological systems. The theory of linear systems is also used to develop control strategies for these systems, such as feedback control, optimal control, and adaptive control. In a linear system, the inputs and outputs are related by linear equations. The behavior of the system can be analyzed using various tools and techniques from linear algebra, such as matrix multiplication, determinants, eigenvalues, and eigenvectors. For example, the eigenvalues and eigenvectors of the system matrix A can be used to determine the stability and frequency response of the system.

The eigenvectors of the system matrix A are the directions in which the system response is amplified or attenuated. They can be used to determine the frequency response of the system, which is the ratio of the output to the input in the frequency domain.

Other tools from calculus, such as Laplace transforms and transfer functions, can also be used to analyze the behavior of linear systems. The transfer function is the ratio of the output to the input in the Laplace domain, and it can be used to determine the frequency response of the system.

Linear systems are used in many areas of science and engineering, such as electrical engineering, mechanical engineering, control theory, signal processing, and communications. They are used to model a wide range of physical systems, such as circuits, mechanical systems, chemical processes, and biological systems. The theory of linear systems is also used to develop control strategies for these systems, such as feedback control, optimal control, and adaptive control.

Linear systems in neural networks are systems that can be described by linear equations or linear transformations. In the context of neural networks, linear systems are often used as building blocks for more complex networks or as models for specific phenomena such as linear filters or linear classifiers.

One common example of a linear system in neural networks is the linear neuron model, which describes the behavior of a neuron that computes a linear combination of its inputs and produces an output based on this computation. Linear neurons are often used in the input layers of neural networks, where they can be used to extract simple features or to preprocess the input data before it is passed to more complex layers. Another example of a linear system in neural networks is the linear transformation, which is a function that maps a set of inputs to a set of outputs using a linear equation or matrix multiplication. Linear transformations are often used in the hidden layers of neural networks, where they can be used to combine and transform the features extracted by the input layer into higher-level representations that are more suitable for classification or other tasks.

Linear systems in neural networks have a number of important properties that make them useful for a wide range of applications. For example, linear systems are often easy to analyze mathematically, which can make it easier to design and optimize neural networks. They are also computationally efficient, which makes them well-suited for large-scale applications such as image or speech recognition. Additionally, linear systems can often be combined with nonlinear systems to create more complex models that can capture a wider range of phenomena.

15.2 Nonlinear System

A nonlinear system is a system in which the output is not directly proportional to the input. Nonlinear systems can exhibit a wide range of complex behaviors, such as chaos, bifurcations, and multiple equilibria, that cannot be modeled or predicted using linear systems theory.

In a nonlinear system, the relationship between the inputs and outputs is described by nonlinear equations, which can take many different forms, such as polynomials, exponential functions, or trigonometric functions. Nonlinear systems can also have time-varying parameters, which can further complicate the modeling and analysis of the system. The behavior of nonlinear systems can be analyzed using a variety of techniques from nonlinear dynamics, such as phase space analysis, bifurcation analysis, and chaos theory. These techniques involve the use of advanced mathematical tools, such as differential equations, dynamical systems theory, and chaos theory.

One of the key concepts in nonlinear dynamics is the idea of the phase space, which is a multi-dimensional space that represents all possible states of the system. The behavior of the system is described by trajectories in the phase space, which can exhibit a wide range of complex behaviors, such as periodic orbits, strange attractors, and chaotic behavior. Bifurcation analysis is another important tool in nonlinear dynamics, which involves the study of how the behavior of the system changes as the parameters of the system are varied. Bifurcations can lead to the emergence of new behaviors, such as the creation of new periodic orbits or the onset of chaotic behavior.

Chaos theory is another important area of nonlinear dynamics that involves the study of deterministic systems that exhibit unpredictable and complex behavior, such as the butterfly effect and sensitive dependence on initial conditions. Chaos theory has applications in many areas of science and engineering, such as weather forecasting, economics, and biology. The equations governing nonlinear systems are generally more complex than those governing linear systems and may involve terms with higher orders of the variables. Nonlinear systems can be represented using state-space models, which describe the evolution of the system's state over time. The equations for a nonlinear state-space model are:

$$x(t + 1) = f(x(t), u(t)) \, y(t) = h(x(t), u(t)), \tag{15.2}$$

where $x(t)$ is the state vector at time t, $u(t)$ is the input vector at time t, $y(t)$ is the output vector at time t, and f and h are nonlinear functions that describe the system dynamics and the output equation, respectively. In addition to the state-space model, nonlinear systems can also be represented using differential equations, which describe how the state variables change over time as a function of their current values and the inputs to the system. Nonlinear differential equations can be written in a general form as:

$$\frac{dx}{dt} = f(x, u), \tag{15.3}$$

where x is the vector of state variables and u is the vector of inputs. The function f describes the dynamics of the system and is generally nonlinear.

Solving nonlinear equations or differential equations analytically is often not possible, and numerical methods such as numerical integration or iterative methods are used to obtain approximate solutions. Nonlinear systems are important in many areas of science and engineering, including control theory, physics, biology, and economics. Nonlinear systems are used in many areas of science and engineering, such as physics, chemistry, biology, and engineering. They are used to model a wide range of physical systems, such as fluid dynamics, population dynamics, and chemical reactions. The theory of nonlinear systems is also used to develop control strategies for these systems, such as feedback control, adaptive control, and nonlinear control. However, the analysis and control of nonlinear systems are typically more complex and challenging than those of linear systems due to their complex behavior and mathematical complexity.

Nonlinear systems in cybernetical intelligence refer to systems that cannot be described by linear equations or linear transformations. These systems are often used to model complex and nonlinear phenomena such as chaotic systems, neural networks, and biological systems.

In the context of cybernetical intelligence, nonlinear systems are often used to model and control complex systems, such as robotics, transportation systems, and industrial processes. The behavior of nonlinear systems can be highly complex and difficult to predict and may exhibit phenomena such as bifurcations, chaos, and nonlinear resonances. Nonlinear systems can be analyzed and controlled using a variety of techniques. One approach is to use mathematical models, such as differential equations or difference equations, to describe the behavior of the system. These models can be analyzed using numerical methods or analytical techniques, such as bifurcation analysis, Lyapunov stability analysis, or phase space analysis. Another approach to controlling nonlinear systems is to use machine learning techniques, such as neural networks or fuzzy logic systems, to model and control the system. These techniques can be used to create models that can adapt to changing conditions or to learn from data and make predictions about the behavior of the system.

Nonlinear systems in cybernetical intelligence can be challenging to analyze and control, but they offer a powerful tool for modeling and controlling complex systems. By using mathematical models, machine learning techniques, and advanced control algorithms, it is possible to create intelligent systems that can adapt and learn in complex and dynamic environments.

15.3 Stability Theory

Stability analysis of a dynamic system is concerned with the behavior of the system over time, particularly how it responds to disturbances or changes in the initial conditions. The behavior of a system can be described by its response function, which is a mathematical expression that relates the output of the system to its input and initial conditions. In general, the response function can be represented by a differential equation:

$$\frac{dx}{dt} = f(x, u), \tag{15.4}$$

where x is the vector of state variables, u is the vector of input variables, and $f(x, u)$ is the vector of system dynamics. The stability of a system can be analyzed by studying the behavior of the system around its equilibrium points, which are the values of x and u where the system does not change over time. There are two main types of stability: asymptotic stability and Lyapunov stability.

Asymptotic stability: A system is said to be asymptotically stable if its response decays to zero over time, regardless of the initial conditions. Mathematically, this can be expressed as:

$$\text{limit} \rightarrow \infty \Longrightarrow x(t) = 0, \tag{15.5}$$

where $x(t)$ is the response of the system at time t. Lyapunov stability: A system is said to be Lyapunov stable if its response remains bound within a certain range, regardless of the initial conditions. This type of stability is more general than asymptotic stability and can be applied to nonlinear systems as well as linear systems. The Lyapunov stability analysis involves finding a Lyapunov function, which is a scalar function that is positive definite and has a global minimum at the desired equilibrium point of the system. The Lyapunov function is used to determine whether the system will remain within a certain region of stability or not.

The stability of linear systems can be analyzed using several techniques, including the root locus method, the frequency response method, and the state-space method. These methods rely on mathematical models of the system dynamics, which can be represented by linear differential equations of the form:

$$\frac{dx}{dt} = Ax + Bu, \tag{15.6}$$

where A is the matrix of system dynamics, B is the matrix of input coefficients, and x and u are the vectors of state and input variables, respectively.

The root locus method is a graphical technique for analyzing the stability of a linear system. It involves plotting the roots of the system's characteristic equation in the complex plane as a function of a parameter, such as the gain of a feedback loop. The stability of the system can be determined by examining the location of the roots relative to the imaginary axis.

The frequency response method is another graphical technique for analyzing the stability of a linear system. It involves calculating the system's response to sinusoidal inputs of different frequencies and plotting the amplitude and phase of the output as a function of frequency. The stability of the system can be determined by examining the gain and phase margins of the frequency response.

The state-space method is a mathematical technique for analyzing the stability of a linear system. It involves representing the system dynamics in a matrix form and analyzing the eigenvalues of the system matrix. The stability of the system can be determined by examining the location of the eigenvalues in the complex plane.

Stability theory in cybernetical intelligence refers to the study of the stability of dynamical systems in the context of control theory and cybernetics. The goal of stability analysis is to determine whether a system will converge to a stable equilibrium or exhibit unstable behavior and to design control algorithms that ensure stability in the presence of disturbances or uncertainty.

In cybernetical intelligence, stability theory is used to analyze and design control systems for a wide range of applications, such as robotics, aerospace systems, and industrial processes. Stability analysis involves studying the behavior of a system over time and analyzing its response to various disturbances or inputs.

There are several techniques used in stability analysis, including Lyapunov stability analysis, input–output stability analysis, and passivity-based stability analysis. Lyapunov stability analysis is one of the most widely used techniques, which involves analyzing the stability of a system based on a function called the Lyapunov function. This function measures the energy of the system and its rate of change and is used to determine whether the system will converge to a stable equilibrium or not.

Input–output stability analysis involves analyzing the stability of a system based on its input–output behavior, while passivity-based stability analysis involves analyzing the stability of a system based on its energy storage and dissipation properties. Stability theory is essential in cybernetical intelligence as it ensures the stability of control systems, which are used to regulate and optimize the behavior of complex systems. By using advanced stability analysis techniques, it is possible to design control algorithms that ensure stability in the presence of disturbances, uncertainties, and nonlinearities.

15.4 Observability and Identification

Observability and identification are important concepts in control theory that deal with the ability to measure and estimate the state of a system. Observability refers to the ability to infer the internal state of a system by only measuring its input and output signals. In other words, if a system is observable, it is possible to reconstruct its internal state using only the available measurements.

Identification, on the other hand, involves estimating the internal parameters of a system based on input–output measurements. In other words, given a set of input–output data, identification seeks to determine the unknown parameters that govern the behavior of the system. Mathematically, observability and identification are described using state-space models. A state-space model represents a dynamic system as a set of first-order differential equations, where the state vector contains the internal variables of the system and the input and output vectors represent the external inputs and measured outputs of the system, respectively. The state-space model can be written as follows:

$$\dot{x}(t) = f(x(t), u(t), t) \tag{15.7}$$

$$y(t) = h(x(t), u(t), t), \tag{15.8}$$

where $x(t) \in \mathbb{R}^n$ is the state vector, $u(t) \in \mathbb{R}^m$ is the input vector, $y(t) \in \mathbb{R}^p$ is the output vector, $f(x(t), u(t), t)$ is the system dynamics function, and $h(x(t), u(t), t)$ is the output function.

Observability can be determined by checking whether it is possible to reconstruct the state vector $x(t)$ from the available output measurements $y(t)$ over a finite time interval $[t_0, t_f]$. Identification involves estimating the parameters of the system dynamics function $f(x(t), u(t), t)$ based on input–output data. This can be done using various techniques, such as system identification algorithms or machine learning methods. One common approach is to use least-squares regression to estimate the parameters of the system dynamics function. Given a set of input–output data $(u(t), y(t))$ over a time interval $[t_0, t_f]$, the objective is to minimize the error between the measured output $y(t)$ and the output predicted by the model $\hat{y}(t)$, which is given by:

$$\hat{y}(t) = h(\hat{x}(t), u(t), t), \tag{15.9}$$

where $h(\hat{x}(t)$ is the estimated state vector obtained by solving the state equations using the estimated parameters. The least-squares solution for the system dynamics function parameters can be obtained by minimizing the following cost function:

$$J = \frac{1}{2} \int_{t_0}^{t_f} (y(t) - \hat{y}(t))^T Q(y(t) - \hat{y}(t)) dt, \tag{15.10}$$

where Q is a positive definite weighting matrix. In intelligent control, observability and identification are two important concepts that are essential for developing effective control strategies. Observability refers to the ability to measure or infer the internal state of a system based on its observable inputs and outputs. A system is said to be observable if its state can be estimated accurately using only its input and output signals. Observability is important because it enables us to design controllers that can regulate the behavior of the system in a desired manner, even when the internal states are not directly measurable. Observability can be enhanced by carefully choosing the system inputs and outputs, as well as by using appropriate measurement techniques.

Identification, on the other hand, refers to the process of estimating the unknown parameters of a system based on its input–output data. Identification is important because it enables us to develop accurate mathematical models of the system, which can be used to design controllers that can effectively regulate the system's behavior. Identification techniques can be used to estimate various system parameters, such as the transfer function coefficients, the time delays, the system order, and the noise characteristics.

Together, observability and identification form the basis of intelligent control. By making a system observable and identifying its parameters, one can develop effective control strategies that can regulate the system's behavior in real-time. This is particularly important for complex systems, such as those encountered in robotics, aerospace, and manufacturing, where accurate and reliable control is critical for safe and efficient operation.

15.5 Controllability and Stabilizability

Controllability is a concept in control theory that refers to the ability to steer the state of a system from an initial state to a desired final state in a finite time through the application of control inputs. It is a fundamental property of a control system and is closely related to the ability to stabilize a system.

In general, a system is said to be controllable if, for any initial state x_0 and any desired final state x_f, there exists a control input $u(t)$ that can steer the system from x_0 to x_f in a finite time. The controllability of a system can be analyzed mathematically using the concept of the controllability matrix. The controllability matrix C of a linear time-invariant system can be defined as:

$$C = \begin{bmatrix} B & AB & A^{2B} \dots A^{n-1}B \end{bmatrix},$$ (15.11)

where A and B are the state and input matrices, respectively, and n is the order of the system. The controllability matrix is a square matrix of dimension $n \times nm$, where nm is the number of input channels.

If the rank of the controllability matrix is equal to the order of the system, then the system is said to be controllable. This means that every state of the system can be reached by applying appropriate control inputs. If the rank of the controllability matrix is less than the order of the system, then the system is uncontrollable, and some states cannot be reached by any control input. Controllability is important in control system design because it allows the designer to determine whether or not the system can be controlled to achieve a desired response. If the system is controllable, the designer can then design a control law that will steer the system to the desired state. If the system is uncontrollable, the designer must either modify the system or the control objectives in order to achieve the desired response.

Stabilizability is a property of a system that ensures that it can be stabilized by a control input. In other words, if a system is stabilizable, then it is possible to design a control law that will drive the system to a desired equilibrium point or a desired trajectory. Mathematically, a linear time-invariant system is said to be stabilizable if there exists a feedback control law that can stabilize the system. The stabilizing control law is typically designed using the state-feedback control approach, which involves finding a feedback gain matrix K that can be used to compute the control input $u(t)$ as:

$$u(t) = -Kx(t), \tag{15.12}$$

where $x(t)$ is the state of the system at time t. The Stabilizability of a system can be analyzed using the concept of controllability, which is the ability to steer the system from any initial state to any desired state using a control input. If a system is controllable, then it is possible to design a control law that can drive the system to any desired state. However, even if a system is controllable, it may not be stabilizable, as there may not exist a feedback control law that can stabilize the system. Stabilizability can be checked using various methods, such as the Lyapunov stability analysis, the pole placement method, or the LQR control design. These methods involve analyzing the stability of the closed-loop system, which is obtained by applying the feedback control law to the original system. In summary, Stabilizability is a key property of a control system that ensures that the system can be stabilized by a feedback control law. It is closely related to the concept of controllability and can be analyzed using various methods based on the stability analysis of the closed-loop system.

The Stabilizability of a system can be determined by analyzing its controllability and observability properties. If a system is controllable and observable, then it is said to be stabilizable. Mathematically, a linear time-invariant (LTI) system can be represented as:

$$\dot{x} = Ax + Bu \tag{15.13}$$

$$y = Cx, \tag{15.14}$$

where x is the state vector, u is the control input, y is the output, A is the state matrix, B is the input matrix, and C is the output matrix. To determine the Stabilizability of the system, one can use the Kalman controllability matrix:

$$K_c = \left[B, AB, A^{2B}, ..., A^{n-1}B\right], \tag{15.15}$$

where n is the order of the system. The system is said to be controllable if the rank of the Kalman controllability matrix is equal to the order of the system. If the system is controllable, then one can design a control input u that can steer the system from any initial state to a desired final state or equilibrium point.

However, controllability does not guarantee Stabilizability. A system may be controllable but may not be stabilizable if it has unstable poles or if the desired equilibrium point is not reachable by any control input. To determine Stabilizability, one needs to analyze the eigenvalues of the system. If all the eigenvalues of the system are stable (i.e. have negative real parts), then the system is said to be stabilizable. If there are any unstable eigenvalues, then the system is not stabilizable.

Stabilizability can also be determined by analyzing the system's transfer function. A system is stabilizable if all the poles of its transfer function are in the left half of the complex plane. In summary, Stabilizability refers to the ability of a control system to stabilize a given unstable system by using a control input. It can be determined by analyzing the controllability and observability properties of the system, as well as the eigenvalues and transfer function of the system.

15.6 Optimal Control

Optimal control is a branch of control theory that deals with finding the control inputs for a system to optimize a certain objective function, subject to certain constraints. The goal of optimal control is to determine the control inputs that will drive the system from an initial state to a final state while minimizing or maximizing a certain performance measure. The main idea of optimal control is to use mathematical optimization techniques to find the control inputs that will produce the best possible outcome. This involves minimizing or maximizing an objective function, which is typically a measure of the system's performance or cost. There are two main types of optimal control: open-loop and closed-loop. Open-loop control involves determining the control inputs based on a predetermined plan or trajectory, while closed-loop control involves adjusting the control inputs in real-time based on feedback from the system.

The mathematical framework for optimal control is provided by the calculus of variations and the theory of partial differential equations. The basic approach is to formulate the problem as an optimization problem, where the objective function is typically a cost function that depends on the state of the system and the control inputs. The optimal control problem can be solved using various methods, including dynamic programming, Pontryagin's minimum principle, and the maximum principle. These methods involve solving a system of differential equations, known as the Hamiltonian equations, which describe the evolution of the system's state and the adjoint variables that are used to calculate the gradients of the objective function with respect to the control inputs.

The optimal control problem can also be solved using numerical methods, such as gradient descent, conjugate gradient, or the Nelder–Mead simplex method. These methods involve iteratively adjusting the control inputs to minimize or maximize the objective function.

Optimal control is a mathematical method used to find the best control inputs for a system to achieve a desired output. The problem is formulated as a minimization problem of a cost function. The cost function is defined as the sum of a running cost and a terminal cost, which is evaluated over a finite time horizon. The running cost is a measure of the performance of the system at each instant of time, and the terminal cost is a measure of the performance of the system at the end of the time horizon. The general form of the optimal control problem is given by:

$$\min_j = \int_{t_0}^{t_f} L(x(t), u(t), t)dt + M(x(t_f)), \tag{15.16}$$

where j is the cost function, which is a scalar function that is to be minimized. L is the running cost, which is a scalar function of the state $x(t)$, control $u(t)$, and time t. $x(t)$ is the state of the system at time t. Note that $u(t)$ is the control input at time t. f is the dynamics of the system, which relates the state and control input to the time derivative of the state. Once the value function is obtained, the optimal control input can be computed using Pontryagin's minimum principle. The optimal state trajectory can be obtained by solving the system dynamics using the optimal control input. Optimal control is widely used in many fields, such as aerospace, robotics, and process control, to design controllers that achieve optimal performance. It is a powerful tool for solving complex control problems, where traditional control methods may not be effective.

15.7 Linear Quadratic Regulator Theory

Linear Quadratic Regulator (LQR) is a popular control design technique that is used to derive optimal feedback control laws for linear systems. The LQR theory considers a linear time-invariant system with a quadratic cost function. The objective of the LQR is to find a feedback control law that minimizes the quadratic cost function over a finite time horizon. The LQR theory is widely used in various applications, including aerospace, automotive, and robotics. The LQR theory is based on the solution of the Linear Quadratic (LQ) optimal control problem. The LQ problem involves finding a feedback control law that minimizes a quadratic cost function subject to the dynamics of the system. The cost function typically includes the control input and the deviation of the state from a desired set point.

The LQR theory extends the LQ problem to include an observer that estimates the system state based on the measured output. The observer is typically designed using the Kalman filter, which is a method for estimating the state of a linear system based on noisy measurements. The LQR control law is obtained by solving a Riccati equation, which is a matrix equation that describes the optimal control law for the system. The solution of the Riccati equation provides the feedback gain matrix that minimizes the cost function. The LQR problem can be formulated as follows: Given a linear system described by the state equation

$$\dot{x}(t) = Ax(t) + Bu(t), \tag{15.17}$$

where $x(t) \in \mathbb{R}^n$ is the state vector, $u(t) \in \mathbb{R}^m$ is the control input, A is an $n \times n$ matrix, and B is an $n \times m$ matrix. The objective is to design a control law of the form.

$$u(t) = -Kx(t), \tag{15.18}$$

where K is an $m \times n$ gain matrix, that minimizes the following quadratic cost function over a finite time horizon $[0, T]$:

$$J = \frac{1}{2} \int_0^T \left(x^T(t)Qx(t) + u^T(t)Ru(t) \right) dt + x^T(T)Q_f x(T), \tag{15.19}$$

where $Q \geq 0$ is an $n \times n$ positive semidefinite matrix, $R \geq 0$ is an $m \times m$ positive semidefinite matrix, and $Q_f \geq 0$ is an $n \times n$ positive semidefinite matrix. The optimal gain matrix K can be obtained by solving the following algebraic Riccati equation:

$$A^T P + PA - PBR^{-1}B^T P + Q = 0, \tag{15.20}$$

where P is an $n \times n$ positive semidefinite matrix called the solution of the Riccati equation. Once the optimal gain matrix K is obtained. The stability of the closed-loop system under the LQR control law can be guaranteed if the matrix pair $(A - BK, B)$ is stabilizable.

The LQR theory has several advantages, such as its ability to handle state and control constraints, its simplicity in implementation, and its ability to provide robust control in the presence of model uncertainties. However, it is limited to linear systems and may not always provide the optimal control solution for nonlinear systems.

The LQR theory is a widely used technique in intelligent control for designing optimal control systems. It is based on the use of a cost function that measures the trade-off between the control effort and the system's performance. In LQR theory, the system is modeled as a linear time-invariant system, and the control input is designed to minimize the cost function over a finite time horizon. The optimal control input is obtained by solving the associated Riccati equation. The LQR controller is known for its ability to provide optimal control solutions that are both stable and robust.

Neural networks, on the other hand, are a powerful tool for approximating complex nonlinear functions. They can be used in conjunction with LQR theory to design optimal controllers for nonlinear systems. The basic idea is to use a neural network to approximate the nonlinear dynamics of the system and then apply the LQR technique to the resulting linearized system. This approach is known as the neural network LQR (NNLQR) controller. The NNLQR controller has several advantages over traditional LQR controllers. First, it can handle nonlinear systems, which are common in many real-world applications. Second, it can adapt to changes in the system's dynamics, making it more robust to disturbances and uncertainties. Finally, it can learn from experience, making it a powerful tool for autonomous control.

In summary, LQR theory is a powerful technique for designing optimal control systems, and it can be extended to handle nonlinear systems using neural networks. The resulting NNLQR controllers are stable, robust, and adaptive, making them well-suited for a wide range of applications in intelligent control.

15.8 Time-Optimal Control

Time-optimal control is a control theory that aims to find the control input that will minimize the time taken by a system to move from an initial state to a final state while satisfying a set of constraints. The objective is to find the control input that will minimize the time taken to achieve a desired state while ensuring that the state variables remain within certain bounds.

Time-optimal control problems can be formulated as optimal control problems, where the objective is to minimize the time taken subject to the constraints of the system dynamics and the control input. The solution to the time-optimal control problem provides the optimal control input that will take the system from the initial state to the final state in minimum time. The formulation of a time-optimal control problem depends on the type of system under consideration. For linear systems, the time-optimal control problem can be formulated as a LQR problem. For nonlinear systems, the problem can be formulated as an optimal control problem subject to state and control constraints.

The solution to the time-optimal control problem for linear systems is given by the LQR control law, which provides a feedback control law that minimizes a quadratic cost function. The LQR control law is based on the solution to the Riccati equation, which is a matrix differential equation that relates the control input to the state variables. For nonlinear systems, the solution to the time-optimal control problem can be obtained using Pontryagin's maximum principle, which provides the necessary conditions for optimality. The maximum principle relates the optimal control input to the Hamiltonian function, which is a function of the state variables, the control input, and the cost function. The solution to the time-optimal control problem is an important topic in control theory and has applications in various fields, including aerospace, robotics, and manufacturing.

Time-optimal control refers to the problem of finding a control signal that minimizes the time required to reach a specified final state while satisfying system constraints. The time-optimal control problem is usually formulated as an optimal control problem, and the solution to this problem is called the time-optimal control law.

To solve this problem, various techniques such as Pontryagin's maximum principle, dynamic programming, and numerical methods like nonlinear programming can be used. In time-optimal control, the control signal is typically "bang–bang," meaning that it switches between two extreme values, such as on/off, in order to minimize the time required to reach the final state. This type of control strategy is commonly used in robotics, aerospace, and other applications where quick and precise control is required. Time-optimal control is a concept in control theory that seeks to minimize the time required to bring a system from an initial state to a desired final state. In the context of neural networks, time-optimal control can be used to design controllers that achieve a desired output as quickly as possible, subject to constraints on the control inputs and the dynamics of the system.

One approach to time-optimal control in neural networks is to use the Pontryagin Maximum Principle, which is a powerful mathematical tool for optimizing control systems. The principle provides a set of necessary conditions for a control input to be optimal, which can be used to derive a set of differential equations that describe the optimal control trajectory. These equations can then be solved using numerical methods to obtain the optimal control input. Another approach to time-optimal control in neural networks is to use MPC, which is a control strategy that uses a model of the system to predict its future behavior and optimize the control input over a finite time horizon. In this approach, a neural network is used to model the dynamics of the system, and the MPC algorithm is used to compute the optimal control input at each time step.

Time-optimal control in neural networks has a wide range of applications in areas such as robotics, autonomous vehicles, and aerospace engineering. For example, it can be used to design controllers for unmanned aerial vehicles (UAVs) that can achieve high-speed maneuvering and obstacle avoidance, or to design controllers for robotic systems that can perform complex tasks quickly and efficiently.

15.9 Stochastic Systems with Applications

Stochastic systems are mathematical models used to describe systems that are subject to random fluctuations or noise. These systems are commonly used in various fields such as finance, engineering, physics, biology, and many others. In general, stochastic systems are more challenging to analyze and control than deterministic systems, as they involve uncertainty and randomness. One of the key concepts in stochastic systems is probability theory, which provides a mathematical framework for analyzing and modeling random events. In stochastic systems, probability theory is used to describe the likelihood or probability of different outcomes based on the randomness and uncertainty in the system.

Stochastic systems can be classified into two main categories: discrete-time systems and continuous-time systems. Discrete-time systems are characterized by a sequence of random variables that evolve over discrete time steps, while continuous-time systems are described by stochastic differential equations that describe how a continuous process evolves over time.

Stochastic systems are often used to model real-world systems that are inherently stochastic, such as financial markets, weather systems, and biological processes. In finance, stochastic models are used to model asset prices and value financial derivatives such as options and futures. In engineering, stochastic models are used to model the behavior of complex systems such as control systems, communication networks, and manufacturing processes. In physics, stochastic models are used to describe the behavior of systems at the quantum level, and in biology, stochastic models are used to describe the behavior of biological systems such as population dynamics and epidemiology. Applications of stochastic systems include risk management in finance, optimization of complex systems in engineering, and modeling of complex biological systems in biology. In addition, stochastic systems are used in artificial intelligence and machine learning algorithms such as stochastic gradient descent, which is used to optimize the parameters of neural networks.

Stochastic systems are also used in control theory, which is the study of how to design controllers that can control a system's behavior. Stochastic control theory is concerned with the design of controllers that can handle the uncertainty and randomness in stochastic systems. Stochastic control theory is used in many applications such as finance, economics, and engineering, where the systems being controlled are inherently stochastic.

15.9.1 Stochastic System in Control Systems

Stochastic systems are commonly used in control systems where random fluctuations are expected or desired. In such systems, the objective is to control the system's behavior despite the presence of random disturbances, measurement errors, or other uncertainties.

One common application of stochastic control is in the control of noisy systems, such as those encountered in signal processing, communications, and robotics. In such systems, the control objective is often to minimize the effects of noise and interference on the system's performance. Stochastic control techniques can be used to design controllers that are robust to these uncertainties and can adapt to changing noise conditions.

Another application of stochastic control is in the control of complex systems with multiple interacting components, such as in biological systems or traffic networks. In such systems, the interactions between components can lead to complex and unpredictable behavior. Stochastic control can be used to design controllers that can adapt to these uncertainties and maintain stable behavior despite the complex interactions.

Stochastic control is also used in finance and economics to model and control the behavior of financial systems and markets. In such systems, the stochastic behavior of prices, interest rates, and other variables can be modeled using stochastic differential equations. Stochastic control techniques can be used to design optimal trading strategies or to control the risk of financial portfolios. Overall, stochastic control provides a powerful framework for designing controllers that can cope with uncertainties and adapt to changing conditions, making it an essential tool for control systems in a wide range of applications.

15.9.2 Stochastic System in Robotics and Automation

Stochastic systems play a vital role in robotics and automation. In robotics, the stochastic system is used to model the uncertainty in the robot's environment, sensors, and actuators. For example, a robot may have uncertainty in its sensors such as noise, which can be modeled using a stochastic system. Similarly, the robot's motion can also be modeled using a stochastic system to account for the uncertainties in the control inputs.

Stochastic control theory can be used to design controllers that are robust to uncertainties in the robot's environment. One such approach is the use of a Kalman filter, which is a mathematical technique that uses a stochastic model to estimate the state of a system. In robotics, the Kalman filter can be used to estimate the robot's position and velocity based on noisy sensor measurements. Another application of stochastic systems in robotics is motion planning. In this case, the stochastic system is used to model the robot's environment and the uncertainty in the robot's motion. The goal is to find a trajectory that maximizes the probability of the robot reaching its target while avoiding obstacles and other constraints. In automation, stochastic systems are used to model the uncertainty in the manufacturing process. For example, the variability in the manufacturing process can be modeled using a stochastic system. This can be used to design controllers that are robust to the variability in the manufacturing process.

Overall, stochastic systems are essential in robotics and automation to account for the uncertainties in the system and environment and design controllers that are robust to these uncertainties.

15.9.3   Stochastic System in Neural Networks

A stochastic system in neural networks is a system that exhibits random behavior or variability in its inputs, parameters, or outputs. These systems can be characterized by probability distributions that describe the random processes that govern their behavior. In the context of neural networks, stochastic systems are often used to model complex phenomena such as noise in sensory inputs, variability in neural firing rates, or uncertainty in system parameters.

Stochastic systems in neural networks can be analyzed using a variety of mathematical tools, including probability theory, statistical inference, and stochastic processes. One common approach to modeling stochastic systems in neural networks is to use probabilistic models such as Bayesian networks or Markov models. These models can capture the probabilistic dependencies between the different components of the system and can be used to make predictions about the system's behavior or to infer the underlying parameters from observed data.

Another approach to modeling stochastic systems in neural networks is to use Monte Carlo methods, which involve generating large numbers of random samples from the system's probability distributions and using these samples to estimate the system's behavior or parameters. Monte Carlo methods can be particularly useful for analyzing complex systems where analytical solutions are not available or are too difficult to compute.

Stochastic systems in neural networks have a wide range of applications in areas such as machine learning, robotics, and neuroscience. For example, they can be used to model the variability in neural firing rates observed in experimental data or to generate synthetic data for training machine learning models that are robust to noise and uncertainty. They can also be used to design controllers for robotic systems that can adapt to changing environments or perform tasks in the presence of uncertainty.

Summary

This chapter covered a wide range of topics related to dynamic system control. From the basics of linear and nonlinear systems to the more advanced concepts of stability theory and optimal control, one discussed how these concepts can be applied to various real-world applications. One also highlighted the importance of mathematical modeling and the use of stochastic systems to handle uncertainties and noise in the system. As technology continues to advance, these concepts will become increasingly important in developing advanced control systems for complex and challenging problems.

In the future, dynamic system control will continue to play a critical role in various fields, such as robotics, automation, aerospace, and transportation systems. As the complexity of these systems increases, the need for efficient and effective control strategies will also increase. One potential future direction is the development of more sophisticated and intelligent control algorithms that incorporate advanced machine learning and artificial intelligence techniques. Another potential area of research is the application of control theory to emerging technologies such as quantum computing and quantum control. Overall, dynamic system control will continue to be an active and important area of research with significant potential for future advancements and applications.

Exercise Questions

Q.15.1 How can nonlinear systems be represented mathematically, and what are some common techniques used for their analysis and control?

Q.15.2 What is the mathematical equation for the transfer function of a linear time-invariant (LTI) system, and how does it relate to the input–output behavior of the system?

Q.15.3 Explain controllability, and how can it be used to design control systems for dynamic systems?

Q.15.4 How can optimal control theory be used to design control systems, and what are some of its limitations?

Q.15.5 What is stochastic control, and how can it be used to handle uncertainties and noise in dynamic systems?

Q.15.6 Explain how can the LQR theory be used to design optimal control systems, and what are some of its advantages and limitations?

Q.15.7 What are some common challenges associated with designing control systems for robotics and automation applications, and how can they be overcome?

Q.15.8 Can you provide the mathematical equation for the stability criterion of a dynamic system, such as the Routh–Hurwitz stability criterion, and how it helps to determine the stability and convergence properties of the system?

Q.15.9 How can feedback control be used to regulate the performance of dynamic systems, and what are some common feedback control techniques?

Q.15.10 How does the concept of optimal control use the cost function to find the input that minimizes the performance index, and what is the mathematical equation for the optimal control problem, such as the LQR problem?

Further Reading

Franklin, GF., Powell, JD. and Workman, ML. *Digital control of dynamic systems* (Vol. 3). Addison-wesley, Reading, MA; 1998.

Goldberg DE. Dynamic system control using rule learning and genetic algorithms. In IJCAI 1985 Aug 18 (Vol. 85, pp. 588–592). ACM Digital Library.

Kalman RE. Contributions to the theory of optimal control. *Boletín de la Sociedad Matemática Mexicana*. 1960 Apr;5(2):102–19.

Russell DL. Controllability and stabilizability theory for linear partial differential equations: recent progress and open questions. *SIAM Review*. 1978 Oct;20 (4):639–739.

Slemrod M. A note on complete controllability and stabilizability for linear control systems in Hilbert space. *SIAM Journal on Control*. 1974 Aug;12(3):500–8.

16

Deep Learning

Deep learning is a subset of machine learning that uses neural networks with numerous layers in order to learn from complex data. It is a powerful technique that has revolutionized various fields, including computer vision, natural language processing, speech recognition, and robotics. Deep learning models are trained using large datasets, and they have the ability to learn and generalize from the data to make accurate predictions.

The basic unit of a deep learning model is a neural network, which is a collection of nodes or neurons that are organized into layers. Each neuron receives input from other neurons, processes it using an activation function, and produces an output that is sent to other neurons in the next layer. The output of the final layer represents the prediction of the model. Deep learning models can be trained using supervised, unsupervised, or semi-supervised learning techniques. In supervised learning, the model is trained using labeled data, where the input data is paired with the correct output. In unsupervised learning, the model is trained on unlabeled data, where the objective is to learn the underlying structure of the data. Semi-supervised learning is a combination of both techniques, where the model is trained on a small amount of labeled data and a large amount of unlabeled data. The training of deep learning models is done using optimization techniques such as gradient descent, where the objective is to minimize the loss function. The loss function measures the difference between the predicted output of the model and the actual output.

One of the strengths of deep learning is its ability to learn high-level representations of the data automatically. This is achieved through the use of convolutional neural networks (CNNs) in computer vision and recurrent neural networks (RNNs) in natural language processing. CNNs are designed to recognize spatial patterns in images, while RNNs are designed to process sequential data. Deep learning has many applications in various fields, including image and speech

Cybernetical Intelligence: Engineering Cybernetics with Machine Intelligence, First Edition.
Kelvin K. L. Wong.
© 2024 The Institute of Electrical and Electronics Engineers, Inc.
Published 2024 by John Wiley & Sons, Inc.
Companion website: www.wiley.com/go/cyberintel

recognition, natural language processing, self-driving cars, and robotics. It has also shown promising results in healthcare, finance, and social sciences. However, the use of deep learning also raises ethical and social concerns, such as data privacy, algorithmic bias, and the impact on the job market.

Deep learning is a type of machine learning that is based on artificial neural networks with multiple layers. It has become a popular tool in intelligent control due to its ability to learn complex patterns and relationships in data.

In intelligent control, deep learning can be used in various ways. One common application is in predictive maintenance, where the neural network is trained on historical data to predict when a system is likely to fail. This can help prevent equipment downtime and reduce maintenance costs.

Another application of deep learning in intelligent control is in anomaly detection. By analyzing patterns in data, a neural network can learn what is normal behavior for a system and detect any anomalies that may indicate a fault. This can help prevent equipment damage and improve safety.

Deep learning can also be used in control systems to optimize performance. By using the neural network to learn the relationship between system inputs and outputs, it can be used to identify the best control actions to achieve the desired results. Overall, deep learning has proven to be a powerful tool in intelligent control, with numerous applications in predictive maintenance, anomaly detection, and control optimization. Its ability to learn from data and identify complex patterns makes it a valuable asset in improving the performance and efficiency of control systems.

Deep learning is a powerful tool for cybernetical intelligence, which refers to the integration of control systems with intelligent algorithms to improve system performance. In the context of cybernetics, deep learning algorithms can be used to create intelligent systems that can learn and adapt to changing environments in real-time. Deep learning algorithms can be used to create neural network-based controllers that can learn the system dynamics directly from data. This approach is called data-driven control and can be used for complex systems where traditional control methods are difficult to apply. By using deep learning for control, the system can adapt to changes in the environment and learn from experience to improve performance. Another application of deep learning in cybernetical intelligence is in the design of intelligent decision-making systems. Deep learning algorithms can be used to learn from data and make predictions or decisions based on the learned patterns. This can be applied to a range of cybernetical systems, such as autonomous vehicles, robotics, and smart cities.

Furthermore, deep learning can also be used in the design of intelligent sensor systems. By combining deep learning algorithms with advanced sensor technologies, it is possible to create systems that can accurately detect and interpret complex patterns in the environment. This can be applied to a range of cybernetical systems, such as surveillance systems, smart homes, and environmental monitoring.

16.1 Neural Network Models in Deep Learning

Neural network models are an essential component of deep learning. They are mathematical models inspired by the structure and functionality of the human brain. These models consist of layers of artificial neurons that process information in a hierarchical manner. In this section, one will discuss neural network models in deep learning in detail, including their architecture, training, and applications.

Neural network models are composed of layers of interconnected neurons, which receive input data and produce output predictions. The number of layers and neurons in each layer depend on the complexity of the problem at hand. The three main types of layers used in neural network models are:

- Input layer: This layer receives the input data and passes it to the next layer.
- Hidden layer: This layer performs computations on the input data and passes the results to the next layer. Neural network models can have multiple hidden layers.
- Output layer: This layer produces the final output prediction based on the computations performed by the hidden layers.

The basic equation for computing the output of a neuron in a neural network model is:

$$y = f\left(\sum_{i=1}^{n} w_i x_i + b\right), \tag{16.1}$$

where y is the output of the neuron, x_i are the input values, w_i are the weights assigned to each input, b is the bias term, and f is the activation function.

The weights and biases of the neurons are learned during the training process. The training process involves presenting the neural network model with a set of input data and corresponding output labels. The model then adjusts its weights and biases to minimize the difference between its output predictions and the actual output labels. This process is repeated iteratively until the model achieves a satisfactory level of accuracy. There are several types of neural network models used in deep learning, including:

- Feedforward neural networks: These are the simplest type of neural network models, where the information flows only in one direction, from the input layer to the output layer.
- Convolutional neural networks (CNNs): These are commonly used for image and video recognition tasks. They use specialized layers, such as convolutional and pooling layers, to extract relevant features from the input data.
- Recurrent neural networks (RNNs): These are used for processing sequential data, such as natural language processing and speech recognition. They use loops to process the data and maintain a memory of previous inputs.

- Generative adversarial networks (GANs): These are used for generating new data samples that are similar to the training data. They consist of two networks, a generator network that produces the new data samples, and a discriminator network that evaluates the similarity of the generated samples to the training data.

Neural network models have been successfully applied to various intelligent control applications, such as robotics, autonomous vehicles, and process control. They can learn complex patterns and relationships in the input data, making them suitable for handling nonlinear and dynamic systems. However, the training process can be computationally expensive, and the models can be prone to overfitting, which is when the model memorizes the training data and performs poorly on new data.

One of the main advantages of neural networks in cybernetical intelligence is their ability to learn complex patterns and relationships from data. Neural networks can be trained using data from the system and can then use this learned information to make predictions or control decisions. This is particularly useful in systems with complex and non-linear dynamics, where traditional control methods are difficult to apply.

Neural networks can be used in a range of cybernetical applications, such as control, decision-making, and sensor systems. For example, in control systems, neural networks can be used to create controllers that can learn the system dynamics directly from data, without the need for a mathematical model. This approach, called data-driven control, is particularly useful in complex systems where traditional control methods are limited. In decision-making systems, neural networks can be used to learn from data and make predictions or decisions based on the learned patterns. This can be applied to a range of cybernetical systems, such as autonomous vehicles, robotics, and smart cities. For example, a neural network could be trained to predict traffic patterns in a smart city and make decisions to optimize traffic flow. Neural networks can also be used in sensor systems, where they can be combined with advanced sensor technologies to create systems that can accurately detect and interpret complex patterns in the environment. This can be applied to a range of cybernetical systems, such as surveillance systems, smart homes, and environmental monitoring.

16.2 Methods of Deep Learning

Deep Learning is a subset of machine learning that uses artificial neural networks to model and solve complex problems. There are several methods used in deep learning, each with its unique characteristics and applications. Here one describe some of the main methods in detail:

16.2.1 Convolutional Neural Networks

Convolutional Neural Networks (CNNs) are a specialized type of neural network commonly used in deep learning for image and video recognition, natural language processing, and other applications that require high-dimensional inputs. CNNs are designed to learn and extract features from input data by convolving them with a set of learned filters.

In a CNN, the input data is typically a matrix of pixel values for an image. The convolutional layers apply a set of filters to this input data to produce a set of feature maps. Each filter is a matrix of weights that is applied to a small region of the input matrix. This operation is known as convolution, and it can be thought of as a sliding window that moves over the input matrix and performs a dot product at each location. The output of the convolutional layers is then passed through a non-linear activation function, such as a rectified linear unit (ReLU), which introduces non-linearity into the model. The output of the activation function is then typically passed through one or more pooling layers, which downsample the feature maps by taking the maximum or average value within a small region of the feature map. The output of the pooling layers is then passed through one or more fully connected layers, which are similar to the layers in a traditional neural network. These layers perform a weighted sum of the input values, followed by an activation function, to produce the final output. The math equations for a single convolutional layer can be expressed as follows:

$$y_{i,j} = \sigma \left(\sum_m \sum_n x_{i+m,j+n} \, w_{m,n} \right), \tag{16.2}$$

where $y_{i,j}$ is the output at position (i, j), $x_{(i+m, j+n)}$ is the input value at position $(i+m, j+n)$, $w_{(m,n)}$ is the weight at position (m, n), and σ is the activation function. The complete basic structure of CNN is shown in Figure 16.1.

Convolutional Neural Networks (CNNs) have been applied in various fields of intelligent control, including robotics, computer vision, and autonomous vehicles. The use of CNNs in intelligent control systems allows for the processing of complex and high-dimensional data, such as images and videos, to make intelligent decisions and actions.

In the context of robotics, CNNs have been used for object detection and recognition, which is an important task for robots that operate in dynamic environments. The CNN can be trained on a dataset of images with annotated objects, allowing it to recognize and identify objects in real-time, enabling the robot to make more informed decisions. Similarly, in the context of autonomous vehicles, CNNs have been used for tasks such as lane detection and traffic sign recognition. By training a CNN on a dataset of road images, the model can recognize and

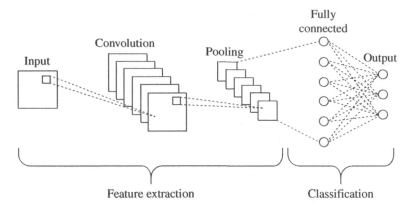

Feature extraction   Classification

Figure 16.1 Basic convolutional neural networks structure.

interpret road markings and traffic signs, allowing the vehicle to make intelligent decisions about its course of action.

CNNs can also be used for anomaly detection in industrial processes, such as predictive maintenance. By analyzing sensor data from industrial machinery, CNNs can detect anomalies that may indicate a fault or failure in the system, allowing for preemptive maintenance to be performed to avoid downtime and costly repairs. Overall, the use of CNNs in intelligent control systems has shown great potential in improving the accuracy and efficiency of decision-making processes in various fields.

The ConvLSTM, or convolutional long short-term memory, is a type of neural network architecture that combines the convolutional neural network (CNN) and the long short-term memory (LSTM) network. ConvLSTM was first introduced by Shi et al. in 2015 and has since become a popular choice for sequence-to-sequence prediction tasks, such as video frame prediction, weather forecasting, and natural language processing. The ConvLSTM network consists of multiple layers, each of which includes a convolutional layer, an LSTM layer, and a set of activation functions. The convolutional layer extracts features from the input sequence, while the LSTM layer processes the temporal information and maintains a memory of the past inputs. The activation functions help to introduce non-linearity into the network. The Network structure of ConvLSTM is shown in Figure 16.2.

The main advantage of ConvLSTM is its ability to handle both spatial and temporal dependencies in the input sequence. The convolutional layer helps to capture spatial features in each frame of the sequence, while the LSTM layer maintains a memory of the past frames and captures temporal dependencies between them. This makes ConvLSTM well-suited for tasks that require modeling of complex sequences with long-term dependencies, such as video prediction.

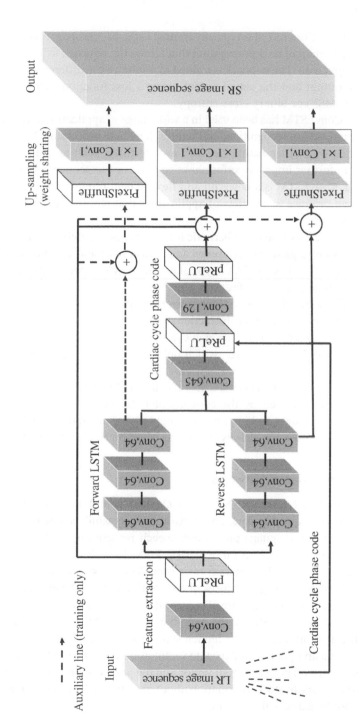

Figure 16.2 Network structure of ConvLSTM.

During training, ConvLSTM is typically trained using backpropagation through time (BPTT), a variant of backpropagation that allows the network to learn over a sequence of input data. The network is trained to minimize the difference between the predicted output and the actual output, using a loss function such as mean squared error (MSE) or binary cross-entropy.

In practice, ConvLSTM has been used in a wide range of applications, including video prediction, action recognition, and natural language processing. It has also been combined with other neural network architectures, such as the attention mechanism, to further improve performance in sequence-to-sequence prediction tasks. Overall, ConvLSTM is a powerful and flexible neural network architecture that has shown promise in a variety of applications that require the modeling of complex sequences.

One of the challenges faced in cybernetic intelligence is the ability to accurately classify and recognize patterns in complex data. This can be addressed using Convolutional Neural Networks (CNN), a type of neural network specifically designed for image recognition and classification.

CNNs are highly effective in identifying patterns in images due to their ability to learn features at different levels of abstraction, from simple edges and lines to more complex shapes and structures. They achieve this by using convolutional layers that apply filters to the input image, which helps to highlight important features and reduce noise.

In addition to convolutional layers, CNNs also use pooling layers to downsample the feature maps generated by the convolutional layers, further reducing the dimensionality of the data and improving computational efficiency. Finally, fully connected layers are used to classify the image based on the learned features.

16.2.2 Recurrent Neural Networks

Recurrent Neural Networks (RNNs) are a class of neural networks that are designed to process sequential data. They have been successfully applied in various fields such as natural language processing, speech recognition, and time series analysis. Unlike feedforward neural networks, RNNs have feedback connections that allow them to retain information over time. This makes them suitable for tasks that require processing sequences of data with temporal dependencies.

The key feature of RNNs is the use of recurrent connections that allow information to be passed from one step to the next in a sequence. At each time step, the network takes an input vector and a hidden state vector as input, and produces an output vector and an updated hidden state vector as output. The hidden state vector is updated based on both the input vector and the previous hidden state vector, allowing the network to store information about past inputs. The basic equations of an RNN can be expressed as follows:

$$h_t = f(w_{hx} x_t + w_{hh} h_{t-1} + b_h) \tag{16.3}$$

$$y_t = g(w_{hy} h_t + b_y), \tag{16.4}$$

where x_t is the input vector at time step t, h_t is the hidden state vector at time step t, and y_t is the output vector at time step t. The w_{hx} and w_{hh} are weight matrices, b_h is the bias vector for the hidden state, w_{hy} is the weight matrix for the output, and b_y is the bias vector for the output. The f and g are activation functions such as the sigmoid function or the hyperbolic tangent function. The basic structure of RNN is shown in Figure 16.3.

There are several variants of RNNs, such as Long Short-Term Memory (LSTM) networks and Gated Recurrent Unit (GRU) networks, which have been developed to address the problem of vanishing gradients during training. These networks have additional mechanisms that allow them to selectively retain or forget information over time, making them more effective for longer sequences. In the context of intelligent control, RNNs have been used for a variety of tasks such as time series prediction, anomaly detection, and control of nonlinear systems. For example, RNNs have been used to model and control complex systems such as power grids and robots. They have also been used for fault diagnosis and predictive maintenance in industrial processes.

Recurrent Neural Networks (RNNs) are a powerful type of neural network used in intelligent control systems. They are used for time-series analysis, sequence prediction, and natural language processing. In intelligent control systems, RNNs are used to model and control systems with a time-varying behavior, where the current state of the system depends on the past states. RNNs are designed to handle sequential data, such as time-series data or data with a temporal component. They are also capable of handling data with variable lengths, making them useful for natural language processing and speech recognition. In intelligent control systems, RNNs are used to predict the future state of the system based on past observations.

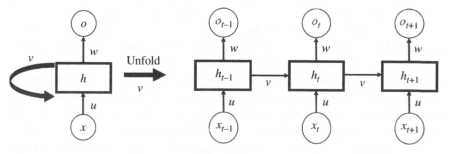

Figure 16.3 The basic recurrent neural networks.

One of the most popular types of RNNs is the Long Short-Term Memory (LSTM) network. LSTMs are designed to overcome the limitations of traditional RNNs, such as the vanishing gradient problem, which can make it difficult to learn long-term dependencies. LSTMs are well-suited for tasks that require the network to remember information over a long period, such as predicting the behavior of a complex system over time.

In intelligent control systems, RNNs can be used for a range of applications, such as predictive maintenance, process control, and anomaly detection. For example, an RNN can be used to predict the future behavior of a machine based on its past behavior, allowing for proactive maintenance before a failure occurs. RNNs can also be used to detect anomalies in a system by comparing the predicted behavior to the actual behavior, allowing for early detection of potential problems. Overall, RNNs are a valuable tool in intelligent control systems, providing a powerful method for modeling and predicting the behavior of complex systems over time.

16.2.3 Generative Adversarial Networks

Generative Adversarial Networks (GANs) are a class of deep learning models that are used for generative tasks such as image, audio, and text generation. The basic idea behind GANs is to train two neural networks, a generator and a discriminator, in a two-player minimax game. The generator network is trained to produce fake data that looks similar to real data, while the discriminator network is trained to distinguish between real and fake data.

During training, the generator network tries to produce data that can fool the discriminator network into believing it is real, while the discriminator network tries to correctly classify whether the data is real or fake. This adversarial training process helps the generator network learn to produce increasingly realistic data. The architecture of GANs typically consists of a generator network and a discriminator network, both of which are usually deep neural networks. The generator network takes a random noise vector as input and produces fake data that is intended to look like real data. The discriminator network takes either real or fake data as input and produces a binary output, indicating whether the input is real or fake. The loss function used in GANs is a combination of two terms: the generator loss and the discriminator loss. The generator loss measures how well the generator network is able to fool the discriminator network, while the discriminator loss measures how well the discriminator network is able to distinguish between real and fake data. GANs have many applications in various fields, including image generation, data augmentation, style transfer, and anomaly detection. In the context of intelligent control, GANs can be used for tasks such as generating synthetic data for training models, predicting future system behavior, and detecting anomalies in system performance. The general workflow of GAN is shown in Figure 16.4.

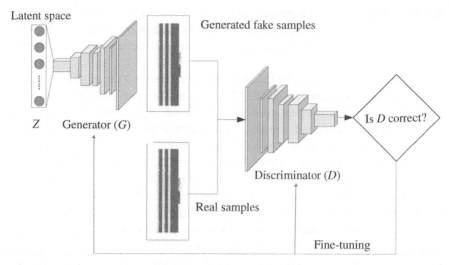

Latent space
Generated fake samples
Z Generator (*G*)
Discriminator (*D*)
Real samples
Is *D* correct?
Fine-tuning

Figure 16.4 The general workflow of GAN.

Generative Adversarial Networks (GANs) have a wide range of applications in cybernetical intelligent control, including computer vision, robotics, and natural language processing. In computer vision, GANs can be used for image and video synthesis, object detection, and recognition. For example, GANs can be trained on a large dataset of images and can generate new images that are similar to the ones in the training set. In robotics, GANs can be used for motion planning and control, reinforcement learning, and robot perception. For instance, GANs can be used to generate simulated environments that can be used to train robots to perform tasks in the real world.

GANs have been used in a variety of applications in cybernetic intelligence, including image and video generation, text-to-image synthesis, and data augmentation. They have also shown promise in areas such as anomaly detection, where they can be used to detect unusual patterns in data. However, GANs can be challenging to train and require careful tuning of hyper parameters. There is also a risk of mode collapse, where the generator produces limited variation in its output, leading to a loss of diversity in the generated data. Overall, GANs are a powerful tool in cybernetic intelligence for generating synthetic data and have potential applications in a wide range of fields. However, their success depends on careful design and training to avoid common pitfalls.

The p-GANs, or projected gradient descent generative adversarial networks, are a type of generative model that use adversarial training to learn to generate realistic samples from a given dataset. The key idea behind p-GANs is to use a projected gradient descent approach to enforce a constraint on the generator function, ensuring that it generates only samples that lie within a given range or subspace. This approach addresses one of the key limitations of traditional GANs, which can sometimes generate samples that are unrealistic or outside the range of the original dataset.

In practice, p-GANs work by training two neural networks in parallel: a generator network *G* as shown in Figure 16.5 and a discriminator network *D* which is shown in Figure 16.6. The generator network takes as input a random noise vector *z* and produces a generated sample *x*. The discriminator network takes as input either a real sample from the original dataset or a generated sample from the generator network, and outputs a probability value indicating whether the input is real or fake. The overall generic architecture of p-GAN is shown in Figure 16.7.

During training, the generator network tries to generate samples that can fool the discriminator network, while the discriminator network tries to correctly distinguish between real and fake samples. The two networks are trained iteratively, with the generator network updating its weights to minimize the difference between the discriminator's output for its generated samples and the expected output (i.e. 1 for real samples and 0 for generated samples), and the discriminator network updating its weights to better distinguish between real and fake samples.

To enforce the constraint on the generator function, p-GANs use a projected gradient descent approach to project each generated sample onto the subspace defined by the range of the original dataset. This helps ensure that the generated

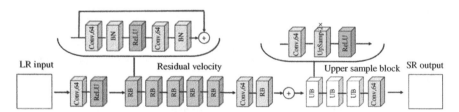

Figure 16.5 Structure diagram of p-GANs generator *G* network.

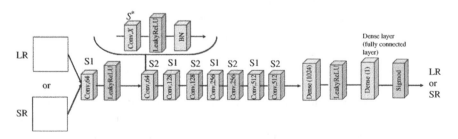

Figure 16.6 Network structure diagram of p-GANs discriminator *D*.

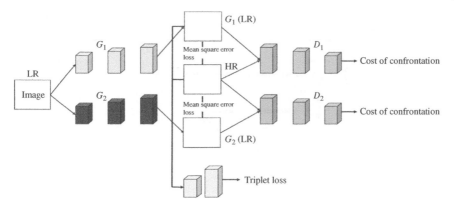

Figure 16.7 Architecture of the p-GANs.

samples remain within a reasonable range and avoids generating unrealistic samples. Overall, p-GANs are an effective approach to generative modeling that can generate high-quality samples while addressing some of the limitations of traditional GANs. They have applications in a wide range of areas, including image and video synthesis, data augmentation, and data privacy. In natural language processing, GANs can be used for text generation, summarization, and translation. For example, GANs can be trained on a large dataset of text and can generate new text that is similar to the ones in the training set. Overall, GANs can be used to generate new data that can be used to train and improve the performance of various intelligent control systems. However, due to their complex nature, GANs require extensive computational resources and expertise in training and fine-tuning the models for specific tasks.

16.2.4 Deep Learning Based Image Segmentation Models

Deep learning image segmentation models are a type of neural network architecture that can segment an input image into multiple regions or objects based on their characteristics. Image segmentation is a critical task in computer vision applications, such as medical imaging, autonomous vehicles, and object detection. The UNet is a popular deep learning image segmentation model based on a fully convolutional neural network (FCN) architecture, which enables it to learn and predict pixel-level segmentation maps.

The UNet architecture consists of an encoder network and a decoder network, which are connected by a series of skip connections as shown in Figure 16.8. The encoder network is similar to a traditional CNN, consisting of multiple convolutional and pooling layers that gradually reduce the spatial resolution of the input

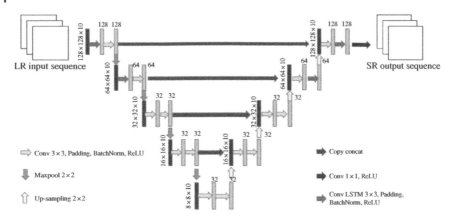

Figure 16.8 Structural principle of U-Net.

image while increasing the number of feature maps. The decoder network is designed to recover the spatial information and produce a segmentation map that has the same resolution as the input image. The skip connections between the encoder and decoder networks are a unique feature of UNet. They enable the network to preserve the high-resolution spatial information learned in the encoder network while also allowing the decoder network to recover the finer details of the segmentation map. Specifically, the skip connections connect each layer of the encoder network to a corresponding layer of the decoder network, allowing the decoder to use information from the encoder at multiple scales to refine the segmentation map. In the decoder network, each layer consists of an upsampling layer followed by a concatenation layer and several convolutional layers. The upsampling layer increases the spatial resolution of the input feature map, while the concatenation layer combines the feature map with the corresponding feature map from the encoder network. This concatenation operation helps the decoder network to learn more accurate segmentation boundaries by incorporating the high-resolution features learned in the encoder network.

Finally, the output layer of UNet is a softmax layer that produces a probability distribution over the different classes in the segmentation map. During training, the network is trained to minimize a loss function, such as cross-entropy loss, between the predicted segmentation map and the ground truth segmentation map. UNet has shown excellent performance on a variety of image segmentation tasks, including medical image segmentation and object detection. Its ability to capture both global and local features and its efficient use of computation and memory resources make it a popular choice for many image segmentation applications.

Moreover, 3D Residual U-Net is a neural network architecture for volumetric medical image segmentation. It is an extension of the popular U-Net architecture that was originally designed for 2D image segmentation. The 3D Residual U-Net consists of a contracting path and an expanding path, similar to the U-Net architecture. The contracting path consists of a series of convolutional layers followed by max pooling layers. This path reduces the spatial resolution of the input volume while increasing the number of feature maps. The expanding path is where the residual connections are introduced as shown in Figure 16.9. It consists of a series of up-convolutional layers followed by concatenation layers and residual blocks. The up-convolutional layers increase the spatial resolution of the feature maps while reducing the number of feature maps. The concatenation layers combine the feature maps from the corresponding layer in the contracting path with the feature maps from the up-convolutional layers.

The residual blocks in the expanding path are similar to those used in the ResNet architecture. They consist of two convolutional layers, each followed by a batch normalization layer and a Rectified Linear Unit (ReLU) activation function. The residual connection is then introduced by adding the input to the output of the second convolutional layer. This enables the network to learn the residual mapping between the input and output of the block. The 3D Residual U-Net architecture also includes several skip connections that connect the contracting path to the expanding path. These skip connections allow the network to capture both high-level and low-level features in the input volume and refine the segmentation map. During training, the 3D Residual U-Net is trained using a dice loss function, which measures the overlap between the predicted segmentation map and the ground truth segmentation map.

Overall, the 3D Residual U-Net architecture has shown promising results in various medical imaging segmentation tasks, such as brain tumor segmentation, lung

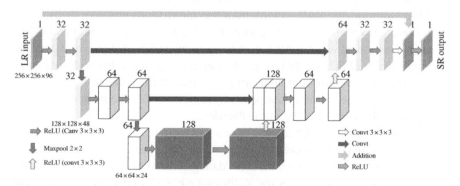

Figure 16.9 Schematic diagram of the network structure principle of 3D residual U-Net.

segmentation, and cardiac segmentation. Its ability to capture both global and local features and its efficient use of computation and memory resources make it a popular choice for many volumetric medical image segmentation applications.

16.2.5 Variational Auto Encoders

Variational autoencoders (VAEs) are generative models that can learn a low-dimensional representation of high-dimensional data, such as images, videos, or audio. VAEs are a type of neural network that consists of two main parts: an encoder and a decoder. The encoder maps the high-dimensional input data to a lower-dimensional latent space, while the decoder maps the latent space back to the original high-dimensional space.

The VAEs use a probabilistic approach to learning the latent space by assuming that the data is generated from a probabilistic distribution with some mean and variance. The encoder learns to map the input data to a distribution in the latent space, while the decoder learns to map the latent space back to the distribution of the original data. The training process for a VAE involves maximizing a lower bound on the log-likelihood of the data given the model. This lower bound, also known as the evidence lower bound (ELBO), can be expressed as:

$$ELBO = E[\log p(x|z)] - KL[q(z|x) \,|\, |p(z)], \tag{16.5}$$

where x is the input data, z is the latent variable, $p(x \,|\, z)$ is the likelihood of the data given the latent variable, $q(z \,|\, x)$ is the approximate posterior distribution over the latent variable given the data, and $p(z)$ is the prior distribution over the latent variable. The first term in the $ELBO$ is the reconstruction loss, which encourages the decoder to reconstruct the input data accurately. The second term is the KL divergence between the approximate posterior and the prior distribution, which encourages the encoder to learn a distribution over the latent variables that is close to the prior distribution. The general architecture of VAE is shown in Figure 16.10.

During training, the VAE samples from the approximate posterior distribution over the latent variable to generate a latent code z for each input data point. The decoder then generates a reconstruction of the input data using this latent code. By minimizing the $ELBO$, the VAE learns to map input data to a lower-dimensional latent space that captures the underlying structure of the data. This latent space can be used to generate new data points by sampling from the prior distribution and passing the samples through the decoder.

The loss function of VAEs consists of two parts: the reconstruction loss and the regularization loss. The reconstruction loss measures the difference between the original input data and the reconstructed data generated by the decoder. The regularization loss, also known as the Kullback-Leibler (KL) divergence, measures the difference between the distribution of the latent space and a predefined prior

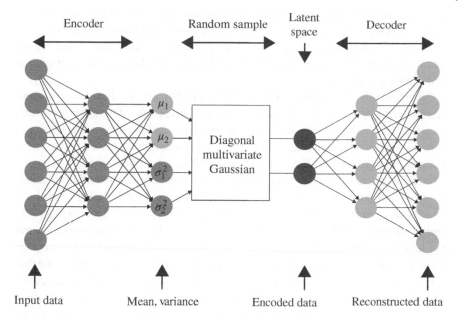

Figure 16.10 The general architecture of variational autoencoders.

distribution, usually a standard Gaussian distribution. The total loss function of VAEs is given by:

$$L = L_{rec} + L_{reg}, \tag{16.6}$$

where L_{rec} is the reconstruction loss and L_{reg} is the regularization loss. The reconstruction loss is calculated using the mean squared error (MSE) between the original input data and the reconstructed data:

$$L_{rec} = \frac{1}{N} \sum (x - \hat{x})^2, \tag{16.7}$$

where N is the number of data points, x is the original input data, and $\hat{x}$ is the reconstructed data generated by the decoder. The regularization loss is calculated using the KL divergence between the distribution of the latent space and the prior distribution:

$$L_{reg} = -0.5 \sum 1 + \log_2(\sigma^2) - \mu^2 - \sigma^2, \tag{16.8}$$

where μ and σ are the mean and standard deviation of the distribution of the latent space, respectively. The final objective of VAEs is to minimize the total loss function L with respect to the weights of the encoder and decoder networks, using stochastic gradient descent (SGD) or other optimization algorithms. In summary, VAEs are a type of generative model that can learn a low-dimensional representation of high-dimensional data. VAEs use a probabilistic approach to learning the latent space and minimize a loss function that includes both reconstruction loss and regularization loss.

Cybernetically, Variational Autoencoders (VAEs) are used to learn a compressed representation of input data that can be used for data generation and reconstruction. The process starts with an encoder network that maps the input data to a lower-dimensional latent space representation. This latent space is defined by a probability distribution learned during training, which is typically a Gaussian distribution. The VAE then uses this probability distribution to generate new data points by sampling from the latent space and decoding them back into the original input space using a decoder network. By sampling from this probability distribution, the VAE is able to generate new data points that are similar but not identical to the original input data. One of the key benefits of VAEs in cybernetic intelligence is their ability to perform unsupervised learning. This means that VAEs can learn useful features and representations of data without requiring labeled examples. This makes VAEs particularly useful in applications where labeled data is scarce or expensive to obtain. Another benefit of VAEs is that they can be used for data compression and reconstruction. By learning a compressed representation of the input data, VAEs can store and transmit data more efficiently, reducing storage costs and improving processing efficiency.

16.2.6 Transformer Models

Transformer models are a type of neural network architecture that have gained popularity in natural language processing tasks such as language translation, language modeling, and text generation. () First introduced the Transformer in the paper "Attention Is All You Need."

The Transformer consists of two main components: the encoder and the decoder. Both the encoder and the decoder are composed of a series of identical layers. The encoder takes an input sequence of tokens and produces a sequence of hidden states. Each token is first embedded into a vector representation and then passed through multiple layers of self-attention and feed-forward neural networks. The self-attention mechanism allows each token to attend to all other tokens in the sequence and compute a weighted sum of their representations, capturing the importance of each token for the current token.

The decoder takes the encoder's output and produces an output sequence of tokens. At each step, the decoder attends to the encoder's output and the previously generated tokens to produce a new hidden state. The new hidden state is then used to generate a probability distribution over the vocabulary of possible

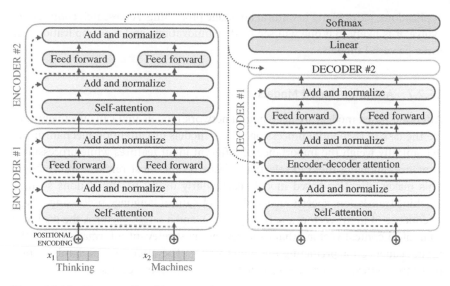

Figure 16.11 The overall architecture of transformer encoder.

tokens, from which the next token is sampled. The overall architecture of transformer encoder is shown in Figure 16.11.

The feed-forward neural network consists of two linear transformations with a ReLU activation function in between:

$$FFN(x) = ReLU(xw_1 + b_1)w_2 + b_2 FFN(x) = ReLU(xw_1 + b_1)w_2 + b_2, \tag{16.9}$$

where x is the input vector, w_1 and w_2 are weight matrices, b_1 and b_2 are bias vectors, and $ReLU(x) = \max(0, x)$ is the rectified linear unit activation function. The Transformer model also includes positional encoding to provide information about the position of each token in the sequence. The positional encoding is added to the token embeddings before being passed to the encoder and decoder layers.

Transformer models are a type of neural network used in cybernetic intelligence that were first introduced in the field of natural language processing (NLP). The Transformer architecture was designed to address some of the limitations of traditional recurrent neural networks (RNNs), which can struggle with long-term dependencies. One of the key benefits of Transformer models in cybernetic intelligence is their ability to process large amounts of data in parallel, making them much faster and more efficient than traditional RNNs. This has enabled researchers to train and deploy larger, more complex models that can handle increasingly complex tasks. Overall, Transformer models have had a significant impact on the field of cybernetic intelligence and have enabled major advances in many applications, particularly in natural language processing. As research continues to evolve, it is likely that one will see further innovations and new applications for these powerful models.

16.2.7 Attention-Based Models

Attention-based models are deep neural network models that can effectively handle the task of sequential processing. These models use attention mechanisms to dynamically weigh the importance of different input features while processing a sequence, allowing them to selectively focus on the most relevant information. This makes attention-based models particularly useful in applications such as machine translation, speech recognition, and natural language processing. Given a sequence of input vectors $x = (x_1, x_2, ..., x_n)$, and a target vector y, the goal is to compute a context vector c that captures the most relevant information from the input sequence for predicting the target vector. The attention mechanism computes the context vector as a weighted sum of the input vectors:

$$c = \sum_i a_i x_i, \tag{16.10}$$

where a_i is the attention weight assigned to the ith input vector. The attention weight a_i is computed as a function of the target vector y and the ith input vector x_i:

$$a_i = \text{softmax}(f(y, x_i)), \tag{16.11}$$

where softmax is the softmax function that ensures that the attention weights sum to one, and f is a function that maps the target vector and the input vector to a scalar value. The basic architecture of attention based models is shown in Figure 16.12.

One common type of attention-based model is the self-attention mechanism used in Transformer models. The self-attention mechanism allows the model to compute the attention weights for all input vectors simultaneously, based on their pairwise similarities. This is achieved by computing a score for each pair of input vectors using a learned matrix of parameters, and then normalizing the scores using the softmax function. The normalized scores serve as the attention weights for each input vector. The self-attention mechanism can be represented mathematically as follows:

Given a sequence of input vectors $X = (x_1, x_2, ..., x_n)$, the self-attention mechanism computes a new sequence of output vectors $Y = (y_1, y_2, ..., y_n)$, where each output vector y_i is a weighted sum of the input vectors:

$$y_i = \sum_j a_{ij} x_j, \tag{16.12}$$

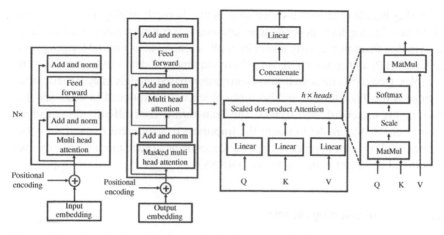

Figure 16.12 The basic architecture of attention based models.

where a_{ij} is the attention weight assigned to the jth input vector for computing the ith output vector. The attention weight a_{ij} is computed as follows:

$$a_{\{i,j\}} = \text{softmax}\left(\frac{e_{ij}}{\sqrt{d_k}}\right),$$
(16.13)

where e_{ij} is the score assigned to the jth input vector for computing the ith output vector, and d_k is the dimensionality of the query and key vectors used to compute the score. The score e_{ij} is computed as the dot product of the query vector q_i and the key vector k_j

$$e_{ij} = q_i\, k_j,$$
(16.14)

where q_i and k_j are learned linear transformations of the input vectors x_i and x_j, respectively.

Overall, attention-based models provide a powerful and flexible mechanism for handling sequential processing tasks by selectively focusing on the most relevant input features. The self-attention mechanism used in Transformer models has been particularly effective in a wide range of natural language processing tasks, and has become a widely adopted technique in the field.

Attention-based models are a type of neural network used in cybernetic intelligence that allow the model to selectively focus on specific parts of the input data when making predictions. This is achieved through the use of an attention mechanism, which assigns weights to different parts of the input data based on their relevance to the task at hand.

The key benefit of attention-based models in cybernetic intelligence is their ability to handle long-term dependencies and capture complex patterns in the data. This makes them particularly useful in applications such as natural language processing (NLP) and computer vision, where sequences of data can be very long and complex. One of the most well-known attention-based models in cybernetic intelligence is the Transformer architecture, which was introduced in 2017 and has been highly successful in NLP tasks. The Transformer uses self-attention mechanisms to enable the model to weigh the importance of different parts of the input sequence, allowing it to process long sequences of data much more efficiently than traditional recurrent neural networks (RNNs).

16.2.8 Meta-Learning Models

Meta-learning models, also known as learning-to-learn models, aim to learn a learning algorithm that can generalize well to new tasks with minimal training. These models leverage prior knowledge gained from previous related tasks to quickly adapt and learn new tasks with limited training data. Meta-learning models can be divided into two main categories: model-based and optimization-based meta-learning.

Model-based meta-learning models learn a model of the learning process, such as a recurrent neural network (RNN), that can effectively capture and generalize patterns in the data across different tasks. The model is trained on a meta-training dataset that consists of multiple related tasks, and its weights are optimized to minimize the loss across all tasks. During meta-testing, the learned model is used to adapt to a new task with limited training data.

Optimization-based meta-learning models learn an optimization algorithm that can quickly adapt to a new task. These models aim to find a set of initialization parameters that can be fine-tuned quickly to achieve good performance on a new task. The model is trained on a meta-training dataset by optimizing the initialization parameters to minimize the loss on a small subset of the training data. During meta-testing, the learned optimization algorithm is used to fine-tune the initialization parameters for the new task.

One popular type of meta-learning model is the Model-Agnostic Meta-Learning (MAML) algorithm, which is an optimization-based approach. MAML learns a good initialization point that can be fine-tuned to a new task quickly. The goal is to optimize the initialization point such that it performs well on a small subset of the training data from each task. The optimization is done by minimizing the average loss across all tasks. Consider D be the set of tasks, with each task d consisting of a training set Sd and a test set Td. Let $f\theta$ be a neural network with parameters θ, and L be a loss function. MAML aims to learn an initialization point θ

such that, after one or a few gradient updates on the training set of a new task d, the model can achieve good performance on the test set of that task.

The MAML algorithm consists of two loops: an outer loop and an inner loop. In the outer loop, the initialization point θ is optimized to minimize the loss on the test sets of all tasks in D. In the inner loop, the model is fine-tuned to a new task by taking one or a few gradient steps on the training set of that task. The MAML update rule for the outer loop can be formalized as:

$$\theta' = \theta - \alpha \nabla_\theta \frac{1}{N} \sum_{i=1}^{N} L(T_i, f_{\theta_i}), \qquad (16.15)$$

where θ is the initial parameter vector of the model, θ' is the updated parameter vector of the model, α is the meta-learning rate, which determines the step size of the update in the outer loop N is the number of tasks in the meta-training set, T_i is the training set of task I, f_{θ_i} is the fine-tuned model on task I, and L is the loss function used to evaluate the model's performance on the task-specific validation set. In the inner loop, the model is fine-tuned to a new task by taking one or a few gradient steps on the training set of that task, which can be formalized as:

$$\theta'' = \theta' - \beta \nabla_{\theta'} L(f_{\theta'}(S_d), T_d), \qquad (16.16)$$

where β is the fine-tuning learning rate, and θ'' is the updated parameters after fine-tuning. The updated initialization point θ'' is used for the next task, and the process repeats. Another common approach to meta-learning is the use of gradient-based optimization methods such as MAML, which learns a good initialization point for the model's parameters that can be quickly adapted to new tasks with few gradient updates. MAML involves first training a model on a distribution of tasks, then fine-tuning the model on a specific task by taking a small number of gradient steps with respect to the task-specific loss.

Meta-learning models can be used for a wide variety of applications, including few-shot learning, reinforcement learning, and natural language processing. They have shown promising results in situations where data is scarce or expensive to collect, and they hold great potential for enabling more efficient and adaptive learning in complex real-world settings. The math equations used in meta learning models can vary depending on the specific approach being used. For example, in the case of MAML, the meta-learning process can be formulated as follows:

- Initialize model parameters theta with some initial values
- Sample a batch of tasks T from some distribution $p(T)$
- For each task i in T: a. Compute a few gradient steps to obtain a new set of parameters $\theta a_i' b$. Evaluate the performance of the new parameters on a validation set

- Compute the meta-objective as the average loss across all tasks on the validation set
- Compute the meta-gradient of the meta-objective with respect to θ
- Update the parameters theta using the meta-gradient
- In this formulation, the meta-objective is the average loss across all tasks on the validation set, which measures how well the model is able to generalize to new tasks. The meta-gradient is computed using the chain rule of differentiation, and it provides information about how to update the model parameters to improve performance on future tasks.

Overall, meta-learning models offer a promising approach to improve the generalization and adaptation of machine learning algorithms, especially in scenarios with limited training data.

In cybernetic intelligence, meta-learning is a technique that allows models to learn how to quickly adapt to new tasks with minimal training data. This approach is particularly useful in scenarios where there is limited labeled data available or when the model needs to adapt quickly to changes in the data distribution. Meta-learning can be applied in several ways in cybernetic intelligence. For example:

- Few-shot learning: In few-shot learning, the goal is to classify objects or perform other tasks with very few labeled examples. Meta-learning can be used to train a model to quickly adapt to new tasks with only a small amount of labeled data.
- Reinforcement learning: In reinforcement learning, the agent learns from interacting with the environment and receiving rewards for certain actions. Meta-learning can be used to help the agent learn more quickly and efficiently by adapting to new environments and tasks.
- Transfer learning: In transfer learning, knowledge learned from one task is transferred to another related task. Meta-learning can be used to optimize the transferability of the learned knowledge between tasks, allowing the model to adapt more quickly to new tasks.
- Hyper parameter tuning: Meta-learning can be used to optimize hyper parameters across different tasks, resulting in better performance overall.

The key advantage of meta-learning in cybernetic intelligence is its ability to accelerate the learning process and reduce the need for large amounts of labeled data. This makes it a powerful technique in domains where data is scarce, expensive to obtain, or rapidly changing. As research in meta-learning continues, one are likely to see further innovations and applications in cybernetic intelligence, including the development of more sophisticated meta-learning algorithms and the integration of meta-learning with other AI techniques like deep learning and reinforcement learning.

16.2.9 Capsule Networks

Capsule Networks, also known as CapsNets, are a type of neural network architecture that aim to overcome the limitations of traditional convolutional neural networks (CNNs) in handling hierarchical relationships between features. The concept of CapsNets was introduced in a 2017 (). Capsule Networks represent objects in the form of "capsules," which are groups of neurons that encode different properties of an object, such as its pose, deformation, and texture as shown in Figure 16.13. These capsules are arranged in a hierarchical structure, where lower-level capsules represent features that are more primitive and higher-level capsules represent objects that are more complex.

The output of a capsule is a vector that represents the probability that the object represented by that capsule is present in the input. The length of this vector encodes the probability of the presence of the object, while the orientation of the vector encodes the pose or transformation of the object. The main equations used in Capsule Networks are:

- Prediction: The prediction of a capsule j for the presence of an object is calculated as the weighted sum of the predictions of all the capsules i in the lower layer, where the weight is given by the coupling coefficient c_{ij}.

$$s_j = \sum_i c_{ij}\, a_i, \tag{16.17}$$

where s_j is the output of capsule j, a_i is the output of capsule i in the lower layer, and c_{ij} is the coupling coefficient between capsules i and j.

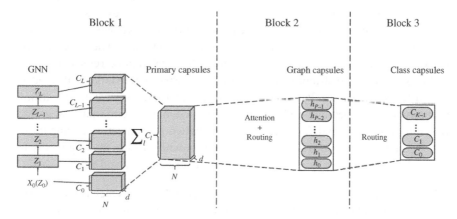

Figure 16.13 Generic architecture of capsule network.

- Routing: The coupling coefficients are calculated based on the agreement between the prediction of capsule i and the output of capsule j. The coupling coefficients are updated through a dynamic routing algorithm that iteratively adjusts the weights to ensure that capsules with similar predictions are coupled together.

$$c_{ij} = \text{softmax}(b_{ij}), \tag{16.18}$$

where b_{ij} is the log prior probability that capsule i should be coupled with capsule j.

Capsule Networks have shown promising results in several tasks, including image classification, object detection, and natural language processing. They offer a novel approach to modeling hierarchical relationships between features and have the potential to improve the interpretability and robustness of deep learning models.

16.3 Deep Learning Frameworks

Deep learning frameworks are software libraries that allow developers to build and train deep neural networks. They provide a set of high-level APIs for defining the network architecture, configuring the training process, and deploying the model to production. Deep learning frameworks are designed to be highly scalable and efficient, making it possible to train and deploy large-scale models on clusters of GPUs or CPUs.

Some of the most popular deep learning frameworks include TensorFlow, PyTorch, Keras, Caffe, and Theano. Each of these frameworks has its unique features and strengths, and developers can choose the one that best fits their needs. TensorFlow is an open-source deep learning framework developed by Google. It provides a wide range of tools and APIs for building and training deep neural networks, including support for both CPU and GPU acceleration. TensorFlow also includes support for distributed training, making it easy to train large-scale models on clusters of machines. PyTorch is another popular open-source deep learning framework, developed by Facebook. It provides a dynamic computational graph, which makes it easy to define and modify the network architecture during training. PyTorch also provides a seamless integration with Python, making it easy to use with other scientific computing libraries such as NumPy and SciPy.

- Keras is a high-level neural network API written in Python, which runs on top of TensorFlow, Theano, or CNTK. It provides a simple and easy-to-use interface for building and training deep neural networks, making it a popular choice for beginners.

- Caffe is a deep learning framework developed by Berkeley Vision and Learning Center. It is optimized for image classification tasks and provides a C++ API, making it a popular choice for real-time image processing applications.
- Theano is a deep learning framework developed by the Montreal Institute for Learning Algorithms (MILA). It provides a low-level Python API for building and training deep neural networks, making it a popular choice for researchers who want fine-grained control over the network architecture and training process.

Overall, deep learning frameworks are essential tools for developing and deploying deep neural networks in various applications, including cybernetical intelligent control systems. Deep learning frameworks are increasingly used in cybernetical intelligent control applications to design and implement complex neural network models. These frameworks provide a high-level programming interface that enables the user to define and train complex neural network architectures easily.

For example, TensorFlow is a widely used deep learning framework that provides an open-source library for numerical computation and data flow graphs. Tensor-Flow allows the user to define a computational graph, which represents a series of operations that need to be executed on the data. The framework automatically performs backpropagation to compute the gradients of the operations in the graph, allowing for efficient optimization of the neural network model. Another popular deep learning framework is PyTorch, which provides a dynamic computation graph that allows for easier debugging and faster prototyping of neural network models. PyTorch is particularly well-suited for applications that require dynamic control flow, such as recurrent neural networks and generative models.

Keras is another widely used deep learning framework that provides a high-level interface for building and training neural network models. Keras is built on top of TensorFlow and allows for rapid prototyping of neural network models with minimal coding. Keras provides a wide range of pre-built layers and loss functions, making it easier for the user to define complex neural network architectures. In cybernetical intelligent control applications, deep learning frameworks are used to design and train complex neural network models for tasks such as control, prediction, and classification. These models can then be integrated into a cybernetical control system to provide intelligent and adaptive control of the system.

16.4 Applications of Deep Learning

Deep learning has been widely applied in cybernetical intelligent control systems to improve the accuracy, efficiency, and adaptability of various control tasks. Deep learning is a powerful technique in the field of cybernetic intelligence that has numerous applications across various domains. One of the most significant application areas of deep learning is computer vision. Deep learning is widely used in computer vision applications, such as object detection, image recognition, and video analysis. For example, convolutional neural networks (CNNs) can be trained to detect objects in images or videos, while generative adversarial networks (GANs) can be used for tasks like image synthesis. Another important area where deep learning is applied in cybernetic intelligence is natural language processing (NLP). Deep learning is used in NLP applications, such as sentiment analysis, text classification, and machine translation. Recurrent neural networks (RNNs), long short-term memory (LSTM) networks, and transformers are commonly used architectures for these tasks. Deep learning is used in cybersecurity applications to detect threats and anomalies in network traffic and user behavior. This includes tasks such as intrusion detection, malware detection, and fraud detection. Finally, deep learning is used in autonomous vehicle applications to enable vehicles to perceive their surroundings and make decisions. Deep neural networks can be used to detect objects on the road and predict their trajectories. Overall, deep learning is a versatile technique in cybernetic intelligence with a wide range of applications. As research continues in this field, one are likely to see further advances and innovations that will enable even more applications of deep learning in cybernetic intelligence.

Some of the applications of deep learning in cybernetical intelligent control include:

16.4.1 Object Detection

Object detection and recognition is a fundamental task in computer vision and has numerous applications in cybernetical intelligent control. Deep learning approaches have shown significant improvement in this task over traditional computer vision techniques.

Convolutional Neural Networks (CNNs) are widely used for object detection and recognition tasks in deep learning. These models can learn to identify different objects in images by analyzing their visual features. The model takes an image as input and produces an output that includes the object class and the location of the object in the image.

The most commonly used approach for object detection is the region-based CNN (R-CNN) family of algorithms. R-CNN performs object detection by first generating region proposals using an algorithm such as selective search. These regions are then passed through a CNN to extract features, and a classifier is trained to identify the object within the region.

Faster R-CNN is an extension of R-CNN that uses a single deep network for generating region proposals and identifying objects. This approach combines the region proposal network (RPN) and the Fast R-CNN network to achieve real-time object detection.

Another popular approach for object detection and recognition is You Only Look Once (YOLO). YOLO divides an image into a grid of cells and predicts bounding boxes and class probabilities for each cell. The network is trained end-to-end to optimize detection performance.

Object detection and recognition have numerous applications in cybernetical intelligent control, including autonomous vehicles, robotics, and security systems. For example, in autonomous vehicles, object detection is used to identify other vehicles, pedestrians, and obstacles on the road to ensure safe driving. In robotics, object detection is used for object manipulation, object recognition, and scene understanding. In security systems, object detection is used for surveillance and threat detection.

16.4.2 Intelligent Power Systems

Intelligent control using deep learning has been applied in various domains, including power systems. Power systems are complex networks that require efficient control to ensure safe and reliable operation. Deep learning techniques can help to improve the performance of power systems by providing more accurate and efficient control.

One of the significant applications of deep learning in power systems is in the area of fault detection and diagnosis. Faults can occur in power systems due to various reasons, including equipment failure, weather conditions, or human error. Early detection and diagnosis of faults are critical to prevent system failures and ensure safe and reliable operation.

Deep learning algorithms such as Convolutional Neural Networks (CNNs) and Recurrent Neural Networks (RNNs) can be used to analyze the data collected from power systems and detect faults accurately. CNNs can be used to analyze the data from sensors such as current and voltage sensors to detect abnormal patterns, while RNNs can be used to detect temporal patterns in the data.

Another application of deep learning in power systems is in the area of load forecasting. Load forecasting involves predicting the future demand for electricity, which is essential for power system planning and operation. Deep learning algorithms such as Long Short-Term Memory (LSTM) networks can be used to forecast the load accurately based on historical data and external factors such as weather conditions and time of day.

Overall, deep learning techniques have shown promising results in improving the performance and efficiency of power systems. By providing accurate and efficient control, deep learning can help to ensure safe and reliable operation of power systems.

16.4.3 Intelligent Control

Deep learning has various applications in intelligent control, and it can be used to improve efficiency, productivity, and safety in industrial processes. Here are some of the examples of how deep learning can be used in industrial intelligent control:

- Predictive maintenance: Deep learning models can analyze sensor data from machines and predict when they are likely to fail, allowing for proactive maintenance and reducing downtime.
- Quality control: Deep learning models can be trained on images of defective products to recognize patterns and identify defects quickly, reducing the time and cost of manual inspection.
- Process optimization: Deep learning models can analyze large amounts of data from industrial processes to identify patterns and optimize production parameters, improving efficiency and reducing waste.
- Supply chain management: Deep learning models can analyze supply chain data to identify bottlenecks and inefficiencies, allowing for more efficient and cost-effective supply chain management.
- Robotics and automation: Deep learning models can be used to train robots to perform complex tasks, such as picking and placing objects, improving the efficiency and safety of industrial processes.

Deep learning is closely linked to cybernetics, the study of control and communication in living organisms and machines. Both fields aim to understand and model complex systems, and use feedback loops to improve their performance over time. In the context of deep learning, intelligent control involves using algorithms to learn from data and improve the accuracy and efficiency of decision-making processes. This can be applied to a wide range of applications, including image and speech recognition, natural language processing, and robotics. By integrating deep learning with cybernetics principles, researchers are able to develop intelligent systems that can adapt and evolve in response to changing environments and input. Ultimately, this can lead to more efficient and effective solutions in areas such as autonomous vehicles, medical diagnosis, and predictive maintenance. Overall, the use of deep learning in industrial intelligent control can lead to significant improvements in efficiency, safety, and cost-effectiveness in various industrial applications.

Summary

This chapter covered the concept of deep learning and its applications in the field of intelligent control. It started with an overview of deep learning and its various methods, including Convolutional Neural Networks, Recurrent Neural Networks,

Generative Adversarial Networks, and Deep Belief Networks. It also discussed the various deep learning frameworks and their applications in cybernetical intelligent control. Furthermore, the chapter explored the different applications of deep learning in intelligent control, including object detection and recognition, power systems control, and industrial control. The use of deep learning in these areas can help to enhance automation, improve efficiency, and optimize the control of complex systems. Overall, deep learning has become an essential tool in the field of intelligent control, and its continued development and integration with control systems will lead to more advanced and effective control solutions in various applications.

As deep learning continues to evolve and mature, it is likely to become an even more integral part of cybernetical intelligent control systems. Advancements in deep learning frameworks, such as the development of more efficient algorithms and hardware, will further improve the performance and capabilities of deep learning-based systems. Additionally, as more data becomes available and the amount of computational power continues to increase, the potential applications of deep learning in intelligent control will expand. However, challenges such as ethical considerations, data privacy concerns, and the need for explainable AI will need to be addressed in order to ensure that deep learning-based systems are developed and deployed responsibly. Overall, the future of deep learning in cybernetical intelligent control looks promising, and it is expected to play a critical role in advancing automation, robotics, and other fields.

Exercise Questions

Q.16.1   What are some of the potential ethical concerns around the use of deep learning in intelligent control systems?

Q.16.2   How does the transformer architecture use attention to improve natural language processing tasks?

Q.16.3   How can deep learning be applied to improve the efficiency and safety of industrial processes?

Q.16.4   What are some of the challenges involved in integrating deep learning into cybernetical intelligent control systems?

Q.16.5   How can deep learning be used to improve the reliability and security of power systems?

Q.16.6   Explain the role of transfer learning in deep learning for intelligent control systems?

Q.16.7   What is the role of regularization in encoder training, and how can one choose an appropriate regularization method?

Q.16.8   Based on the following Equation,

$$\Delta w_{ij} = -\eta \cdot \frac{\partial E}{\partial w_{ij}}.$$

How does the learning rate (η) affect the weight update in the back-propagation algorithm?

Q.16.9   In what ways can deep learning be used to improve cybersecurity?

Q.16.10   How can one mitigate the problem of catastrophic forgetting during transfer learning?

Q.16.11   Explain how transfer learning can be applied to unsupervised learning tasks?

Q.16.12   Below is the equation of softmax is given, how does it convert the output logits into probabilities for multi-class classification?

$$\text{softmax}(z_i) = \frac{e_i^z}{\sum_{J=1}^{K} e_J^z}.$$

References

1 Vaswani A, Shazeer N, Parmar N, Uszkoreit J, Jones L, Gomez AN, Kaiser Ł, Polosukhin I. Attention is all you need. *Advances in Neural Information Processing Systems*. 2017;30:6000–10.

2 Jordan MI, Kearns MJ, Solla SA, editors. *Advances in neural information processing systems 10: proceedings of the 1997 conference*. Mit Press; 1998.

Further Reading

Arora A, Corchado JM. Face detection and recognition, face emotion recognition through NVIDIA jetson nano. In Ambient Intelligence–Software and Applications: 11th International Symposium on Ambient Intelligence 2020 Sep 9 (Vol. 1239, p. 177). Springer Nature.

Bryson AE. *Applied optimal control: optimization, estimation and control.* CRC Press; 1975.

Chorowski JK, Bahdanau D, Serdyuk D, Cho K, Bengio Y. Attention-based models for speech recognition. *Advances in Neural Information Processing Systems.* 2015;28:577–585.

Stanko I. The architectures of Geoffrey Hinton. In *Guide to deep learning basics: logical, historical and philosophical perspectives*; 2020 Jan 24; pp. 79–92. Cham: Springer International Publishing.

17

Neural Architecture Search

Neural Architecture Search (NAS) is an automated approach for finding the best neural network architecture for a given task. The idea is to use machine learning algorithms to automatically search through a large space of possible architectures and identify the one that performs the best on a given dataset. The general approach to NAS involves the following steps:

- Define the search space: The first step is to define the space of possible neural network architectures. This can include the types of layers, the number of layers, the number of nodes in each layer, and any other architectural parameters that may be relevant.
- Generate candidate architectures: Next, the algorithm generates a set of candidate architectures to evaluate. This can be done randomly or using a more sophisticated approach, such as Bayesian optimization or evolutionary algorithms.
- Train and evaluate the candidate architectures: Each candidate architecture is trained on the training dataset and evaluated on the validation dataset. The performance metrics, such as accuracy or loss, are recorded for each architecture.
- Update the search space: Based on the performance of the candidate architectures, the search space is updated to include the architectures that performed well.
- Repeat the process: The above steps are repeated until a stopping criterion is met, such as a specified number of iterations or a convergence of the performance metric.

There are several variations of the NAS approach, including:

- Reinforcement learning-based NAS: This approach treats the search for the optimal architecture as a Markov decision process and uses reinforcement learning to guide the search process.

Cybernetical Intelligence: Engineering Cybernetics with Machine Intelligence, First Edition.
Kelvin K. L. Wong.
© 2024 The Institute of Electrical and Electronics Engineers, Inc.
Published 2024 by John Wiley & Sons, Inc.
Companion website: www.wiley.com/go/cyberintel

- Evolutionary algorithms-based NAS: This approach uses evolutionary algorithms, such as genetic algorithms or differential evolution, to search for the best architecture.
- Gradient-based NAS: This approach uses gradient descent to optimize the architecture directly.

NAS has become an active area of research, with many variations and extensions being proposed. It has the potential to automate the tedious and time-consuming process of manual neural network architecture design, allowing researchers to focus on higher-level tasks such as model interpretation and analysis. Neural Architecture Search (NAS) can be applied in the context of cybernetical control intelligent systems to optimize the architecture of the neural network used for control. In a cybernetical control system, a neural network is used to control a process based on input data and output feedback. The performance of the system depends heavily on the architecture of the neural network. However, designing an optimal architecture manually can be a challenging and time-consuming task. NAS can automate the process of designing the optimal neural network architecture for a cybernetical control system. The general approach to NAS is to define a search space of possible architectures, generate candidate architectures, train and evaluate them, update the search space based on performance, and repeat the process until a satisfactory architecture is found. The generic working of NAS is shown in Figure 17.1.

For instance X be the input data, and Y be the output data. Let W be a matrix of weights that govern the connections between the nodes in the network, and let b be a vector of biases that are added to the outputs of each node. For a single layer of the network, the output can be calculated as shown in Equation (17.1).

$$Y = f(WX + b), \tag{17.1}$$

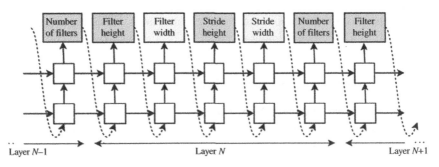

Figure 17.1 The generic working of NAS.

where f is an activation function that introduces nonlinearity into the output of the layer. Common activation functions include the sigmoid function, the rectified linear unit (ReLU) function, and the hyperbolic tangent function. The equation for a sigmoid function is shown in Equation (17.2):

$$f(x) = \frac{1}{1 + e^{-x}}.$$ (17.2)

To build a deep neural network with multiple layers, this equation can be recursively applied to each layer, with the output of one layer becoming the input to the next layer:

$$Y = f(W_2(f(W_1X + b_1) + b_2) + b_3),$$ (17.3)

where W_1 and W_2 are weight matrices for the first and second layers, b_1, b_2, and b_3 are bias vectors, and f is the activation function. In the context of cybernetical control, the search space may include architectural parameters such as the number of layers, the types of layers, the number of neurons in each layer, and the activation functions. The evaluation of the candidate architectures may be based on performance metrics such as the speed of convergence, stability of the control, or accuracy of the predictions. One potential challenge in applying NAS to cybernetical control is the need for real-time control. The search and evaluation process can be time-consuming, and a delay in control can result in unstable or ineffective control. To address this challenge, specialized hardware such as Field Programmable Gate Arrays (FPGAs) can be used to accelerate the search and evaluation process.

Overall, NAS can be a powerful tool for optimizing the neural network architecture used in cybernetical control systems. By automating the architecture design process, it can improve the performance and efficiency of the system and allow researchers to focus on higher-level tasks such as model interpretation and analysis.

17.1 Neural Architecture Search and Neural Network

Neural network and Neural Architecture Search (NAS) are closely related as NAS is used to automatically search for and optimize neural network architectures for a given task. Neural networks are a type of machine learning model that is inspired by the structure and function of the human brain. They are composed of multiple layers of interconnected nodes or neurons, which can learn and generalize patterns from the data. Traditionally, the architecture of neural networks has been manually designed and optimized by human experts. However, this process is time-consuming, expensive, and often limited in its ability to explore the vast space of possible architectures. This is where NAS comes in—it uses machine learning algorithms to automate the process of designing neural network architectures, making it faster, more efficient, and more effective.

NAS algorithms search for optimal neural network architectures by exploring the space of possible architectures using search algorithms such as evolutionary algorithms, reinforcement learning, Bayesian optimization, gradient-based optimization, or meta-learning. These algorithms evaluate the performance of each architecture by training and testing the network on a given task, and then selecting the best-performing architectures based on some optimization criteria. Once the optimal architecture is found, the network is trained using standard backpropagation algorithms to learn the weights and biases of the neural network. The trained neural network can then be used to perform the task it was designed for, such as image classification, speech recognition, or control tasks in cybernetical intelligent systems.

Traditionally, the design of control systems has relied on expert knowledge and trial-and-error methods to determine the optimal architecture for a given task or environment. However, this approach can be time-consuming and costly, and may not always result in the most effective system. NAS, on the other hand, uses machine learning techniques to automatically design neural network architectures that are optimized for a specific task or environment. By using algorithms such as reinforcement learning, evolutionary algorithms, or Bayesian optimization, NAS can search through a space of possible architectures and find the best one for a given task. This can greatly reduce the need for expert knowledge in network design, as well as improving the efficiency and effectiveness of the resulting control system. Furthermore, NAS can also facilitate the development of adaptive cybernetical intelligent systems, which are able to learn and adapt to new tasks or environments over time. This is particularly important in applications such as robotics, autonomous vehicles, and industrial control systems, where the ability to adapt to changing conditions is crucial for success.

In summary, neural networks and NAS are closely related and work together to create more efficient and effective machine learning models. Neural networks provide a flexible and powerful framework for modeling complex patterns in data, while NAS algorithms help to optimize the architecture of the neural network to achieve better performance on a given task. Together, these tools enable us to build more accurate, reliable, and scalable machine learning models that can help to solve a wide range of real-world problems. Table 17.1 presents the comparison of the Neural Architecture Search and Neural Networks

Table 17.1 Comparing neural architecture search and neural networks.

Feature	Neural Architecture Search	Neural Networks
Design process	Automated	Manual
Architecture complexity	Large, often with many layers and complex connections	Small, often with few layers and simple connections
Model performance	Generally better than manually designed networks	Generally worse than NAS-designed networks
Time required	High, due to extensive search through complex design space	Low, due to simpler design process
Human intervention	Limited	High
Exploration space	Large, with extensive search through potential architectures	Small, with limited exploration of design space
Scalability	Good, as NAS can be applied to a wide range of neural network tasks	Limited, as manual design may be required for specific tasks
Explainability	Limited, due to the complexity of NAS-generated architectures	Good, as human-designed networks are often easier to understand
Adaptability	Good, as NAS can be used to generate specialized architectures for specific tasks	Limited, as manual redesign may be required for new tasks

17.2 Reinforcement Learning-Based Neural Architecture Search

Reinforcement learning-based Neural Architecture Search (NAS) is an approach to automatically search for an optimal neural network architecture by formulating the search process as a reinforcement learning problem. In this approach, a reinforcement learning agent learns to generate neural network architectures by maximizing the expected reward signal. The reward signal is typically a function of the performance of the network architecture on a given task.

Let's break down the reinforcement learning-based NAS approach into its core components:

- State: The state in reinforcement learning-based NAS is typically represented as a vector of features that describes the current state of the search process. For example, the state vector might include the current architecture being evaluated, the performance of the architecture on the current task, and other relevant features. The state at time t is represented as a vector s_t, which contains relevant information about the current architecture and the performance of the network on the task at hand. The state vector can be defined as:

$$s_t = f(a_{t-1}, p_{t-1}, r_{t-1}), \tag{17.4}$$

where a_{t-1} is the previous action taken, p_{t-1} is the previous architecture evaluated, and r_{t-1} is the reward received for the previous architecture.

- Action: The action in reinforcement learning-based NAS is the generation of a new neural network architecture. The action space typically includes a set of architectural operations that can be applied to the current architecture, such as adding or removing a layer, changing the activation function, or adjusting the number of neurons in a layer. The action at time t is represented as a vector a_t, which specifies the architectural operations to be applied to the previous architecture p_{t-1}. The action vector can be defined as:

$$a_t = [o_1, o_2, ..., o_k], \tag{17.5}$$

where o_i is the ith architectural operation in the action space, and k is the number of operations in the action space.

- Reward: The reward in reinforcement learning-based NAS is a function of the performance of the neural network architecture on the given task. The reward function can be defined in many ways, depending on the task at hand. For example, the reward might be the accuracy of the network on a classification task, or the negative mean squared error on a regression task. The reward function is a function $R(p_t)$, which maps the performance of the network on the task to a scalar reward value. The reward function can be defined in many ways depending on the task at hand. For example, in a classification task, the reward might be the accuracy of the network on the training set, while in a regression task, the reward might be the negative mean squared error on the training set.
- Expected Reward: The expected reward of the policy π can be computed as:

$$J(\theta) = E_\pi [R(p_t)|\theta], \tag{17.6}$$

where E_π denotes the expectation over the distribution of architectures generated by the policy π. The objective of reinforcement learning-based NAS is to maximize the expected reward over a set of training tasks.

- The policy parameters θ can be learned using gradient-based optimization techniques such as policy gradient methods or actor-critic methods. The gradient of the expected reward with respect to the policy parameters can be computed using the policy gradient theorem as:

$$\nabla_\theta J(\theta) = E_\pi \left[\nabla_\theta \log \pi(a_t \,|s_t, \theta) Q(s_t, a_t) \right], \tag{17.7}$$

where $Q(s_t, a_t)$ is the state-action value function, which estimates the expected reward of taking action a_t in state s_t and following the policy π. The state-action value function can be estimated using a critic network, which is trained to minimize the mean squared error between the estimated and actual rewards. The actor-critic method combines the policy gradient method with the critic network to improve the stability of the optimization process.

- Policy: The policy in reinforcement learning-based NAS is a function that maps the current state to a probability distribution over the actions. The policy can be represented as a neural network, where the input is the state vector and the output is a probability distribution over the architectural operations.

The objective of the reinforcement learning-based NAS approach is to find the optimal policy that maximizes the expected reward over a set of training tasks. The NAS implementation using reinforcement learning is shown in Figure 17.2.

The optimization problem can be solved using gradient-based optimization techniques, such as policy gradient methods or actor-critic methods. The policy gradient method updates the policy parameters using the gradient of the expected reward with respect to the policy parameters, while the actor-critic method combines the policy gradient method with a critic network that estimates the value function of the policy. In summary, reinforcement learning-based NAS is an approach to automatically search for an optimal neural network architecture by formulating the search process as a reinforcement learning problem. The approach involves defining the state, action, reward, and policy components of the problem, and optimizing the policy using gradient-based optimization techniques.

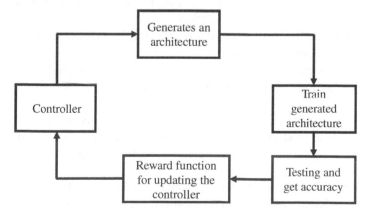

Figure 17.2 NAS implementation using reinforcement learning.

17.3 Evolutionary Algorithms-Based Neural Architecture Search

Evolutionary algorithms-based Neural Architecture Search (NAS) is a class of optimization algorithms that use principles of natural selection to search for optimal neural architectures. In evolutionary algorithms-based NAS, a population of neural architectures is iteratively evolved through a process of selection, mutation, and crossover, with the goal of finding architectures that maximize the performance on a given task. Here are some key equations and concepts related to Evolutionary algorithms-based NAS:

- Encoding: The first step in Evolutionary algorithms-based NAS is to encode the neural architectures in a format that can be used by the optimization algorithm. A common encoding scheme is to represent the architecture as a vector of binary or real-valued numbers, where each number corresponds to a specific architectural decision (e.g. the number of filters in a convolutional layer).
- Fitness Function: The fitness function is a function that evaluates the performance of a neural architecture on a given task. The fitness function can be defined in many ways depending on the task at hand. For example, in a classification task, the fitness function might be the accuracy of the network on the training set, while in a regression task, the fitness function might be the negative mean squared error on the training set. $F(I_i) =$ The fitness function that evaluates individual I_i based on some predefined criteria.
- Selection: The selection step involves choosing the fittest architectures from the current population to produce the next generation. The selection process can be implemented using various selection strategies, such as tournament selection or roulette wheel selection. The fitness function is used to assign a probability of selection to each architecture in the population.
- Mutation: The mutation step involves randomly changing the architecture of the selected individuals to produce new architectures. The mutation process can be implemented using various mutation operators, such as random addition or deletion of architectural components, or random modification of existing components.
- Crossover: The crossover step involves combining the architecture of two selected individuals to produce new architectures. The crossover process can be implemented using various crossover operators, such as one-point or two-point crossover.
- Elitism: The elitism step involves preserving a small fraction of the fittest individuals from the previous generation in the next generation to ensure that the best individuals are not lost during the evolutionary process.

- Fitness-based Probability: The probability of an architecture being selected for reproduction is proportional to its fitness value. This is known as fitness-based probability and can be expressed as:

$$P_i = \frac{f_i}{\sum_j f_j},\tag{17.8}$$

where P_i is the probability of selecting architecture i, f_i is the fitness value of architecture i, and $\sum_j f_j$ is the sum of fitness values over all architectures in the population.

Fitness Function Optimization: The goal of Evolutionary algorithms-based NAS is to optimize the fitness function over a set of training tasks. This can be achieved by iteratively evolving the population of architectures until the fitness function converges to an optimal solution. An example of the two types of mutations in evolutionary NAS is shown in Figure 17.3.

Convergence Criteria: The convergence criteria determine when to stop the evolutionary process. The convergence criteria can be based on various factors, such as the number of generations, the fitness values of the best architectures, or the similarity of the architectures in the population.

These equations and concepts provide a more detailed mathematical formulation of Evolutionary algorithms-based NAS, which can be used to design and implement more sophisticated NAS algorithms. A candidate architecture is a potential solution in the search space that represents a neural network with a specific set of hyper parameters. It can be represented as a vector of values that

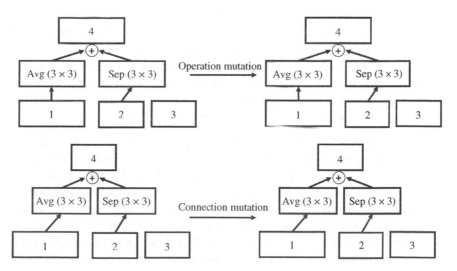

Figure 17.3 An example of the two types of mutations in evolutionary NAS.

describe the architecture, such as the number of layers, the number of neurons per layer, and the type of activation function used as shown in Equation (17.9).

$$A = [h_1, h_2, ..., h_n], \tag{17.9}$$

where h_i represents a hyper parameter for the ith layer of the network. Genetic operators, such as mutation and crossover, are used to create new candidate architectures from existing ones in the population. Mutation involves randomly changing the value of one or more hyper parameters in the architecture, while crossover involves combining two architectures to create a new one as shown in Equations (17.10) and (17.11) respectively.

$$\text{mutation} : A' = \text{mutate}(A) \tag{17.10}$$

$$\text{crossover} : A' = \text{crossover}(A1, A2). \tag{17.11}$$

The selection is the process of choosing which candidate architectures will be used to create the next generation of the population. Selection is typically based on the fitness function, with higher fitness architectures being more likely to be selected as shown in Equation (17.12).

$$A' = \text{select}(A_1, A_2, ..., A_n). \tag{17.12}$$

17.4 Bayesian Optimization-Based Neural Architecture Search

Bayesian optimization-based Neural Architecture Search (NAS) is a class of optimization algorithms that uses Bayesian optimization to search for optimal neural architectures. Bayesian optimization-based NAS is particularly useful for optimizing black-box functions, such as the validation accuracy of a neural network, where the underlying function is unknown and expensive to evaluate. Here are some key equations and concepts related to Bayesian optimization-based NAS and the complete workflow of Bayesian optimization is shown in Figure 17.4.

- Surrogate Model: The first step in Bayesian optimization-based NAS is to construct a surrogate model that approximates the unknown function. The surrogate model is typically a Gaussian Process (GP) model that models the function as a Gaussian distribution with a mean and a covariance function.
- Acquisition Function: The acquisition function is a function that quantifies the usefulness of evaluating a point in the search space. The acquisition function is typically defined in terms of the posterior distribution of the surrogate model and aims to balance the exploration of new architectures with the exploitation of promising architectures.

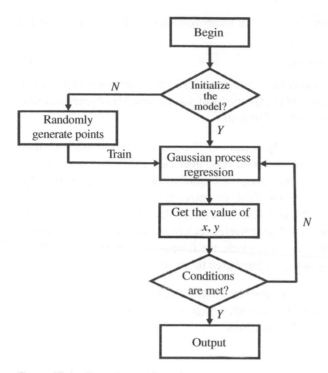

Figure 17.4 Flow chart of Bayesian optimization.

- Bayesian Optimization Loop: The Bayesian optimization loop consists of iteratively updating the surrogate model and selecting the next architecture to evaluate based on the acquisition function.
- Gaussian Process Regression: The Gaussian Process (GP) model is a non-parametric regression technique that models the function as a Gaussian distribution with a mean and a covariance function. The mean function represents the expected value of the function at a given point, while the covariance function captures the correlation between different points in the search space.

$$f(x) \sim GP(m(x), k(x, x')), \tag{17.13}$$

where $f(x)$ is the function value at point x, $m(x)$ is the mean function, $k(x, x')$ is the covariance function between points x and x', and $\sim GP$ denotes that the function is modeled as a Gaussian Process.

- Acquisition Functions: The acquisition function is a function that quantifies the usefulness of evaluating a point in the search space. There are several popular acquisition functions, such as Upper Confidence Bound (UCB), Expected

Improvement (EI), and Probability of Improvement (PI). The UCB acquisition function can be expressed as:

$$a(x) = m(x) + \beta\sigma(x), \tag{17.14}$$

where $a(x)$ is the acquisition value at point x, $m(x)$ is the mean function at point x, $\sigma(x)$ is the standard deviation of the GP model at point x, and β is a hyperparameter that balances exploration and exploitation.

- Bayesian Optimization Loop Optimization: The goal of Bayesian optimization-based NAS is to optimize the fitness function over a set of training tasks. This can be achieved by iteratively optimizing the acquisition function and updating the surrogate model until the fitness function converges to an optimal solution.
- Convergence Criteria: The convergence criteria determine when to stop the Bayesian optimization loop. The convergence criteria can be based on various factors, such as the number of iterations, the fitness values of the best architectures, or the similarity of the architectures in the search space.

These equations and concepts provide a more detailed mathematical formulation of Bayesian optimization-based NAS, which can be used to design and implement more sophisticated NAS algorithms.

17.5 Gradient-Based Neural Architecture Search

Gradient-based Neural Architecture Search (NAS) is a class of optimization algorithms that uses gradient descent to search for optimal neural architectures. Gradient-based NAS can be used for optimizing both continuous and discrete search spaces, and has been shown to achieve state-of-the-art performance on various benchmark datasets. Here are some key equations and concepts related to gradient-based NAS:

- Differentiable Architecture Search: Differentiable Architecture Search (DARTS) is a popular gradient-based NAS algorithm that uses a continuous relaxation of the discrete search space to enable gradient-based optimization. The DARTS algorithm can be summarized as follows:
  - Represent the search space as a directed acyclic graph (DAG) $G(V, E)$, where V is the set of nodes and E is the set of edges.
  - Represent the architecture as a set of continuous variables α that determine the edges and the operations between nodes.
  - Define a proxy loss function $L(w, \alpha)$ that depends on the network weights w and the architecture variables α.

– Optimize the network weights w and the architecture variables α using stochastic gradient descent (SGD) with backpropagation.

• Continuous Relaxation: The key idea behind DARTS is to use a continuous relaxation of the discrete search space to enable gradient-based optimization. The continuous relaxation is achieved by using a softmax function to convert the architecture variables α to a probability distribution over the possible edges and operations. The continuous relaxation can be expressed as:

$$p\left(e_{ij}\right) = \frac{e^{\alpha_{ij}}}{\sum_k e^{\alpha_{ik}}}, \qquad (17.15)$$

where $p(e_{ij})$ is the probability of including edge e_{ij} in the DAG, α_{ij} is the architecture variable corresponding to edge e_{ij}, and $\sum_k e^{\alpha_{ik}}$ is the sum of the exponentials of all architecture variables α_{ik} that correspond to the incoming edges to node j.

• Gradient Computation: The gradient of the proxy loss function $L(w, \alpha)$ with respect to the architecture variables α can be computed using the chain rule of calculus and the continuous relaxation. The gradient can be expressed as:

$$\frac{dL}{d\alpha_{ij}} = \sum_k \left(\frac{dL}{dw_k}\right)\left(\frac{dw_k}{d\alpha_{ij}}\right), \qquad (17.16)$$

where $\frac{dL}{dw_k}$ is the gradient of the proxy loss function with respect to the kth weight, and $\frac{dL}{d\alpha_{ij}}$ is the gradient of the kth weight with respect to the architecture variable α_{ij}.

Weight Sharing: To reduce the computation cost of gradient-based NAS, DARTS introduces weight sharing, which allows sharing the weights across different architectures during the training process. Weight sharing is achieved by computing the gradients of the weights with respect to the architecture variables using the validation set, and then using these gradients to update the architecture variables. These equations and concepts provide a more detailed mathematical formulation of gradient-based NAS, which can be used to design and implement more sophisticated NAS algorithms.

17.6 One-shot Neural Architecture Search

One-shot Neural Architecture Search (NAS) is a type of NAS algorithm that is designed to reduce the computational cost of searching for optimal neural architectures. The key idea behind One-shot NAS is to train a single "supernet" that contains all possible architectures in the search space, and then use weight sharing and architecture selection to identify the optimal architecture. Here are some key equations and concepts related to One-shot NAS:

- Supernet Training: The first step in One-shot NAS is to train a supernet that contains all possible architectures in the search space. The supernet is trained using a combination of stochastic gradient descent (SGD) and weight sharing, which allows the supernet to learn a good initialization for all possible architectures. The supernet can be represented as follows:

$$f(x, \alpha) = \sum_i w_i op_i(x), \tag{17.17}$$

where $f(x, \alpha)$ is the output of the supernet for input x and architecture variables α, w_i are the weights of the supernet, $op_i(x)$ are the operations of the supernet, and i ranges over all possible architectures.

- Architecture Selection: Once the supernet is trained, the next step is to select the optimal architecture from the search space. This is done by selecting a subgraph of the supernet that corresponds to the desired architecture, and then training the weights of that subgraph using SGD.
- Weight Sharing: To reduce the computational cost of One-shot NAS, weight sharing is used to share the weights of the supernet across different architectures. Weight sharing is achieved by using a single set of weights for all possible architectures, and then computing the gradients of the weights with respect to the architecture variables during the optimization process.
- Optimization: The optimization process in One-shot NAS consists of two stages: supernet training and architecture selection. The supernet training stage involves training the weights of the supernet using SGD and weight sharing. The architecture selection stage involves selecting the optimal architecture from the search space using architecture selection and SGD.

In the context of cybernetical intelligence, One-shot NAS can be seen as a technique for automating the design of neural networks, which can help to improve the efficiency and effectiveness of cybernetical control systems. By using One-shot NAS, cybernetical control systems can be designed to adapt to changing environments and new data, without the need for manual reconfiguration or redesign of the neural network architecture. This can help to improve the overall performance and robustness of cybernetical control systems, and enable them to operate more effectively in complex and dynamic environments. The generic architecture of one-shot neural network is shown in Figure 17.5.

In cybernetical intelligent systems, One-shot NAS can be used to automatically design neural network architectures that are optimized for specific control tasks. This can help to improve the performance of cybernetical control systems, by

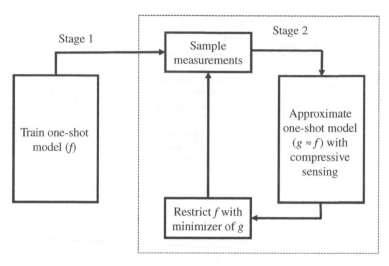

Figure 17.5 One-shot neural network model.

enabling them to learn more efficiently from data and adapt to changing environmental conditions. By using One-shot NAS, can also reduce the time and cost required for manual design and optimization of neural network architectures, while ensuring that the resulting architectures are well suited to the specific control task at hand.

17.7 Meta-Learning-Based Neural Architecture Search

Meta-learning-based Neural Architecture Search (NAS) is a type of NAS algorithm that leverages meta-learning techniques to learn a search strategy that can efficiently explore the space of neural architectures as shown in Figure 17.6. The key idea behind Meta-learning-based NAS is to use a meta-learner to learn an optimization algorithm that can quickly find the optimal architecture for a given task. Here are some key equations and concepts related to Meta-learning-based NAS:

- Meta-Learner: The first step in Meta-learning-based NAS is to train a meta-learner that can learn an optimization algorithm for finding optimal neural architectures. The meta-learner takes as input a set of tasks, each of which is associated with a training set and a validation set. The meta-learner can be represented as $\theta = \text{meta\_learn}(D)$, where θ is the set of meta-parameters learned by the meta-learner, D is the set of tasks, and meta_learn is the meta-learning algorithm used to train the meta-learner.

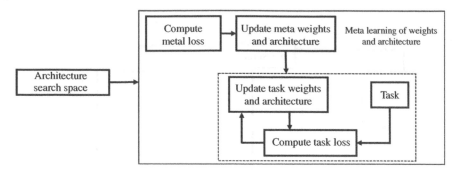

Figure 17.6 Meta learning for NAS.

- Search Strategy: Once the meta-learner is trained, the next step is to use it to learn a search strategy that can efficiently explore the space of neural architectures. The search strategy is learned by optimizing the architecture variables α using the meta-learner's optimization algorithm.
- Optimization: The optimization process in Meta-learning-based NAS involves two stages: meta-learning and search. During the meta-learning stage, the meta-learner is trained on a set of tasks using a variety of optimization algorithms. During the search stage, the search strategy learned by the meta-learner is used to find the optimal architecture for a given task.

The objective of Meta-learning-based NAS is to find a neural network architecture that performs well on a given task. To achieve this, there is need to define an objective function that takes into account the performance of the network on a validation set during the search process. The meta-learning objective function can be written as:

$$L_{meta}(\theta, \varnothing) = \sum_i L(T_i, \theta_i, \varnothing), \tag{17.18}$$

where L_{meta} is the meta-learning objective function, θ represents the model parameters that are updated during meta-training, $\varnothing$ represents the hyper parameters that are optimized during meta-training, T_i represents a task i sampled from a distribution of tasks, θ_i represents the parameters of the model trained on task $I, L(T_i, \theta_i, \varnothing)$ represents the loss on task i, which is computed using the model parameters θ_i and the hyper parameters $\varnothing$. To optimize the policy network, the meta-learning algorithm minimizes the expected loss, which can be defined as:

$$L(\theta, \omega) = -E[\log p(a | \theta, \omega) R(\theta')], \tag{17.19}$$

where $p(a|\theta, \omega)$ is the probability distribution over actions given the architecture parameterization θ and the policy network parameters ω, and θ' is the architecture parameterization obtained by taking the action a. To solve the optimization problem, the meta-learning algorithm uses a gradient-based approach, such as the Reinforce algorithm, to compute the gradient of the expected loss with respect to the policy network parameters ω. The gradient can be computed as follows:

$$\nabla \omega L(\theta, \omega) = -E[\nabla \omega \log p(a \,|\, \theta, \omega) R(\theta')]. \tag{17.20}$$

The policy network parameters ω can then be updated using the gradient descent algorithm to maximize the expected reward $R(\theta)$ by taking small steps in the direction of the gradient.

In the context of cybernetical intelligent systems, Meta-learning-based NAS can be used to improve the efficiency and effectiveness of neural network design and optimization for control tasks. By leveraging meta-learning techniques, Meta-learning-based NAS can learn a search strategy that can quickly find the optimal architecture for a given control task, without the need for manual tuning or intervention. This can help to reduce the time and cost required for designing and optimizing neural network architectures for control tasks, while also improving the overall performance and adaptability of these systems.

17.8 Neural Architecture Search for Specific Domains

Neural Architecture Search (NAS) can be used to design and optimize neural networks for specific domains, such as computer vision, natural language processing, and cybernetical control. In each of these domains, the design and optimization of neural network architectures can be challenging, requiring domain-specific knowledge and expertise. Here are some key concepts and equations related to NAS for specific domains:

- Domain-specific constraints: Each domain has its own specific constraints that must be taken into account when designing and optimizing neural network architectures. For example, in computer vision, the size of the input image and the complexity of the object recognition task may influence the optimal architecture. In cybernetical control, the dynamics of the control system and the requirements for stability and performance may influence the optimal architecture.
- Fitness function: The fitness function is used to evaluate the quality of a given neural network architecture for a specific task in a domain. In computer vision, the fitness function may measure the accuracy of object recognition on a test set. In cybernetical control, the fitness function may measure the performance and stability of the control system under different conditions. The fitness function can be represented as follows:

$$f(\alpha) = \text{fitness}(\alpha, D), \tag{17.21}$$

where α is the architecture variable, D is the task-specific data, and fitness is the function used to evaluate the quality of the architecture.

- Optimization: The optimization process in NAS for specific domains involves exploring the space of possible architectures and evaluating them using the fitness function. The optimization can be performed using a variety of algorithms, including Reinforcement Learning-based NAS, Evolutionary algorithms-based NAS, and Gradient-based NAS.

17.8.1 Cybernetical Intelligent Systems: Neural Architecture Search in Real-World

NAS techniques can be used to address many challenges in intelligent control systems, including those related to optimization, adaptation, and robustness. By leveraging the power of machine learning and optimization algorithms, NAS can generate high-quality neural network architectures that can efficiently and effectively control complex systems in a wide range of environments. The generic overview of intelligent control is shown in Figure 17.7.

One of the key challenges in intelligent control is optimization, where the goal is to find the optimal set of control parameters that can achieve a specific

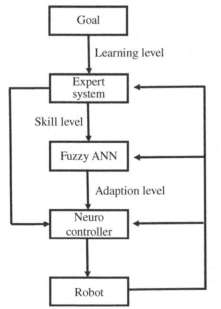

Figure 17.7 Generic overview of intelligent control system.

performance objective. NAS can be used to automatically generate neural network architectures that are optimized for specific control objectives, such as minimizing energy consumption or maximizing throughput. By leveraging advanced optimization techniques such as RL and EA, NAS can efficiently explore the vast space of possible neural network architectures and identify the most effective solutions.

Another challenge in intelligent control is adaptation, where the control system must be able to adapt to changing environmental conditions and feedback. NAS techniques such as One-shot NAS and Meta-learning-based NAS can be used to generate neural network architectures that are flexible and adaptable, allowing the control system to learn and improve in real-time based on changing environmental conditions and feedback. This can improve the performance and robustness of the control system, as well as reduce the need for manual tuning and adjustment. Finally, robustness is another important challenge in intelligent control systems, where the system must be able to maintain its performance and stability in the face of unexpected disturbances and uncertainties. NAS can be used to generate robust neural network architectures that can handle a wide range of disturbances and uncertainties, by leveraging techniques such as BO-based NAS and Gradient-based NAS. These approaches can optimize the architecture to be more robust to perturbations and uncertainties, improving the overall reliability and stability of the control system.

In summary, NAS techniques can be a powerful tool for addressing many challenges in intelligent control systems, including optimization, adaptation, and robustness. By generating high-quality neural network architectures that are optimized, flexible, and robust, NAS can help to improve the performance, reliability, and efficiency of intelligent control systems, making them more effective in a wide range of environments and applications.

17.8.2 Neural Architecture Search for Specific Cybernetical Control Tasks

Neural Architecture Search (NAS) can be used to design and optimize neural network architectures for specific cybernetical control tasks, such as robot navigation, drone control, or autonomous vehicle control. These tasks typically involve complex dynamics and uncertainties, which can make it challenging to manually design and optimize neural network architectures. NAS can help to overcome these challenges by automatically searching for the optimal architecture that is well-suited to the specific task at hand. Here are some key concepts and techniques related to NAS for specific cybernetical control tasks:

- Task-specific constraints: Each cybernetical control task has its own specific constraints that must be taken into account when designing and optimizing neural network architectures. For example, in robot navigation, the size of the robot and the environment may influence the optimal architecture. In drone control, the aerodynamics of the drone and the control objectives may influence the optimal architecture. These constraints must be encoded in the search space for NAS.
- Fitness function: The fitness function is used to evaluate the quality of a given neural network architecture for the specific cybernetical control task. The fitness function may measure the performance of the control system, such as the speed and accuracy of the robot navigation or the stability and precision of the drone control. The fitness function can be represented as follows:

$$f(\alpha) = \text{fitness}(\alpha, D), \tag{17.22}$$

where α is the architecture variable, D is the task-specific data, and fitness is the function used to evaluate the quality of the architecture.

- Search space: The search space for NAS in cybernetical control tasks typically includes various types of layers, activation functions, and connections between the layers. The search space may also include specific types of modules or building blocks that are well-suited to the task at hand. For example, in drone control, the search space may include modules that encode the aerodynamics and flight dynamics of the drone.
- Optimization: The optimization process in NAS for specific cybernetical control tasks involves exploring the space of possible architectures and evaluating them using the fitness function. The optimization can be performed using a variety of algorithms, including Reinforcement Learning-based NAS, Evolutionary algorithms-based NAS, and Gradient-based NAS.

By applying NAS to specific cybernetical control tasks, researchers can design and optimize neural network architectures that are well-suited to the specific task and environment. This can help to improve the performance and adaptability of cybernetical control systems, and enable them to operate more efficiently and effectively in complex and uncertain environments. Additionally, NAS for specific cybernetical control tasks can help to reduce the time and cost required for manual design and optimization of neural network architectures, while ensuring that the resulting architectures are well-suited to the task at hand.

17.8.3 Neural Architecture Search for Cybernetical Intelligent Systems in Real-World

Neural Architecture Search (NAS) can be used to design and optimize neural network architectures for cybernetical intelligent systems in real-world environments with constraints and uncertainties. Real-world environments can be complex and dynamic, with changing conditions and unforeseen events, which can make it challenging to design and optimize neural network architectures manually. NAS can help to overcome these challenges by automatically searching for the optimal architecture that is well-suited to the specific environment and task. Here are some key concepts and techniques related to NAS for cybernetical intelligent systems in real-world environments:

- Real-world constraints: Cybernetical intelligent systems operating in real-world environments often have constraints that must be taken into account when designing and optimizing neural network architectures. These constraints may include hardware limitations, power constraints, and communication bandwidth constraints. The search space for NAS must be designed to take these constraints into account.
- Uncertainties: Real-world environments are often characterized by uncertainties, such as sensor noise, communication delays, and unpredictable events. The neural network architecture must be designed to be robust to these uncertainties and to adapt to changing conditions.
- Reinforcement learning: Reinforcement Learning-based NAS can be used to optimize neural network architectures for cybernetical intelligent systems operating in real-world environments. Reinforcement learning involves learning a policy that maps observations to actions based on feedback in the form of rewards or penalties. The neural network architecture can be optimized using reinforcement learning to maximize the reward function.
- Transfer learning: Transfer learning can be used to transfer knowledge learned in one environment to another related environment. This can be useful in real-world environments where data is scarce or expensive to collect. The neural network architecture can be optimized using transfer learning techniques to leverage knowledge from related environments.
- Cybernetical Intelligent Systems: The objective function for Meta-learning-based NAS for cybernetical intelligent systems can be written as:

$$J(\theta) = E_{P(D)}[L(\theta - \alpha \nabla_\theta L(\theta, D), D)], \tag{17.23}$$

where D is the dataset, α is the step size, and L is the loss function used for the given task. The optimization problem for Gradient-based NAS for cybernetical intelligent systems can be written as:

$$\theta^* = \mathrm{argmin}_\theta L(f_\theta(x), y), \tag{17.24}$$

where $f_\theta(x)$ is the neural network architecture, x is the input, y is the output, and L is the loss function used for the given task. One-shot NAS can also be applied to cybernetical intelligent systems, where the binary gates can be used to decide which operations to use in each layer of the neural network architecture.

17.8.4 Neural Architecture Search for Adaptive Cybernetical Intelligent Systems

Adaptive Cybernetical Intelligent Systems (ACIS) refer to intelligent systems that can adapt their behavior and decision-making strategies in real-time based on changing environmental conditions and feedback. Such systems must be able to adjust their neural network architectures to learn from new experiences and data. Neural Architecture Search (NAS) can be used to design and optimize the architecture of the neural network for ACIS, allowing it to adapt and learn in real-time. Here are some key concepts and techniques related to NAS for ACIS:

- Continual Learning: Continual Learning is a type of machine learning that focuses on training a neural network on a sequence of tasks, allowing it to learn and adapt to new tasks without forgetting previously learned tasks. NAS for ACIS must incorporate continual learning to enable the system to learn from new experiences and adapt to new tasks.
- Meta-Learning: Meta-Learning is a type of machine learning that focuses on learning how to learn. In the context of NAS for ACIS, meta-learning can be used to learn the optimal neural network architecture for a given task in a fast and efficient manner, reducing the time and resources required for manual architecture design.
- Transfer Learning: Transfer Learning can be used to transfer knowledge learned from one task or environment to another related task or environment. This can be useful in ACIS, where data may be scarce or expensive to collect. Transfer Learning can help to optimize the neural network architecture for new tasks and environments, while leveraging the knowledge learned from previous tasks and environments.
- Reinforcement Learning: Reinforcement Learning-based NAS can be used to optimize the neural network architecture for ACIS, enabling the system to learn and adapt in real-time based on feedback in the form of rewards or penalties. Reinforcement Learning-based NAS can be combined with Continual Learning to enable the system to learn and adapt to new tasks in real-time, without forgetting previously learned tasks.
- Online Learning: Online Learning is a type of machine learning that focuses on learning from data that is generated in real-time. NAS for ACIS must incorporate online learning to enable the system to learn and adapt in real-time to changing environmental conditions and feedback.

For the fine-tuning consider, $W_{\{pre\}}$ be the weights of a pre-trained neural network, $W_{\{new\}}$ be the weights of a new neural network, and L be the loss function for the new task. The fine-tuning objective can be expressed as:

$$\theta' = \text{argmin}_\theta L(\theta, D_{train}) + \lambda \Omega_\theta, \tag{17.25}$$

where θ is the parameters of the pre-trained model, θ' is the updated parameters after fine-tuning $L(\theta, D_{train})$ is the loss function on the training dataset, which measures the difference between the predicted outputs of the model and the actual outputs, λ is the regularization parameter, which controls the trade-off between the model's performance on the training dataset and its generalization to new data, Ω_θ is the regularization term, which penalizes complex models that may overfit to the training data, and D_{train} is the training dataset used for fine-tuning. For feature extraction consider, w_{pre} be the weights of a pre-trained neural network and $h(x)$ be the output of the pre-trained network for input x. The feature extraction objective can be expressed as:

$$f(x) = g(w_{new}h(x))f(x) = g(w_{new}h(x)), \tag{17.26}$$

where w_{new} is the weight matrix for a new neural network, and $g(.)$ is a non-linear activation function that maps the output to the desired range.

By applying NAS to ACIS, researchers can design and optimize the architecture of the neural network, enabling the system to learn and adapt in real-time based on changing environmental conditions and feedback. This can help to improve the performance and reliability of ACIS, enabling them to operate more efficiently and effectively in complex and dynamic environments. Additionally, NAS for ACIS can help to reduce the time and resources required for manual architecture design and optimization, while ensuring that the resulting architecture is well-suited to the task and environment.

17.9 Comparison of Different Neural Architecture Search Approaches

The field of Neural Architecture Search (NAS) for Cybernetical Intelligent Systems (CIS) has seen the development of several different approaches, each with its own strengths and weaknesses. Here are some key factors to consider when comparing and evaluating different NAS approaches for CIS:

- Efficiency: The efficiency of an NAS approach refers to its ability to quickly and effectively generate high-quality neural network architectures. Efficiency can be measured in terms of search time, computation resources required, and the number of architectures evaluated.

- Performance: The performance of an NAS approach refers to the quality of the generated neural network architectures, as measured by metrics such as accuracy, speed, and energy efficiency. Performance can also be measured in terms of how well the neural network architecture performs on a specific task or set of tasks.
- Generalizability: The generalizability of an NAS approach refers to its ability to generate neural network architectures that perform well on a variety of tasks and environments, rather than being optimized for a specific task or environment.
- Flexibility: The flexibility of an NAS approach refers to its ability to adapt and learn in real-time based on changing environmental conditions and feedback, allowing it to continuously improve its performance.
- Explainability: The explainability of an NAS approach refers to its ability to provide insight into the decision-making process and the underlying mechanisms of the generated neural network architecture. Some of the most common NAS approaches for CIS include:
- Reinforcement Learning (RL)-based NAS: RL-based NAS uses an agent to iteratively generate and evaluate neural network architectures based on feedback in the form of rewards or penalties. RL-based NAS can be effective at generating high-quality neural network architectures, but can be computationally expensive and time-consuming.
- Evolutionary Algorithms (EA)-based NAS: EA-based NAS uses genetic algorithms to evolve and optimize neural network architectures. EA-based NAS can be more efficient than RL-based NAS, but may struggle to generate complex architectures.
- Gradient-based NAS: Gradient-based NAS uses gradients to optimize neural network architectures, allowing it to efficiently generate high-quality architectures. However, gradient-based NAS may struggle with non-differentiable architecture components.
- Bayesian Optimization (BO)-based NAS: BO-based NAS uses probabilistic models to optimize neural network architectures. BO-based NAS can be effective at generating high-quality architectures with limited computational resources, but may struggle with scalability.
- One-shot NAS: One-shot NAS generates a single architecture that is trained and evaluated on multiple tasks, allowing it to learn and adapt in real-time. One-shot NAS can be effective at generating flexible and adaptable architectures, but may struggle with performance on specific tasks.

When comparing and evaluating different NAS approaches for CIS, it is important to consider the specific requirements and constraints of the task and environment, as well as the trade-offs between efficiency, performance, generalizability, flexibility, and explainability. Additionally, it is important to consider the scalability of the NAS approach, as well as its ability to learn and adapt in real-time based on changing environmental conditions and feedback. Ultimately, the choice of NAS approach will depend on the specific needs and goals of the CIS application.

Summary

This chapter presents the Neural Architecture Search (NAS) and its application in cybernetical intelligent systems. It has covered various NAS approaches such as Reinforcement Learning-based NAS, Evolutionary Algorithms-based NAS, Bayesian Optimization-based NAS, Gradient-based NAS, One-Shot NAS, Meta-Learning-based NAS, and NAS for specific domains. The chapter has also discussed how NAS can help solve challenges in intelligent control by automating the design and optimization of neural network architectures. Overall, NAS and neural networks are closely related and work together to create more efficient and effective machine learning models.

In the future, NAS continue to play an important role in the development of cybernetical intelligent systems. As the complexity and size of neural networks continue to increase, the need for more efficient and effective NAS algorithms will become even more critical. It is also expected from NAS to become more domain-specific, with algorithms tailored to specific tasks and applications. Additionally, the integration of NAS with other machine learning techniques such as transfer learning, unsupervised learning, and multi-task learning is likely to lead to even more powerful and adaptive cybernetical intelligent systems. With these advancements, it is expected to see significant progress in the fields of intelligent control, robotics, and autonomous systems, leading to new and innovative applications in a wide range of industries.

Exercise Questions

Q.17.1   What is the mathematical equation for the performance metric used to evaluate different neural network architectures, such as classification accuracy or mean squared error?

Q.17.2   How can reinforcement learning be used for Neural Architecture Search, and what is the mathematical equation for the objective function and policy gradient used in this approach?

Q.17.3   Can Evolutionary Algorithms-based NAS be used to find optimal neural network architectures? If yes, how?

Q.17.4   How can Bayesian Optimization-based NAS aid in the development of artificial intelligence?

Q.17.5   What is the role of Gradient-based NAS in the development of machine intelligence?

Q.17.6   What is the mathematical equation for the hyper parameters that control the search space and optimization algorithm used in Neural Architecture Search, such as the number of layers, number of neurons, and learning rate?

Q.17.7   What is Meta-Learning-based NAS and how can it be beneficial for these systems?

Q.17.8   In what ways can NAS be used to address specific cybernetical control tasks?

Q.17.9   How can NAS contribute to the development of adaptive machine learning?

Q.17.10   Can you describe the concept of gradient-based Neural Architecture Search, and how it uses the gradients of the validation loss with respect to the architecture parameters to optimize the architecture, and what is the mathematical equation for this gradient computation?

Further Reading

Batista GE, Prati RC, Monard MC. A study of the behavior of several methods for balancing machine learning training data. *ACM SIGKDD Explorations Newsletter*. 2004 Jun 1;6(1):20–9.

Lewis DD, Catlett J. Heterogeneous uncertainty sampling for supervised learning. In Machine Learning Proceedings 1994 1994 Jan 1 (pp. 148–156). Morgan Kaufmann.

Meek C, Thiesson B, Heckerman D. The learning-curve sampling method applied to model-based clustering. *Journal of Machine Learning Research*. 2002;2(Feb):397–418.

Schaffer C. Overfitting avoidance as bias. *Machine Learning*. 1993 Feb 10:153–78.

Tippets WE, Moyle PB. Epibenthic feeding by rainbow trout (*Salmo gairdneri*) in the McCloud River, California. *The Journal of Animal Ecology*. 1978 Jun 1:549–59.

Final Notes on *Cybernetical Intelligence*

The contemporary world is characterized by uncertainty, where the ability to predict events accurately bestows the power to influence and shape consequential actions. This influence extends to the masses, who heed the predictions akin to the authority held by prophetic figures.

Artificial intelligence (AI) transcends a mere tool status, embodying a culture grounded in the philosophy of predictions. The allure of AI in this context is comparable to the fascination evoked by Nostradamus's Les Prophéties (published in 1555), a collection of 942 poetic quatrains reputedly foretelling future occurrences.

Utilizing AI poses significant challenges, and achieving mastery in this domain has been my lifelong pursuit. To propel AI technology forward optimally, I firmly advocate for developing a tool that democratizes AI model creation based on machine learning algorithms. This tool should be accessible to a broad audience without stringent requirements for advanced mathematical or software engineering knowledge. I believe such a powerful tool could have transformative potential for society. In 2023, I proudly introduced "Deep Red," a graphical programming environment (accessible at https://www.deepredsys.com) engineered as a cloud-based platform. Deep Red empowers ordinary individuals to construct and deploy their AI applications seamlessly. User-friendliness has been a primary design principle, rooted in the belief that prioritizing consumer benefits is paramount. Additionally, I decided to write *Cybernetical Intelligence*, envisioning it as a valuable resource for Deep Red users seeking to delve into the more intricate facets of machine learning.

In conjunction with *Cybernetical Intelligence*, Deep Red is dedicated to tackling global challenges and mitigating human suffering. Among its primary applications, medical diagnostics stands out, where medical professionals and radiologists are empowered to specialize in developing diagnostic tools tailored to patient's

Cybernetical Intelligence: Engineering Cybernetics with Machine Intelligence, First Edition.
Kelvin K. L. Wong.
© 2024 The Institute of Electrical and Electronics Engineers, Inc.
Published 2024 by John Wiley & Sons, Inc.
Companion website: www.wiley.com/go/cyberintel

specific medical needs. Adequate support materials are available to facilitate this process, with *Cybernetical Intelligence* serving as an advanced resource for AI-based medical diagnosis education. Furthermore, the technology finds critical use in environmental protection, offering predictive capabilities and pollution control mechanisms to alleviate respiratory distress.

The overarching objective of Deep Red based on cybernetical intelligence is to minimize human suffering across diverse domains. AI extends its reach beyond medical and environmental applications to other scientific and engineering disciplines. For instance, AI is pivotal in creating speech-recognition systems, image and video recognition tools, and autonomous vehicles. This multifaceted field of AI continues to hold immense potential, and its impact on society is continuously under exploration.

Moreover, AI-driven data-driven decision-making and automation revolutionize numerous industries. AI algorithms effectively combat fraud, enhance credit scoring, and facilitate investment analysis in finance. In manufacturing, AI enables predictive maintenance and quality control processes, while in transportation, it facilitates intelligent routing, traffic management, and the development of autonomous vehicles. The breadth of AI applications appears virtually limitless, and its profound influence on society holds significant promise for the future.

From a broad perspective, I strongly believe that the advancements in AI have a transformative impact on various technological domains. AI catalyzes research and development across different scientific and engineering disciplines, fostering accelerated improvements in these fields. Each milestone achieved in AI research generates a significant surge in progress across corresponding domains, contributing to a profound transformation of scientific and technological landscapes.

An illustrative example of AI's catalytic effect is observed with the advent of ChatGPT, a prominent AI language model. This development has expedited critical processes in programming, information organization, data analysis, and data mining, thereby substantially accelerating advancements in numerous scientific and technological sectors.

Introducing large language models (LLMs) in healthcare has unlocked new and impactful applications in Natural Language Processing (NLP). The latest release of healthcare-specific LLMs presents a suite of highly accurate tools for production use. These advanced LLMs offer versatile capabilities, including medical question answering, research comprehension, clinical text generation, and summarization of clinical encounters and patient inquiries.

In summary, the dynamic progression of AI exerts a far-reaching influence, driving advancements in diverse scientific and engineering domains, thus holding the potential to revolutionize various sectors for the betterment of society.

A simple model can be formulated to establish a mathematical representation of the interdependence between AI advancement and the progress in other fields of science and engineering. Let us consider two variables: ξ, denoting the level of AI advancement, and ϖ, representing the level of improvement in other science and engineering fields. We propose the following relationship:

$$\varpi(t) = k * \xi(t)^n.$$

In this equation, t represents time, $\varpi(t)$ signifies the level of advancement in other science and engineering domains at time t, and $\xi(t)$ denotes the level of AI advancement at time t. The proportionality constant k characterizes the fundamental relationship between AI advancement and progress in other fields. The exponent n signifies the rate at which advances in other science and engineering fields change in response to AI advancement. Anticipated to be greater than 1, n is expected to increase as our technology across diverse scientific and engineering disciplines progresses to higher levels over time.

The model suggests a nonlinear relationship between AI advancement and progress in other fields, implying that as the level of AI advancement increases, the advancement in other science and engineering domains will experience exponential growth. Nonetheless, it is essential to acknowledge that this model is a simplification, and the actual situation is likely to be more intricate. Real-world progress in various science and engineering domains is influenced by multifaceted factors, encompassing economic conditions, policies, resource availability, and more. Therefore, while this mathematical representation provides insights into the interconnectedness of AI and technological advancements, it should be treated as a foundational framework subject to refinement and expansion in light of complex real-world dynamics.

Moreover, it is essential to recognize that the efficacy of powerful AI systems is contingent on robust hardware capabilities. In this context, the Deep Red system, harnessing AI technology, augments hardware performance, thereby facilitating the creation of more potent AI models. This interplay between AI and hardware exemplifies a reciprocal relationship, underscoring a symbiotic dependence where AI propels hardware advancements while advanced hardware empowers AI.

Nevertheless, upholding human control as the ultimate authority over AI systems remains paramount. While AI can generate novel ideas and innovations, it is crucial to emphasize that humans must retain possession and take responsibility for the direction and consequences of AI-driven advancements. By incorporating human controllers, we can ensure that AI functions as a tool shaped by human intentions to improve society. Mathematically, this symbiotic relationship between AI and hardware can be articulated as follows:

Hardware Capability $\propto$ AI Power

AI Power $\propto$ Hardware Capability

These equations elucidate the interdependence between AI and hardware, manifesting their reciprocal influence. They underscore the imperative for a harmonious integration, with human control as the driving force behind responsible AI development. This alignment ensures that AI's potential benefits are realized while potential risks are mitigated, and AI's trajectory remains aligned with the broader objectives of societal well-being and progress.

I envision that the integration of Deep Red with Cybernetical Intelligence holds the potential to significantly accelerate the progress of AI, representing a contribution that I aspire to make on a global scale. However, developing a comprehensive understanding of how to regulate this technological advancement is imperative, as unsupervised management of AI could lead to a loss of complete control over human destiny. While my proposed AI application seeks to enhance the quality of life and alleviate human suffering, it is essential to recognize the inherent complexity of this endeavour. Pursuing these goals presents a dual nature, akin to a double-edged sword, where achieving an ideal world may have unforeseen consequences. To safeguard against such risks, I strongly advocate that the AI research community's future generations establish an indispensable human controller at the highest level of authority in all fully implemented AI systems.

This call for human control aligns with the principles of responsible AI development, emphasizing the importance of human oversight to ensure AI technology's ethical and beneficial deployment. By placing human controllers at the helm, we can steer AI advancements toward a trajectory that serves the greater good, fostering an environment where AI is harnessed to improve society while being directed away from potential harm. This balance of power between human controllers and AI systems is fundamental to shaping AI's impact that aligns with our collective aspirations for a better and more equitable world.

The future of AI, robotics, and cybernetics integration promises a paradigm shift with the emergence of cutting-edge technologies that will redefine industries and revolutionize human–machine interactions. Envision a world where cyber-physical systems (CPS) synergistically combine AI algorithms, smart sensors, and human–machine interfaces to create intelligent entities capable of autonomous decision-making (ADM) and self-regulating behaviours. These CPS will embody artificial general intelligence (AGI), enabling them to learn, reason, and adapt in real time, resulting in more resilient and reliable systems. The equation below lies at the heart of technological advancements in this visionary landscape. The synergy between AI, robotics, and cybernetics creates an integrated network of intelligent systems, elevating the capabilities of each component.

One groundbreaking application is the development of AI-driven cyborg robots equipped with neural networks and reinforcement learning (RL). These AI-enhanced robotic beings can self-learn from their experiences, optimizing their performance and behaviour over time. By integrating neuro-fuzzy systems, they will exhibit sophisticated cognition, mimicking human thought processes and even exhibiting emotional intelligence (EI). As we delve into complex environments, multi-agent systems (MAS) powered by deep learning (DL) and swarm intelligence will coordinate and collaborate seamlessly. This symbolizes the transformative impact of combining CPS with AGI to create AI-cyborg entities capable of surpassing traditional limitations and achieving new frontiers in robotic intelligence. It showcases the integration of neuro-fuzzy systems and emotional intelligence into AI-cyborgs, elevating them into AI-enhanced robots. This amalgamation enables robots to possess logical reasoning and emotional awareness, allowing them to interact more empathetically with humans and respond to dynamic situations with greater nuance. It elucidates the role of DL and swarm intelligence in shaping MAS. As we embrace these advancements, intelligent swarms of robots will collectively achieve tasks with remarkable efficiency and fault tolerance, exemplifying the true power of distributed AI and robotic systems.

In this future landscape, human controllers will play a vital role in steering the course of AI, ensuring ethical and responsible deployment. As we strive for a better and more equitable world, the balance of power between human controllers and AI systems will shape the impact of AI-driven advancements in a manner that aligns with our collective aspirations.

Index

Page numbers in *italics* refer to figures; page numbers in **bold** refer to tables

Cybernetical Intelligence: Engineering Cybernetics with Machine Intelligence, First Edition.
Kelvin K. L. Wong.
© 2024 The Institute of Electrical and Electronics Engineers, Inc.
Published 2024 by John Wiley & Sons, Inc.
Companion website: www.wiley.com/go/cyberintel

Printed and bound by CPI Group (UK) Ltd, Croydon, CR0 4YY

27/10/2024

14580672-0003